DATE DUE

OCT 17			

DEMCO 38-296

Lotus Notes Certification:

Application Development
and
System Administration

Scott L. Thomas

Amy E. Peasley

McGraw-Hill

New York   San Francisco   Washington, D.C
Auckland   Bogotá   Caracas   Lisbon   London
Madrid   Mexico City   Milan   Montreal   New Delhi
San Juan   Singapore   Sydney   Tokyo   Toronto

ss Cataloging-in-Publication Data

tification: Application Development and System Administration /
Scott L. Thomas, Amy E. Peasley.
    p.   cm. — (Certification series)
    Includes index.
    ISBN 0-07-913674-5
    1. Lotus Notes.   2. Groupware (Computer software)   3. Computer
software — Development.   I. Peasley, Amy E.   II. Title.
III. Series.
HF5548.4.L692T474   1997   IN PROCESS
005.369—dc21   97-27735
                                                       CIP

McGraw-Hill

*A Division of The **McGraw-Hill** Companies*

The views expressed in this book are solely those of the author, and do not represent the views of any other party or parties.

1 2 3 4 5 6 7 8 9 0 DOC/DOC   9 0 2 1 0 9 8 7

ISBN   0-07-913674-5

The sponsoring editor for this book was Judy Brief. It was set in New Century Schoolbook by E. D. Evans, freelance designer for McGraw-Hill's Professional Book Group composition unit. The Chapter opener art and icons were created by David Evans, freelance illustrator for McGraw-Hill's Professional Book Group composition unit.

Printed and bound by R.R. Donnelley & Sons Company.

McGraw-Hill books are available at special quantity discounts to use as premiums and sales promotions, or for use in corporate training programs. For more information, please write to the Director of Special Sales, McGraw-Hill, 11 West 19th Street, New York, NY 10011. Or contact your local bookstore.

Product or brand names used in this book may be trade names or trademarks. Where we believe that there may be proprietary claims to such trade names or trademarks, the name has been used with an initial capital or it has been capitalized in the style used by the name claimant. Regardless of the capitalization used, all such names have been used in an editorial manner without any intent to convey endorsement of or other affiliation with the name claimant. Neither the author nor the publisher intends to express any judgement as to the validity or legal status of any such proprietary claims.

 This book is printed on recycled, acid-free paper containing a minimum of 50% recycled de-inked fiber.

With love to my family: Mom, Dad, Bill, and Brad.

—Scott Lawrence Thomas

With love to my family: Dad, Mom, Matthew,
John, Beth, Marcus, and Isaac;
and to Michael, for all of your patience.

—Amy Elizabeth Peasley

TABLE OF CONTENTS

Contents

Contents

Acknowledgments

With the writing of a book of this magnitude comes the combined efforts of many individuals. This book is certainly no exception.

We would like to thank our technical reviewers William Thompson of Whittman-Hart, Inc., and Aaron Voyles also of Whittman-Hart for providing technical feedback of our work.

Additional thanks go to Judy Brief, our editor at McGraw-Hill, Gwynne Jackson, copyeditor, Edie Evans, design and production manager, David G. Evans, illustrator, and all the other members of McGraw-Hill who made this book possible.

And finally, many thanks go out to our families and friends who have given us the incentive and drive necessary to make this book a success. Without their encouragement, we would have never made it.

Scott L. Thomas
Amy E. Peasley

Introduction
Purpose and Objective

With your purchase of this book, you have realized the explosion of Lotus Notes in recent years and with that, the demand for qualified Notes professionals. The Lotus Notes Certified Professional program indeed provides individuals the recognition that is demanded by companies that use or are planning to deploy a Lotus Notes network. There are many different publications available to individuals that describe how to effectively design both Lotus Notes applications and infrastructures. However, no publication to date is available to help those individuals striving to obtain Lotus Notes certification. Instead, the only option available is material obtained through expensive Lotus Notes certification classes. What we are hoping to provide you, the reader, is a comprehensive study guide to help you pass the version 4 core Lotus Notes certification exams.

The purpose of this book is not to instruct a user on how to develop Notes applications or administer a Notes infrastructure. Many points in both areas will not be covered within this material at all. Instead, the intention is to give you a good idea of what areas of Notes Application Development and Notes System Administration to study in preparation for becoming a version 4 Certified Lotus Professional.

It should be noted that this reference specifically deals with the certification exams related to Lotus Notes version 4.0. The questions in this book as well as those found on the tests will not reflect any enhancements made to later releases. To the best of our knowledge, Lotus does not plan to distribute any additional exams until the release of Lotus Notes 5.0. We do not anticipate those exams being available until second or third quarter of 1998.

Lotus Notes has become the dominant and defining product in the Groupware market. Companies are now beginning to deploy Notes for a variety of reasons such as electronic mail, document collaboration, and Web deployment to name a few. Knowledgeable professionals are needed to implement and maintain these systems. Certification by the software vendor is a way to verify a professional is truly an expert.

People prepare for exams in different ways. Some take classes, some study on their own, while others rely on their working knowledge of a product. This resource will help people who feel they need some additional guidance in the best way to tackle these exams.

What you will find within this publication includes comprehensive reviews for the four core Lotus Notes version 4 certification examinations. These include:

- **Notes Application Development I**

- **Notes Application Development II**

- **Notes System Administration I**

- **Notes System Administration II**

Notes Application Development I

The first section of this book concentrates on the Application Development I certification exam. The content is geared towards the individual with a strong grasp of basic development techniques and skills. This section will concentrate on the major areas of study for the Application Development 1 exam:

- Developing Notes Applications

- Forms, Fields & Formulas

- Agents, Actions & Hotspots

- Documenting Your Application

- Troubleshooting Application Problems

Following the end of each chapter, you will find sample questions geared towards the topics of that particular chapter.

Notes Application Development II

The second section of this book focuses on the more advanced skills required for the Application Development II certification exam. Many of the Application Development I topics are included, but a greater depth of knowledge about each topic is required. Some additional topics are also covered.

Application Development II will concentrate on the following areas:

- Developing & Maintaining Advanced Notes Applications

- Working with Advanced Forms, Fields & Formulas

- Advanced Views

- Agents & Actions

- Developing Secure Applications

- Advanced Troubleshooting

Again, following the end of each chapter, you will find sample questions geared towards the topics of that particular chapter.

Notes System Administration I

The third section of this book focuses on the skills required for the System Administration I certification exam.

System Administration I will concentrate on the following areas:

- Infrastructure Planning and Design

- Installation and Setup

- Server Administration

- The public Name and Address Book

- Infrastructure Security

Sample questions that relate to topics associated with each System Administration chapter can be found at the end of each chapter.

Notes System Administration II

The fourth section of this book focuses on the more advanced skills required for the System Administration II certification exam. Many of the System Administration I topics are included, but a greater depth of knowledge about each topic is required. Some additional topics are also covered.

System Administration II will concentrate on the following areas:

- Advanced Server Installation and Setup

- Advanced Server Configuration

- Advanced System Security

Like all other chapters, sample test questions can be found at the end of each chapter.

Also included within this publication are 7 sample tests on the included CD-ROM. The tests are located within the Notes database on the CD-ROM.

The Certified Lotus Professional Program

The Certified Lotus Professional (CLP) Program provides a measure of technical knowledge and skills with Lotus Notes and Lotus cc:Mail. Certification demonstrates that a person has achieved a professional level of expertise within a particular arena. Selected competencies are tested through Sylvan Prometric exams, which require not only technical training, but also practical experience. Classes are available for obtaining structured training, but this book will allow you to identify the skills required to pass the exams regardless of whether you have taken any coursework or not.

Currently, two Notes certification tracks are offered by Lotus:

- **Certified Lotus Professional Application Developer:** This track is designed for individuals designing Notes applications consisting of multiple databases and complex design concepts. Individuals who complete this track will have demonstrated an in-depth knowledge of competencies including application architecture, development, security, and documentation. Some System Administration skills are also required to complete this track.

An advanced level of certification, Principal Application Developer, is also available. This requires an understanding of advanced development concepts including complex application design and security issues as well as object-oriented programming skills.

- **Certified Lotus Professional System Administrator:** This track is designed for individuals seeking expertise in running a Notes network. Individuals who complete this track will have demonstrated an in-depth knowledge of Notes infrastructure, planning and design, server configuration, maintenance and setup, as well as system and application security.

An advanced level of certification is also available for the system administrator as a Principal System Administrator. This requires additional expertise in advanced communication technology such as integration between Lotus Notes and Lotus cc:Mail.

Notes

The Principal level of certification in Application Development and System Administration requires additional exams and competencies which are NOT covered in this book. We will be only covering those tests necessary for the Certified Lotus Professional level.

The following table outlines the required exams for each certification track:

Table 1
Certification Exam
Requirements

Notes V4 Certification	Required Exams	Exam Number
CLP Application Developer	Application Development I (AD1) Exam	190-171
	Application Development II (AD2) Exam	190-172
	System Administration I (SA1) Exam	190-174
CLP System Administrator	System Administration I (SA1) Exam	190-174
	System Administration II (SA1) Exam	190-175
	Application Development I (AD1) Exam	190-171

Note that these requirements have changed for version 4 from prior versions of Lotus Notes. Also, if certification has already been achieved in version 3, update exams are available for a limited time. Principal level certification requires an additional elective exam for each track.

Concurrent Application Exams

Lotus has recently started offering two types of testing methods: **Multiple Choice** or **Concurrent Application**. Multiple choice is the standard exam format used for all exams where the candidate is presented with a question and several possible answers. Concurrent application testing is task based, which allows the candidate to perform actual tasks within a Notes environment. For example, a CLP Application Developer candidate would be presented with an actual Notes database that must be modified based on the exam questions. According to Lotus sources, concurrent application testing became available at certain sites in April, 1997. Multiple choice exams will continue to be offered.

Notes

Only multiple choice exam questions and information will be covered in this book. Concurrent application testing within the Notes environment will NOT be covered. For more information on concurrent application testing, please see the Lotus Notes CLP Exam Guide, available from Lotus.

Testing Format

The multiple choice format for Notes examinations offers the candidate 40–60 multiple choice questions per test that may have one or multiple answers. There is a time limit for the test of which is dependent on the examination itself. For most candidates, the time limit will be sufficient enough time to complete the examination.

The testing environment is computerized and follows examinations similar to Microsoft certification exams, where the student may traverse through the examination and either answer and/or mark troublesome questions. The candidate then has the ability to go back to questions and review answers. The Lotus Notes tests are not adaptive like Novell certification examinations. You will have a set number of questions that will quiz on all topics associated with that particular examination.

Questions will be direct and related to a certain topic or will be based upon a given scenario in which the candidate must gather pertinent information.

All examinations are closed book format and no external notes, calculators, or computers are allowed. A blank, scratch sheet of paper will be provided to you at the examination center that will have to be turned back to the center once the examination is completed.

Once the examination is completed, the user will be notified immediately of the score on-screen on the computer. A print-out of the score will also be provided to user. The user must pass a certain percentage of questions for a passing grade of which will be told to the user upon startup of the examination. Scores will then be automatically forwarded to the Lotus Education department within five business days.

Notes

If you do not pass an examination, you will be required to re-register for the examination and re-pay the registration fee.

Study Methods

Many candidates ask us what is the best method for studying for the certification examinations. We always answer with the standard consulting answer—it depends. The best method is what makes the candidate the most comfortable with the material. For some, this includes memorizing all available information on a particular topic. For others it is hands-on experimentation with the product itself. For others still, it is sample test questions. For most it is a combination of all three methods. We hope this publication will help all three types of certification test takers.

Cheating Policies

The candidate should completely understand the testing rules of the facility and the repercussions of failing to abide by those rules. If an examination is passed by questionable means and is indeed proven by the testing center along with Lotus, then the candidate's test will be nullified and the candidate will not be permitted to take another certification examination for six months.

Registering for Examinations

At present, Lotus Certification examinations are offered by Sylvan Prometric Testing Centers, which may be found world-wide. For information about testing centers or to register for a Lotus examination, call one of the following numbers:

800-74-LOTUS (800-745-6887)

or

612-896-7000

The Sylvan Prometric testing center will need the following items when you call:

- Name

- Social Security Number (this will be your Sylvan Prometric ID number)

- Mailing Address and Phone Number

- Company Name

- Name and Code Number of the examination you will be taking

- Date you wish to take the examination

- Method of Payment (Credit Card, Money Order, or Check)

The testing center will instruct you on location of the testing center and brief you on the cancellation policy.

Notes

If you leave your current employer, your certification will follow you to your next employer.

Notes

At publication time of this book, Lotus has not yet re-signed Sylvan Prometric for its testing center. Lotus' Web site (www.lotus.com) should be reviewed to ensure the current testing center.

Other Contacts

Other information on Lotus Education may be obtained from Lotus' Web site at:

www.lotus.com

or by calling the Lotus Education Helpline at:

800-346-6409

Notes

As stated before, it should be noted that this reference specifically deals with the certification exams related to Lotus Notes version 4.0. The questions in this book as well as those found on the tests will not reflect any enhancements made to later releases. To the best of our knowledge, Lotus does not plan to distribute any additional exams until the release of Lotus Notes 5.0. We do not anticipate those exams being available until second or third quarter of 1998.

Application

Development I

Chapter 1

Developing Notes Applications

The Application Development I exam focuses on the key competencies of designing a basic Lotus Notes application. These competencies include working with forms, views, formulas, navigators and agents. The next four chapters will cover each of these topics, focusing on the points which are most important for the Application Development I exam. These chapters assume that the exam candidate has some experience working with Lotus Notes, and therefore does not go into detail on every aspect of every topic. Some concepts are not covered until the Application Development II exam; those will be noted throughout the chapters.

This chapter focuses on the competencies related to creating and maintaining a Notes database as part of a Notes application. We will cover creating the database, setting database properties, setting security on the database, creating graphical navigators, and documenting the design of the database.

Designing a Notes Application

Lotus Notes applications are designed to store information. Different types of applications store information in different ways. Notes applications consist of one or more databases designed to work together to manage and store data.

There are five main types of databases:

- **Broadcast:** Broadcast databases update users about new information. These databases allow time-critical information to be disseminated to a large audience via mail messages. The information is usually static, such as a new policy or newsletter distribution. This type of database is **new** to version 4 of Lotus Notes.

- **Discussion:** Discussion databases track main documents and responses. These databases are very helpful in a group information-sharing environment.

- **Reference:** Reference databases are frequently called Document Libraries. These types of databases store information that can be referred to and updated as necessary.

- **Tracking:** Tracking databases move an activity from paper-based to electronic format. These databases track status or categorize documents automatically. Usually, many users are actively involved with the information. Tracking databases are especially beneficial when integrated with workflow databases to create complex dataflow applications.

- **Workflow:** Workflow databases move information through a process or cycle. This is applicable when several people must approve or review the information. Notifications and reminders can be sent out on a scheduled basis to facilitate the workflow process. Documents can be restricted to the creator and approvers for additional security.

An application can be composed of several of these different types of databases, all functioning together to meet the user's needs.

Tips

In the Application Development I exam, you will be provided with a description of an application and asked to select one of these types. It is important to note that the Broadcast application type is new to Lotus Notes version 4, and there will most likely be questions related to this item.

Although Lotus Notes is an excellent way to manage and store data, certain applications are *not* well suited to Lotus Notes:

- **Real-time transactions:** Notes data distribution relies on replication. Replication occurs on a scheduled basis and data may have to be moved through several servers to reach its final destination. Thus, data that needs to be accessed on a real-time basis from distributed locations should not be stored in a Notes application.

- **Large amounts of data:** Notes databases are limited to four gigabytes in size, thus limiting the usefulness of Notes for extremely large amounts of data. Based on the speed of users' machines and the functionality of the application, the practical size limit is much less.

- **Complex mathematical computations:** Applications requiring complex queries or statistical calculations are not appropriate for Lotus Notes.

Database Components

Lotus Notes databases are composed of four key elements: Forms, Fields, Documents, and Views.

- **Forms:** The form is the basic structure of a Notes document. It contains all of the design elements associated with the document's functionality including actions, sections, and fields, which allow users to enter data.

- **Fields:** The fields on a form contain data. This data is entered by the user or calculated automatically by Notes. Various types of data can be stored in a field, including:

- Text

- Rich text

- Numbers

- Times & Dates

- Keywords

- Names

- Authors

- Readers

Fields can also be shared between forms.

- **Documents:** Each document in a database consists of information entered into the fields, as well as the properties of the document itself. Documents are displayed to the user through views.

- **Views:** Views are document collections. A selection formula determines which of the database's documents are displayed. The view's columns determine the information displayed from each document. Data in views can also be sorted and categorized.

Databases also include design elements which are not directly related to the data residing in the database. This includes functionality such as database security, navigators, and documentation.

Creating a Database

Creating a database is the first step in building a Notes application. To create a database from the menu, select **File – Database – New**. This opens the New Database dialog box, shown Figure 1-1:

Figure 1-1

New Database
Dialog Box

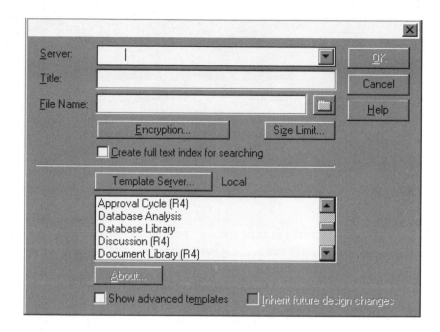

Select the server where the new database will reside. *Local* appears as the default server. Select a descriptive title and filename for the database. The filename will fill in automatically as the title is entered, but can be changed to suit the designer's preferences.

Each of the following elements must be determined when creating the database: size, index, and template.

- **Set the database size:** The database designer has the option of setting the maximum amount of disk space the database can utilize on a server. This is the only point where a designer can set the maximum size of a database. Once the absolute size limit is selected, it can never be changed, unless you make a new copy of the database. To set the database size, click on the **Size Limit...** button (shown in Figure 1-2). The drop-down box allows you to select one, two, three, or four gigabytes as the maximum absolute size of the database.

Figure 1-2
Size Limit
Dialog Box

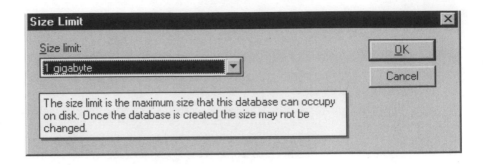

Notes

This is a key item! The Application Development I exam will include a question related to the maximum size of a database. Remember that four gigabytes is the absolute maximum size a designer can set for a Notes database. This size limit can not be changed once it is set, unless a new copy of the database is created.

- **Create a full text index for searching:** At creation time, a full text index can be created for the database. For the Application Development I exam, it is important to note that the default settings will be used to create the index, including **Index Encrypted Fields** and **Index Breaks—Word Breaks Only**. No other options are set automatically. To select other options, create the full text index after the database is created. For more information about creating full text indexes, see the "Database Properties" section in this chapter.

- **Select a Template:** At this point, the designer must decide whether the database should be based on a template or designed from scratch. Templates can be selected from any available server or the local workstation. To show advanced templates, select the **Show advanced templates** option. Designing databases based on templates is covered in preparation for the Application Development II exam later in this book. This information is not required for the Application Development I exam.

Database Properties

Database properties are a main focus of the Application Development I exam. The database properties infobox is comprised of several tabs, each one specifying different types of information. To access any of the below tabs for a Notes database, highlight the Notes database icon and select **File – Database – Properties** from the menu.

Notes

Lotus likes to confuse the candidate by listing different types of properties and different tabs as the alternative answers to a question. Be sure you understand exactly the type of property the question is referring to (e.g. a database, a form, or a field property) as well as the location (tab) where the property is accessible.

The Basics Tab

Figure 1-3

Database Basics Tab

The Basics tab (Figure 1-3) provides general database information. The title of the database can be changed as well as the Database type, Encryption and Replication Settings. The database title will appear on the icon on the user's workspace as well as in the Open Database dialog box.

- **Database Type:** The database type can be one of three options: Standard, Library, or Personal Journal. Most databases are Standard type. Other types can be used in conjunction with special templates. It is not necessary to know the details of these types for the Application Development I exam, only what the types are.

- **Encryption:** Local databases can be encrypted. This prevents anyone sitting at the computer from accessing the database without the correct Notes ID. This is useful when several people will share the machine. Figure 1-4 shows the local encryption dialog box:

Figure 1-4
Local Encryption
Dialog Box

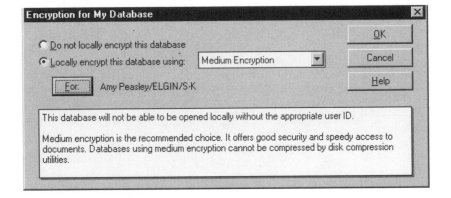

Three levels of encryption are available:

1. **Simple:** Simple encryption is the least secure type of encryption. It prevents other users from opening the database. Documents can still be accessed quickly and the database can be compressed using disk compression utilities.

2. **Medium:** Medium encryption is the default level of encryption (shown in Figure 1-4). Documents can be accessed quickly, but the database cannot be compressed by disk compression utilities. Medium encryption offers a stronger level of security than simple encryption.

3. **Strong:** Strong encryption should be utilized when the database contains sensitive information and security is a primary concern. Documents will take a little longer to open than when using medium encryption. The database cannot be compressed using disk compression utilities. This is the most secure level of encryption.

- **Replication Settings:** The **Replication Settings** button allows the database creator to select various options related to replicating the database. The creator can decide which documents are replicated, how long documents will remain in the database, the replication priority, which features of the database will be replicated, and other options. These are not stressed on the Application Development I exam. For more information on replication, see Chapter 10.

- **Replication History:** The replication history can also be viewed from this tab. The replication history tracks the last successful replication with each server, including the number of documents added, modified, or deleted in the database. The replication history is used to track the date the servers last replicated and which documents should be added to the replica. Notes checks the replication history of the database on each server before replicating. If the replication histories don't agree, the entire database is replicated.

The designer can disable background agents and allow the use of stored forms by selecting or deselecting these options. The **Allow use of stored forms** option must be selected in order to store the form in the document which is frequently used when documents are mailed to users from a database.

The Information Tab

Figure 1-5
Database
Information Tab

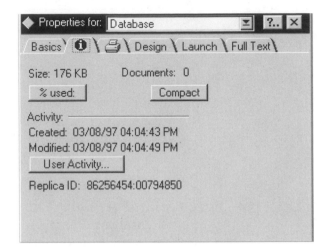

The Information tab (Figure 1-5) provides information about the size of the database, including the number of documents and percent used (this tracks the amount of white space contained in the database). The **Compact** button allows the user to compact the database and eliminate any unused white space that may be in the database from deletions, etc. Compacting can be done automatically on the server, but users can also compact the database using this button. If the database is not at least 90 percent used, it should be compacted. The user can also track when a database was created, modified, and used (via the **User Activity** button). Every Notes database has an associated Replica ID, which provides a unique identifying code for the database. This replica ID can be used in formulas to refer to the database.

The Print Tab

The Print tab (Figure 1-6) is standard for all types of InfoBoxes (i.e. the Form Properties Print Tab shows the same options). Header, footer, font, size, style, and first page printing can all be set here.

Figure 1-6

Database Print Tab

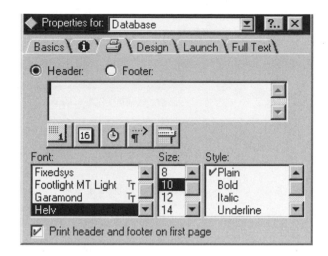

The Design Tab

Figure 1-7

Database Design Tab

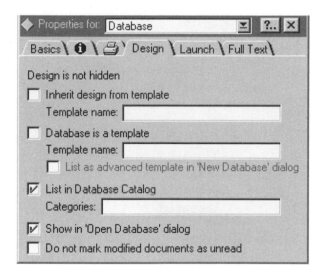

The Design tab (Figure 1-7) sets the properties for the database's design. Even after the database is created, it can inherit the design of a template or become a template (templates are discussed later in this chapter). This tab provides the ability to prevent the database from displaying in the catalog or the Open Database dialog box. **Do not mark modified documents as unread** is a helpful attribute if an agent modifies documents in the background, but the changes should be transparent to the user.

The Launch Tab

Figure 1-8
Database Launch Tab

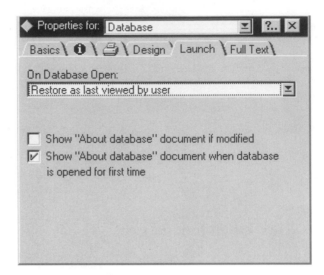

The Launch tab sets the database opening properties. Several options are available from the **On Database Open** drop down list.

- **Restore as last viewed by user:** This is the default setting. The "About database" document attributes may be set to determine when a user views the About document. The default selection only shows the document the first time the database is opened.

- **Open "About database" document:** This option provides no other selections. The "About database" document will open every time a user enters the database.

- **Open designated Navigator:** A specific navigator must be selected. This navigator will open every time a user enters the database. The "About database" document options are also available here.

- **Open designated Navigator in its own window:** A specific navigator must be selected. No "About database" document options are available. This selection is especially useful for databases containing a full-screen navigator used as the "front door" to access other information.

- **Launch 1st attachment in "About database":** When a user opens a database, the first attachment will automatically launch. The "About database" document may still be viewed by selecting **Help – About this Database.** This option is beneficial when the database is used as the front end for another application.

- **Launch 1st doclink in "About database":** When a user opens a database, the first doclink listed in the "About database" document will launch, sending the user to a particular document, view, or database, depending on the type of link. No other "About database" selection options are available here.

The Application Development I exam questions related to this information generally set up a scenario where one of the above actions is happening and ask the candidate to identify how the result was achieved. It will be important to note that this functionality is set on the Launch tab in the database properties infobox.

The Full Text Tab

Figure 1-9
Database Full Text Tab

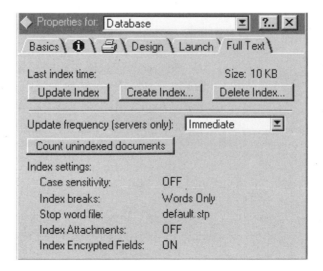

Full text indexes can be created, updated, and deleted from this tab so that users may perform Boolean searches on the data within the application. The update frequency can be changed; however, this functionality only applies to servers. Unindexed documents can be counted, and the index settings can be viewed. The index must be deleted and recreated to change these settings unless the user has selected the **Enable local background indexing** in the **File – Tools – User Preferences** menu option. If this option is selected, Notes will automatically update local full-text indexes on a workstation at startup.

The following options are available when creating a full text index on a database:

- **Case sensitive index:** When a case sensitive index is created, each case is indexed separately. For example, "Excel" and "excel" would both be listed in the index. Note that this option will increase the size of the full text index by 5–10%.

- **Index attachments:** This option indexes any text in attachments. This is helpful if users will want to search through attached text documents within the database without having to open each attachment individually. This will increase the size of the index depending on the number of attachments in the database.

- **Index encrypted fields:** This option allows text located in encrypted fields to be included in the index. This option increases the size of the index depending on the number of encrypted fields. It is important to note that including encrypted fields in the index will compromise the security on the field.

- **Exclude words in Stop Word file:** This option decreases the size of the full text index because words contained in the Stop Word file are not indexed. The Stop Word file includes words such as *an*, *be*, *to*, and *the*. Designers have the option of using the default Stop Word file, **DEFAULT.STP** or creating a customized Stop Word file.

- **Index breaks:** Full text indexing contains two options for index breaks. The designer can index based on **word breaks only,** which finds all words regardless of their location. The index can also be based on **Word, Sentence,** and **Paragraph** breaks. This allows the user to specify a proximity for two or more words. For example, the search "IBM sentence Lotus" would return the documents containing the words "IBM" and "Lotus" in the same sentence. The search "IBM paragraph Lotus" would return any documents containing the words "IBM" and "Lotus" in the same paragraph.

Database Security

Lotus Notes contains various levels of security, from Notes ID authentication to field level security. Databases are secured based on their Access Control List (ACL). The ACL determines:

- **Who can access the database:** The "Default" entry in the ACL determines what level of access users have to the database. When Default is set to "No Access," users will receive an "Access has been denied" message when trying to open the database unless they are listed in the ACL individually or as a group.

- **What functions each person or group can perform:** Each user or group is given a level of access which allows them to perform certain functions within the database, such as reading, authoring, editing, designing, or managing. These access levels are described in detail in the next section.

- **Each person's roles:** Roles can be set up which include certain individuals and groups listed in the ACL. Roles are used to refine access levels within the database.

To view the ACL for the database, select **File – Database – Access Control** from the menu (or right-click on the database and select **Access Control**). The Access Control List dialog box appears, as shown in Figure 1-10.

Figure 1-10

Database ACL
Dialog Box

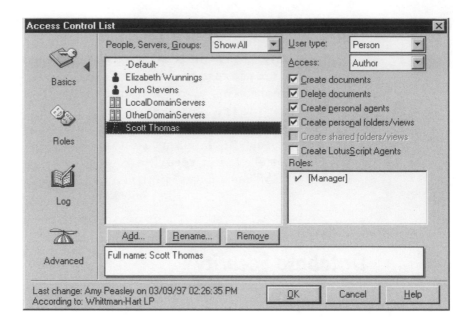

The ACL dialog box Basics pane allows the manager of the database to add, rename, or remove people or groups from the Access Control List. When the database is created, the creator is given manager access. The **-Default-** group controls access for all users not specified in the ACL. **Designer** access is automatically given to the Default group on creation of the database. Set the Default access level to **No Access** to restrict who can open the database. The Default group cannot be removed or renamed.

To add a user or group to the ACL of the database, click the **Add...** button. A prompt will appear, allowing the manager to type a name or select from the Name & Address Book. When adding a group to the ACL, it should exist in the Public Name & Address Book; otherwise, it will be useless.

Access Levels

The manager of a Notes application can select from seven different levels of access to grant to users and/or groups. Within these levels, additional options are also available; that level of detail is not required for this exam.

- **Manager:** Users with Manager access can do things allowed by no other access level, such as:

  - Modify ACL settings

  - Modify replication settings

  - Encrypt a database for local security

  - Delete the database

Managers can also perform all tasks allowed by all other access levels.

- **Designer:** Users with Designer access can modify all design elements, including fields, forms, views, agents, the database icon, and About and Using documents. Designers can create full text indexes and perform all tasks allowed by lower access levels.

- **Editor:** Users with Editor access can create documents and edit all documents in the database.

- **Author:** Users with Author access can create documents and edit any documents they created. Give users Author access rather than Editor access to reduce Replication and Save Conflicts. With Editor access, any user can be editing any document at any time, which increases the likelihood that two users will be editing the same document at the same time. This causes replication and save conflicts. If users can only edit their own documents, the chances of two people editing the same document at the same time are greatly reduced.

- **Reader:** Users with Reader access can read existing documents in a database, but cannot create or edit documents.

- **Depositor:** Users with Depositor access can create documents, but cannot read any documents in the database, even documents they create. This type of access is useful for mail-in databases, such as surveys.

- **No Access:** Users with No Access cannot access the database. They cannot even add the icon for the database to their workspace.

Notes

> *This is only a general introduction about Access Control Lists for purposes of the Application Development I exam. Users taking the Application Development II exam should see Chapter 9—Securing Notes Applications for additional information required for that exam. Users taking the System Administration I exam should see Chapter 14—Notes Infrastructure Security for a more detailed discussion on the topic. Security topics for the System Administration II exam are covered in Chapter 16—Advanced Notes Infrastructure Security.*

Creating Navigators

Navigators are new to version 4 of Lotus Notes. The designer can create a completely graphical user interface to automate much of the functionality within Notes. Navigators can be displayed in their own window or on the left side of the view in the navigation pane. If no custom navigator is designed and displayed, Notes displays a default navigator consisting of folders and magnifying glasses, which help users navigate between views. However, it is sometimes beneficial to use full-screen navigators or graphically enhanced navigators, which are designed with the users' needs in mind.

To create a navigator, select **Create – Design – Navigator** from the menu. An empty navigator and the design pane appear with the Navigator Properties infobox. Set the navigator's properties, including a name, an initial view or folder, and a background color. The navigator can be automatically resized at run time by selecting the **Auto adjust panes at runtime** option. The navigator properties infobox is shown in Figure 1-11:

Figure 1-11

Navigator Basics Tab

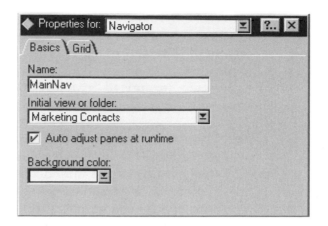

Navigators can be created using several different tools, including graphic backgrounds, graphic buttons, and hotspots. Graphic backgrounds can be copied and pasted into the navigator from any graphic product. To create a graphic button, copy the graphic from the original product and select **Create – Graphic Button** from the menu. Select **Create – Hotspot Rectangle** from the menu or use the SmartIcon bar to add hotspots to the navigator. Hotspots can be programmed to run simple actions, @formulas, or LotusScript.

Tips

For the Application Development I exam, it is most important to understand that navigators help users navigate through the application. For example, it might be useful for a department in charge of the facility to have a graphical layout of the floor in a navigator. When the user selects a particular section of the floor, another navigator appears which provides a more detailed graphic of a room. The user can then click on different parts of the room to view documents related to that piece of furniture, etc.

Database Documentation

About and Using documents within a Notes database enable the designer to provide basic database documentation. These documents can only be created and modified by a person with Designer or Manager access to the database. Once these documents are created, they can be accessed by selecting the **Help – About this Database** or **Help – Using this Database** options on the Notes menu.

To create an About or Using document, select **View – Design** from the menu. In the navigator pane, select **Design – Other – About Database Document** or **Design – Other – Using Database Document**. The designer is presented with a blank slate which can contain formatted text, graphics, links, buttons, hotspots, and objects.

- **The About Database Document:** The About document usually provides information related to the purpose of the database as well as the intended audience, the name and phone number of the person to contact with questions about the database, the version number, and some basic guidelines for using the database. About documents can contain formatted text, graphics, links, buttons, hotspots, and objects. The About document can be launched based on the database properties. See "The Launch Tab" under the "Database Properties" section of this chapter for details on launching the About document.

- **The Using Database Document:** The Using document is geared toward the user. It usually provides an overview of the database, including how the database fits into the application as a whole, a description of any navigators, an explanation of each form and view, and an explanation of the agents contained in the database.

The information in this chapter provides the basic design of the database. However, the database itself is only a shell for forms, views and documents. In the next chapter we will discuss forms, which allow data to be entered into the database.

Chapter 1 Sample Questions

Objective: Writing Notes Applications which are appropriate for a company.

Nikolas wants to design an application to update all users about new Accounting Policies. The information is static, but it is very important that it be distributed quickly because it is time sensitive. Which type of application should Nikolas design?

      A. Broadcast

      B. Discussion

      C. Reference

      D. Workflow

Answer: A

Broadcast databases allow time-critical information to be disseminated to a large audience via a mail message.

Objective: Using the properties infobox.

When a user opens the database, Janet wants to trigger an event. Which one of the following choices is not an option when the database is launched?

      A. Launch 1st doclink in About document

      B. Open designated Navigator in its own window

      C. Launch 1st document in default view

      D. Restore as last viewed by user

Answer: C

The options when launching a database include: Restore as last viewed by user, Open About document, Open designated Navigator, Open designated Navigator in its own window, Launch 1st doclink in About document, and Launch 1st attachment in About document.

Objective: Writing Notes Applications which are appropriate for a company.

The Safe–N–Clean Company wants to leverage their use of Lotus Notes. Which of the following types of applications are not well suited to Notes?

A. A report generating application which generates 30,000 documents per month

B. A project request database where users want to track the status of their request

C. A statistical processing application which performs complex mathematical calculation on the information

D. A sales tracking information where sales reps need real-time, up-to-the-minute information about the status of the client at locations all over the world

Answer: A, C & D
Notes is not a good solution for business problems which require large amounts of data, complex mathematical or statistical calculations, or real-time access to distributed data.

Objective: Writing Notes Applications which limit database sizes.

Jean-Luc wants to limit the absolute size of his Notes database from growing over 1 gigabyte. How does he set this attribute?

A. By selecting the **Size Limit** button in the Database Properties InfoBox

B. By selecting the **Size Limit** button when originally creating the database

C. He cannot do this; a size cannot be set for the database

D. He cannot do this; the size limit can only be set to 4 gigabytes

Answer: B
The absolute size limit can be set to 1, 2 ,3, or 4 gigabytes when the database is created.

Objective: Creating Notes Databases.

Drew is creating a new Notes database. What are his database type options?

A. Standard, Personal Journal, Library

B. Normal, Discussion, Document Library

C. None, Tracking, Personal Journal

D. Standard, Discussion, Tracking

Answer: A
On the Database Properties Basics tab, the database creator can select the database type. The options are Standard (by default), Library, or Personal Journal. These can be utilized in conjunction with Notes Templates.

Objective: Writing Notes Applications which are secure.

The Accounting Department has a laptop computer running Lotus Notes, which is shared between several individuals when they travel. One of the databases replicated locally should only be used by the manager of the department and the information is highly confidential. What is the most secure thing the manager can do to the database to secure it on the laptop from unauthorized users?

A. Set the ACL to not allow any other users to access the database

B. Set up strong encryption for each document in the database

C. Set up strong encryption in the Database Properties

D. Remove the icon from the workspace so none of the other users can see it

Answer: C
Strong encryption on the local copy of the database will protect it from unauthorized access by other users of the machine. Strong encryption is the most secure of the encrypting option, but it can increase the time required to open documents in the database.

Objective: Using the properties infobox.

Marcus has designed a Notes discussion database so he and his co-workers can share ideas concerning a project they are all working on. When someone creates a response to a main document within the application, Marcus wants the OriginalSubject field on the response document to automatically inherit the value of the Subject field on the main document. How does he accomplish this?

A. He sets a field property in the Subject field in the main document

B. He sets a field property in the OriginalSubject field in the response document

C. He sets a form property on the main document form

D. He sets a form property on the response document form

Answer: D
Marcus needs to select the **Formulas inherit values from selected document** property in the Form properties of the response document.

Objective: Using the properties infobox.

Marie is working on a database which will only be used by the managers of the department to track financial data. She doesn't want everyone in the company to see that this database exists. When users select **File – Database – Open** from the Notes menu, she does not want her database to be displayed. How can Marie accomplish this?

A. Deselect **Show in 'Open Database'** dialog in the form properties infobox

B. Place parentheses around the title of the database

C. Select **Hide Database when opening** from the database settings dialog box

D. Deselect **Show in 'Open Database' dialog** in the database properties infobox

Answer: D
The **Show in 'Open Database'** dialog option should be deselected in the database properties infobox. There is no such setting as **Hide Database when opening**, and parentheses around the title have no effect.

Objective: Writing Notes Applications which allow for full text indexing.

The users have requested that the How to Train Your Dog Reference Database is full-text indexed in order for users to perform Boolean searches. Allie, the database designer, selects **Create full-text index for searching** when creating the database. What default settings will be used to create the index?

> A. Case Sensitive Index and Index Encrypted Fields
>
> B. Index Encrypted Fields and Index Breaks—Word Breaks Only
>
> C. Case Sensitive Index and Index Breaks—Word, Sentence and Paragraph
>
> D. Index Encrypted Fields and Index Breaks—Word, Sentence and Paragraph

Answer: B
When a full-text index is created at the same time as the database, the default settings are **Index Encrypted Fields** and **Index Breaks—Word Breaks Only**.

Objective: Writing Notes Applications which control database access.

Jigneth is setting up the Access Control list for his Site-For-Sore-Eyes Glasses Sales Tracking Database. He wants users to be able to create new sales documents, but not edit other people's documents. What level of access should he give to the -Default- group?

> A. Creator
>
> B. Author
>
> C. Editor
>
> D. No Access

Answer: B

Author access will enable users to create documents, but not edit any documents other than their own.

Objective: Understanding Database Properties.

Antonio needs to know the Replica ID of the Men's Hair Products Discussion Database for a formula he is writing. Where would he look for this information?

    A. The Basics Tab in the Database Properties InfoBox, under **Replication Setting**

    B. The Design Tab in the Database Properties InfoBox

    C. The Launch Tab in the Database Properties InfoBox

    D. The Information Tab in the Database Properties InfoBox

Answer: D

The Information Tab provides the Replica ID.

Objective: Diagnose and fix navigator problems.

Lizzie created a graphical main navigator which shows a blueprint of the office layout. What type of functionality should she incorporate into the navigator in order to view more details of one section of the office?

    A. A hotspot which opens a detailed section navigator

    B. A layout region which shows the details of the section

    C. An expandable section to show details of the section

    D. An action button which opens a view

Answer: A

None of the design elements listed in the other answers are available in a navigator.

Objective: Write About and Using documents.

When Becky releases a new version of her database, she makes a change to the About document reflecting all of the new enhancements. At no other time does she modify this document. How can Becky automatically notify the users that they are using a new version of the database?

A. Select **Show About database document if modified** on the document properties launch tab

B. Select **Show About database document if modified** on the database properties launch tab

C. Select **Show About database document if modified** on the form properties launch tab

D. She must send out an e-mail to notify the users

Answer: B
The **Show About database document if modified** option is only available on the database properties launch tab.

Objective: Create About Documents which use optional launching parameters.

Tony created a database which automatically follows a document link to a particular document in the database when the database is first opened. Which of the following design elements allowed this?

A. A button on the main navigator

B. A navigator within the About Document

C. A doclink in the About Document

D. A doclink in the main navigator

Answer: C
The **Launch 1st doclink in About database** option on the launch tab of the database properties allows this.

Objective: Diagnose and fix navigator problems.

Lynn created a navigator in her State Tax Tracking database. She wants this navigator to appear full-screen when the database is opened. What does she need to do?

    A. Select **Open designated Navigator** in the database properties

    B. Select **Open designated Navigator** in the navigator properties

    C. Select **Open designated Navigator in its own window** in the database properties

    D. Select **Open designated Navigator in its own window** in the navigator properties

Answer: C

To open the navigator full screen, the **Open designated Navigator in its own window** option must be selected. This is a database property found on the Launch tab.

Chapter 2

Working with Forms

Forms are the backbone of a Notes database. They provide the structure for inputting and viewing data contained in a document. The Application Development I exam questions related to forms focus on form properties. Thus, this chapter will describe each tab in the form properties infobox in detail. Other design elements, including static text, hotspots, hide-when formulas, actions, subforms, and window titles are discussed in this chapter as well. Fields, the most integral design element on a form, are addressed in Chapter 3.

Form Properties

Several key areas covered in the Application Development I exam center around form properties. To view form properties within a Notes database, enter the database and open the form. Select **Design – Form Properties...** The form properties infobox will appear. This infobox consists of several tabs, covered in the following sections.

The Basics Tab

Figure 2-1
Form Basics Tab

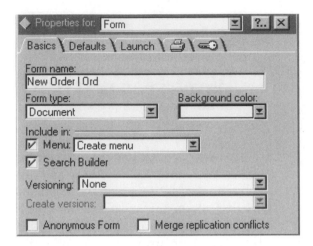

The Basics tab (Figure 2-1) provides key information about the form.

The following properties can be set in the basics tab:

- **Form Name:** The form name should be a descriptive title indicating the purpose of the form or the type of information contained on the form. Form names are case sensitive, cannot exceed 256 characters, and can contain any combination of characters, spaces, and punctuation.

Form names can also use *synonyms*. Synonyms are used internally by Notes. These are helpful in several situations, such as when the form name is too long and cumbersome to be easily used in formulas; when you want to change the form name; or when you want the form to have multiple names. To create a synonym, use the | (vertical bar) symbol after the form name and add a synonym name. The first name listed will be displayed in the Create menu, and the synonym will be used internally in formulas or as an additional way to refer to the form. In the illustration above, the form name is *New Order* and the synonym is *Ord*. Synonyms are also utilized in other types of design elements, including keyword choices.

- **Form Type:** A form can be specified as a Document, Response, or Response to Response.

- **Document:** Document is the default type and should be used unless you want to create a document hierarchy with a parent-child relationship. The Document form type means the document will be a parent rather than a child of another document.

- **Response:** Response documents are associated with a main document. The response (child) document frequently inherits information from the main (parent) document. For example, if John creates a new main document in a discussion database, Beth might want to respond to his comments. When Beth creates her response, she might want her document to automatically contain certain information from John's document, such as the subject. Inheritance is discussed more thoroughly in the next chapter.

A view can also demonstrate the parent-child relationship. Responses can be indented to show how the discussion flows between the respondents. Figure 2-2 demonstrates how response documents can be displayed in a view:

Figure 2-2

Example of a
Discussion View

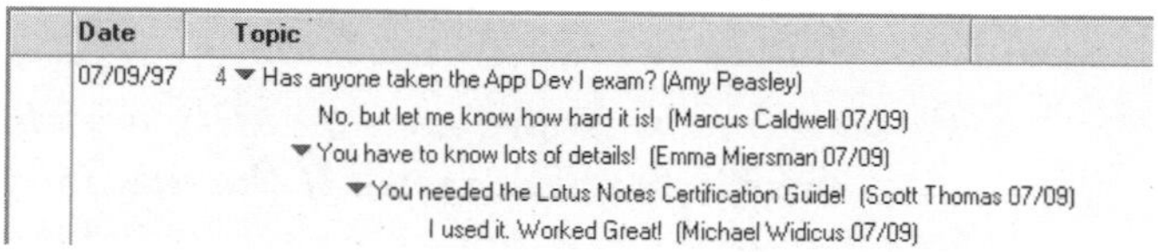

Date	Topic	
07/09/97	4 ▼ Has anyone taken the App Dev I exam? (Amy Peasley)	
	No, but let me know how hard it is! (Marcus Caldwell 07/09)	
	▼ You have to know lots of details! (Emma Miersman 07/09)	
	▼ You needed the Lotus Notes Certification Guide! (Scott Thomas 07/09)	
	I used it. Worked Great! (Michael Widicus 07/09)	

- **Response to Response:** Response to response documents can be associated with a main document or a response document. This document type allows an additional level in the parent-child relationship by enabling a response document, which is a child, to also be a parent to a response to response document.

Response and Response to Response type documents are most frequently used in discussion databases to track the history of the discussion, as displayed in Figure 2-2 above.

- **Background Color:** The background color can be set to any color available on users' systems.

Tips

It is important to understand what types of monitors your audi-ence is using. Some monitors can't handle all of the color options available, and the form should look consistent for all users. If the monitor cannot display the color the form was designed in, the form may be very difficult for the user to see.

- **Include in Menu & Search Builder:** The designer has the choice of including the form in the Create Menu, the Create – Other Dialog Menu, or neither. If the form is included in the menu options, the form name (not the synonym) will appear.

The form is included in the Search Builder by default. This option allows users to search for information by form. Deselect this option if the form will be hidden.

- **Version tracking:** When version tracking is enabled, both the original document and the new, edited version of the docu-ment are saved. Users can track the original document as well as all new versions by using the version tracking options.

Notes

Version tracking can only be utilized when the specified form is used to edit the document. If the document is displayed using another form and the user edits the document, the version track-ing functionality will not track the change.

There are four options for version tracking:

- **None:** Version tracking is off. This is the default selection.

- **New versions become responses:** In the view, all succes-sive new versions will show as responses to the original docu-ment. With this option, if users on different servers modify the same document, the versions each become separate documents when replication occurs. This option should be used when the focus in the view should remain on the original document rather than the responses.

- **Prior versions become responses:** The most recent version becomes the main document. All prior versions show as responses in the view. The original document will always be the last response. Replication and save conflicts cannot be prevented with this option. This option is most useful when the users' focus is on the most recent version of the document.

- **New versions become siblings:** In the view, the original document is listed first. All subsequent versions are listed below as additional main documents (rather than response documents). This option makes it more difficult to find the original document, since all documents are main documents. This option is useful when the timing of revisions is irrelevant.

Version tracking is covered on the Application Development I exam, but it is not a primary focus. It is most important to understand that it is a property of a form on the basics tab.

- **Create Version:** When versioned documents are edited and saved there are two options:

  - **Automatic—File, Save:** This option will automatically create a new version when the document is saved.

  - **Manual—File, New Version:** This gives the user an option at save time. A new version is created only when the user selects **File – Save As New Version**.

- **Anonymous Form:** Version 4 allows documents to be truly anonymous even to the application designer. This is beneficial in applications such as surveys or discussion databases where the author wishes to remain unknown. This option replaces the $UpdatedBy field with an $Anonymous field containing the value "1." The names of the authors and editors are eliminated from the form. However, the designer should be careful not to utilize any @UserName computed fields in the form, as this would display the user's name even if the form is set to be anonymous.

- **Merge replication conflicts:** Replication conflicts occur when the same document is edited on two different servers.

When these servers replicate, a Replication Conflict document is created. A Save Conflict occurs when the same document is edited on the same server by two different people at the same time. In Notes version 4, replication works at the field level rather than the document level as in prior versions. Instead of replicating the entire document when something changes, only the changed fields are replicated. This allows documents where changes were made in *different* fields to be merged together, rather than creating a replication conflict. The following examples demonstrate this concept:

Example 1:

Kevin and Kiki are working on the same document on different servers. Kevin makes a change to the Name field and Kiki makes a change to the Address field. If **Merge replication conflicts** is *not* selected, when the two servers replicate, a replication conflict is created. However, if **Merge replication conflicts** *is* selected, the changes in both fields would be replicated and no replication conflict would be created. The document would contain both Kiki and Kevin's changes.

Example 2:

Kevin and Kiki are working on different servers. They both make changes to the Address field on the same document. Regardless of whether **Merge replication conflicts** is selected or not, a replication conflict will be created, because they both edited the same field within the same document.

Notes

*Creating an anonymous form and avoiding replication conflicts are both very prominent topics on the Application Development I exam. For a more comprehensive discussion on replication, see Chapter 10—*Notes Infrastructure Planning and Design.

The Defaults Tab

The Defaults tab determines the settings for basic aspects of the form. Figure 2-3 shows all of the available selections:

Figure 2-3

Form Defaults Tab

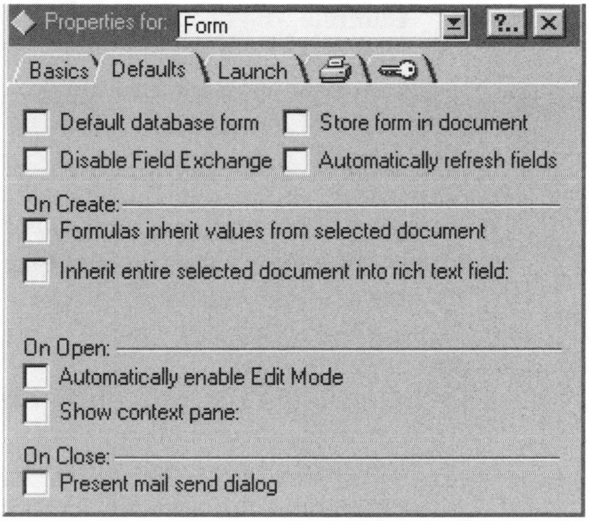

By default, no options are selected. In the top section, the following four options are available:

- **Default database form**: This option sets the current form as the default form in the database. The default form is used to display documents when the form associated with the document can't be found in the current database. Only one form per database can be the default form. It is marked with an asterisk (*) in the forms list in the design navigator.

- **Disable Field Exchange (Disable Notes/FX)**: Notes/FX enables Notes and OLE server applications to exchange field information. By selecting this option, field exchange is disabled, but the fields can remain on the form. Using field exchange is not covered on the exam, but it is important to know how to disable it. For more information about Notes/FX, see Lotus Notes Help.

- **Store form in document**: In Notes, the data and the form are stored separately. However, by selecting this option, the form is stored with the data. This must be selected if the form is going to be mailed to a user or to another database where the receiving mail-in database does not contain the form. There are drawbacks to storing the form in the document. For example, the document size will increase since every document contains a copy of the form. Also, if any changes are made to the design of the form, the documents created with the old version will not reflect the form changes.

Notes

The **Allow the use of stored forms in this database** *option must be selected on the Basics tab of the Database properties infobox for this option to work correctly.*

- **Automatically refresh fields**: If it is necessary for users to see field calculations or the result of field changes immediately, select this option. All fields on the form will be recalculated every time the user moves from one field to another. However, this will slow down data entry, especially on forms containing several calculated fields.

Lotus Notes documents have the ability to pull information stored in fields on one document into fields on another document. This functionality is referred to as *inheritance*. Inheritance can only occur when documents are being composed. Once the document has been created, information from fields in other documents must be accessed programmatically rather than via inheritance. A document must be selected in the view before the user selects **Create – *formname*** from the menu for either of the following inheritance options to work.

- **Formulas inherit values from selected documents**: This option allows fields to inherit their value from fields on a selected document or from fields within the document. This avoids unnecessary typing and keeps documents consistent when dealing with related information. The default value of the field must be set to the field name from which it should inherit its value. For example, if the designer wants the Subject field on a response document to automatically contain the information in the Subject field of the main document, this option should be selected and the default value in the field should be "Subject."

- **Inherit entire selected document into rich text field**: This selection allows the entire selected document to be automatically copied into a rich text field on the form in one of three ways: link, collapsible rich text, or rich text. In Figure 2-4, Body is the rich text field and the display options are also shown.

Figure 2-4
Inherit Selected
Document Option

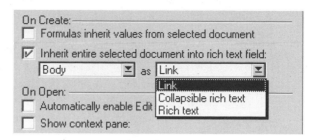

A rich text field must exist on the form for this option to work.

If **Link** is the selected option, a doclink will be placed in the rich text field that leads to the document. The **Collapsible rich text** option copies the contents of the selected document into a section in the rich text field, which can be expanded or collapsed. The **Rich text** option copies the selected document into the rich text field as rich text.

When a document created with this form is opened, two possible options are available:

● **Automatically enable Edit Mode**: By default, documents are opened in read mode. If this option is selected, the document will automatically open in edit mode. This is useful whenever users are going to make changes to a document every time it is opened.

● **Show context pane**: A context pane can be opened at the bottom of the screen to show the contents of either a **doclink** included in the document, or the **parent** of the current document.

When the user closes the document, the mail send dialog box can be displayed by selecting the **Present mail send dialog** option on the Defaults tab. This gives the user the option of sending, saving, or disregarding changes when the document is closed. If the send option is selected, the document must have the required mail fields for the document to be mailed correctly.

The Launch Tab

The Launch Tab provides a way to automatically launch links, attachments, and objects, which are part of the form. By default, this is set to **-None-** so nothing will be automatically launched. A list of options to automatically launch are available including the first attachment, first document link, the first OLE object, a URL, and all OLE enabled applications on the local workstation. If the designer selects the first attachment, document link, or URL, the first of these in the form will be automatically launched when the user selects **Create – *formname***. Figure 2-5 shows the additional options provided for all OLE related selections:

Figure 2-5
Form Launch
Properties—
Launching OLE
Objects

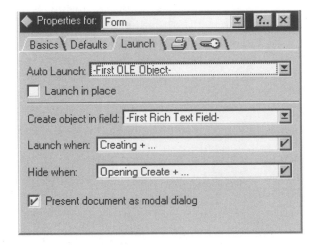

Several options are provided for launching, creating, and hiding the object:

- **Launch in place**: Objects can be launched in or out of place. By default, they are launched out of place. This shifts the focus from Notes to the application in which the document was created. If this option is selected and the object is launched in place, the application is opened within Notes.

- **Create object in field**: To create a new object in a field, select the field where the object will be placed when the document is composed. The **-First rich text field-** option is selected by default. This will add the new object to the first rich text field it finds on the form. **-None-** can also be selected if the object should not be displayed in the document. The designer can also select from any rich text field on the form.

- **Launch when**: The object can be launched when **Creating, Editing,** or **Reading** the document. By default, all three are selected. These can be toggled on or off. If a new object is automatically launched when the document is created, **Creating** must be selected in the Launch when options. Launch when **Editing** and **Reading** don't take effect until the document is saved and reopened. If the document is set to automatically open in edit mode, the launch when **Editing** option must be selected. If only **Reading** is selected, and the document always opens in edit mode, the object will never be automatically launched. For the purposes of the exam, it is not necessary to have an in-depth understanding of these items. This information is provided as a general overview.

- **Hide when**: Hiding the document allows the user to move seamlessly between Notes and another application. There are several options for hiding the document:

    - **Opening Create:** Hide when the user creates a document (selected by default).

    - **Opening Edit**: Hide when the user opens a document to edit it (selected by default).

    - **Opening Read**: Hide when the user opens a document to read it (selected by default).

    - **Closing Create**: Hide when the user closes a document after creating it (available only if **Opening Create** is selected).

    - **Closing Edit**: Hide when the user closes a document after editing it (available only if **Opening Edit** is selected).

    - **Closing Read**: Hide when the user closes a document after reading it (available only if **Opening Read** is selected). This option is selected by default.

These options can be mixed, based on what the designer wants to present to the user and the role of the Notes document in the application.

- **Present document as modal dialog**: This option prevents users from accessing the Notes menu. The only options available to the user are entering/modifying data, launching the first embedded OLE object by clicking on the **Launch** button in the dialog box, or selecting an action from the list at the bottom of the dialog box. The designer can control which actions are available to the user from the Action menu, as well as create custom commands.

The Print Tab

The Print tab in the form properties infobox is identical to the Print tab in the database properties infobox, as seen in Figure 2-6:

Figure 2-6
Form Print Tab

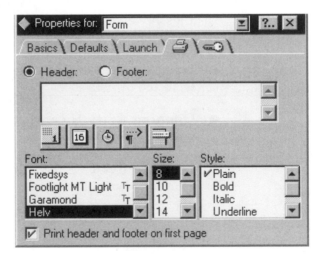

Any print options set here will affect all documents created with this form. However, these options can be changed on an individual document basis in the document properties infobox once the document is created. The document properties will override the form properties.

The Security Tab

The information listed on the Security tab is not covered on the Application Development I exam. For more information about security issues in application development, see Chapter 9—*Securing Notes Applications*.

Sections

The form itself is only a blank slate; there are very few restrictions on the length of this slate. The bottom of the form is set when there are no more design elements. If the designer continues to add design elements, the user will be forced to scroll down until the bottom of the form is reached. Most users find scrolling down a form cumbersome. Adding collapsible sections to a form enables the designer to include a lot of design elements, without adding length to the form. Two types of sections are available: Standard and Controlled access.

Standard Sections

To create a standard section on the form, open the form and select **Create – Section – Standard** from the menu. The section title properties, expanding/collapsing properties, font, and hide-when formula can be set in the section properties infobox shown in Figure 2-7:

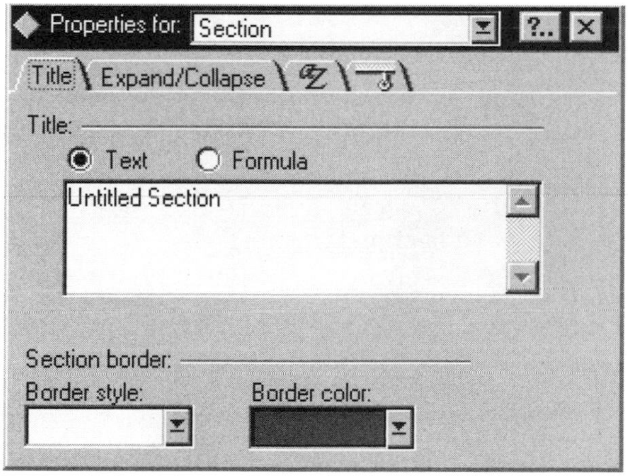

Figure 2-7
Section Title Tab

App. Dev. I

- **Title**: The title of the section appears in the section header. This can be text or a formula specified by the designer. On this tab, the border style and color can also be selected. By default, no border is selected and Dark Cyan is the color.

- **Expand/Collapse**: The section can be set to expand or collapse automatically on four document events: Previewed, Opened for reading, Opened for editing, and Printed. By default, all of the options are set at **Don't auto expand or collapse**. The user can select auto-expand or auto-collapse for any or all of the sections. This tab also allows the designer to hide the section title when expanded or only show the section when the document is being previewed.

- **Font**: The font tab allows the designer to specify the font, size, and color of the section title.

- **Hide When**: The section title can be hidden based on a formula or the state of the document. Hide-when formulas are covered later in this chapter.

Tips

To create a section from information already contained on the form, highlight the fields, then select Create – Section – Standard from the Notes menu. This will automatically move the selected fields into the section and create a section title .

Controlled Access Sections

To control access to an area on the form, create a Controlled Access section. To add a controlled access section to the form, open the form and select **Create – Section – Controlled Access**. The section properties for a controlled access section differ slightly from a standard section. In the Title tab, the section title can be entered, as well as a section field name. There are two tabs for setting expand/collapse options: one for editors, one for non-editors. These tabs provide the same options as the standard section's expand/collapse tab, with the exception of the **Preview Only** option. Also, there is no option for hiding the title when the section is expanded for the Editors of the section. The formula tab is shown in Figure 2-8.

Figure 2-8

Controlled Access
Section Formula Tab

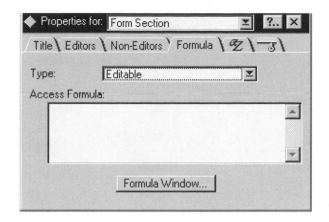

The formula type can be **Editable**, **Computed**, **Computed for Display**, or **Computed when Composed**. The formula must evaluate to a name or list of names. Also, the section access cannot override the Access Control List of the database. This access controls who can edit the fields within the section, but allows anyone with access to the document to read the information in the section. To prevent users from reading the information contained in a section, use a hide-when formula (hide-when formulas are covered later in this chapter).

Working with Design Elements

Forms only provide a shell for the information in a Notes document. All other parts of the form add functionality. In this section, we will cover some of the design elements which enable the designer to enhance the form, including static text, hotspots, actions, hide-when formulas, subforms, and window titles.

Static Text

Static text provides additional information to the user and adds readability to the form. It also determines what type of look and feel the form will have. Fields are labeled using static text to help the user understand what type of information should be placed in the field. Static text can also be used to break up different areas of the form. This information is displayed on all documents created with the form, and cannot be changed by the user. The text infobox shown in Figure 2-9 determines static text characteristics:

Figure 2-9

Text Font Tab

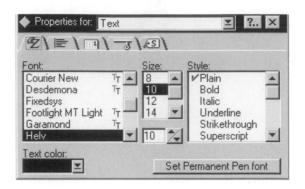

All text characteristics are determined here. On the Font tab shown above, the font, size, style, and color can be selected. The following tabs allow the designer to select the tabs, spacing, hide-when formula, and style. We will not cover these tabs in detail, as they are not covered on the Application Development I exam.

Hotspots

Hotspots come in different types, providing the designer with a myriad of choices. Hotspots can link to another document, display text in a pop-up box, run a formula, or perform an action. Hotspots are added to the form by selecting **Create – Hotspot – *Hotspot Type***. Hotspots can be created on forms or in rich text fields on documents. The different types of hotspots are listed below:

- **Link Hotspot**: Link hotspots are used to link a document, view, folder, or database. The user clicks on the text or graphic hotspot, and Notes switches them to the linked item. This functionality is similar to using a doclink, but instead of clicking on the Notes doclink icon to get to the link, the user clicks on the text or graphic hotspot.

- **Text Pop-Up**: When the user clicks on a text pop-up hotspot, text is displayed while the mouse is held down. This is not useful for large amounts of text, since the user cannot scroll through the information. The text is entered in the hotspot properties infobox. The normal text formatting options are available, including font, spacing, hiding, and style.

- **Button**: Buttons automate Notes actions. They are similar to buttons on the action bar, but can be placed anywhere on the form (or in a rich text field of a document). Buttons can be programmed to run simple actions, formulas, or a script. When the user clicks the button, the action, formula, or script runs.

- **Formula Pop-Up**: A formula pop-up works exactly like a text pop-up, except that instead of the designer typing the text into the hotspot properties infobox, the design pane appears and the designer can add an action, formula, or script that results in text.

- **Action Hotspot**: When the user clicks on an action hotspot, a Notes action is performed. The action can run a simple action, formula, or script.

Notes

Links and text pop-up hotspots are considered "manual" hotspots and are the focus of the hotspot questions on the Application Development I exam. It is also important to note that a button on a form is considered a hotspot. Buttons are created by selecting Create – Hotspot – Button from the menu.

Hide-When Formulas:

Design elements can be hidden based on a formula or document event. In the Hide tab of the infobox for the design element (shown in Figure 2-10), the designer can select from document events or write a formula to hide the design element.

Figure 2-10
Text Hide Tab

![Properties for: Text infobox showing the Hide tab. "Hide paragraph when document is:" with checkboxes for Previewed for reading, Previewed for editing, Opened for reading, Opened for editing, Printed, Copied to the clipboard. "Hide paragraph if formula is true:" checkbox with formula text area and Formula Window... button.]

Note that this infobox enables the hide-when setting for previewing, opening, printing, and copying the document. Hiding is available for hotspots, buttons, sections, objects, text, and graphics.

Actions

Actions can be associated with forms or views. They are available via the **Actions** menu item or on the **Action Bar** of the form or view (View actions are discussed in Chapter 4). Notes provides a set of default actions on all forms. These actions include common form functionality: editing the document, moving the document to a folder, forwarding the document, or removing the document from a folder. The designer can also create new actions by selecting **Create – Action** on the menu. These actions can use simple actions, formulas, or script.

Actions have their own set of properties (Figure 2-11) which can be set by the designer:

Figure 2-11
Action Properties
InfoBox

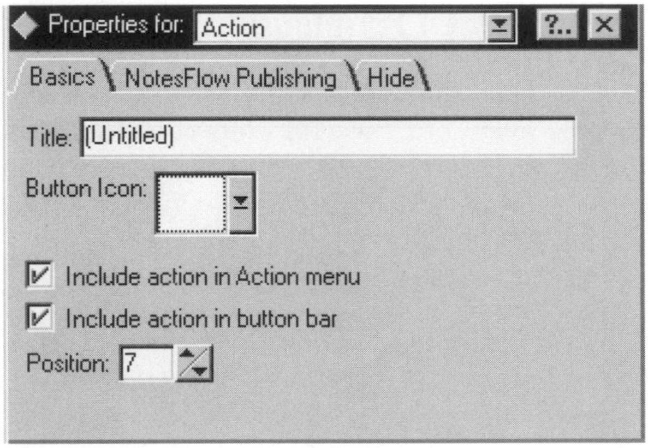

The title contains the text that will appear in the menu and on the button in the button bar. The button icon can be selected from the drop-down list. This provides a distinguishing graphic on the button. The designer has the option of displaying the action in the Actions menu or in the button bar. The position determines where the action is displayed in relation to other actions.

The action properties infobox also allows actions to be hidden, based on document events or hide-when formulas.

Subforms

Subforms are similar to forms in that they can contain all of the same design elements. Subforms are inserted into forms as a way to enable forms to share multiple design elements. The subform is considered one design element on the form. Subforms are similar to shared fields in that a change to a subform will affect all forms that include the subform. Subforms also enable the designer to quickly create new forms, rather than starting from a blank slate. To create a subform, select **Create – Design – Subform** from the Notes menu.

The subform properties infobox is shown in Figure 2-12:

Figure 2-12
Subform Properties
InfoBox

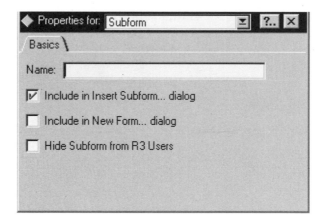

Three options are available when designing a subform:

● **Include in Insert Subform... dialog**: By default, this option is selected. By deselecting this option, the subform can only be used in computed subform properties and not when forms are created.

● **Include in New Form... dialog**: Select this option if the subform should appear immediately when designers choose **Create – Design – Form** from the menu.

- **Hide Subform from R3 users**: This option allows the designer to hide the subform from anyone using version 3.x of Lotus Notes. This is beneficial if there is a mixed environment and designers want to add R4 functionality to the form.

Window Titles

The window title appears in the title bar of the document. The title also appears in the Window menu when the user switches between Notes windows. If no title is set, **(Untitled)** appears.

The window title is set in the design pane of the form. This title can be static text, or can change dynamically based on a formula. For example, the window title formula for a Call Tracking form might be:

```
@If(@IsNewDoc;"New Call";CallSubject)
```

This formula sets the window title to **New Call** if the document is being composed; otherwise, it uses the value of the CallSubject field as the window title.

Chapter 2 Sample Questions

Objective: Writing Notes Applications using properties.

Isaac created a Question & Answer database which allows new mothers to post questions about their newborns. How can he associate the answer documents with the appropriate question?

    A. Create a form and select **Response** as the document type

    B. Create a form and name it "Response"

    C. Select the **Response Form** option in the Document Properties Basics Tab

    D. Select the **Allow Response Hierarchy** option in the From Properties infobox

Answer: A

Parent/child hierarchies are created by using Response and Response to Response type forms. A Response type form is created by selecting Response or Response to Response in the form type options on the Basics tab of the form properties infobox.

Objective: Writing Notes Applications which allow for anonymity.

Monique has created a survey to gather information about the effectiveness of her department. However, people don't want their names associated with the survey when they complete it. How can Monique make the survey remains anonymous?

    A. Select the **Anonymous Form** option in the Form Properties Default Tab

    B. Select the **Anonymous Form** option in the Form Properties Basics Tab

    C. Select the **Anonymous Form** option in the Field Properties Basics Tab

    D. This feature is not available because of the $UpdatedBy field

Answer: B

By selecting the **Anonymous Form** property, the $UpdatedBy field is replaced by an $Anonymous field.

Objective: Writing Notes Applications which allow for anonymity.

Monique decides she wants people to put their name on the survey. She creates a computed field which has the @UserName formula in it so the user's name is automatically saved on the document. However, she forgets to deselect the Anonymous Form option. What will happen?

> A. The Anonymous Form option will override the field and the user's name will not be stored
>
> B. Notes will generate an error when Monique tries to save the form
>
> C. The user's name will be stored in the computed field, but not in the $UpdatedBy field
>
> D. The user's name will be stored in the computed field and the $UpdatedBy field will store the user's name (the Anonymous Form option will be ignored)

Answer: C

Although the @UserName field defeats the purpose of the Anonymous Form selection, the field will be filled out and the name stored. However, the user's name will not be stored in the $UpdatedBy field, because the Anonymous Form selection is still in effect. This is something to be careful of when creating Anonymous forms—an @UserName field will still store the person's name.

Objective: Writing Notes Applications which merge replication conflicts.

The TPC Company has three servers in different locations which replicate every four hours. Tom makes a change to the Comments field on a document on the Des Moines server. At the same time, Chip makes a change to the Comments field on the same document on the Cleveland server. **Merge replication conflicts** is selected on the form. When the servers replicate, is a replication conflict created?

A. No, because the **Merge replication conflicts** property solves replication conflicts

B. No, only Chip's change would replicate because his change was made after Tom's change

C. No, because the documents were changed on different servers

D. Yes, because the same field on the same document was changed on different servers

Answer: D
Since **Merge replication conflicts** was selected, a conflict would not have occurred if the users had edited different fields. Since the users edited the same field, a replication conflict was created.

Objective: Writing Notes Applications which merge replication conflicts.

Michael creates a document and saves it. Amy opens the document on the same server and starts revising it. While Amy has the document open, Michael goes back into the document, makes a change, and saves the document. What will happen when Amy saves the document? Merge replication conflicts is not selected.

A. Multiple copies of the document will be saved in the database. No error will be generated

B. Amy's changes will be ignored; only Michael's changes will be saved

C. A Save Conflict will be generated

D. Amy and Michael's changes will both be saved because they are on the same server

Answer: C
Since Michael changed the document while Amy was editing it, a Save Conflict document will be created. If Michael and Amy were on different servers, a replication conflict would have been created.

App. Dev. I

Objective: Writing Notes Applications which allow for version control.

Pedro is developing a Notes database for document review. He wants the most recent revision to show as the main document in the view. What option will achieve this?

> A. Set versioning to **Prior versions become responses** in the View Properties
>
> B. Set versioning to **New versions become responses** in the Document Properties
>
> C. Set versioning to **Prior versions become responses** in the Form Properties
>
> D. Set versioning to **New versions become responses** in the Form Properties

Answer: C

The **Prior versions become responses** setting in the form properties will set the most recent version of the document as the main document. All prior versions will show as responses to the main document in the view.

Objective: Writing Notes Applications using Default properties.

Joey wants to mail a survey to all Notes users in the company, have them fill it out, and return it to a mail-in database. However, when he mails it out, an error is generated when the users open the document and they only see an empty mail message. What can Joey do to fix this problem?

> A. Joey needs to create a field called Form in the document to store the name of the form
>
> B. Joey must select **Store Form in Document** in the Form Properties
>
> C. Joey must select **Store Form in Document** in the Document Properties
>
> D. The sending formula must include the name of the form

Answer: B

Assuming users do not have a copy of the survey form in their mail database, the form must be stored in the document. The error is generated because Notes cannot find the form and tries to use the default form.

Objective: Writing Notes Applications which automatically enable edit mode.

Luci is designing a Call Tracking application for the MIS department's Help Desk. The users have specified that once the document is created, they should be able to edit it without any special keystrokes every time it is opened. What should Luci do to meet the users' specifications?

    A. Enable the **Automatically enable edit mode** selection in the Default Tab in the Form Properties InfoBox

    B. Enable the **Automatically enable edit mode** selection in the Launch Tab in the Form Properties InfoBox

    C. Enable the **Automatically enable edit mode** selection in the Launch Tab in the Document Properties InfoBox

    D. Enable the **Automatically enable edit mode** selection in the Default Tab in the Document Properties InfoBox

Answer: A

Automatically enable edit mode is an option in the Form Properties InfoBox on the Defaults tab in the "On Open" section.

Objective: Use synonyms for Notes design elements.

When the users go to the Create menu, Maddi wants them to see "Customer Service Complaint Form." However, when she is designing the application, that form name is very cumbersome to work with. What can Maddi do about this problem?

    A. Set the Form Name field to **Customer Service Complaint Form** and the Alias field to **Complaint**

B. Set the Form Name to **Customer Service Complaint Form | Complaint**

C. Set the Form Name to **Complaint | Customer Service Complaint Form**

D. Set the Form Name field to **Complaint** and the Alias field to **Customer Service Complaint Form**

Answer: B
The first entry in the form name is the name used in the Create Menu; Notes uses the second entry internally. There is no **Alias** field available in Form properties, only in View Properties.

Objective: Write Notes Applications which inherit documents.

Lindsey is designing a discussion database. The users have requested the entire original document be shown in a collapsible section within every response document. How can this be accomplished?

A. Notes does not have this capability without the use of LotusScript

B. Set the Body field's Default formula to **Parent Doc—Collapsed**

C. Select the **Formulas inherit values from selected document** attribute

D. None of the above

Answer: D
This capability is available via the **Inherit entire selected document into rich text field** setting. Lindsey must also select the correct rich text field and **Collapsible section**.

Objective: Control section access.

In a form developed to track application problems, Mark wants to add a section that only Managers can edit, but everyone can view. How can he accomplish this task?

A. Add a collapsible standard section with a hide-when formula to the form

B. Add a controlled access section to the form allowing Managers to edit the section

C. Add a collapsible standard section to the form

D. None of the above

Answer: B
A controlled access section prevents users not in the access list from editing the information, but all users can view the information. A hide-when formula would only affect viewing, not editing.

Objective: Create forms which share design attributes using subforms.

Laticia wants to reuse a set of design elements on every form in her database. However, she knows that she may want to add more fields to the set of information in the future. What type of design element should she use which will allow her to reuse the elements and make changes on all forms?

A. Add a section to each of the forms which includes all of the design elements

B. Used shared fields on each form

C. Create a subform and insert it into each form

D. Copy and paste all of the design elements onto each form

Answer: C
Only a subform enables different types of design elements to be inserted and updated on different forms.

Objective: Create forms which use buttons.

Mario wants to add a button to the bottom of his form to automatically send the document to the manager of the database. How can he add a button directly on to the form?

A. Select **Actions – Create** from the menu

B. Select **Create – Hotspots – Action** from the menu

C. Select **Create – Hotspots – Button** from the menu

D. Select the **Show action in button bar** attribute

Answer: C

To place a button directly on the form (rather than in the Action Bar), the designer should select **Create – Hotspots – Button.**

Objective: Write applications which use manual hotspots.

Dierdre created a hotspot on her form which opens a view when the user clicks on it. What type of hotspot did Dierdre create?

A. Link Hotspot

B. Text pop-up Hotspot

C. Action Hotspot

D. Button Hotspot

Answer: A

Link hotspots can open a document, view, folder or database.

Objective: Create forms which use objects with hide-when settings for previewing documents.

Samantha is in a view. She is selecting documents and looking at them in the preview pane at the bottom of the screen. Samantha knows that when she opens the document, it contains a **Send** button in the button bar. However, she is not seeing this action when previewing the document. What did the designer do to accomplish this?

A. Nothing, the form actions are not shown when a document is displayed in the preview pane

B. Selected the **Previewed for reading** attribute in the Action's Hide Properties

C. Selected the **Previewed for opening** attribute in the Action Bar's Hide Properties

D. Deselected the **Show action in button bar** attribute in the Action Properties

Answer: B
Selecting the **Previewed for reading** will prevent the action from showing in the action bar when the document is being previewed in read mode.

Objective: Create forms which use objects with hide-when formulas to control object display.

The TPC Consulting firm has created a database to store all of the consultants' employee records. Each employee's resume is an object on the form. The only people who can see the resumes are the managers. How are other people prevented from seeing the resumes?

A. The resumes are in an access controlled section on the form

B. The managers have Editor access to the forms and everyone else only has reader access

C. Managers are looking at the document through a different form

D. A hide-when formula check to see if the person reading the document is in the Managers role; if not, the resume is hidden

Answer: D
Hide-when formulas can control when objects are hidden.

Objective: Create forms which use window titles.

When Yada creates a document, the word **(Untitled)** appears in the title bar of the form. What does the designer need to change about the form?

A. Nothing, a document does not have a title until it has been saved

B. A form name needs to be provided for the form

C. An alias needs to be provided for the form name

D. A window title needs to be provided for the form

Answer: D
(Untitled) will show in the title bar if no window title is specified for the form.

Objective: Create forms which use manual actions.

Tom designed an action which sends an opened document to the leader of the temple. What type of action did he create?

A. Field Action

B. Form Action

C. View Action

D. Database Action

Answer: B
When a document is opened, form actions are in effect.

3

Working with Fields, Formulas & Agents

Fields contain the individual data elements stored in the document; they enable the user to enter and retrieve data. Each field is associated with a particular type of data. The information in the field can be entered by the user or computed from a formula. Some fields are not shown to the user on the form, but store information to be used in views or for calculations. Fields are defined by five main elements: a name, a data type, the computed or editable attribute, display options and the formulas associated with the field. The Application Development I exam focuses on these attributes, the subject of this chapter.

This chapter also covers the fundamentals of writing formulas. Basic formula components and usage are discussed. The candidate should have a basic understanding of formulas, including how to create and interpret them, for the Application Development I exam.

Agents are covered briefly on the Application Development I exam. This chapter reviews creating and using manual agents within a Notes application.

Field Properties

Field properties dynamically change based on the designer's selections (such as data type). For example, if the designer selects the data type "time," all of the time options appear in the infobox. Figure 3-1 shows the Basics tab when the keywords data type is selected.

Figure 3-1

Field Basics Tab

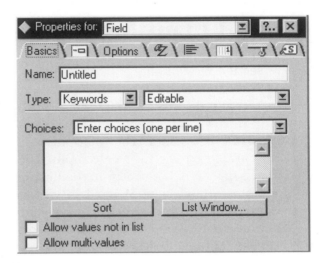

An identifying name should be entered for the field. Field names have the following restrictions:

● No two fields on a form can have the same name

● The field name cannot be longer than 32 characters

● The field name cannot begin with a number, and should not begin with a dollar sign ($) or at symbol (@)

● The field name cannot contain spaces (use underlines or capitalization instead)

● Certain field names are reserved and should not be used by the designer for any other functions than they were intended for. For example, SendTo, CopyTo, Sign, and Encrypt are reserved field names used for mailing. A designer could create fields with these names for other purposes, but if the form was ever mail-enabled, these fields would be used by Notes for mailing rather than the designer's purpose. The reserved field called *Form* is used to store the name of the form. See Notes documentation for a complete list of reserved field names.

At the bottom of the Basics tab, you will find the **Allow multi-values** option. By selecting this option, the user can create lists within the field. Also, by selecting this option, the Multi-value options area on the Options tab can be modified. See the Options tab section for more information.

Keywords & Other Data Types

Notes provides eight different data types for fields: text, time, number, keywords, rich text, authors, names, and readers. In the Application Development I exam, the questions are focused on the keywords data type.

Keywords provide the user with a predefined list of choices. This is useful for forcing consistency in data entry. When the designer selects keywords as the data type, the keywords options appear in the Basics tab (as shown in Figure 3-1). Several options are available for generating the keywords list:

- **Enter choices (one per line):** The designer can manually enter the choices. These choices are the same every time the list is shown to the user. If the designer selects this option, the design must be changed to add or delete a choice. To allow users to enter items not on the list, select the **Allow values not in this list** option. However, any items added by users will not appear the next time the list is generated. To accomplish this, a formula must be used. The **enter choices** option is useful if the list of choices will remain static.

Keyword selection lists are another design element where *synonyms* can be utilized. The same rules apply here as when creating synonyms for form names. The item displayed to the user is listed first, then the internal name. The two elements are separated by a pipe (|) character. For example, the list of keyword options might look like Figure 3-2:

Figure 3-2
Creating Keyword
Synonyms

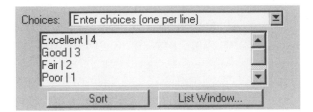

The user will see the items listed on the left as the keyword options (shown in Figure 3-3 as a dialog box), but the designer can use the numeric synonym to refer to the value of the field. This allows the text of the keyword to change without affecting any formulas written based on the keyword selection. For example, if the designer decided to change the keyword "Excellent" to "Wonderful," the text would change but the synonym would continue to be "4," thus, no reprogramming would be required.

Figure 3-3
User's Keyword
Dialog Box

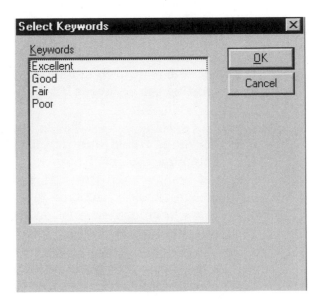

Traps

If keywords are used in column formulas, the synonym *will be displayed, not the text normally displayed to the user! In Figure 3-3, 4, 3, 2, or 1 would show in the view, rather than* Excellent, Good, Fair, *or* Poor.

App. Dev. I

- **Use formula for choices:** Formulas allow the list of keyword choices to change dynamically. The formula must evaluate to a value or list of values that can be stored in the field. Frequently, an @DBColumn formula is used to generate a list of values from a view. When a formula is used to generate the choices for the keywords list, designers still have the option of allowing values not in the list.

- **Use Address Dialog for choices:** The user is presented with the Names dialog box to select a name from the Personal or Public Name and Address Book. **Look up names as they are entered** is available with this option to speed up name entry.

- **Use Access Control List for choices:** The list presented to the user will contain the people, groups, and roles listed in the ACL of the database. This is useful if the only choices available to the user should be names, groups, and roles which have access to the database.

- **Use View dialog for choices:** This option is new to version 4 of Lotus Notes. When the user clicks on the arrow to display the keywords, the data appears in columns in a Notes view. The designer must specify what database, view, and column should be shown. The **Allow values not in this list** option is not available here.

Additional information is available for the display options, but this is not necessary for the Application Development I exam.

On the Basics tab, the designer can allow the user to select multiple keywords based on the **Allow multi-values** selection. Multiple keyword values are stored as a text list in Notes.

The keywords data type allows the designer to specify how the keywords should be shown to the user. The display type selection is made on the Options tab (shown in Figure 3-4). The only time this tab is active in the field infobox is when the keywords data type is selected.

Figure 3-4
Keyword Display
Options Tab

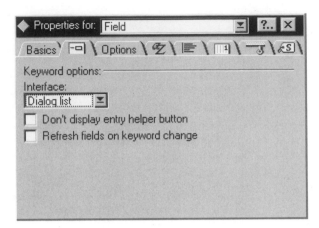

The Interface option is only available if the keyword choices are entered by the designer or generated by a formula. The Address Book, ACL, and View dialog option have a predesigned dialog box used to display the choices. Three different interfaces are available:

- **Dialog List:** In Figure 3-3, the dialog list option was shown. The user can see all of the available keywords by pressing **Enter** or clicking on the entry helper button on the form (the arrow to the right of the field). New keywords are typed at the bottom of the dialog box if **Allow values not in this field** is selected.

Traps

The Dialog List display option is not available if the field is located in a layout region!

- **Checkbox:** A box is provided for each option. Users can select one or more options, but are not allowed to enter any values not listed in the checkboxes. The **Allow values not in this list** and **Allow multi-values** options are ignored if this display option is selected. By selecting **Checkbox** as the display option, multi-values is assumed. The frame can be hidden (using the **None** option), shown in standard mode, or shown in 3D, (see Figure 3-5), and can have up to eight columns.

Figure 3-5
Example of Checkbox
Keyword Display

- **Radio Button:** Radio buttons only allow the user to select one option from the list. The **Allow values not in this list**, and **Allow multi-values** options are ignored if this display option is selected. By selecting **Radio Button** as the display option, it is assumed that only one option is allowed. The frame can be hidden (using the None option), shown in standard mode, or shown in 3D (see Figure 3-6), and can have up to eight columns.

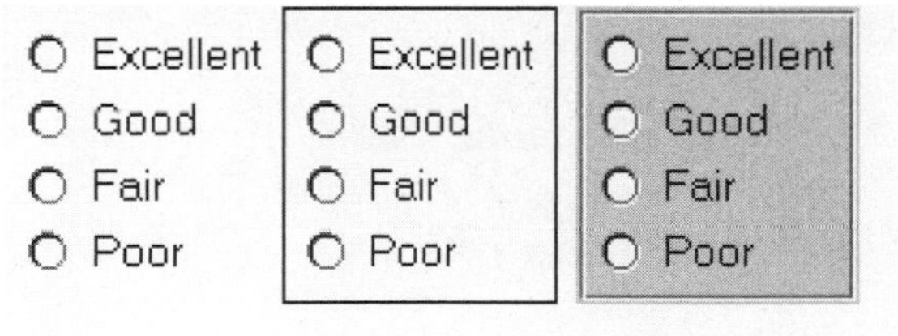

Figure 3-6
Example of Radio Button
Keyword Display

- **Listbox & Combobox:** These options are only available in layout regions and are covered in preparation for the Application Development II exam in Chapter 5—*Workflow Applications & Form Design.*

The other data types used in fields include:

- **Text:** Text includes letters, punctuation, spaces, and numbers not used mathematically. This is the most frequently used field type for entering data.

- **Rich Text:** Rich text fields allow the user to enter formatted text, graphics, hotspots, attachments, or objects. Different text styles can be used within the field. Rich text data cannot be displayed in views or returned in most formulas.

- **Numbers:** Number fields allow the user to enter numbers which can be used in mathematical calculations. Numbers can be formatted as general, fixed, scientific, or currency.

- **Time:** Time fields contain data related to time or date. This information can be displayed in a variety of formats. By default, time data is stored as MM/DD/YYYY HH:MM:SS. Time, date or both can be displayed in a time data type field.

Notes

Lotus Notes is completely Year 2000-compliant. In a time data type field, the century will only be displayed if it is not the current century. For example, if the date to be displayed was June 29, 1997, it would be displayed as 06/29/97 before the year 2000, but after the year 2000 it would be displayed as 06/29/1997, since it is not the current century.

- **Names:** Names fields display server or user names as they appear in a Notes ID file. Names fields are not used for security purposes.

- **Authors:** Authors fields determine who can edit a document. This is useful if users have Author access, but some users need to edit documents they did not create. An in-depth understanding of this type of field is not necessary until the Application Development II exam. See Chapter 9—*Securing Notes Applications* for more information on Authors fields.

- **Readers:** Readers fields restrict access on who can read the document regardless of the user's access level in the ACL. An in-depth understanding of this type of field is not necessary until the Application Development II exam. See Chapter 9—*Securing Notes Applications* for more information on Readers fields.

Notes

It is very important to remember that only one data type can be stored within a field (even if the field is multi-valued). If data is to be combined into one field, it must be converted to all one data type. For example, to create a field that contains the text "This document was created on 06/27/97," where the date is provided by the @Today command, the date must be converted to text. The appropriate formula for this field would be:

```
"This document was created on " + @Text(@Today)
```

If the @Text conversion was not included, the field would generate an error.

The Options Tab

The Options tab (Figure 3-7) allows the designer to provide field-level help. A brief description about the field or what type of data the field expects can be entered in the help description. The information will display at the bottom of the user's screen when they enter the field, if the user's menu option **View – Show – Field Help** is selected.

If the user's cursor should be placed in this field when the document is opened in edit mode, select the **Give this field default focus** option.

Figure 3-7
Field Options
Dialog Box

Within the Multi-value options section, the designer can specify how multiple values within a field can be entered or displayed. The **Separate values when user enters** and **Display separate values with** selections both have the same options, including:

- Space

- Comma

- Semicolon

- New Line

- Blank Line

The designer can select all, one, or any combination of these options. For these options to be enabled, the **Allow multi-values** option must be selected on the Basics tab. Note that in a keywords field which allows multi-values, there are no options to choose from. The comma is used as the separator when values are entered into the field, and no options are allowed for displaying the values.

This tab also allows the designer to select security options. Security options are not covered on the Application Development I exam.

Editable and Computed Fields

Notes provides four options for all fields other than fields of rich text data type. Rich text fields can only be Editable or Computed.

- **Editable:** The user enters the information into the field. The field may have a default value which appears in the field when the document is created. Field labels and field help are beneficial in editable fields to provide the user with guidance in entering the data.

- **Computed:** Information in computed fields is calculated every time a document is created, refreshed, or saved. A formula must be provided for a computed field. Users cannot change the data in a computed field.

- **Computed for display:** If a field is computed for display, it is calculated when the document is opened for reading or editing and when the document is refreshed, but no data is saved in the field. These fields cannot be used in views. This type of field is beneficial when there is no reason to store the data; it is only used for viewing on the form.

- **Computed when composed:** Computed when composed fields are calculated when the document is created and never recalculated. The data is stored in the field and can be referred to in views and formulas.

The Font Tab

The Font tab (Figure 3-8) allows the designer to set the font. You can set the font on fields, text, sections—anywhere a font can be designated. The font type, size, and color are all specified on this tab. The permanent pen can also be set on this tab. The permanent pen function allows the user to switch to a different font at any location on the document. This is helpful for adding comments to a document or using a special font in different areas of a form.

Figure 3-8
Field Font Tab

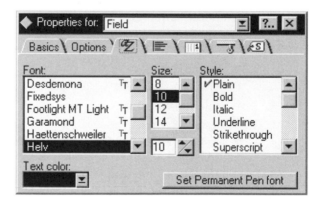

Other Tabs

The spacing, tab, hide-when, and style tabs in the field properties infobox are all related to formatting the information on the form. These tabs are not covered on the exam.

Formulas

Lotus Notes consists of two types of programming languages: Formula Language and LotusScript. Formula language is comprised of constants, variables, operators, keywords, and @functions. LotusScript is a BASIC-compatible, structured, object oriented programming language similar to Visual Basic. LotusScript is not covered in the Application Development I or II exams, so it will not be covered in this discussion.

Formulas are used in all aspects of Notes application design from hide-when formulas to field formulas. They can be very simple or extremely complex. In the Application Development I exam, it is important to understand the basic components of a formulas and how formulas work. Based on the syntax of the formula provided, you should understand what the formula is trying to accomplish and how to evaluate the formula. Note that this is not a comprehensive description of how to use formulas in Notes! If you have never written formulas in Notes, please refer to the Lotus Notes Help documentation.

Formulas are based on the following four basic elements as well as @functions which are covered in the next section:

- **Constants**: Constants are text, time, or numbers that do not change. To refer to a constant in a formula, place it in quotes ("Location").

- **Variables:** Field names are used as variables in Notes. Temporary variables can also be set to store information while the formula is being evaluated. Field names can be used alone, with other operators to create a new result or as part of an @formula. When a field name is being used as a variable in a formula, it is generally not placed in quotes (MyName); however there are exceptions based on the syntax of some formulas.

- **Operators:** Operators take action on variables and constants. Five different types of operators are available in Notes (listed in order of evaluation):

- Assignment (:=)

- Concatenation (:, +)

- Arithmetic (+,-,*,/)

- Comparison (=,<,>,!=)

- Logical (!,&, |)

The order of evaluation follows standard mathematical procedure:

- Parentheses

- Exponents

- Multiplication and Division

- Addition and Subtraction

- **Formula Keywords:** Notes contains certain words which perform special functions when used in formulas:

  - **REM:** (REM "remark"): Used to remark out lines in the formula as well as add comments to the code. These lines are ignored when Notes evaluates the formula.

  - **SELECT:** (SELECT Form = "Main Topic"): Defines which documents should be included in a view, agent, or replication. If a SELECT statement is needed in the formula and is not included by the designer, SELECT @ALL is appended to the formula automatically.

  - **DEFAULT:** (DEFAULT *fieldname* := *value*) If the field does not exist in the document being processed by the formula, the field is treated as though it does exist and the specified value is associated with it. The default keyword is not necessary when specifying a value in the Default value, event for a field. Field events are explained later in this chapter.

- **FIELD:** (FIELD *fieldname* := *value*): If the field exists, its value is replaced. If the field does not exist, it is created.

- **ENVIRONMENT:** This is not covered on the Application Development I exam.

@Functions

At functions (@functions) are built-in formulas that provide the Notes programmer with a means of enhancing the functionality of the application, without requiring knowledge of a complex object-oriented programming language. Notes includes about 200 @functions which can perform a variety of tasks, including formatting text and dates, evaluating conditional statements, calculating numeric values or values in a list, or activating agents and actions.

This text assumes you have a basic knowledge of @functions. It is important to know how to spot problems in formula syntax and basic structure. It is especially helpful to understand @If functions.

The @If function evaluates a series of conditions, then performs the specified action. The syntax of the @If function is:

```
@If(condition1; action1; condition2; action2;else
action)
```

Example of a computed field formula:

```
@If(Status = "Approved";"Completed";"In Process")
```

which translates to: *If the Status field equals the word Approved then the current field's value will be set to Completed; otherwise, the field's value is set to In Process.*

Example 2:

```
@If(color = "Red";"Apple";color = "Yellow"; "Lemon";
"Unknown Fruit")
```

App. Dev. I

which translates to: *If the value of the color field is equal to Red then the value of the field is Apple, if the value of the color field is equal to Yellow, then the value of the field is Lemon, otherwise the field is set to Unknown Fruit.*

Note that @If statements must always have an odd number of arguments, can be nested, and can take up to 99 conditions.

The exam focuses on some of the @functions new to version 4 listed below. Additional @functions are covered in the table at the end of this chapter.

- **@AllChildren:** This @function is used in view selection and selective replication formulas. All response documents that match the parent documents are included in the view. However, only the immediate responses and no response-to-response documents will be included. This differs from @IsResponseDoc in that only responses to parent documents included in the view are selected or replicated.

  Example: `SELECT` *selection formula* `| @AllChildren`

- **@AllDescendents:** This @function is used in view selection and selective replication formulas. All response and response-to-response documents that match the parent documents are included in the view. This differs from @IsResponseDoc in that only responses to parent documents included in the view are selected or replicated. This differs from @AllChildren in that ALL responses at any level are returned rather than only the immediate responses.

  Example: `SELECT` *selection formula* `| @AllDescendents`

- **@IsDocBeingEdited:** This @function is used in button, hide-when, action, and field formulas. The function checks whether the document is in edit mode or read mode. If the document is being edited, the formula returns 1 (True). If the document is not being edited, the formula returns 0 (False).

  Example: `@If(@IsDocBeingEdited;"You are in EDIT MODE";"You are in READ MODE")`

● **@Sum:** This @function adds a list of numbers. The numbers can be constants or numbers contained in field values. A number is returned.

Example: `@Sum(NumApples; NumOranges; NumGrapes; 10)`

This formula will result in the sum of the number in each of the NumApples, NumOranges, and NumGrapes fields plus 10.

● **@PickList:** This @function prompts the user with a dialog box that contains either a view specified by the designer or the Address dialog box. @PickList will return either the column value from the selected document or the name selected from the address dialog box. The syntax for @PickList is:

@PickList([Custom] ; *server* : *file* ; *view* ; *title* ; *prompt* ; *column* **)**

or

@PickList([Name] : [Single])

Although @PickList is very similar to @DBLookup and @DBColumn formulas, it has several benefits:

● @PickList can store more data than an @DB formula. There is no 64K limitation.

● @PickList performs the lookup faster, however, there is no **NoCache** option with @PickList so the lookup is performed every time.

● @PickList has QuickSearch capability which allows the user to find a document by typing the first few letters.

Notes

@PickList is covered much more comprehensively in Chapter 7—Advanced View Concepts. It is more important for the Application Development II exam.

Tips

See the @Function Table at the end of this chapter to review some of the most common @functions used in the Application Development exams.

@Commands

@Commands are a special type of @function designed to automate Notes menu commands that affect the user interface. @Commands are used in action, button, hotspot, SmartIcon, and some agent formulas. @Command formulas are written using the following syntax:

```
@Command([CommandName];parameters)
```

where [*CommandName*] is the keyword command you are sending. An @command can utilize any number of parameters, depending on the @command used. A semicolon is always used to separate parameters.

Notes version 4 contains two types of @commands differentiated only by when they are executed:

- **@Commands:** These run in the sequence they appear in the formula: top to bottom, left to right.

- **@PostedCommands:** These run after **all** other @functions and @commands in the formula have run, regardless of their location within the formula.

For example, the following example will execute differently based on the type of @command specified:

```
@Command([Compose];"Contact");FIELD Name :
= "Amy Peasley";

@Command([FileSave]);@Command([FileCloseWindow]);
```

Written this way, a Contact document would be composed, the name field would be assigned the value "Amy Peasley" and the document would be saved, and the window closed. If the formula was written this way:

```
@PostedCommand([Compose];"Contact");FIELD Name :
= "Amy Peasley";

@PostedCommand([FileSave]);@PostedCommand
([FileCloseWindow]);
```

Notes would try to assign the value first before composing the document. Then the document would be composed, the document would not be saved because it is blank, and the window closed.

The only difference between the two types of @commands is the order of execution. Both take the same type of keyword commands and use the same syntax.

Field Events

Field event formulas are one example where formulas are used. There are three types of field event formulas used in editable fields. *Default formulas* programmatically enter data into editable fields when the document is composed. *Input translation formulas* edit data after the user has entered information into the field. *Validation formulas* verify that the data passes the designer's specification. If the validation formula fails, the user receives a failure message and returns to the field.

Earlier in this chapter we discussed the options for creating an editable or a computed field. Computed fields do not have any field events because users are not entering data. The three types of formula driven events available in editable fields are shown in Figure 3-9:

Figure 3-9

Field Events in
the Notes
Design Pane

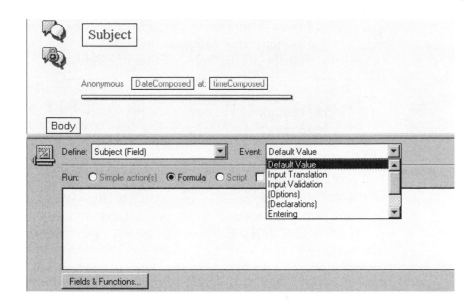

- **Default Value Formula:** Default values provide an initial value for the field when the document is created. Since the field is editable, users can change the value that is initially computed. Text strings must be enclosed in quotation marks. *Beware!* If an error is created by a default formula, users will not be able to create documents using the form.

- **Input Translation Formula:** Input translation formulas modify the data entered by the user. This is useful for standardizing and formatting information in fields (such as trimming extra spaces, or setting a name to the proper case). Input translation formulas are calculated when the document is refreshed or saved.

- **Input Validation Formula:** Input validation formulas perform data entry checking. This is useful for requiring users to fill in fields or check that the data entered fits the required specifications. These formulas are evaluated when the document is saved or refreshed. If the designer has the **Automatically refresh fields** form property selected, the formula is evaluated as soon as the user leaves the field. Validation formulas are written using the @Success and @Failure functions. For example, an Input Validation formula to verify that the status field is filled in might be:

```
@If(Status = "";@Failure("Please provide a status!")
;@Success)
```

This field checks the value of the status field. If it is blank, a prompt box informs the user that a status must be provided, and will not allow the user to save the document until this requirement is met. If the status field contains information, then the document can be saved.

Notes

Input Validation Formulas are especially emphasized on the Application Development I exam. It is important to understand that they are used to require users to enter data, as well as understanding the actual syntax of the formula!

Field Types

Two additional types of fields are available in Lotus Notes: *shared fields* and *categories fields*.

Shared Fields

Notes design attributes can be shared. One way we have already discussed is through subforms which share a group of design elements between forms. Shared fields allow fields to be shared between forms. Shared fields can be distinguished from single-use fields by a heavy border. They can be created in three ways:

● **Create a new shared field:** In the database, select **Create – Design – Shared Field** from the menu. The field can be designed and used later.

- **Single-use fields can be shared:** Go to the field you want to share with another form. Click on it and select **Design – Share This Field**. To stop sharing a field, cut and paste it back onto the form.

- **Copy a shared field from another database:** In the navigation pane of the database you want to copy the shared field from, select **Design – Shared Fields**. Highlight the fields you want to copy and select **Edit – Copy**. Go to the navigator pane of the database you are pasting the shared fields into and select **Edit – Paste**.

The important item to remember is that shared fields allow a change in the field to be made in one location and all the forms in the database which contain the field will reflect the change. This saves development time and adds consistency between forms. It is also important to understand that shared fields allow one design element, a field, to be shared. Subforms allow a group of design elements to be shared between forms.

Categories

Forms can be created which make use of Notes automatic categorization features. The Categorize action allows documents to automatically be placed in selected categories by the user. This is very helpful in views. To use the **Action – Categorize** menu option, a field named **Categories** must be included in the form. This field can be a keywords field which allows users to manually select a Category from a list, or the field can be computed to automatically set the value of the Categories field, based on other data in the form. This Categories field can then be used in the view to group like documents.

Creating Agents

To create a new agent, select **Create – Agent** from the menu. The agent design window appears, as shown in Figure 3-10.

Figure 3-10

Agent Design
Window

This window sets all design attributes for the agent including the name, schedule, document selection, and formula.

The agent's **name** should be descriptive and understandable. The name will appear in the menu list under the **Actions** menu. Users must be able to distinguish between agents to understand which one to run.

The agent can be shared or private. It is important to understand the difference for the exam:

● **Shared Agents:** These can only be created by someone with Designer or above access to the database. If the agent is shared, it can be used by other people.

- **Private Agents:** These can be created by anyone with Reader or above access who has the **Create personal agents** option checked in the Access Control List. Private agents can only be used by the creator.

Notes

Once the agent has been created as shared, it cannot be changed to private. If the agent is initially created as private, it cannot be changed to shared.

Agents can be triggered by several different events. The designer selects the trigger in the **When should this agent run** combo box. The following options are available:

- Manually From Actions Menu

- Manually From Agent List

- If New Mail Has Arrived

- If Documents Have Been Created or Modified

- If Documents Have Been Pasted

- On Schedule Hourly, Daily, Weekly, Monthly, or Never

Agents can be run from action buttons used in forms and views. The Application Development I exam focuses only on running agents manually. You will not be tested on scheduled agents.

The designer can also decide which documents the agent should run on. The following options are available in the **Which document(s) should it act on?** drop-down list:

- All documents in database

- All new and modified documents since last run

- All unread documents in view

- All documents in view

- Selected documents

- Run Once (@Commands may be used)

A search query can also be built to select which documents the agent should run on.

The agent design pane allows the designer to use simple actions, @formulas, or LotusScript to write the agent. Simple actions can be used to perform many of the common functionalities of agents such as:

- Managing documents in databases and folders

- Managing read and unread marks

- Modifying fields

- Sending messages

- Sending newsletters

- Running other agents

- Archiving documents

Formulas written with @functions can also be used to perform these and other functions. LotusScript can be used, but is not covered in this exam.

Example of an Agent Used to Modify a Field

Michael wants to write an agent to change the value of the status field to "Completed." He creates an agent called "Update Status" which runs manually from the actions menu on selected documents. He wants to use a simple action to modify the status field. He selects the **Add Action** button and opens the Add Action dialog box. He selects the **Modify Field** action, selects the **Status** field as the one he wants to modify, places **Completed** in the Value box and selects the **Replace value** option. Michael's completed dialog box is shown in Figure 3-11.

Figure 3-11

Add Action Agent
Example

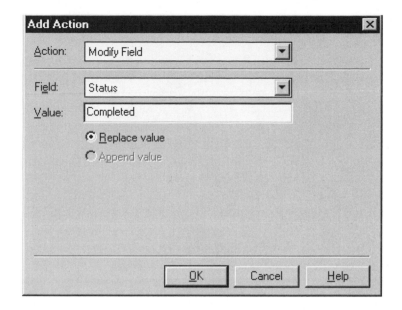

There are limits to using simple actions. For example, a field name cannot be used in the Value box; only text can be entered. To automate this functionality even more, an action button could be added to the view to run this agent.

@Function Table

The following table describes a subset of some of the most common @functions used as examples on the test and in common programming. This table does not represent every available @function. The Application Development I exam does not place an emphasis on knowing *every* @function, but this table can be used as basic reference. Some of the questions will refer to various @functions and expect the candidate to be familiar with them. The description is very basic and not all caveats related to the @function are listed. For more information about these @functions, please refer to Chapters 5, 6, and 7 in the official documentation *Lotus Notes Programmer's Guide Part 2* or the on-line help menu option **Help – Contents – Tell me about – @Functions A-Z**.

Table 3.1
@Functions

@Function	Syntax	Description	Example
@Abs	@Abs(*number*)	Returns the absolute value of a number.	@Abs(-134) *returns* 134
@Accessed	@Accessed	Returns the last time the document was opened (for reading or editing).	@Accessed *returns* 06/15/73 1:40:36 PM if the document was last read or edited on June 15, 1973 at 1:40 in the afternoon.
@Adjust	@Adjust(*date;years;months;days;hours;minutes; seconds*)	Adjusts the provided date by the amount listed.	@Adjust([06/15/73];5;-1;0;0;0;0) *returns* 6/14/78
@All	@All	Returns True.	SELECT @ALL *returns* all documents
@AllChildren	SELECT *selectionFormula* | @AllChildren	Used only in view selection formulas to include all response documents for the documents that match the selection formula.	SELECT Form = "Main" | @AllChildren *returns* all documents created using the Main form and any responses to those documents.
@AllDescendents	SELECT *selectionFormula* | @AllDescendants	Used only in view selection formulas to include all response and response-to-response documents for the documents that match the selection formula.	SELECT Form = "Main" | @AllDescendents *returns* all documents created using the Main form and any responses to those documents or responses to the responses.
@Author	@Author	Returns a list of all of the users who have edited the document (From any Authors fields, From fields, or the $UpdatedBy field).	@Author *returns* Amy Peasley; Scott Thomas on a document that contains "Amy Peasley" and "Scott Thomas" in the $UpdatedBy field.
@Begins	@Begins(*string;substring*)	Determines whether the specified subtring is found at the beginning of the string.	@Begins("Hello";"Hello World") *returns* 1 (True).
@Command	@Command([*command*];*parameters*)	Executes an @Command function.	@Command([EditDocument];"1") placed the document into edit mode. *See the @Commands section in this chapter for more information on using @Commands.*

Table 3.1
@Functions
(Cont'd)

@Function	Syntax	Description	Example
@Contains	@Contains(*string;substring*)	Determines whether the specified substring is contained anywhere within the string.	@Contains("Hello World";"llo") *returns* 1 (True).
@Created	@Created	Returns the time and date the document was created.	@Created *returns* 06/15/97 1:55:36 PM if the document was created on June 15, 1997 at 1:55 in the afternoon.
@Date	@Date(*year;month;day*) @Date(*year;month;day;hour minute;second*) @Date([*time-date*])	Returns the date value of the provided value.	@Date(73;06;15) *returns* 06/15/73 @Date(2001;06;21;06;15;49) *returns* 06/21/2001 (Note that the time is left off).
@Day	@Day(*time-date value*)	Returns the day of the month from the date provided.	@Day(@Today) *returns* the number 3 if today is July 3, 1997.
@DbColumn	@DbColumn(*class* : "NoCache" ; *server* : *database* ; *view* ; *columnNumber*)	Returns the information found in the column from the specified view or folder.	@DbColumn("";"Chicago":"Names.nsf":"People";3) *returns* the values found in the third column of the People view in the Names.nsf database on the Chicago Notes server.
@DbLookup	@DbLookup(*class* : "NoCache" ; *server* : *database* ; *view* ; *key* ; *fieldName*) **or** @DbLookup(*class* : "NoCache" ; *server* : *database* ; *view* ; *key* ; *columnNumber*)	Returns the information found in the field or column based on the specified key.	@DbLookup("" : "NoCache" ;"Chicago" : "Names.nsf":"People" ; "Peasley" ;"FirstName") *returns* the value of the FirstName field from the record which contains Peasley in the first column of the People view on the Chicago Notes server.
@DbName	@DBName	Returns the server on which the database resides and the path and filename of the database.	@DBName returns "CHICAGO;MAIL\STHOMAS.NSF" if the current database's filename is STHOMAS in the MAIL subdirectory on the CHICAGO Notes server.

Table 3.1
@Functions
(Cont'd)

@Function	Syntax	Description	Example
@DeleteDocument	@DeleteDocument	In an agent that runs a formula, deletes the document being processed. **Note:** To delete a document via an action button in a view or folder, you must use the @Command([EditClear]) function.	@If(Form = "Temp"; @DeleteDocument;"") deletes document based off the Temp form if the formula is contained in an agent.
@DeleteField	@DeleteField	In an agent that runs a formula, deletes the field.	Field OldInfo := @DeleteField will delete the OldInfo field from any document that the agent processes.
@DialogBox	@DialogBox(*form*; [AutoHorzFit]:[AutoVertFit])	Presents a dialog box based on the specified form which allows the user to input information. **Note:** See Chapter 5 for more information about @DialogBox.	@DialogBox("MyForm"; [AutoHorzFit]:[AutoVertFit]) will present MyForm which the user is still in their original form. The box will be centered vertically and horizontally.
@Do	@Do(*expressions*)	Evaluates the listed expressions from left to right.	@If(Send = "Yes";@Do(@Command([EditDocument]; "1");@Command([FileSave]);@MailSend;@Command([FileCloseWindow));@Command([FileCloseWindow]) will place the document into edit mode, save the document, send the document and close the window if the Send field equals yes, otherwise the document will just close.
@DocChildren	@DocChildren	Used in a column or window title formula, @DocChildren returns the number of direct response documents. **Note:** Response to Response documents are not included in this number.	@DocChildren *returns* 4 if there are 4 response documents to the main document, regardless of how many response to response documents there are.

Table 3.1
@Functions
(Cont'd)

@Function	Syntax	Description	Example
@DocDescendants	@DocDescendants	Used in a column or window title formula, @DocDescendants returns the number of *all* response documents, regardless of level. **Note:** Response to Response documents *are* included in this number.	@DocDescendants *returns* 7 if there are 4 response documents to the main document and 3 response to response documents.
@DocNumber	@DocNumber	Used in a column or window title formula, @DocNumber returns the entry number of the current document.	@DocNumber *returns* 1 for the first document in the view, 2 for the second document, 2.1 for the first response to the second document, etc. These numbers are not stored with the document, they change dynamically based on the view or window title formula. This is the default formula for a new view column.
@Elements	@Elements(*list*)	Returns the number of elements in the list.	@Elements("Hawkeyes"; "Buckeyes";"Wolver-ines") *returns* 3.
@Explode	@Explode(*daterange*) @Explode(*string*) @Explode(*string;separa-tor*) @Explode(*string;separa-tor; includeEmpties*)	Returns a text list of the elements; either the days within a range, or the words/clauses of a string.	@Explode([01/05/95 – 01/19/95]) *returns* 01/05/95, 01/06/95, 01/07/95, 01/08/95, 01/09/95, 01/10/95 @Explode(Fruits;";") *returns* Apple, Banana, Orange if the Fruits field contains Apple;Banana;Orange
@Failure	@Failure(*string*)	Returns a failure message when data doesn't pass validation formula.	@If(Status = "" ; @Fail-ure("You must provide a status!");@Success will prompt the message if the status field is left blank, otherwise the formula or function will continue.
@False	@False	Returns the number 0.	@If(Status = "Complet-ed";@True;@False) would return 0 if the Status field did not equal Completed.

Table 3.1
@Functions
(Cont'd)

@Function	Syntax	Description	Example
@GetDocField	@GetDocField(*documentID;fieldName*)	Returns the contents of the specified field on the document based on the documentID provided.	@If(@IsNewDoc;Title;@GetDocField($Ref;Title) will return the value of the Title field in the parent document.
@Hour	@Hour(*timedatevalue*)	Returns the number of the hour of the provided time-date value.	@Hour(@Now) *returns* 10 if it is 10:23 in the morning.
@If	@If(*condition1;action1; condition2;action2;…..;cc ondition99;action99;else action*)	Evaluates the condition and returns the action if the condition is true, otherwise it evaluates the next action. If none of the conditions evaluate to True, the else action is performed.	@If(Status = "Completed";"Review Completed";"Please Review") *returns* Review Completed if the Status field evaluates to Completed, else it returns Please Review.
@Implode	@Implode(*textlist*) or @Implode(*textlist;separator*)	Concatenates all elements of list and returns a string.	@Implode("Apples"; "Bananas";"Oranges") *returns* Apples Bananas Oranges
@IsMember	@IsMember(*textvalue;te xtlistvalue*)	Determines if one text value (or a list of values) is contained within a text list and returns a Boolean value.	@IsMember("Red"; "Blue":"Red" :"Green") *returns* 1 because Red is contained in the text list.
@IsNewDoc	@IsNewDoc	Determines if the document has been saved to disk.	@If(@IsNewDoc;"New Topic"; Subject) *returns* New Topic if the document has not yet been saved. Otherwise, the contents of the Subject field are returned. This is very useful in Window Title formulas.
@IsResponseDoc	@IsResponseDoc	Determines whether a document is a child of another document.	@If(@IsResponseDoc; "Response"; Subject) *returns* Response if the document is a Response or Response to Response type documents, otherwise the contents of the Subject field are returned.
@Left	@Left(*stringToSearch;nu mberofChars*) or @Left(*stringToSearch;sub-String*)	Searches a string from left to right and returns the leftmost specified number of characters or the specified substring	@Left("Matthew Peasley";4) *returns* Matt. @Left("Matthew Peasley";" ") *returns* Matthew.

Table 3.1
@Functions
(Cont'd)

@Function	Syntax	Description	Example
@LeftBack	@LeftBack(*string-ToSearch;numToSkip*) or @LeftBack(*string-ToSearch;startString*)	Searches a string from right to left and returns the leftmost characters after the number to skip or the number to start.	@LeftBack("Matthew Peasley";4) *returns* Matthew Pea. @LeftBack("Matthew Peasley";" ") *returns* Matthew.
@Length	@Length(*string*) or @Length(*stringlist*)	Returns the number of characters in the string or each string in the list.	@Length("My name is Amy") *returns* 13. @Length("John":"Amy" : "Matthew") *returns* 4;3;7.
@LowerCase	@LowerCase(*string*)	Returns the string in all lowercase letters.	@LowerCase("Hello Everyone!") *returns* hello everyone!
@Member	@Member(*value;stringlist*)	Finds the position of the value in the list.	@Member("Peasley"; "Hart" :"Bennie" : "Bress" :"Peasley") *returns* 4. If the value cannot be found in the list, 0 is returned.
@Modified	@Modified	Returns the last time-date the document was edited and saved. **Note:** When used in a computed field formula, the *next-to-last* time the document was saved is returned. Use a computed for display formula to avoid this problem.	@Modified *returns* 12/01/96 11:45:23 if the document was last edited and saved at that time.
@Month	@Month(*time-date*)	Returns the number of the month of the date specified.	@Month(@Today) *returns* 7 if the current month is July.
@NewLine	@NewLine	Inserts a carriage return into a text string.	"Enter" + @NewLine + "Name:" *returns* Enter Name:
@Now	@Now	Returns the current time and date.	@Now *returns* 07/03/97 10:23:56 AM on July 3, 1997 at 10:23:56 in the morning.
@Responses	@Responses	Returns the number of responses to the document in the view. **Note:** This function can only be used in window title formulas. It will not work in any other formula.	@If(@Responses > 0; "Discussion Item";"Main Topic") *returns* Discussion Item if there are any responses to the document.

Table 3.1
@Functions
(Cont'd)

@Function	Syntax	Description	Example
@Return	@Return(*value*)	Stops executing the formula and returns the value specified.	@If(@Prompt[OK]; "Continue?"; "Do you want to continue?"); @Command([File-Save]);@Return("")) If the user selects **OK**, the document is saved; otherwise they are returned to the document.
@Right	@Right(*stringToSearch;numberofChars*) or @Right(*stringToSearch;subString*)	Searches a string from right to left and returns the rightmost specified number of characters or the specified substring	@Right("Matthew Peasley";4) *returns* sley. @Right("Matthew Peasley";" ") *returns* Peasley.
@RightBack	@RightBack(*stringToSearch;numToSkip*) or @RightBack(*stringToSearch;startString*)	Searches a string from left to right and returns the rightmost characters after the number to skip or the number to start.	@RightBack("Matthew Peasley";4) *returns* hew Peasley. @LeftBack("Matthew Peasley";" ") *returns* Peasley.
@Second	@Second(*time-date*)	Returns the seconds value of the time.	@Seconds(@Now) *returns* 45 if the current time is 11:35:45.
@Set	@Set(*variable;value*)	Sets a temporary variable to be used in a formula.	Total := "";@If(Part1 = "";@Set("Total"; Init + " " + Total);@Set ("Total";Init + Part1 + Total)
@SetDocField	@SetDocField(*documentUNID;fieldName;newValue*)	Sets the value of a specified field on a document based on the document's unique ID.	@SetDocField($Ref; "NumResponses"; ResponseNum) updates the parent document's NumResponses field by the number in the response document's ResponseNum field.
@SetEnvironment	@SetEnvironment(*variablename;value*)	Sets the value of an environment variable stored in the user's **NOTES.INI** file. (Used when the variable must be set from within another formula).	@If(Status = "Completed";@SetEnvironment("ENVStatus"; "Completed";"")

Table 3.1
@Functions
(Cont'd)

@Function	Syntax	Description	Example
@SetField	@SetField(*fieldName; value*)	Used within another formula to set the value of a field. **Note:** The field must be declared before it is used in the @SetField formula.	FIELD Computer := Computer; @If(Type = "IBM";@SetField("Computer";"IBM");@SetField ("Computer";"Clone") sets the value of the Computer field to either IBM or Clone.
@Subset	@Subset(*list;number*)	Searches the specified list from left to right and returns the value in the list corresponding to the number specified. (A negative number will search the list from right to left.)	@Subset(@DBName;1) *returns* CHICAGO if the name of the server is CHICAGO, since the server name is the first element of @DBName. **Note:** This example is used in the Application Development I and II exams.
@Success	@Success	Returns True (1). Usually used in input validation formulas.	@If(Name = "";@Failure("You must provide a name."); @Success. If Name is not blank, the user will continue; otherwise the user will be stopped and prompted with the failure message.
@Sum	@Sum(*numbers*)	Returns the sum of the listed numbers.	@Sum(4: 5: 6) *returns* 15. **Note:** The elements can be separated by colons or semicolons.
@TextToNumber	@TextToNumber(*string*)	Converts a text string to a number. An error will be generated if the string cannot be converted.	@TextToNumber("123") *returns* the number 123.
@TextToTime	@TextToTime(*string*)	Converts a text string to a date-time value. A blank will be generated if the string cannot be converted.	@TextToTime("03/16/63 5:45") *returns* 03/16/63 5:45:00 AM
@Today	@Today	Returns today's date.	@Today *returns* 07/03/97 if today is July 3, 1997.
@Tomorrow	@Tomorrow	Returns tomorrow's date.	@Tomorrow *returns* 07/04/97 if today is July 3, 1997.

Table 3.1
@Functions
(Cont'd)

@Function	Syntax	Description	Example
@True	@True	Returns 1 as a numeric value.	@If(Years >= 21;@True;@False)
@UpperCase	@UpperCase(*string*)	Returns the string in all uppercase letters.	@UpperCase("Hello Everyone!") *returns* HELLO EVERYONE!
@URLGetHeader	@URLGetHeader(*URL-String;headerString*)	Returns the URL's HTTP header information. **Note:** This function should only be used in the Web Navigator database.	@URLGetHeader("http://www.lotus.com"; "Last-modified") *returns* the last time the www.lotus.com Web page was modified.
@URLHistory	@URLHistory ([Command])	Used to navigate, save or reload the URL history list. **Note:** This function should only be used in the Web Navigator database.	@URLHistory([Next]) moves to the next URL listed in the history list.
@URLOpen	@URLOpen	Opens the specified URL.	@URLOpen("http://www.lotus.com") opens the ww.lotus.com web page.
@UserAccess	@UserAccess(*server;file*)	Returns the current user's level (from 1-6) of access for the specified database. Return value also displays whether the user can create and delete documents.	@UserAccess(@DBName) *returns* 5:1:1 if the user has designer access, and can create and delete documents.
@UserRoles	@UserRoles	Returns a list of the current user's roles if the database is located on the server. If the database is local, the **Enforce consistent ACL** option must be selected in the advanced ACL properties of the database.	When used in a hide-when formula for an action button, this formula: !@IsMember("[CPA_Admin]"; @UserRoles) hides the button if CPA_Admin is not included in the current user's list of roles.

Chapter 3 Sample Questions

Objective: Create forms which use keyword lists.

Hart wants to design a keywords field which allows users to enter their own values. Which type of keywords interface can she use?

> A. Dialog List
>
> B. Dialog Box
>
> C. Radio Button
>
> D. Combo Box

Answer: A
Radio Buttons and Combo Boxes don't allow the user to enter their own entries. Dialog Box is not an option for keywords interface. The dialog list interface allows users to enter their own entries if the designer has selected **Allow entries not in this list.**

Objective: Create forms which use keyword lists.

Noreen is editing a document. When she clicks on the entry helper button, a list of choices appears in a dialog box. She adds a new keyword item and saves the document. Tom edits another document and sees Noreen's item in the list of choices. What type of choice did the designer of the Notes application use?

> A. Enter Choices
>
> B. Use Formula for choices
>
> C. Use Address Dialog for choices
>
> D. Use Access Control list for choices

Answer: B
The designer used an @DbColumn formula from a view to enable the list to change dynamically, based on what the user enters.

Objective: Write Notes applications that contain multi-value fields.

Julie Ann designed a field to categorize documents. She wants to allow users to select multiple categories from the list. How can she enable this attribute?

      A. Set the Categories field to display as a Radio Button

      B. Select the **Allow multi-values** option

      C. This is automatically set when the field is created

      D. A and B

Answer: B
Julie Ann could also set the Categories field to display as a Checkbox.

Objective: Write Notes applications that contain multi-value fields.

Gary created a field which lists all of the different types of equipment used to fix the client's bicycle. He wants to display this list in a vertical row where each piece is listed on its own line. How can Gary get this information to display the way he wants?

      A. Create a keywords field which displays the selected items in a dialog list

      B. Select the **Allow multi-values** option on the Basics tab

      C. Select the display separator as New Line on the Basics tab

      D. Select the display separator as New Line on the Options tab

Answer: B & D
The **Allow multi-values** option must be selected in order to use the multi-value options. These options are selected from the **Display separate values with:** option on the Options tab of the field properties.

Objective: Create fields which use reserved field names.

Marilyn wants to refer to the name of the form used to create the document. What is the name of the field used to store this information?

        A. Form

        B. FormName

        C. It is whatever the designer called the field which stores this information

Answer: A

The reserved field Form stores the name of the form.

Traps

If the form is stored in the document, the $Title field contains the name of the form rather than the Form field. The $Title field is only used when the form is stored in the document.

Objective: Use synonyms for Notes design elements.

Tom has set up a keyword field with seven choices. Many formulas are based on what the user selects in this field. Now, one of the choices must be changed and Tom must go back and change all of the formulas. How could Tom have avoided changing the formulas?

        A. By using an alias for the field name

        B. By setting the value of the field to a variable in the formula

        C. By using simple choices

        D. By using synonyms for the choices

Answer: D

Synonyms allow the user's choices to change without affecting what the internal program stores.

Objective: Use forms which use required fields.

Linnea is designing a form to track calls made to the tax hotline. She wants to force the support person to enter the customer's name or the form can't be saved. What type of formula should she use?

      A. Field Formula

      B. Default Formula

      C. Input Translation Formula

      D. Input Validation Formula

Answer: D
Input Validation formulas can be used to require the user to enter information into a field.

Objective: Create forms which use field formulas.

What is the result of this field formula (Num is equal to 4):

`@If(Num < 25;(4 + 5 * 6) + Num; 25 - (Num + @Sum(Num;3;2)))`

      A. 58

      B. 12

      C. 38

      D. None of the above

Answer: C
Remember the order of evaluation for operators: 1) Parentheses, 2) Exponents, 3) Multiplication and Division, 4) Addition and Subtraction. @Sum evaluates to the sum of the components

Objective: Create forms which use field formulas.

Isaac is using a Computed field. When will the formula be evaluated?

        A. When the document is created

        B. When the document is saved

        C. When the document is opened

        D. When the document is refreshed

Answer: A, B & D
Computed formulas are calculated every time a document is created, refreshed, or saved. Computed for display fields are calculated when the document is opened, created or refreshed, but no data is saved in the field. Computed when composed fields are only calculated when the document is created.

Objective: Create forms which use field formulas.

Emily wrote a default formula for a field. When will this formula be refreshed?

        A. When the document is created

        B. When the document is saved

        C. When the document is opened

        D. When the document is refreshed

Answer: A
Default formulas are only evaluated when the document is composed. They are never recalculated *after* the document is composed, including when the document is refreshed.

Objective: Create forms which use field formulas.

Lakshmi can't get the following formula to work. How should it be re-written?
```
"The book is due: " + @Today
```

      A. `The book is due + "@Today"`

      B. `The book is due: + @Date(Today)`

      C. `"The book is due: " + @Text(@Today)`

      D. `(The book is due) + @Date(@Today)`

Answer: C
Different data types cannot be mixed in one formula,

Objective: Create forms which share design attributes.

Matthew has created a form containing many different design elements. He is now creating another form on which he wants to use some of the same fields from different parts of his first form. He knows that the formulas for these fields might change as the application is enhanced. What is Matthew's best design option?

      A. Create a subform for the fields

      B. Share the fields on the original form and use them on the new form

      C. Copy the fields from the original form and paste them onto the new form

      D. Write field translation formulas to inherit the data

Answer: B
Sharing the fields allows the original form to remain the same, and any changes to the design of the fields will be automatically reflected in all forms containing the fields. A sub form would require redesigning the original form, because the fields are spread out. Copy and pasting the fields would require that a change in the design of a field would have to be made on every form containing that field.

Objective: Create forms which use categories.

Roger and Judy are designing an inventory tracking application. They want to design a form which will automatically allow users to group together documents related to types of inventory via a Notes action. What field must be included in the form?

        A.　Inventory

        B.　Groups

        C.　Categories

        D.　DocumentType

Answer: C
A Categories field must be included in the form for the Categorize action to work.

Objective: Create forms which use new @Functions.

The @PickList function is used to:

        A.　Pick a user's name from the Access Control List

        B.　Display a view and pick information from a column of data

        C.　Display a dialog box and pick the desired category

        D.　Create a list of values from a selection dialog box

Answer: B

@PickList can prompt the user to pick a name (or names) from the Address Book dialog box or present the user with a view dialog box and return the value in the specified column.

Objective: Create Notes applications that use @Commands.

What will occur when the following formula is executed?

```
@Command([Compose]; ""; "Main Topic");
@Command([EditGotoField]; "Subject");
@Command([EditInsertText]; "New subject");
@PostedCommand([EditGotoField]; "Body");
@Command([EditInsertText]; "Body Information");
@Command([TextBold]); @Command([EditInsertText];
"This is new information");@Command([FileSave]);
@PostedCommand([FileCloseWindow])
```

    A. A Main Topic document is composed. The cursor goes to the Subject field and inserts the text "New Subject." The cursor goes to the Body field and inserts the text "Body Information" and "This is new information" in bold font. The document is saved and closed.

    B. The cursor will go to the Body field. The document will be closed. Then a Main Topic document will be composed. The cursor goes to the Subject field and inserts the text "New Subject." The document is saved.

    C. A Main Topic document is composed. The cursor goes to the Subject field and inserts the text "New Subject." The text "Body Information" and "This is new information" in bold font is inserted into the Subject field. The cursor goes to the Body field. The document is saved and closed.

    D. A Main Topic document is composed. The cursor goes to the Subject field and inserts the text "New Subject." The text "Body Information" and "This is new information" in bold font is inserted into the Subject field. The document is saved. The cursor goes to the Body field and the document is closed.

Answer: D

@Commands are executed in the order they appear. @PostedCommands are executed after *all* other @functions and @commands have been executed.

Objective: Write macros/agents that run manually.

Aaron is creating an agent in a server-based application to track his favorite sushi restaurants. What does he need to remember about the difference between private and shared agents?

        A. Both can be changed by anyone with Editor access

        B. Only shared agents can be run on all documents in the database

        C. Only private agents can be run by users

        D. Neither can be changed to the other type once the agent has been created

Answer: D

To change the type from shared to private or private to shared, the agent must be re-created.

Objective: Write applications which use manual agents.

Sean wants to track how many chapters of his book he has completed. He has created an agent which automatically changes the status of completed documents. However, he thinks going to the actions menu is too confusing. What are his other options?

        A. Create an action button which runs the agent

        B. Create another agent which runs the status agent

        C. Create a view to display completed documents

        D. Create a form which automatically updates the document

Answer: A
Action buttons can run agents. This provides a more graphical way to run the agent.

Objective: Create agents to change field values.

In the question above, Sean's agent modified the value of a field. How did he accomplish this?

    A. By using the Manually Change Field Value option

    B. By using the @Command([ChangeValue]) statement

    C. By using the Modify Field simple action

    D. By using the @Modify formula

Answer: C
None of the other options provided are Notes functionalities.

Objective: Write applications which use manual agents.

James has created an agent to modify documents in his database. Which option is not a valid agent trigger?

    A. When new mail arrives

    B. When new documents are created or modified

    C. When documents are opened

    D. Once a week

Answer: C
Agents cannot be based on a document being opened. The following triggers are available: Manually from the agent list, manually from the actions menu, if new mail has arrived, if documents have been created or modified, if documents have been pasted, on schedule hourly, daily, weekly, monthly or never.

Chapter

Working with Views

Views in a Notes database provide a means of viewing information. Views can be used to sort and/or categorize data based upon user and designer specifications. Columns can be sorted and data grouped together to create an index of the database contents. Views can be programmed to display particular fields from a subset of the database's documents. A Notes database may contain multiple views which categorize and sort information in different ways.

Views are differentiated from folders by the documents they contain. A view's contents are determined by a selection formula written by the designer. Documents cannot be moved in or out of a view. A folder's contents are determined by the user rather than the designer; folders have no selection formula. Documents can be contained in multiple folders and moved between folders. However, only one copy of the document is stored in the database, regardless of how many folders include it.

Throughout this chapter we will be discussing views and folders. However, the focus of the exam is mostly on views; thus, folders will not be discussed in depth.

Creating Views and Folders

Views are created to display data. When creating a view, it is important to understand the key information which should be highlighted from the document, as well as how documents will be grouped together. Every database must contain at least one view. When a new database is created, it contains a view named **Untitled**. This view contains one column that defaults to the document's position in the view.

To create a view, select **Create – View** from the menu. The Create view dialog box, shown in Figure 4-1, appears:

Figure 4-1
Create View
Dialog Box

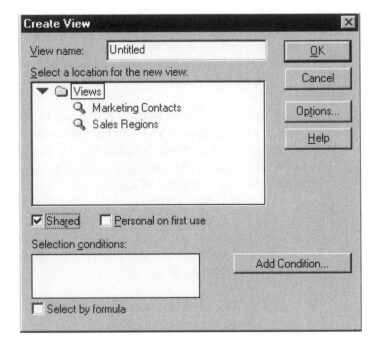

The view name is case sensitive and may contain letters, numbers, spaces, and punctuation. The view name can be changed later through the view properties. The view's location can also be selected here. The **Options** button allows the view's design to be inherited from an existing view.

Three types of views can be created:

- **Shared views:** Shared views can be seen by all users of the database who are not explicitly excluded by the view security. Shared views can only be created by managers or designers of the database. They are stored in the database on the server.

- **Private views:** Users with at least Reader access to the database can create private views. No other user than the creator can see a private view. A user's level of access in the Access Control List of the database determines where the private view is stored. If a user has the **Create personal folders/views** option selected, the view is stored in the database. If this option is not selected, the private view is stored in the user's **DESKTOP.DSK** file.

- **Shared, personal on first use:** This option allows designers to create private views for users. Initially, the view is shared and can be accessed by anyone. As soon as a user enters this view, it is copied to the user's desktop and becomes private for each user. This is beneficial when a view will be specific to each user. For example, if the designer wants to create a view for everyone which will show only the documents that person created, the view can be initially shared. As soon as each user enters the view, it immediately becomes private and contains the documents created by the user. Once the view becomes private, it follows the same storage rules as a private view. If a user has the **Create personal folders/views** option selected, the view is stored in the database. If this option is not selected, the private view is stored in the user's **DESKTOP.DSK** file.

Views frequently display a subset of all of the documents included in the database. The **selection formula** determines which documents are included in a view. The selection formula can be set when the view is created or at a later time. In the **Selection conditions** box in the Create View dialog box shown in Figure 4-1, the designer can select documents in two ways, by writing a customized formula, or using the search builder. The **Add Condition** button opens the Search Builder dialog box. Here the designer can select documents based on the author, date, field, form, or form used.

Writing a selection formula allows for more flexibility and a more complex selection criteria than the Search Builder. The selection formula is written with the @ formula language. **SELECT @ALL** is the default selection formula, which includes all documents in the database in the view.

Creating a folder follows the same basic steps. Select **Create – Folder** from the menu. The Create Folder dialog box appears (shown in Figure 4-2). This looks very similar to the Create View dialog box, with the exception of the Selection Condition formula box.

Figure 4-2
Create Folder
Dialog Box

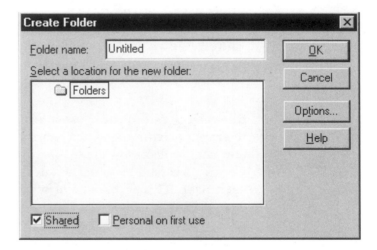

As shown in the dialog box, the same types of folders (shared, private, shared—personal on first use) are available.

View Properties

Properties are key in the view-related questions of the exam. There are extensive questions about view and column properties. In this chapter, we thoroughly review each tab and its contents.

The Basics Tab

The Basics tab is used for naming purposes. As shown in Figure 4-3, a view name, alias, and comments can be associated with the view.

Figure 4-3
View Basics Tab

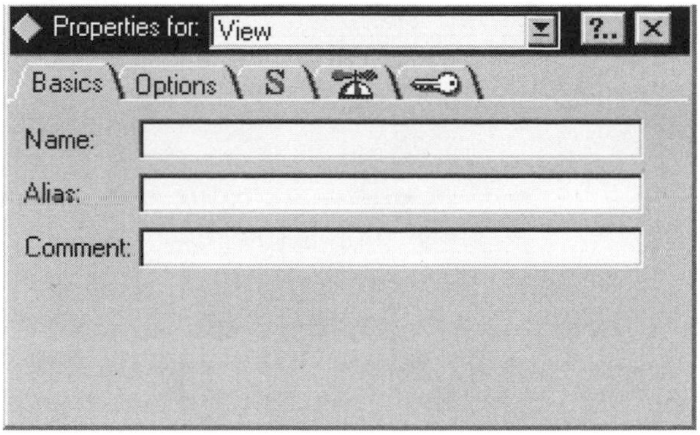

The view name is case sensitive and may contain letters, numbers, spaces, and punctuation. To create **cascading views**, use the backslash, (\), character. Aliases allow a view to have a name for internal use; this is very similar to using a synonym. Note that synonyms can be used in view names or aliases by using the vertical bar (|) symbol. Comments allow the designer to provide additional information about the view. Hidden views can be created by enclosing the view name in parenthesis.

The Options Tab

The Options tab (Figure 4-4) sets several attributes for the view.

Figure 4-4
View Options Tab

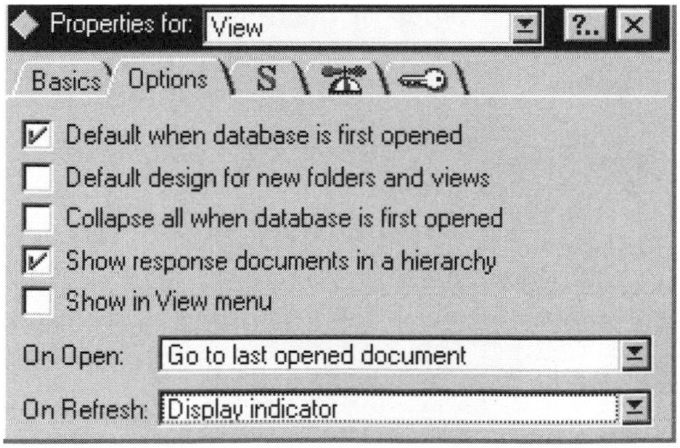

- **Default when database is first opened:** The designer can select the initial view for the database. However, this will be ignored if the database launch property opens a navigator with an associated view. Only one default view is allowed in a database; it is marked with an asterisk (*) in the view list.

- **Default design for new folders and views:** Consistency in views helps the user locate information. Thus it is helpful to have one base view from which all others are designed. By selecting this option, all views will be designed using the same properties and column formulas which can then be modified to meet the specific view's needs. The designer can select a different view as the default design at creation time by selecting the **Options** button on the Create View/Create Folder dialog box.

- **Collapse all when database is first opened:** Documents can be grouped together using categories. From left to right, categorized columns can expand and collapse to display or hide documents. Select this option to automatically collapse all categories when the database is opened.

- **Show response documents in a hierarchy:** Response and response-to-response type documents can be automatically associated with their parent document in views. This is useful in discussion databases where the user will want to track main and response documents via a hierarchy. Deselect this option if it is not necessary to differentiate between different types of documents, such as in a *By Author* view where it is unnecessary to know which documents are responses. A responses only column is frequently used to display the response information in a view using response hierarchy.

- **Show in view menu:** Deselect this option if the view should not appear in the **View** menu.

- **On Open:** The designer of the view can determine where the user is taken when the view opens.

  - **Go to last opened document:** This is the default selection. When the view is opened, the last opened document will be highlighted in the view.

App. Dev. I

- **Go to top row:** The user will be at the top of the view each time the view is opened. This is useful for locating the most current document in views sorted by *descending* date.

- **Go to bottom row:** The user will be at the bottom of the view each time the view is opened. This is useful for locating the most current document in views sorted by *ascending* date.

- **On Refresh:** Views contain an index, which tracks the order of documents in the view. This index must be refreshed to display the most changes in the view. Views can be set to refresh in several different ways:

  - **Display indicator:** The refresh indicator is displayed by default. This indicator (the blue circular arrow in the upper left hand corner) will display when the view should be refreshed. The user can then click on the arrow or press **F9** to refresh the view.

  - **Refresh display:** This option automatically refreshes the view when changes occur.

  - **Refresh display from top row:** The view is refreshed from the top down. This is useful when the view is designed to show updates at the top of the view.

  - **Refresh display from bottom row:** The view is refreshed from the bottom up. This is useful when the view is designed to show updates at the bottom of the view.

Tips

It is especially important to understand the open and refresh options for the exam! Note that these options can be set on the Options tab in the view properties.

The Style Tab

The Style tab determines the presentation of the view. Figure 4-5 shows the available options.

Figure 4-5
View Style Tab

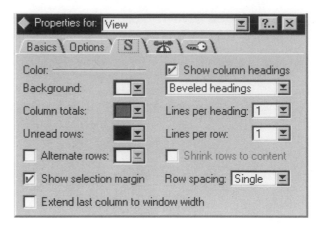

This infobox allows the designer to set the color and display options for columns, rows, and headers. The background, column totals, unread rows, and alternate rows can have a color setting.

- **Background color:** The background is usually a light color for text readability (it is white by default). If desired, the view designer can set each row to be an alternating color where neither of the rows are set to be white. To do so, set the background to one color, and the alternating row's color to the other.

- **Column totals color:** The column total color is only used for columns which have the Total option set. The **Total** option (discussed in the Column Properties section of this chapter) adds the values in the column and creates a total. Sometimes it is beneficial to set this total to a different color in order to draw attention to it. This option is set to dark gray by default.

- **Unread rows color:** The designer may want to set unread documents apart from the rest of the documents in the view. This can be accomplished by setting the text of the document to a different color in the view. The unread rows color will appear if the designer sets the view to display unread marks. This color is black by default.

- **Alternate rows:** Selecting this option sets every other document in the view to a different background color. This is especially useful with the multi-line row functionality. The designer can now enable one document to take up multiple rows and distinguish documents from each other by changing the background color of the rows. An example of this is shown in the mailing list view in Figure 4-6:

Figure 4-6

Multi-line Alternating Rows Example

Name	Company	▲ Address	Business #
Gaskill, Claire	Little Tykes	555 N. Orleans New Orleans, IL 990799	
James, Marcus	Sharks-R-Us	323 W. Pine Grove Key West, FL 99999	989-555-9876
Schmidt, Gwedolyn	CT Workbench	1344 N. Borndear Rd. Denver, CO 998877	819-555-6453

In this example, the address can show on multiple lines. Different documents can be distinguished by their background color. Note that the color must be chosen and the option selected for this to take effect.

Other options available on this tab include:

● **Show selection margin:** Selected by default, this option allows the designer to show or hide the selection margin shown on the left side of the view pane. If the selection margin is hidden, documents can still be selected by holding down the **Shift** key. The selection margin will temporarily be displayed while the user is selecting documents.

● **Extend last column to window width:** This selection enables flexible view windows. Regardless of the width of the view, the rightmost column will extend to the end of the window.

● **Show column headings:** If column titles are unnecessary in the view, the column header bar can be hidden by deselecting this option.

● **Heading display type:** Column headings can be displayed as *beveled headings* (the default setting), which provides a 3D effect. Column headings can also be displayed as the background color of the view without any 3D effects. This is referred to as *simple headings*.

- **Lines per heading:** Headings can have between one and five lines. This allows for a more descriptive column title, without adding width. The text will wrap to the necessary number of rows until the maximum set on this tab is reached.

- **Lines per row:** Each row can be set to a maximum of nine lines. This selection allows for the multi-line functionality shown in the mailing list illustration in Figure 4-6. The **alternate rows** and **shrink rows to content** options are frequently used in conjunction with this option.

- **Shrink rows to content:** This option is only available when the lines per row selection is greater than one. Regardless of the lines per row setting, only the necessary lines are utilized. For example, if lines per row is set at eight, but the document's information only requires four lines, only four lines will be displayed. Empty lines will not be displayed. If another document requires all eight allowable lines, eight lines will be displayed.

- **Row spacing:** Additional space can be inserted between rows if necessary. The designer can set the row spacing to single, $1\frac{1}{4}$, $1\frac{1}{2}$, $1\frac{3}{4}$, or double.

The Advanced Tab

The Advanced tab icon resembles a beanie. This tab provides additional functionality for many of the basic options already selected (see Figure 4-7):

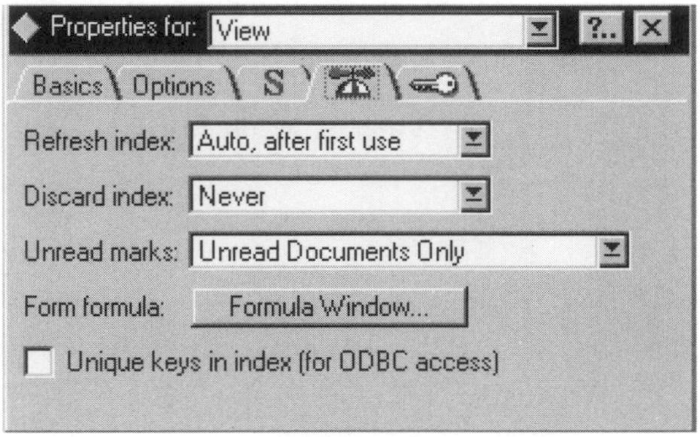

Figure 4-7
View Advanced Tab

The **Refresh Index**: option sets the view refresh rate. The designer can set the index to refresh in the following ways:

- **Auto, after first use:** This is the default option. The view will be updated every time it is opened after the first time. Since the changes are incrementally added to the view's index, the user isn't required to manually update the view, but it takes longer to open the view the first time.

- **Automatic:** The view is updated regardless of whether the view is ever opened. The user isn't required to manually update the view because the changes are incrementally added to the index.

- **Auto, at most every *n* hours:** This option provides a compromise between automatic and manual updating. The view will be updated no more frequently than the specified interval. The refresh icon will appear in the upper left hand corner of the view when the user opens the view and changes have been made since the last time the document was indexed. The user has the option of manually updating or waiting for the view to automatically update.

- **Manual:** This option leaves refreshing in the hands of the user. This is especially useful for large databases where the view can take a long time to open if it has been reindexed. If a user wants to view new documents, she can click on the refresh icon and wait for the view to be re-indexed at that time.

Notes

A view may be manually updated by pressing **F9** *while in the view or by pressing the square in the upper-left corner of the screen where the row and columns intersect.*

The **Discard index** options allow the designer to set the interval for deleting the index. When this occurs, the index must be rebuilt which can be time consuming, especially for large databases. The following discard index options are available:

- **Never:** This option never deletes the index. New updates are added to the existing index. This allows the view to be opened quickly, but takes up the most disk space. This is the default option.

- **After each use:** The view index is built when the view is opened, and discarded when the database closed. This cuts down on disk space, but the view will take longer to open. This is a good option when the view is rarely used.

- **If inactive for *n* days:** This is a compromise between the two previous options. If a view is being used frequently, the index will not be discarded. If users no longer need the view, the index is discarded until used again. This is beneficial for views which have cyclical use.

Unread marks can also be set on this tab. This is especially useful when a color for unread marks is set in the Style tab. Three options are available for unread marks:

- **None:** If the designer selects this option (the default), unread documents are not visually tracked in the database (even if a color is selected in the Style tab). This opens the view fastest, but doesn't allow for any visual notification that the document has not been read. Unread documents can still be located using navigation SmartIcons.

- **Unread documents only:** An asterisk will appear next to any unread documents. However, if the document is included in a collapsed category, no asterisk will appear until the category is expanded to the document level. This option displays documents faster than the Standard option, but slower than if unread marks are not shown at all.

- **Standard (compute in hierarchy):** An asterisk will appear by the document, as well as by a collapsed category if any documents within the category are unread. This option takes the longest to open the view, but provides the most information to the user.

The **Form Formula** allows the designer to control what form is displayed to the user based on a formula. For example, you might want to display one type of form for entering the data, and another form to display the data in a different way. Since the form formula is based on the view, different views can contain different form formulas which in turn allow the form to differ based on the current view. Notes determines which form to display based on the following:

1. If a form is stored in the document, that form is displayed regardless of a form formula.

2. If the form is not stored in the document and a form formula exists for the view, the form formula will be evaluated and the resulting form will be used to display the document.

3. If the form is not stored in the document and no form formula is identified, either the form used to create the document will be displayed, or if that is not available, the default form of the database will be displayed.

The form formula must evaluate to the name of a form available in the database. For example, a form formula might look like this:

```
@If(@IsNewDoc; "New Topic"; "Display Topic")
```

This formula states that if the document is a new document, then use the New Topic form; otherwise, use the Display Topic form.

Tips

For the Application Development I exam, it is important to understand the steps Notes uses to determine which form to use to display the document. It is also important to remember that form formulas are associated with view properties, not the form itself.

The Security Tab

The Security tab determines who can use the view. This is not covered on the Application Development I exam.

Column Properties

The distinction between column and view properties can be difficult, but it is important to understand for the purpose of the exam. Column properties relate to things that can differ in each column. View properties relate to *all* columns or view attributes. Certain column attributes can be unique for each column, such as size, width, and font. The **Basics** and **Sorting** tabs are the most relevant for the Application Development I exam.

The Basics Tab

The Basics tab sets the basic properties of the column such as the name, width, etc. Figure 4-8 shows all available selections for the **basics** tab:

Figure 4-8
Column Basics Tab

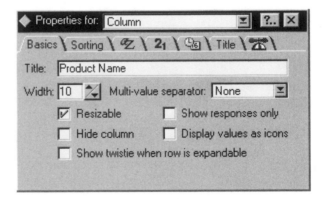

- **Title:** The title of the column is set on this tab. If the width of the column is not wide enough to display the entire name, the name will be cut off.

Traps

Column headers can be set to multiple lines, but that requires changing a view *property. Individual columns cannot be set to display multiple lines; all columns must display the same number of lines. This is an important distinction for the exam!*

- **Width:** The column width is set to 10 by default. The width can be changed by altering this number, or dragging the column's right edge to the right or left.

- **Multi-value separator:** If a column will contain multiple values per document, this option allows the designer to set the separator. The default separator is **None**, which displays the information as it is stored in the field. Other options include: **comma**, **space**, **semicolon**, or **new line**.

- **Resizable:** Deselect this option if you do not want users to be able to manually resize the column. If the **Resizable** option is deselected, no line will appear on the right edge of the column header.

- **Hide column:** Hidden columns can be used for sorting the documents in the view. The sorting criteria may not be pertinent in the view, but necessary to display the documents in the desired order. Hidden columns don't show in the view, but are displayed when the view is in design mode.

- **Show twistie when row is expandable:** This option is used with categorized columns which can be expanded or collapsed. If this option is selected, an arrow (or twistie) is displayed next to the categorized column when the row is collapsed. The arrow points down when the row is expanded (see Figure 4-9):

Figure 4-9

Example of Twisties in Expandable Rows

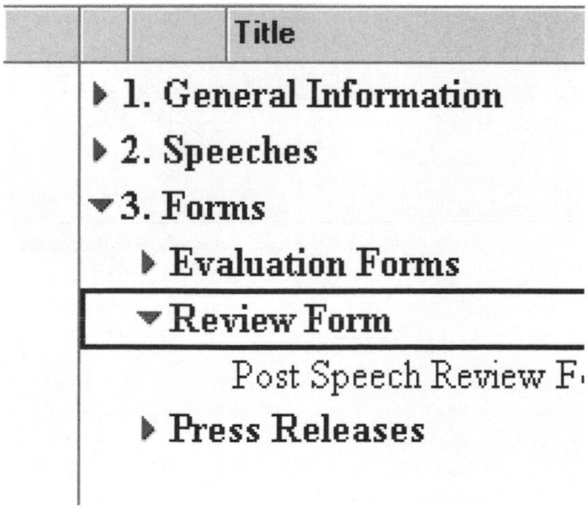

This option is not selected by default. If multiple categorized columns exist (as in Figure 4-9), the setting must be applied to each column. The twistie icon is preset and cannot be changed to a different icon.

- **Show responses only:** If this option is selected, the column will only display response or response-to-response type documents. "Response only" columns are frequently used in discussion views. The response documents will be shown as indented beneath the associated parent document. The view property **Show Response Hierarchy** must be selected to create this discussion-type format.

- **Display values as icons:** Instead of text, Notes icons can appear in the column. Notes provides 170 icons. To display an icon, this option must be selected, and the column formula must evaluate to a number between one and 170.

The Sorting Tab

The **Sorting** tab determines the order in which documents are displayed in the view (see Figure 4-10).

Figure 4-10
Column Sorting Tab

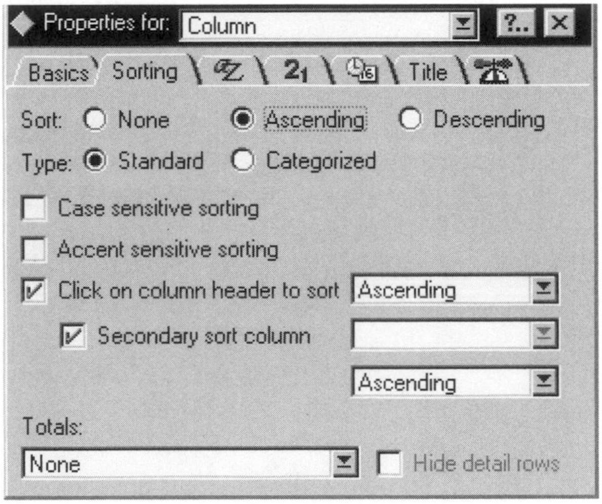

Documents can be sorted, categorized and totaled based on the following selections:

- **Sort:** Documents can be sorted in three ways: **None, Ascending,** and **Descending**. The column defaults to **None** which displays documents in the order they are added to the view. Documents can be sorted by one or many columns.

- **Type:** If the column is sorted (either ascending or descending is selected in the sort options), the designer can select a sorting type. The type can be **Standard**, by default, or **Categorized**. Categorized columns group like data together and can be expanded or collapsed.

- **Case sensitive sorting:** This option enables sorting based on case as well as any other attributes set in the column properties.

- **Accent sensitive sorting:** This option enables sorting based on accents as well as any other attributes set in the column properties.

- **Click on column header to sort:** Selecting this option allows users to sort the documents dynamically. Arrows appear in the column header informing the user they can sort the column in ascending order (up arrow), descending order (down arrow), both (up and down arrows are displayed), or change to a different view (a curved arrow displays). If the designer selects the **Change to View** option, a view from the database must be selected.

- **Secondary sort column:** If the designer selects **Ascending**, **Descending**, or **Both** in the **Click on column header to sort** option, a secondary sorting column can also be selected from the view. This refines the sorting in the user-sorted column without any intervention by the user.

The remaining tabs in the column properties infobox are not tested in the exam. They are used to format the contents of the column. The font, time format, numeric format, and title font and format can be set in the other tabs.

Formulas for Columns and Views

There are two settings where formulas are utilized within views: *selection formulas* and *column formulas*.

Selection Formulas

At the beginning of the chapter, we discussed writing selection formulas when the view is created in the Create View dialog box. Selection formulas can also be written within the view itself after it is created. The same formula creation options are available in the design pane in the view selection event. The formula can be **Easy**—designed by clicking on the **Add Condition** button—or an @function formula can be used. LotusScript is not available for view selection formulas. If no selection formula is written by the designer, SELECT @ALL is used as the default formula. This will include every document in the database in the view.

Column Formulas

Column formulas determine the contents of a column. The formula can be created using simple functions, a field name, or an @formula. Simple functions allow the designer to use common functionality without any programming. This includes information such as the document's creation date or information about attachments. The designer can also select from a list of field names; only fields which can be displayed in the view are included in the list. Computed for display, rich text and encrypted fields cannot be used in views. If the designer writes a formula, a combination of field names, @functions, and operators are available. The formula can only use one data type. For example, to use the chapter number and chapter title in one column, the formula would be:

```
@Text(ChapterNum) + ". " + ChapterTitle
```

If dates or numbers are used by themselves (not within a formula), they do not need to be converted to text. To include static text in the column, place the text in quotes.

Tips

In the Application Development I exam, you will be asked to troubleshoot column formulas as well as determine the results of a column formula.

There is a set of @functions specifically designed to be used with views. Two of the key @functions are listed below:

- **@AllChildren:** This is used in view selection and selective replication formulas. All response documents that match the parent documents are included in the view. However, only the immediate responses (no response-to-response documents) will be included. This differs from @IsResponseDoc in that only responses to parent documents included in the view are selected or replicated.

Example: `SELECT` *selection formula* `| @AllChildren`

- **@AllDescendents:** This is used in view selection and selective replication formulas. All response and response-to-response documents that match the parent documents are included in the view. This differs from @IsResponseDoc in that only responses to parent documents included in the view are selected or replicated. This differs from @AllChildren in that *all* responses at any level are returned, rather than only the immediate responses.

Example: `SELECT` *selection formula* `| @AllDescendents`

These are two of the @functions covered in the exam. You should feel comfortable understanding how @functions work and how they are evaluated. An @function table is located in Chapter 3—*Working with Fields and Formulas*. See the *Lotus Notes Programmers Guide* for a complete description of all @functions.

View Actions

Actions can be associated with forms or views. They are available via the **Actions** menu item, or on the **Action Bar** of the form or view. Form actions are discussed in Chapter 2—*Working with Forms*. Notes provides a set of default actions on all views and forms. These actions provide common functionality, including categorizing the document, editing the document, sending the document, moving the document to a folder, forwarding the document, or removing the document from a folder. The designer can also create new actions by selecting **Create – Action** on the menu. These actions can use simple actions, formulas or script.

Actions have their own set of properties which can be set by the designer (see Figure 4-11):

Figure 4-11
Action Properties
InfoBox

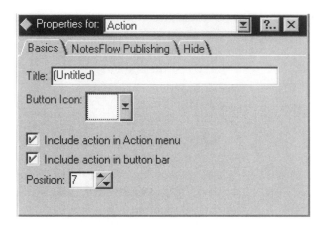

The title contains the text that will appear in the menu and on the button in the button bar. The button icon can be selected from the drop down list. This provides a distinguishing graphic on the button. The designer has the option of displaying the action in the **Action** menu or in the button bar. The position determines where the action is displayed in relation to other actions.

The action properties infobox also allows actions to be hidden, based on document events or hide-when formulas.

Tips

The Application Development I exam focuses on which types of actions are used when. For example, if the action was going to be run on unread documents, it would be a view action. If the action was going to switch the document's form in the display, it would be a form action.

Chapter 4 Sample Questions

■ **Objective:** Create views that use selection formulas.

Eddie wants to create a view that only contains documents which have "Approved" in the Status field. How should he write the selection formula?

      A. FIELD = Approved

      B FIELD Status:= "Approved"

      C. SELECT "Approved"

      D. SELECT Status = "Approved"

Answer: D
Selection formulas must contain a SELECT statement. Without the field name, the formula would not make any sense.

■ **Objective:** Create views which use selection formulas.

What are Eddie's other options for writing a selection formula to specify the documents included in the view?

      A. Add a Condition

      B. Add a Search by Status

      C. Add a Selection

      D. None, he must write a selection formula to specify which documents to include

Answer: A
Selection formulas can be built by adding conditions.

■ **Objective:** Create private/shared folders.

Joan wants to group all of the documents related to financial information together in the database, but she doesn't have any design rights. She wants to be able to decide which financial documents are included, because she only cares about current information. When she is no longer interested in the document, she wants to be able to move it out of the group of documents. What can she do?

    A. Create a private view

    B. Create a private folder

    C. Create a shared folder

    D. Nothing; without design rights Joan is limited to the views provided by the designers

Answer: B
Users can create private folders (assuming they have at least Reader access to the database). Folders allow documents to be grouped together and moved in and out. Views are based on a selection formula.

■ **Objective:** Create views which use shared or private attributes.

Fred is designing a view in a database on the server for his math class. He wants to design a view that is unique for every student. It will show only those documents pertinent to the student viewing the database. However, he wants the design of the view to be the same for each student. How can he accomplish this?

    A. Create a private view

    B. Create a private folder

    C. Create a shared, personal on first use view

    D. Create a shared view

Answer: C
A shared, personal on first use view allows the designer to create a private view for each individual.

■ Objective: Create views which use open option(s).

When Bress opens the Current Sales view, she is always at the top of the view. What property did the designer of the view set?

        A. A document default property

        B. A view options property

        C. A view launch property

        D. A view basics property

Answer: B
The **On Open: Go to top row** property can be set on the Options tab of the view properties infobox.

■ Objective: Create views which use refresh options.

Emma has created a view which is sorted by date created in ascending order. Newly created documents will show at the bottom of the view. What refresh option would refresh the most current documents first?

        A. Display indicator

        B. Refresh display

        C. Refresh display from top row

        D. Refresh display from bottom row

Answer: D
In the view described above, new documents would be displayed at the bottom of the view. To refresh the view to show the newest documents first, the view should be refreshed from the bottom up.

■ **Objective:** Create views which use a response hierarchy.

Elizabeth wants to create a view where child documents are associated with their parent. What property does she need to set?

> A. Documents inherit fields
>
> B. Show response documents in a hierarchy
>
> C. Show response relationship
>
> D. Documents display in hierarchy

Answer: B

The view property **Show response documents in a hierarchy** associates main and response documents in the view.

■ **Objective:** Create views which use alternate row colors.

Scott designed a view to show all of the compact discs he has available for his DJ business. Some documents in the view take up multiple lines. He finds it very difficult to distinguish between the CD titles. What can he do to fix this?

> A. Set a document property to display the document in a
>   different color
>
> B. Set a form property to display the document in a
>   different color
>
> C. Set a view property to display alternating colors
>
> D. Set a view property to display a different background color

Answer: C

Alternating colors allow every other document to appear in a different color to distinguish between documents.

■ **Objective:** Create views which use multiple lines per row.

Dhamba wants to view the entire title of the document. However, some titles are very long and don't fit in the width of the column. What can she do to view more of the title without extending the width of the column?

A. Specify a column property to allow multiple lines in the column

B. Specify a view property to allow multiple lines per row

C. Specify a view property to allow multiple lines per column

D. Specify a column property to allow multiple lines per row

Answer: B
The **lines per row** option in the view properties can be set to greater than one which will allow the information to wrap to multiple lines.

■ **Objective:** Create views which shrink rows to content.

Greta allows seven lines to display in each row. However, some of her documents don't require that many lines and are unnecessarily large. What can she do to fix this?

A. Reduce the number of lines displayed in each row

B. Set a column property to shrink the number of rows displayed

C. Set a column property to set a maximum number of rows displayed

D. Set a view property to shrink the rows to the content of the document

Answer: D
Setting the **Shrink rows to content** property in the view properties will reduce the number of lines used per row to only the amount necessary for the document.

■ **Objective:** Create views which use adjustable row spacing.

Caroline designed a view for her department to track dress sales. Her supervisor has complained that the view seems very crowded. What can Caroline do to spread out the documents?

A. Set the spacing to double in the document properties

B. Set the row spacing to 1¼ in the view properties

C. Set the column spacing to 1½ in the column properties

D. She can deselect the **Shrink rows to content** option

Answer: B
The row spacing option is available in the view properties. The spacing can be set to single, 1¼, 1½, 1¾, or double.

■ **Objective:** Create views which use form formulas.

Alex has designed a database for tracking which dogs have completed the Good Doggy training class. If the dog has completed the course, he wants to view the form which shows the completion information; if not, he wants to view the scheduled class form. How can he accomplish this?

A. Create a view formula in the view properties

B. Create a view formula in the form properties

C. Create a form formula in the form properties

D. Create a form formula in the view properties

Answer: D
Form formulas are contained in the Advanced tab of the view properties.

■ **Objective:** Create views that use form formulas.

Kelly created a document in the Regional Sales database with the New Order form. The default form in the database is Product. The form is not stored in the document. The designer also created the following form formula:

```
@If( Type = "Order"; "New Order"; "Sale")
```

The Type field on Kelly's document is Product. What form will be displayed when this document is opened in the database?

A. New Order

B. Product

C. Type

D. Sale

Answer: D
Notes determines the form to display the document based on whether the form is stored in the document, then on the form formula, which would result in "Sale," then on the form with which the document was created, then the default form.

■ **Objective:** Create views that use multiple-line column headings.

Kareem wants to use very descriptive column headers in the view he is creating. However, this is resulting in very wide columns. What can he do to keep his headers descriptive but shrink the width of his columns?

A. Change the **Lines per heading** in the view properties

B. Change the **Lines per heading** in the column properties

C. Select the **Shrink to content** option in the view properties

D. Select the **Shrink to content** option in the column properties

Answer: A
Column headings can be set to up to five lines in the view properties.

■ **Objective:** Create views that use heading variations.

Mica wants to eliminate the column headers in her view. Can she do this?

      A. Yes, remove all of the titles in the column headers

      B. Yes, select the Simple headers property in the column properties

      C. Yes, deselect the **Show column headings** property in the view properties

      D. No—headers cannot be removed, only titles

Answer: C
The **Show column headings** view attribute allows the headers to be shown or hidden.

■ **Objective:** Create views which use column sorting options.

Griffin has created a view to sort documents in ascending order so the newest documents would be located at the bottom. However, the users have requested the same view in descending order. Does Griffin have to create an additional view?

      A. Yes, but he can set the original view as the default for design so he doesn't have to redesign the entire view

      B. Yes, he will have to copy and paste the view and change the sorting options

      C. No, he can enable the users to resort the view based on the view properties

      D. No, he can enable the users to resort the view based on column properties

Answer: D
Griffin should select the **Click on column header to sort—Descending** option in the column properties.

■ **Objective:** Create views that use resizable columns.

Mitzie has set the column width to 8 in order to maximize the number of columns which can be seen in the view. However, this makes it difficult to view all of the data in a column. How can Mitzie show the most columns, and still allow users to view more of the data if desired?

A. Allow the columns to be resorted by the user in the view properties

B. Allow the columns to be resized by the user in the view properties

C. Allow the columns to be resized by the user in the column properties

D. Allow the view to be expanded by the user in the view properties

Answer: C
The **resizable** option allows the user to change the width of the column. This property is set on the Sorting tab of the column properties.

■ **Objective:** Create views which use preset expandable row symbols.

Joe is using categorized columns in his view. When the view opens, the categories are automatically collapsed. How can Joe notify the user that the row is expandable without using any formulas?

A. Select the **Display value as icon** column property

B. Select the **Show icon when row is expandable** column property

C. Select the **Show icon when row is expandable** view property

D. Select the **Show twistie when row is expandable** column property

Answer: D
The **Show twistie when row is expandable** option displays an arrow when the row is expandable. This attribute is set on the Basics tab of the column properties.

■ **Objective:** Create views that use adjustable title widths.

Basil included 10 columns in his view. However, now all of the title can't be seen. What attributes does Basil need to set in order to allow users to adjust the width of the column title?

> A. The Resizable column attribute
>
> B. The Resizable title attribute
>
> C. The Width view attribute
>
> D. The Width column attribute

Answer: A

The **resizable** column attribute allows users to drag the column header to the right and left to enlarge or decrease the width of the column.

■ **Objective:** Create views which use @functions.

Linda is designing a view for a discussion database to be used by her IS department. If a document has any responses, she wants to include all of them in the view. However, she does not want to show any responses for documents not included in the view. What should she do?

> A. Write a view selection formula using `@IsResponseDoc`
>
> B. Write a view selection formula using `@AllChildren`
>
> C. Write a view selection formula using `@AllDescendents`
>
> D. Select **Show response hierarchy** in the view properties

Answer: C

`@AllDescendents` includes all responses to parent documents in the view. `@AllChildren` only includes the immediate responses. `@IsResponseDoc` shows all responses regardless of whether a parent document is shown in the view.

■ **Objective:** Create views that use column formulas.

Mark is writing a column formula. He wants to show the information in the Status field and if the status is **Completed**, he wants to show the date it was completed. The date completed is stored as a date in the DateCompleted field. What should his formula look like?

A. `@If(Status = Completed;Completed +`
   `DateCompleted;Status)`

B. `@If(Status = "Completed";"Completed" +`
   `DateCompleted;Status)`

C. `@If(Status = Completed;"Completed" +`
   `@Text("DateCompleted");Status)`

D. `@If(Status = "Completed";"Completed" +`
   `@Text(DateCompleted);Status)`

Answer: D
Since you are checking for a particular field value, the value must be in quotes. Any static text must also be in quotes. Since the **DateCompleted** field is in date format, it must be changed to text.

■ **Objective:** Create views that use manual actions.

In Vicky's views, she always deselects the **Show in View menu** option. What design element could she use instead to allow users to switch between views?

A. Create a view action

B. Create a menu action

C. Create a navigator action

D. Create a SmartIcon

Answer: A
A view action could automatically switch the view.

Application

Development II

Chapter 5

Workflow Applications & Form Design

This chapter begins our coverage of the competencies required for the Application Development II exam. In the next five chapters, we will cover advanced development topics including form design, fields and formulas, views, agents, and security. These chapters assume that the candidate has extensive experience working with Lotus Notes; very little basic concept review is provided. The chapters do not cover all possible application development topics, but focus on those concepts important to understand for the exam.

The Application Development II exam focuses on the tools used to create complex multi-database applications. One of the most common types of advanced applications is *workflow*. Workflow applications move documents and information among different users through a process. This chapter will focus on the design elements used to create these types of applications, including using Notes' mailing functionality within a workflow application. We will cover the best practices for designing applications including an overview of the design process. We will also cover the most basic aspect of database design: *the form*.

Advanced design elements related to forms are especially important on the Application Development II exam.

Planning the Application

When designing an application, the designer should spend some time planning out the application and reviewing the design with the users. Otherwise, costly development changes may have to be made in order to meet the users' needs. The following steps outline the recommended procedure for creating an application:

1. Assess the business processes and the organizational requirements.

2. Develop a design specification using a flow diagram.

3. Review the design specification with the users and make any changes.

4. Create a prototype to give the users an understanding of the functionality, as well as the look and feel of the application.

5. Test the prototype and elicit feedback from users.

6. Make any changes based on the response from the users and retest.

7. Provide documentation and training to users.

These steps help ensure that the development cycle will be smooth and users will be happy with the completed product. The Application Development II exam requires an understanding of these steps and the order in which they are completed.

Developing Workflow Applications

Workflow is one of the five main types of applications. The others include broadcast, reference, tracking, and discussion. The focus of the Application Development II exam is primarily on workflow-type applications. It is helpful to have a basic understanding of the terminology used by Lotus within workflow applications:

- **Business Process:** According to Lotus, a business process is a sequence of steps used to reach a specific business goal, such as approving expenditures.

- **Activity:** These are steps within a business process, such as completing the expenditure form.

- **Interaction:** The steps within a business process which move the information from one person or status to another.

- **Workflow:** The activities (work) and interactions (flow) utilized to complete a business process.

Workflow applications can interact with the user in various ways. Lotus has identified three basic models for workflow:

- **Send Model:** The send model takes the information to the user. The form is routed to the user and the user takes action on it from his mail database.

- **Share Model:** The share model assumes users come to the data. Users are responsible for checking the database on a regular basis for the status of the document.

- **Hybrid Model:** The hybrid model uses the best of both models. In a hybrid workflow, the forms are not routed; they are stored within the database. A reminder is sent to the user with a link that points to the database.

Both the send and hybrid workflow models rely on mailing information to the user. The next section of this chapter describes how to implement mailing functionality within the application as it relates to the Application Development II exam.

Automating Notes Applications for Mailing

To route documents within Notes, three different requirements must be met:

- **The form must be mail-enabled:** The form must know how to send the information. This can be controlled by the user or by a formula. The form must also contain a trigger to indicate when the message should be sent and the recipient's address. This is covered in detail in the following section; "Mail-Enabling a Notes Form."

- **A route must exist:** Based on the document's destination, the message must be able to get to the receiver from the sender. For a document to be routed from one database to another, a person or mail-in database document must exist in the Public Name and Address Book.

- **The destination must be able to accept the message:** A document can be sent to a user's mail file or to a mail-enabled database. Mail files are created for the purpose of accepting messages and are already mail enabled by the associated person document in the Public Name and Address Book. Other databases which receive mail must have a mail-in database document in the Public Name and Address Book.

To create a mail-in database document in the Public Name and Address book, open the Public Address Book and select **Create – Server – Mail-In Database**. (The Notes Administrator may have to create this document, since most users are not granted rights to create documents in the Public Name and Address Book.) The document shown in Figure 5-1 appears:

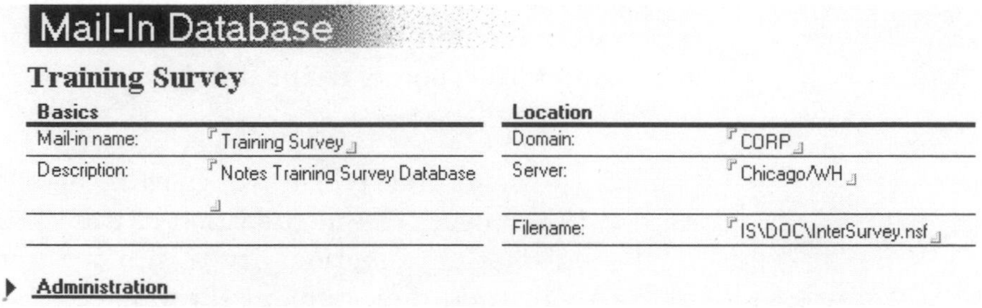

Figure 5-1
Mail-In Database
Document

Provide the name of the database, and a brief description. The database's location information must also be provided, including the domain, server, and file name.

Once these requirements have been met, the document can be routed to the user or mail-in database. The next section provides a detailed description of the requirements for mailing a form.

Mail-Enabling a Notes Form

There are three ways to enable a form for mailing: set the form properties mailing option, add a MailOptions field to the form, or use the @MailSend function to automatically send the document:

Set the Form Properties Mailing Option

On the **Defaults** tab of the form properties infobox, the **On Close: Present mail send dialog** option is available. If this option is selected, the user will be presented with the option to mail, save, sign, or encrypt the form when the document is saved. Figure 5-2 illustrates the form properties infobox where the selection can be made:

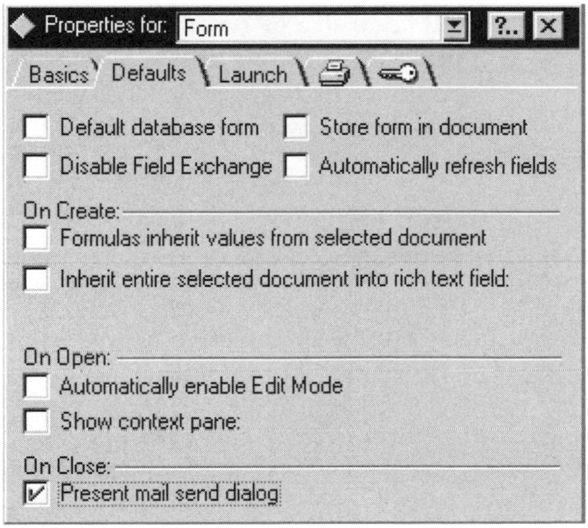

Figure 5-2
Form Properties
Infobox

When this option is selected, the form must contain the reserved fields for mailing. These fields provide the address and mailing options for the message. The **SendTo** field must exist on the form and contain a text value. Multiple values can also be used to address the message to multiple people. The form might also contain the other reserved mailing fields including **CopyTo**, and **BlindCopyTo**. The message will be sent to any names listed in these fields. Although the data in any of these addressing fields must be text, the datatype of the field can be text, keyword, author names, reader names, or names, since all of these data types return text.

Notes

For more information about reserved fields using in mail-enabled forms, see Chapter 6—Advanced Fields and Formulas.

Add a MailOptions Field to the Form

A MailOptions field is a reserved field which can force mailing or prompt the user with mailing options. If the field is set to 1, the document will be mailed to the user(s) specified in the form's **SendTo** field. Setting the field to 0 will not automatically mail the document.

Traps

If the MailOptions field is set to 1, and the **On Close: Present mail send dialog** *option is selected, the form option* **On Close: Present mail send dialog** *will be overwritten. The dialog box appears, but the user's selection will be ignored and the message mailed.*

Use the @MailSend Function

The @MailSend function can be used to automatically mail the document based on parameters specified by the user. The function can be placed in almost any design element including field formulas, buttons, actions, or SmartIcons. However, note that the @MailSend function cannot be used in window title, hide-when, column, or selection formulas.

@MailSend can be used with or without parameters. Without parameters, @MailSend sends the current document and relies on the value of the reserved mailing fields within the form. Thus, if no parameters are used, the document must contain at least a **SendTo** field.

Notes

If the current document is not the memo form and the destination mail file or database does not contain the form, the form must be stored in the document for the recipient to view it in her mail file. Otherwise, the form will not be available and only information in the standard mail fields will be displayed. To store the form in the document, select Store form in document *from the Defaults tab in the form properties infobox.*

Several parameters can be used with @MailSend. When @MailSend is used with parameters, a *new* mail message will be composed and sent based on the information provided in the formula. @MailSend uses the following syntax:

```
@MailSend( sendTo ; copyTo ; blindCopyTo ; subject ;
remark ; bodyFields ; [ flags ])
```

Each parameter is described below:

- **sendTo:** The recipient(s) of the message. This must be text or a text list.

- **copyTo** (Optional): The recipients copied on the message. This must be text or a text list.

- **blindCopyTo** (Optional): The recipients blind copied on the message. This must be text or a text list.

- **subject:** The text placed here will be included in the subject field of the mail memo.

- **remark** (Optional): The text placed here will be placed at the beginning of the message's body field.

- **bodyFields** (Optional): The fields from the current document that should be placed on the new mail message. These fields can be of any datatype. They will appear below the Body field in the order listed.

- **[Sign]** (Optional Flag): This flag adds the user's electronic signature to the memo when it is mailed. (See Chapter 9—*Securing Notes Applications* for more information about electronic signatures).

- **[Encrypt]** (Optional Flag): Including this flag encrypts the document with the recipient's public key from the Public Name and Address Book. The recipient's private key must be used to read the document. (See Chapter 9—*Securing Notes Applications* for more information about encryption).

- **[PriorityHigh]**, **[PriorityNormal]**, or **[Priority Low]** (Optional Flag): One of these can be added to determine the priority level of the mail message. If no priority flag is included, Notes assumes the message should be sent with normal priority.

- **[ReturnReceipt]** (Optional Flag): This flag includes a return receipt with the message. The return receipt will notify the sender when the user has opened the document.

- **[DeliveryReportConfirmed]** (Optional Flag): The sender will be notified regarding the successful delivery of the message.

- **[IncludeDocLink]** (Optional Flag): Adds a doclink to the mail message pointing to the open or selected document where the @MailSend function was launched.

Example:

```
@MailSend("Amy Peasley"; "Scott Thomas";" "; "Meeting
Minutes";" ";"";[Sign]:[ReturnReceipt]:[IncludeDocLink])
```

This formula sends a new document to Amy Peasley, copied to Scott Thomas. The subject of the memo is Meeting Minutes. The message is signed, and includes a doclink back to the document where the message was created. The sender is notified when Amy and Scott open the message.

Although workflow and mailing are key concepts for the Application Development II exam, a detailed understanding of advanced form elements, including subforms, layout regions, controlled-access sections, and hide-when formulas, is also required. The following sections provide more information on these topics.

Subforms

Subforms can contain all of the same design elements as forms. They allow forms to share multiple design elements. A change to a subform will affect all forms that include the subform. Subforms enable the designer to quickly create new forms by reusing design elements, rather than starting from a blank slate.

Figure 5-3 illustrates the properties associated with subforms.

Figure 5-3
Subform Properties
Infobox

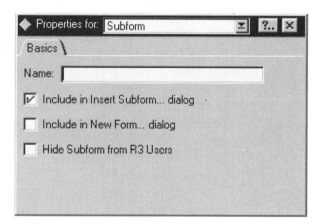

Three options are available when designing a subform:

- **Include in Insert Subform... dialog:** By default, this option is selected. By deselecting this option, the subform can only be used in computed subform properties and not when forms are created.

- **Include in New Form... dialog:** Select this option if the subform should appear immediately when designers choose **Create – Design – Form** from the menu.

- **Hide Subform from R3 users:** This option allows the designer to hide the subform from anyone using version 3.x of Lotus Notes. This is beneficial if there is a mixed environment and designers want to add R4 functionality to the form.

The Application Development II exam focuses on using computed subforms. Computed subforms allow the designer to build forms when they are composed or opened, based on a condition such as the value of a field in the parent document or a user's role. A computed subform formula must evaluate to the name of a subform or Notes will generate a run-time error. Once the form has been composed or opened, the computed subform formulas are *not* dynamically re-evaluated. Thus, refreshing the fields while in the document will not change the result of the computed subform formula.

To insert a computed subform, open the form in design mode. Select **Create – Insert Subform** from the Notes menu. Select the **Insert Subform based on formula** option and create the formula in the design pane using Notes @functions. Note that neither simple actions nor LotusScript is available for writing a computed subform formula. Figure 5-4 shows the insert subform dialog box.

Figure 5-4
Insert Subform
Dialog Box

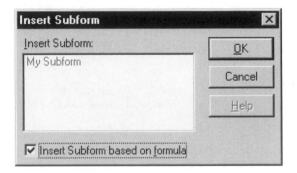

Traps

Subforms are only computed when the form is composed or opened! This is an extremely important concept for the Application Development II exam. Many questions focus on this topic and the understanding that once the form is composed or opened, the subforms cannot be changed. See the sample questions at the end of the chapter for examples.

Layout Regions

Layout regions are a new design element in Notes version 4. They provide a graphical interface which provides more flexibility for laying out fields and other design elements on a form. Text, fields, graphics, buttons, and graphic buttons can be placed anywhere within the layout region by clicking and dragging the element to the desired location.

To create a layout region on a Notes form, open the form in design mode and place the cursor at the desired location layout region. Select **Create – Layout Region – New Layout Region**. The layout region is placed on the form.

Design elements can be layered within the layout region to control how a user tabs through the fields. By default, elements are layered in the order they are created rather than left to right, top to bottom as in a regular form. To change the tab order or element layering, select **Design – Bring to Front** or **Design – Send to Back** from the Notes menu.

For the Application Development II exam, it is important to be familiar with some of the specialized functionality and caveats surrounding the use of layout regions. Layout regions *cannot* contain certain design elements including:

- Links

- Tables

- Attachments

- Pop-ups

- Sections

Keywords data type fields have different interface options when used within layout regions. The following interface options are available:

- **Check Box:** This has the same functionality as a non-layout region keywords field.

- **Radio Button:** This has the same functionality as a non-layout region keywords field.

- **List Box:** List boxes allow the options to be displayed in a list. The number of options displayed depends on the size of the field in the layout region. Users click on the item they wish to select. Multiple items can be selected if the **Allow multi-values** option is selected for the field. Figure 5-5 shows an example of a listbox.

Figure 5-5
List Box Example

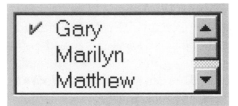

- **Combo Box:** Combo boxes display the keyword options in a drop-down list box. By clicking on the arrow on the right side of the field, all of the available options are displayed. Only one option can be selected with the combo box interface. Figure 5-6 illustrates a keywords combo box:

Figure 5-6
Combo Box
Example

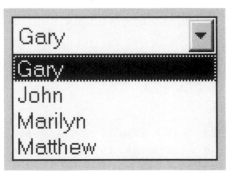

It is important to remember that the Dialog Box option is not available within a layout region for a keywords field. The **Allow values not in this list** option is never provided. Thus, there is no way for users to add values which are not included in the predefined list of a keywords field within a layout region.

Text fields have some additional features within layout regions. When a new field is created on a layout region, it appears as an **edit control**. The designer can select options for the edit control as shown in the edit control properties infobox in Figure 5-7.

Figure 5-7
Field Properties
Within a
Layout Region

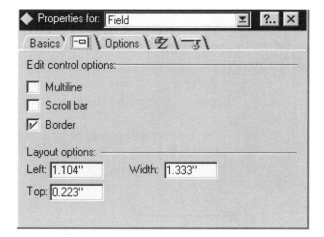

There are also special design restrictions when working with layout regions on a field. The designer must remember that when a field is copied from a layout region, the entire layout region is copied, not just the field. Thus, elements can be copied from a form and placed on a layout region, but elements on a layout region cannot be pasted back onto the form.

Tips

The Application Development II exam places a lot of emphasis on layout regions and their related caveats. It is important to have a strong understanding of this section.

Using @DialogBox with Layout Regions

Layout regions can also provide a dialog box interface for the user. A dialog box can prompt the user for additional information that is then saved with the document. The dialog box provides an additional type of user interface.

The @DialogBox function can display a form, a subform or layout region. The syntax for @DialogBox is:

```
@DialogBox("Dialog"; [AutoVertFit] : [AutoHorzFit])
```

`AutoVertFit` and `AutoHorzFit` size the dialog box to the size of the form. **OK** and **Cancel** buttons are displayed in the dialog box. The text and functionality of these buttons cannot be changed. Values entered into the fields in the dialog box are entered into the document. Figure 5-8 illustrates a dialog box used to gather information from the user:

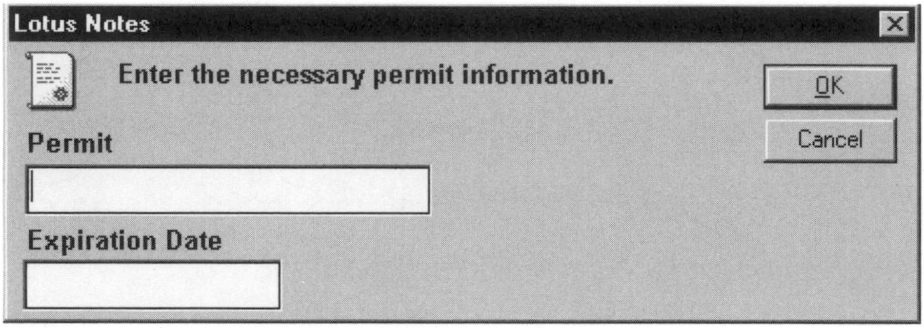

Figure 5-8
Example of a
Dialog Box

Controlled Access Sections

Sections allow the user to collapse an area of the form into a single line. Adding collapsible sections to a form enables the designer to include many design elements, without adding length to the form. Two types of sections are available: standard and controlled access. Standard sections are covered in Chapter 2—*Working with Forms*. They can be expanded or collapsed by the user. The Application Development II exam focuses on controlled access sections.

To control access to an area of the form, create a controlled access section. The expand/collapse options can be set explicitly for editors versus non-editors. To add a controlled access section to the form, open the form and select **Create – Section – Controlled Access**. The section properties for a controlled access section differ slightly from a standard section. Each tab in the controlled access section properties infobox is described below:

- **Title:** The title of the section appears in the section header. On a controlled access section, this cannot be a formula, only text. The section field name is also set on the Title tab. The section field name is used to identify the section. On this tab, the border style and color can also be selected. By default, no border is selected and Dark Cyan is the color.

- **Editors & Non-Editors Tabs:** These two tabs allow the designer to predefine whether the section is expanded or collapsed automatically when the document is previewed, opened for reading, opened for editing, or printed. By default, all of the options are set at **Don't auto expand or collapse**. The Editors tab controls the settings for anyone included in the allowable editors formula. The Non-Editors tab controls the setting for anyone who is not allowed to edit the section. The Non-Editors tab also allows the designer to hide the section title when expanded.

- **Formula:** The formula determines who can edit the section. The formula tab is shown in Figure 5-9.

Figure 5-9
Controlled Access
Section Formula Tab

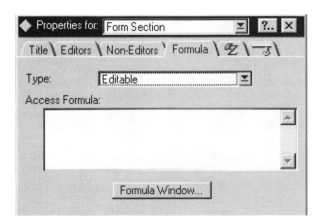

The formula type can be Editable, Computed, Computed for Display, or Computed when Composed. The formula must evaluate to a name or list of names. Also, the section access cannot override the Access Control List of the database. This access controls who can edit the fields within the section, but does not prevent anyone with access to the document from reading the information in the section.

- **Font:** The Font tab allows the designer to specify the font, size, and color of the section title.

- **Hide When:** The section title can be hidden based on a formula or the state of the document.

Tips

The Application Development II exam includes several questions contrasting controlled access sections and subforms. It is important to understand that subforms are utilized to create customized forms. The display of a subform is controlled by a formula. Controlled access sections will always be displayed, but the formula controls who can edit the information within the section.

Using Hide-When Formulas

Design elements can be hidden based on a formula or document event. In the Hide tab of the infobox for the design element (shown in Figure 5-10), the designer can select from document events or write a formula to hide the design element.

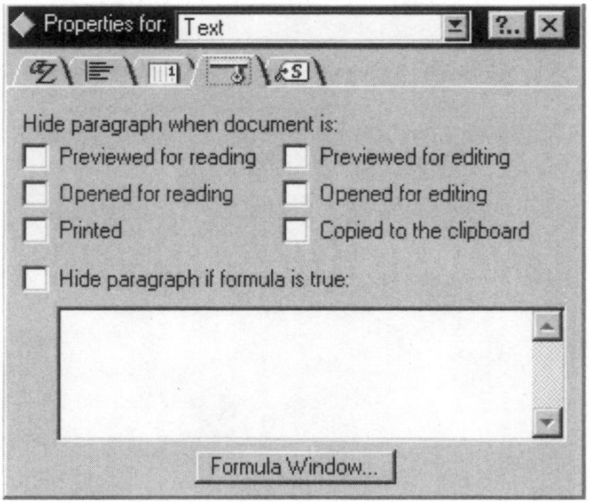

Figure 5-10
Text Hide Tab

Note that this infobox enables the hide-when setting for previewing, opening, printing and copying the document. Hiding is available for hotspots, buttons, sections, objects, text, and graphics. Hide-when formulas can also be used on layout regions or controlled access sections. On layout regions, each design element can be hidden independently. The entire paragraph isn't hidden as it is on a form, only the selected design element.

This chapter covered creating a workflow application using mailing and advanced form design elements. The next chapter goes into more detail about using advanced fields and formulas.

Chapter 5 Sample Questions

■ **Objective:** Plan Notes standards.

As an application designer, you have been asked to create a multi-database application. You have assessed the user and organizational requirements, developed a design specification, held review meetings and had the design approved. What should you do next?

      A. Document your work

      B. Create the first database and place it in production

      C. Create a prototype

      D. Train the users

Answer: C
A prototype will allow the users to review the design and make any changes before you complete the entire application.

■ **Objective:** Understand workflow terminology.

What is a sequence of steps used to accomplish a specific business objective called?

      A. Business goal

      B. Activity

      C. Business process

      D. Workflow

Answer: C
Lotus' definition of a business process is "a sequence of steps that accomplishes a specific business goal..." The workflow terminology will be covered on the Application Development II exam!

■ **Objective:** Create forms which generate mail.

Sharon has a button which automatically creates a new document, then mails the new document to Bill with a copy to Aaron. When Bill reads the message, a note is sent back to Sharon. Bill sees that the subject is Dinner Plans and follows a link back to the document Sharon used to create the message. The mail message was not signed. Which one of the following formulas could have been used to send this message to Bill?

A. @MailSend("Bill"; "Aaron";""; "Dinner Plans";
   "";""; [Sign]:[PriorityNormal]:[ReturnReceipt]:
   [IncludeDocLink])

B. @MailSend

C. @MailSend("Bill"; "Aaron";"Dinner Plans";
   [Return Receipt] : [IncludeDocLink])

D. @MailSend("Bill"; "Aaron";""; "Dinner Plans";
   "";"";[PriorityHigh]:[ReturnReceipt]:
   [DeliveryReportConfirmed] :[IncludeDocLink])

Answer: D
The correct syntax for the @MailSend command is:

```
@MailSend( sendTo ; copyTo ; blindCopyTo ;
subject ; remark ; bodyFields ; [ flags ])
```

All items (other than flags) must be included, even if they are blank. The additional items listed in answer D will not affect the scenario described in the questions. @MailSend without any parameters is not acceptable because a *new* document was created. @MailSend without parameters sends the current document.

■ **Objective:** Create forms which generate mail.

Kramer saves a document which prompts him with sending options. He is still working on the document, so he selects the **Save Only** option. However, the document is sent regardless. Why is the message getting sent?

> A. The designer selected **On Close: Present send dialog**
>
> B. The form contains a **MailOptions** field set to **0**
>
> C. The form contains a **MailOptions** field set to **1**
>
> D. The form contains a **SaveOptions** field set to **Send**

Answer: C

Setting the **MailOptions** to **1** overrides any other settings and sends the document, regardless of the user's selection in the send dialog.

■ **Objective:** Create forms which share design attributes using Subforms.

The CityMap form contains the following formula for a computed subform:

`@If(City = "Marshalltown"; "Mtown"; "OtherTown")` where `Mtown` and `OtherTown` are subforms. The City field is an editable field on the CityMap form containing the default formula `Metamora`. What will be shown when the form is composed?

> A. Nothing
>
> B. The Mtown subform
>
> C. The OtherTown subform

Answer: C

Since the default value of the City field is **Metamora**, not **Marshalltown**, the OtherTown subform will be used.

The same scenario applies as the previous question. What happens when the user changes the value of the **City** field to **Marshalltown** and refreshes the form?

> A. Nothing is displayed, a run-time error is generated
>
> B. The Mtown subform is now displayed
>
> C. The OtherTown subform is displayed

Answer: C
Once the form has been composed, the formula is not recalculated even if the form is refreshed. Thus, even though the formula would now evaluate to the Mtown subform, the OtherTown subform is still displayed because the formula is not recalculated.

■ **Objective:** Create forms which share design attributes using Subforms.

The computed subform contains the following formula:

`@If(Form = "Main"; "MainSub"; "ResponseSub")`. However, the true name of the subform is **RespSub**. What will happen when the user composes a document with the Main form?

> A. The MainSub subform will be included
>
> B. The ResponseSub subform will be included
>
> C. The RespSub subform will be included
>
> D. A run-time error will be generated

Answer: A
The subform will correctly evaluate to the MainSub subform. However, if any other form was used, a run-time error would have been generated because no ResponseSub subform exists in the database.

■ **Objective:** Minimize the impact of Notes architectural limitations.

Bennie is designing a form to track her workouts. She is having some trouble deciding whether to use a section or a subform. What must Bennie remember about the differences between sections and subforms?

        A. Subforms can be displayed using a formula; sections cannot

        B. Subforms can be hidden; sections cannot

        C. Subforms can use layout regions; sections cannot

        D. Sections can display rich text; subforms cannot

Answer: A
Computed subforms allow a subform to be included on the form based on a formula. Sections do not have this flexibility. There is no such thing as a computed section.

■ **Objective:** Create forms which use objects to control sections for viewing.

Wendy is completing a medical school application form within the database. However, about half way down the form there is an area she cannot edit, because it is for office use only. How did the designer create a non-editable area on the form?

        A. The designer created a subform which was not editable

        B. The designer used an access-controlled section

        C. The designer used a controlled access layout region

        D. The designer used a hide-when formula on that area of the form

Answer: B
An access-controlled section allows people included in the result of the formula to edit the section, but only allows others to read the section.

■ **Objective:** Create forms which use keyword lists.

Brent has designed a keywords field on a layout region. Which interface is not available for use here?

> A. Dialog Box
>
> B. List Box
>
> C. Combo Box
>
> D. Check Box

Answer: A
Within a layout region, the only available interfaces are the Radio Button, Check Box, List Box, and Combo Box.

■ **Objective:** Create forms which use keyword lists.

Ackmei is designing a layout region which includes a keywords field. If Ackmei wants to be able to control the height of the list, which interface should he *not* use?

> A. Dialog List
>
> B. Radio Button
>
> C. List Box
>
> D. Combo Box

Answer: D
There is no height option available for the combo box interface—it will be the height of one entry. There is no limit to the length of the drop down list. The height can be controlled on the other options. However, note that a dialog list cannot be used in a layout region, and the check box and radio button height will be determined by the number of entries and columns the designer selects.

■ **Objective:** Using layout regions on forms.

Which of the following items can be used within a layout region?

        A. Attachments

        B. Buttons

        C. Links

        D. Tables

Answer: B
Buttons are the only design element that can be used within a layout region. Layout regions cannot contain links, tables, attachments, pop-ups, or sections.

■ **Objective:** Create forms which use objects with hide-when settings for previewing documents.

Hannah included a letterhead graphic at the top of her memo form. However, when users preview the document, she doesn't want to show the graphic because of its size. What is the best way to display the graphic only when users open the document?

        A. Place the graphic in a computed subform

        B. Place the graphic in a controlled access section

        C. Place the graphic at the bottom of the form

        D. Select the hide-when previewing option on the graphic's properties

Answer: D
A hide-when option is the best solution to this problem. A section could be used, but it is not the best solution. Since the graphic is meant to be a letterhead, moving it is not a desirable solution.

Chapter 6

Advanced Fields and Formulas

The field and formula questions on the Application Development II exam focus on user interaction with a Notes application. In this chapter, we will review some basics such as field types and formula writing. The chapter then moves into different types of fields such as internal and reserved fields. The chapter also focuses on data manipulation through lists, environment variables, lookups, and dialog boxes. Note that although we will attempt to cover the most important formulas for the exam, you should have an understanding of basic formula syntax and usage. For more detailed information and official documentation regarding formulas, see the *Lotus Notes Programmer's Guide*, Chapters 5, 6, and 7.

Reviewing the Basics

The Application Development II exam assumes that the candidate is well versed in fields and formulas. You will be required to understand how and when formulas are evaluated. Recall that there are four types of fields within Lotus Notes: editable, comput-ed, computed for display, and computed when composed. Each type has specific characteristics and associated formulas that are evaluated at various times:

- **Editable:** In an editable field, the user enters the information into the field. Three types of formulas are associated with editable fields:

  - Default Value: A default value is calculated once when the document is created. This is the initial value of the field presented to the user.

  - Input Translation: Input translation formulas modify the information input by the user—for example, removing any unwanted spaces from the input. This is helpful for standardizing input. Input translation formulas are evaluated when the document is refreshed or saved.

  - Input Validation: Input validation formulas are used to verify that valid data has been entered into the field. For example, an input validation formula could be used when the designer wants to check that a specific field is filled in before saving the document. Input validation formulas are evaluated when the document is refreshed or saved. Note that input validation formulas are calculated after input translation formulas.

- **Computed:** Computed fields are recalculated every time a document is created, refreshed, or saved. A formula must be provided for a computed field. Users cannot edit the data in a computed field.

- **Computed for display:** If a field is computed for display, it is calculated when the document is composed, loaded, refreshed, or saved. These fields cannot be used in views. This type of field is beneficial when it is unnecessary to store the data because it is only used to display information on the form.

- **Computed when composed:** These fields are calculated when the document is created, and are never recalculated. The data is stored in the field and can be referred to in views and formulas.

Within a formula, the statements are evaluated from the top down. The only exception to this is `@PostedCommands`, which are calculated after all other statements have been run.

Chapter 3—*Working with Fields and Formulas* covers `@If` as a function used in many Notes formulas. The Application Development II exam expands on the @If function by demonstrating how other @functions can be used in conjunction with @If to control calculations. The following functions are frequently used with @If to control calculations based on the status of the document:

- **@Return:** @Return immediately stops the evaluation of a formula and returns the specified value. This can be used within an @If statement as a condition. For example:

```
@If(fruit = "Banana";@Return("");@Prompt([OK];
"Bananas"; "Please select Banana as the fruit!"))
```

This formula checks the fruit field. If it is equal to Banana, stop executing the formula. If it is equal to anything else, prompt the user.

- **@IsNewDoc:** If the document has not been saved, this returns "1," otherwise it returns "0." This is used when a formula condition is based on whether a document is new (1) or an already existing document (0).

- **@IsDocBeingSaved:** If the document is currently being saved, this returns "1," otherwise it returns "0." This is useful if the designer wants to track the number of times a document has been edited and saved.

- **@IsDocBeingMailed:** If the document is currently being mailed, this returns "1," otherwise it returns "0." This can be used to set a flag that determines whether or not the document has been mailed.

- **@IsDocBeingLoaded:** If the document is being loaded into memory for display, this returns "1," otherwise it returns "0." This can be used to track when the document is being opened.

- **@IsDocBeingRecalculated:** If the document is being recalculated, this returns "1," otherwise this returns "0." This can be utilized to prevent certain fields from being recalculated when the document is refreshed, such as with a time-date stamp.

Tips

For a more comprehensive list of @ functions, see the table in Chapter 3—*Working with Fields and Formulas** or the official documentation in **Lotus Notes Programmers Guide, *Chapters 5, 6, and 7.

Internal and Reserved Fields

The previous section reviewed editable and computed fields. Two other types of fields used in Notes include internal and reserved fields. Notes uses these fields to track information and store data to manipulate the document.

Internal Fields

Internal fields begin with a dollar sign ($). Notes automatically generates the value of these fields. Internal fields can be viewed by opening the document properties and viewing the Fields tab, as shown in Figure 6-1:

Figure 6-1
Internal Fields Listed in
Document Properties

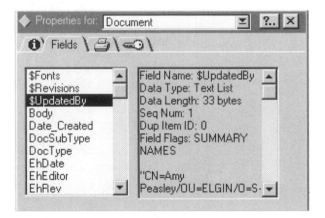

Internal fields are shown at the top of the list beginning with a dollar sign. In the example above, $Font, $Revisions, and $Updated-By are all internal fields. Internal fields can be referenced by Notes formulas. However, the value of an internal field should not be changed as this could corrupt the document.

Although this is not a complete listing of all internal fields, a few examples include:

- **$Title:** Stores the name of the form when the form is stored in the document.

- **$Ref:** Used on response type forms. The parent's document ID is stored in this field in order to maintain the parent/child relationship.

- **$Revisions:** Tracks each time and date the document is revised. This is useful in an edit history.

- **$UpdatedBy:** Lists all users who have edited the document. The @Author function returns the values stored in this field.

Reserved Fields

Reserved fields are specially named fields that Notes recognizes as utilized for a specific purpose. In Chapter 2—*Working with Forms*, several reserved fields were used when mailing documents. For example, the **SendTo** field is used by Notes to determine the recipients of a mail message.

On a mail-enabled form, reserved fields can be used to automate the mailing functionality. Almost all mail settings can be determined using the following reserved fields.

- **SendTo:** Lists all recipients. This is a required field on all mail-enabled forms.

- **CopyTo:** Lists all recipients copied on the document.

- **BlindCopyTo:** Lists all recipients blind copied on the document.

- **DeliveryPriority:** Specifies the delivery priority of the document: high, normal, or low.

- **DeliveryReport:** Specifies when a delivery report will be returned to the sender. By default, delivery reports are returned only when delivery fails.

- **ReturnReceipt:** Specifies whether the sender is notified when the recipients open the document.

- **MailOptions:** Allows the designer to force the document to be mailed. By setting the **MailOptions** field to "1," the document is automatically mailed, regardless of the user's selection in the mail send dialog box. If the field is set to "0," the document will not be mailed.

- **SaveOptions:** Allows the designer to force the document to be saved when it is mailed. This setting will override the user's selection in the document save dialog. By setting the value to "1," the document will be saved. Setting the **SaveOptions** field to "0" will not save the document.

- **Sign:** Allows the designer to force the document to be signed when it is mailed. By setting this field equal to "1," the document will be saved when it is mailed. If the field is set to "0," the document won't be signed.

- **Encrypt:** Adding an **Encrypt** field to the document will specify whether the document should be encrypted when it is sent. Setting this field to "1" will encrypt the document, setting it to "0" will leave the document unencrypted.

To use a reserved field to encrypt a document which is *not* mailed, the designer should use the **SecretEncryptionKeys** field. This will encrypt the document and identify which key is used for the encryption.

There is also a reserved field not related to mailing:

- **FolderOptions:** This field automates the **Actions – Move to Folder** menu option. By setting the value to "1," Notes will prompt the user with the Add to Folder dialog box when the document is saved. By setting the value to "2," the document will automatically be placed in the current folder when the document is saved.

Working with Document IDs

Although document IDs are not stored in internal or reserved fields, they are created and utilized within Notes. Document IDs cannot be altered.

Every Notes document contains a unique document ID. This ID can be used to link documents together or retrieve field values. Several @functions work directly with document IDs:

- **@DocumentUniqueID:** This function returns the 32-character unique ID of the document. By including this formula in a field formula, a link is created to the current document. However, this link is only useful within the current database—if the document is mailed, the link will no longer be valid.

- **@InheritedDocumentUniqueID:** This function returns the unique ID of the current document's parent. Response documents utilize this function to maintain a link to their parent. To utilize this function, the **Inherit values from selected document** form property must be selected.

- **@GetDocField:** This function returns the contents of a field within a document specified by its unique ID.

Syntax: `@GetDocField(documentUNID; fieldname)`

The `documentUNID` parameter refers to the unique ID of the document you want to retrieve the data from. The `fieldname` must be enclosed in quotes unless a variable name is used.

- **@SetDocField:** This function sets the value of a field within a document specified by its unique ID.

Syntax: `@SetDocField(documentUNID; fieldname; newvalue)`

The `documentUNID` parameter refers to the unique ID of the document you want to set the value on. The `fieldname` must be enclosed in quotes unless a variable name is used. The `newvalue` is the value you wish to give to the field.

Working with Lists

Lotus Notes provides many ways to manipulate data by using lists. The elements of a list can be referenced individually or as a whole. All elements of the list must be of the same data type. A colon (:) separates each element within a list.

App. Dev. II

There are several @functions designed to work with lists. You should be familiar with these functions for the Application Development II exam.

- **@Contains:** Determines whether a specified substring is included anywhere within a string.

- **@Elements(list):** Returns the number of elements included in the list.

- **@Explode:** Returns a list composed of the elements of a text string or date range.

- **@Implode:** Concatenates all elements of a list into a single text string.

- **@IsMember/@IsNotMember:** Determines whether or not an element is contained within a list.

- **@Member:** Returns the position of an element within the text list.

- **@Subset:** Searches a string from left to right and returns the specified number of elements.

- **@Unique:** Returns only the first occurrence of an element in the list.

Tips

For more information on @ functions, please refer to the table in Chapter 3—Working with Fields and Formulas, or the Lotus Programmers Guide.

Using Environment Variables

Environment variables store information within an individual's **NOTES.INI** file so that it can be accessed from another database or Notes session. This location provides a permanent storage area for the information. Figure 6-2 illustrates how environmental variables look within a user's **NOTES.INI** file:

Figure 6-2

Environmental
Variables Stored
Within a User's
NOTES.INI File

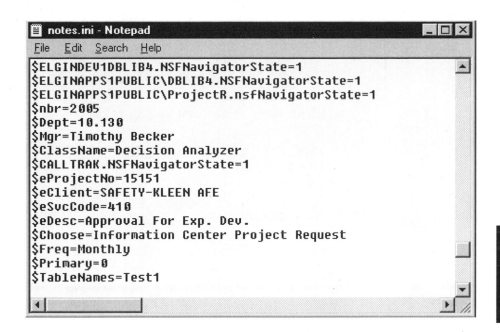

```
📄 notes.ini - Notepad                                    _ □ ✕
File   Edit   Search   Help
$ELGINDEV1DBLIB4.NSFNavigatorState=1
$ELGINAPPS1PUBLIC\DBLIB4.NSFNavigatorState=1
$ELGINAPPS1PUBLIC\ProjectR.nsfNavigatorState=1
$nbr=2005
$Dept=10.130
$Mgr=Timothy Becker
$ClassName=Decision Analyzer
$CALLTRAK.NSFNavigatorState=1
$eProjectNo=15151
$eClient=SAFETY-KLEEN AFE
$eSvcCode=410
$eDesc=Approval For Exp. Dev.
$Choose=Information Center Project Request
$Freq=Monthly
$Primary=0
$TableNames=Test1
```

App. Dev. II

You can see from the illustration above that environmental variables within the **NOTES.INI** file are preceded by a dollar sign ($) character.

Environmental variables are most frequently used to store user-specific information that will be reused on a continuous basis. Using environmental variables avoids forcing the user to continually enter the same information. Other common uses for environmental variables include passing data among formulas and database (since Notes version 4.1 and below cannot use global variables), and generating sequential numbers for one user.

Three methods are available in the @formula language for setting environment variables:

- **@SetEnvironment(*variable;value*):** Use the @SetEnvironment function when you want to set an environment variable from within another @function such as @If. This will place the variable in the user's **NOTES.INI** file. The `variable` parameter is the name of the environment variable. The `value` is the text you want to store in the variable. (Note that although the variable is stored with a dollar sign ($) in the **NOTES.INI** file, the dollar sign should not be used when referencing the variable.)

- **@Environment(*variable;value*):** When used with both parameters, this sets an environmental variable in a formula. The **variable** parameter is the name of the environment variable. The **value** is the text you want to store in the variable. Note that if the @Environment function is used within another @function, @SetEnvironment must be used instead.

- **ENVIRONMENT:** This keyword can be used to begin an expression in a formula. The syntax is: **ENVIRONMENT variable := textvalue**

  The **variable** parameter is the name of the environment variable. The **textvalue** is the text you want to store in the variable.

Notes

There are several caveats to remember when using environmental variables. Environmental variables cannot be set in column or selection formulas or agents running on a server. If an environmental variable is set in an agent running on the server, the server's NOTES.INI file will be affected, not the user's NOTES.INI file! Also, the value must be converted to text before being placed in the variable.

To retrieve the value stored in an environment variable, use the **@Environment(*variable*)** function. A text value of the data stored in the variable will be returned. Remember that when using @Environment with two parameters, you are setting the variable, and @Environment with one parameter retrieves the value.

Using @Db Functions

If information is not user specific, it is not beneficial to store it in an environmental variable. @Db functions allow information to be stored in one location and retrieved from another location. @Db functions allow the user to access data stored in Notes (and non-Notes) databases. This type of function is useful in field formulas, keyword lists, agents (other than mail agents), buttons, SmartIcons, and pop-ups. However, @Db Functions cannot be utilized in mail agents, or view selection or column formulas.

One of the caveats when using @Db functions is mismatched data types. The field being looked up must have the same data type as the field containing the formula. Thus, if Notes expects the @Db formula to return a numeric value and the formula returns text, the function will fail.

The Application Development II exam only focuses on the @DbColumn and @DbLookup formulas. You are not required to understand the parameters required for the @DbCommand function, which returns the results of a query made to a non-Notes database.

@DbColumn

@DbColumn uses a view to locate data within a column. The view can be in the current database or a different one. It is frequently used to populate keyword lists.

The syntax for @DbColumn is:

```
@DbColumn( class : "NoCache" ; server : database ;
view ; columnNumber )
```

Each of the parameters is described below:

- **class:** Distinguishes between Notes and non-Notes databases. If you are referencing a Notes database, use *""* or *"Notes."*

- **"NoCache"**(Optional): Determines whether the information returned by the lookup will be cached or re-searched every time. If *"NoCache"* is included, the results will not be cached. If not included, the results will be cached and re-used during subsequent lookups. If the most recent data must always be returned, use the *"NoCache"* option. If the lookup is time consuming and the data is static, it is better to omit this parameter.

- **server : database:** The server parameter indicates the server of the database you wish to search. For a database on a server or on a local drive, the full path must be used (not including the notes\data directory). To refer to the current database, use "" in place of the server and database name. To refer to a database stored on the user's workstation, use "": "database.nsf". This parameter can be replaced by using the database's replica ID. @DbName can also be used in place of this parameter.

- **view:** The name of the view which contains the column. If the view is cascaded, two backslashes must be provided: "Lookup\\NotesName".

- **columnNumber:** The number of the column whose values are being returned. Columns are counted from left to right, excluding any hidden columns. Review the view in design mode to verify you can see all of the columns. Columns which display a constant value such as **"Received From:"** should not be included in the count. Remember that a formula which always results in the same value is not considered a constant. Columns which contain certain @functions should also be ignored when counting columns. Any column which uses only the following formulas should be discounted: @DocChildren, @DocDescendants, @DocLevel, @DocNumber, @DocParentNumber, @DocSiblings, @IsCategory, or @IsExpandable. If the column number specified in the formula does not exist, Notes will return a null value rather than an error.

@DbLookup

@DbLookup retrieves data from a field based on a specified key. The key is based on the first sorted column within the specified view. Once the key is found, the formula can return the value stored in a view column or field on the document

The syntax for @DbLookup is:

```
@DbLookup( class : "NoCache" ; server : database ;
view ; key ; fieldName ) or

@DbLookup( class : "NoCache" ; server : database ;
view ; key ; columnNumber )
```

Each of the parameters is described below (`class`, `"NoCache"`, `server:database`, and `view` are the same as in the @DbColumn function):

- **class:** Distinguishes between Notes and non-Notes databases. If you are referencing a Notes database, use `""` or `"Notes."`

- **"NoCache"** (Optional): Determines whether the information returned by the lookup will be cached or re-searched every time. If `"NoCache"` is included, the results will not be cached. If not included, the results will be cached and re-used during subsequent lookups. If the most recent data must always be returned, use the `"NoCache"` option. If the lookup is time consuming and the data is static, it is better to omit this parameter.

- **server : database:** The server parameter indicates the server of the database you wish to search. For a database on a server or on a local drive, the full path must be used (not including the notes\data directory). To refer to the current database, use `""` in place of the server and database name. To refer to a database stored on the user's workstation, use `""`: `"database.nsf"`. This parameter can be replaced by using the database's replica ID. `@DbName` can also be used in place of this parameter.

- **view:** The name of the view which contains the key in the first sorted column. If the view is cascaded, two backslashes must be provided: `"Lookup\\NotesName"`.

- **key:** The value to match in the first sorted column of the view. This is the identifier for the lookup that tells Notes which information should be returned. The key must be a text string placed in quotes, a field name, or a variable containing a text string. Time/dates cannot be used as a key unless they are converted to text. The match between the key and the information in the column must be exact.

- **fieldName:** The field containing the value which will be returned. The field name must be placed in quotes.

- **columnNumber:** The number of the column within the specified view containing the value to be returned. Specifying a column number rather than a field is more efficient. The column number is not in quotes. Columns are counted from left to right excluding any hidden columns. Review the view in design mode to verify you can see all of the columns. Columns which display a constant value such as **"Received From:"** should not be included in the count. Remember that a formula which always results in the same value is not considered a constant. Columns which contain certain @ functions should also be ignored when counting columns. Any column which uses only the following formulas should be discounted: @Doc-Children, @DocDescendants, @DocLevel, @DocNumber, @Doc-ParentNumber, @DocSiblings, @IsCategory, or @IsExpandable. If the column number specified in the formula does not exist, Notes will return a null value rather than an error.

Example: A customer master database contains the name, address, and phone number of each customer. The order database tracks each order placed with the company. When an order form is completed, the users want customer's information shown on the order without re-entering the data. On the order form, the name is selected from a keywords list whose values are calculated using an @DbColumn formula. Once a customer has been selected, the address and phone number are automatically filled in using computed fields containing @DBLookup formulas. The customer's name is the key. You will always have an exact match with the key because the name was selected from a list generated from the database.

The Application Development II exam expects the candidate to be able to understand and interpret @Db formulas.

Collecting User Input with @Prompt

The @Prompt function allows interaction between the application and the user. @Prompt displays a dialog box requiring action by the user. The designer uses various parameters based on what type of information is desired from the user. The user's input is returned as a text string when the user enters a value, or a boolean value if the user clicks on the **Yes** or **No** buttons. If the user selects the **Cancel** button, formula evaluation stops.

@Prompt should be used in design elements where the user can interact with the application. Use @Prompt in field formulas, buttons, manual agents, and form and view actions. @Prompt should not be used in any formula which runs in the background or does not interact with the user, such as column formulas, selection formulas, mail agents, scheduled agent formulas, hotspot text pop-ups, or hide-when formulas.

Tips

The Application Development II exam places a great deal of emphasis on @Prompt. You should be familiar with the syntax as well as the various styles.

The syntax for @Prompt is:

```
@Prompt( [ style ] : [ No Sort ] ; title ; prompt ;
defaultChoice ; choiceList )
```

Nine styles are available for use with @Prompt. The required parameters and return value vary based on the selected style. The standard parameters are described below:

- **style:** There are nine styles used with @Prompt.

  - Ok

  - YesNo

  - YesNoCancel

  - OKCancelEdit

  - OKCancelList

  - OKCancelCombo

  - OKCancelEditCombo

  - OKCancelListMult

  - Password

- **[NoSort]:** This is an optional keyword which can be used any time a list of choices is provided. By default, Notes sorts the items in the list. Adding this parameter displays the choices in the same order as they were entered.

- **title:** The text to display in the title bar of the dialog box.

- **prompt:** The text to display in the dialog box.

- **defaultChoice:** The default value for the dialog box. This parameter is not used in the OK, YesNo, YesNoCancel, or Password styles, since no choices are provided for the user.

- **choiceList:** The options displayed in the dialog box. This parameter is required when using the OKCancelList, OKCancelCombo, OKCancelEditCombo, or OKCancelListMult styles.

The style of @Prompt to use depends on the information required from the user. Each style is described below:

- **OK:** This style provides information to the user. Nothing is returned by the user. This style only requires a title and prompt. See Figure 6-3.

Example:

```
@Prompt([OK]; "Notice"; "The message has been sent!")
```

Figure 6-3
Example of
@Prompt([OK])

- **YesNo:** This style provides information to the user. The user has the option of selecting the **Yes** or **No** button. This style only requires a title and prompt. See Figure 6-4.

Example:

```
@Prompt([YesNo]; "Change Status"; "Do you want to
update the status of the document?")
```

Figure 6-4
Example of
@Prompt([YesNo])

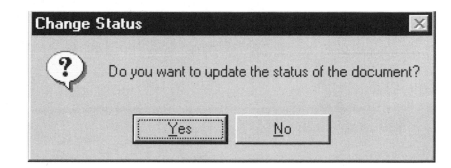

- **YesNoCancel:** This style also provides information to the user. The user has the option of selecting the **Yes**, **No**, or **Cancel** button. If the user selects **Yes**, the formula returns 1, **No** returns 0, and **Cancel** returns,1. This style only requires a title and prompt. See Figure 6-5.

Example:

```
@Prompt([YesNoCancel]; "Update Document"; "Do you want
to modify all selected documents?")
```

Figure 6-5
Example of
@Prompt([YesNoCancel])

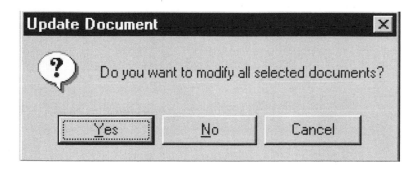

● **OKCancelEdit:** This style retrieves a text string from the user. A default value can be provided. See Figure 6-6.

Example:

```
@Prompt([OKCancelEdit]; "Lotus Notes Classes"; "Please
enter the trainer's name:"; "Tracy Trainer")
```

Figure 6-6
Example of @Prompt
([OKCancelEdit])

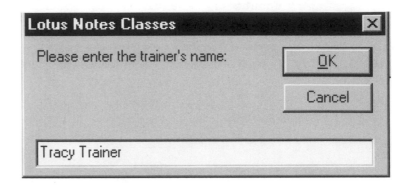

● **OKCancelList:** This @Prompt style provides the user with a list of options using the list box interface. The `choiceList` parameter provides the list of choices in the list box. See Figure 6-7.

Example:

```
@Prompt([OKCancelList]; "Color Options"; "Please
select a color from the list:"; "Red"; "Red":
"Orange": "Yellow" : "Green" : "Blue")
```

Figure 6-7
Example of @Prompt
([OKCancelList])

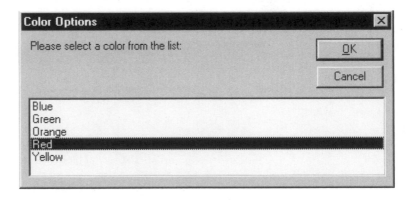

- **OKCancelCombo:** This @Prompt style provides the user with a list of options using the combo box interface. The `choiceList` parameter provides the list of choices in the combo box. This is similar to the OKCancelList style, except a combo box is used to display the list rather than a list box. Only the default value is initially displayed. See Figure 6-8.

Example:

```
@Prompt([OKCancelCombo]; "Color Options"; "Please
select a color from the list:"; "Red"; "Red":
"Orange": "Yellow" : "Green" : "Blue")
```

Figure 6-8

Example of @Prompt
([OKCancelCombo])

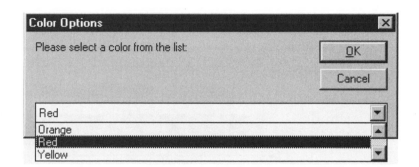

- **OKCancelEditCombo:** This is similar to the OKCancelCombo style, but users can also enter a value not listed in the options provided by the formula.

Example:

```
@Prompt([OKCancelEditCombo]; "Color Options"; "Please
select a color from the list or type your own color:";
"Red"; "Red": "Orange": "Yellow" : "Green" : "Blue")
```

Figure 6-9

Example of @Prompt
([OKCancelEditCombo])

● **OKCancelListMult:** This @Prompt style provides the user with a list of options using the list box interface. The user can select multiple values from the list. See Figure 6-10.

Example:

```
@Prompt([OKCancelListMult]; "Color Options"; "Please
select your colors from the list:"; "Red"; "Red":
"Orange": "Yellow" : "Green" : "Blue")
```

Figure 6-10
Example of @Prompt
([OKCancelListMult])

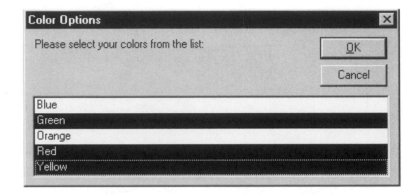

● **Password:** This style is different in that the user is allowed to enter a password. The password is not displayed on the screen; the formula returns the password. See Figure 6-11.

Figure 6-11
Example of
@Prompt([Password])

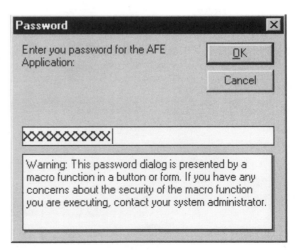

Notes

This is not the user's Notes ID password. There is no interaction with the Notes ID password function. In fact, you do not want users to type in their Notes password since the value typed in is captured by the formula.

This function should not be confused with the @Password function, which is used to encode a string. In the Application Development II exam, this function is often provided as an alternative answer, but it is usually just a decoy.

Example:

```
@Prompt([Password]; "Password"; "Enter you password
for the AFE Application:")
```

Notes

As shown in **Figure 6-11,** *Notes automatically displays a warning when using the @Prompt([Password]) function.*

App. Dev. II

Chapter 6 Sample Questions

■ **Objective:** Create forms which use required fields.

Michael created a field called Activity containing the following formulas:

Default Value: "White-Water Rafting"

Input Validation:
```
@If(Activity = "White-Water Rafting";@Failure("Sorry, your activity is not valid!");@Success)
```

Input Translation:
```
@If(@Contains(Activity; "Rafting"); "Rafting";Activity)
```

If the user does not modify this field, what will happen when the document is saved?

      A. The Activity field will equal Activity

      B. The Activity field will always fail the validation

      C. The Activity field will equal "White-Water Rafting"

      D. The Activity field will equal "Rafting"

Answer: D
Since the user did not interact with the field, the default value is used. When the document is saved, the Input Translation formula is executed. This formula will evaluate to "Rafting". The Input Validation formula is then executed to check the data's validity. Since the field now equals "Rafting", the field will be valid and the document saved.

■ **Objective:** Create forms which use required fields.

Gabby's Name field contains the following Input Validation formula:

Input Validation:
```
@If(Name = "";@Failure("Please provide the user's name!");
@Success)
```

When will this formula be executed? (Select all answers that apply)

>   A. When the document is created
>
>   B. When the document is saved
>
>   C. When the document is refreshed
>
>   D. When the user exits the field

Answer: B & C
Input Validation formulas are evaluated when the document is refreshed or saved. If the **Refresh fields automatically** option was selected in the form properties, the formula would be evaluated when the user leaves the field, but this option is not selected by default.

■ **Objective:** Create formulas which control calculation.

Rory wants to stop his formula from evaluating and return a value if certain conditions are met. Which @function allows him to do this?

>   A. @Return
>
>   B. @Exit
>
>   C. @Failure
>
>   D. @Error

Answer: A
@Return immediately stops the evaluation of a formula and returns the specified value.

■ **Objective:** Create forms which use internal and reserved fields.

Abulae wants to track each time the document has been updated. What internal field can he place in a formula to access this information?

A. $Modified

B. $Updated

C. $Revisions

D. $Ref

Answer: C
$Revisions tracks the time and dates the document has been revised. $Ref links child and parent documents. $Updated and $Modified are not valid internal fields.

■ **Objective:** Create forms which use internal and reserved fields.

Molly uses an @MailSend formula on her form. She does not use any parameters, but wants to include the following mail functionality:

- A blind copy of the message should go to her boss.

- She wants to receive a memo when each recipient opens the memo.

- The memo should be signed and encrypted when it is mailed.

- The document should save automatically when it is sent.

Which reserved fields *must* be included on her form?

A. SendTo

B. SendTo, CopyTo, BlindCopyTo, DeliveryPriority, DeliveryReport, ReturnReceipt, MailOptions, SignOptions, Encrypt

C. SendTo, BlindCopyTo, SaveOptions, Encrypt, Sign, ReturnReceipt

D. SendTo, BlindCopyTo, SaveOptions, SecretEncryptionKeys, SignOptions, Return Receipt

Answer: C

When @MailSend is used without parameters, the reserved field must be included on the form for any special mail functionality. If no special mailing functionality is needed, the **SendTo** field is still required.

■ **Objective:** Create formulas which use internal and reserved fields.

Sele wants to find the contents of a field within another document. However, he only knows the document's unique ID. Which function should he use to retrieve the data?

    A. @DbLookup

    B. @DBColumn

    C. @GetDocField

    D. @DocumentUniqueID

Answer: C

@GetDocField returns the contents of a field within a document specified by its unique ID. @Db functions do not use unique IDs to locate documents. @DocumentUniqueID returns the document's unique ID, not a field value.

■ **Objective:** Create Notes applications that incorporate environment variables.

Lexi wants to store information about a user which can be used in several different applications. She captures the data, but does not want to store it in a Notes database. What can she use to store the information?

    A. Temporary variables

    B. Environmental variables

    C. Notes variables

    D. @SetDocField

App. Dev. II

Answer: B
Environmental variables store information which can be accessed from another Notes database or session.

■ **Objective:** Creating formulas that incorporate environmental variables.

Which of the following formulas can be used to retrieve information stored in an environmental variable (select all that apply)?

> A. `@Environment(variable)`
>
> B. `@Environment(variable; value)`
>
> C. `@GetEnvironment`
>
> D. `ENVIRONMENT keyword`

Answer: A
@Environment (with one parameters) is the only @function which retrieves data. @SetEnvironment, @Environment(variable; value), and the ENVIRONMENT keyword are all used to set environment variables. @GetEnvironment is not a valid @function (but Lotus likes to use it as a decoy answer).

■ **Objective:** Create forms which get information from Notes databases.

Willie is creating an order form. He wants to retrieve the customer's phone number from the CustomerInfo view in the Customer database. The customer's name is stored in the Name field on the current document. Which @Db function will return the correct value?

> A. `@DbColumn("";@DbName; "CustomerInfo";3)`
>
> B. `@DbColumn(""; "": "Customer.nsf";`
>   `"CustomerInfo";Name)`
>
> C. `@DbLookup("" ; @DbName; "CustomerInfo";Name;`
>   `"Phone")`
>
> D. `@DbLookup("" ; "CHICAGO": "Customer.nsf";`
>   `"CustomerInfo";Phone; 3)`

Answer: C
The correct syntax for @DbLookup is:

```
@DbLookup( class : "NoCache" ; server : database ; view ; key ;
fieldName ) or @DbLookup( class : "NoCache" ; server : database
; view ; key ; columnNumber )
```

@DbColumn will not work in this instance because a key is required to locate the specific information. @DbName can be used in place of the `server : database` parameter.

■ **Objective:** Create forms which get information from Notes databases.

Bollero wants to use an @DbColumn formula to populate a keywords list. However, the view he uses frequently changes. What can Bollero do to make sure that a new list is generated every time the user views the keyword list?

    A. Include the "NoCache" parameter in the @DbColumn formula

    B. Eliminate the "NoCache" parameter from the @DbColumn formula

    C. Select the **Automatically refresh fields** form option

    D. Verify that the view automatically refreshes each time it is used

Answer: A
The "NoCache" parameter determines whether the results of the query will be stored. If this parameter is included in the formula, the results are not cached and the lookup is refreshed each time.

■ **Objective:** Create forms which prompt for user input.

Which of the following prompts is not valid?

    A. OKCANCELEDIT

    B. OKCANCELLISTMULT

App. Dev. II

C. OKCANCELEDITLIST

D. OKCANCELCOMBO

Answer: C

There is no such prompt as OKCancelEditList. When a list box is used, the user cannot add new entries.

■ **Objective:** Create forms which prompt for user input.

Which of the following prompts cannot use the [NoSort] parameter?

A. OKCANCELLIST

B. OKCANCELEDIT

C. OKCANCELCOMBO

D. OKCANCELEDITCOMBO

Answer: B

In order to utilize the [NoSort] parameter, there must be a list of choices. OKCancelEdit does not provide the user with any selection options.

■ **Objective:** Create forms which prompt for user input.

Based on Figure 6-12 below, which @Prompt formula was used?

Figure 6-12
@Prompt Example

A. @Prompt([OKCancelCombo] : [NoSort] ; "Entrees";
"Please select an entree from the list:"; "New
York Strip Steak"; "New York Strip Steak": "Pasta
Primavera" : "Pork Tenderloin" : "Smoked Salmon")

B. @Prompt([OKCancelEditList]; "Entrees"; "Please
select an entree from the list:"; "New York
Strip Steak"; "New York Strip Steak": "Smoked
Salmon": "Pasta Primavera" : "Pork Tenderloin")

C. @Prompt([OKCancelList]; "Entrees"; "Please
select an entree from the list:"; "New York
Strip Steak"; "New York Strip Steak": "Smoked
Salmon": "Pasta Primavera" : "Pork Tenderloin")

D. @Prompt([OKCancelEditCombo] : ; "Entrees";
"Please select an entree from the list:";"New
York Strip Steak": "Smoked Salmon": "Pasta Pri-
mavera" : "Pork Tenderloin")

Answer: C
The illustration shows a list box which cannot be edited. (There is no such prompt as OKCancelEditList). Answer A is valid; however, the illustration did not show a combo box but a list box.

■ **Objective:** Create forms which prompt for user input.

Which of the following functions can be used to prompt for the user's Notes ID password?

A. @Password

B. @Prompt([Password])

C. @DialogBox("Password";[AutoVertFit];[AutoHorzFit])

D. None of the Above

Answer: D
There is no @function designed to capture the user's Notes ID. The @Prompt([Password]) function will hide what the user types in, but should not be used for the Notes ID as the function would return the password and thus be a security risk. @Password will encode the information the user enters, but it does not do any comparison with the user's Notes ID.

Chapter 7

Advanced View Concepts

The Application Development II exam requires a more in-depth understanding of views. Whereas in the Application Development I exam the properties of the view were important, the Application Development II exam expects the candidate to integrate advanced view functionality into the application and troubleshoot view design problems.

The Application Development II exam focuses on selection formulas, form formulas, sorting options, using hidden columns, and using the @Picklist command. This chapter provides you with a detailed review of each of these topics.

View Selection Formulas and Using the Search Builder

Selection formulas determine which documents within the database are displayed in the view. This criteria can be based on any information stored in the document as well as the author names, dates, forms, or fields.

Notes provides two different ways to create a selection formula: using the search builder or creating a selection formula with the @formula language. LotusScript cannot be utilized to create a selection formula.

Using the Search Builder

Notes contains an automatic search builder which builds the selection formula for the designer. This allows the designer to rapidly create a view without requiring a detailed understanding of the @formula language. To utilize the search builder, select **View – Design**. In the navigation pane, select **Design – Views** and select your view from the view pane. In the design pane, **Easy** is selected by default. Press the **Add Condition...** button at the bottom of the design pane. This will open the Search Builder window, as shown in Figure 7-1 below.

Figure 7-1
Search Builder
Dialog Box

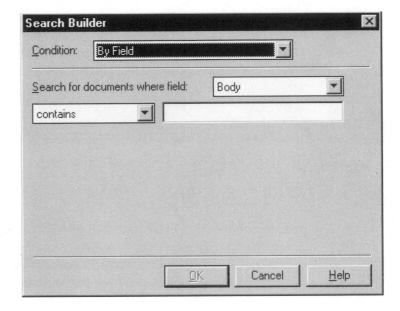

The search builder dialog box allows the view designer to select from the following five conditions:

● By Author

● By Date

- By Field (default)

- By Form

- By Form Used

Traps

Don't get confused between the **By Form** *and* **By Form Used** *options. The* **By Form** *option presents the selected form and allows you to use fields and other form attributes to set the search criteria. Use* **By Form Used** *when you want to search by the form used to create the document.*

Each of these conditions allows the user to specify the criteria for the condition. For example, if the designer selects **By Form Used** as the condition, the dialog box provides a list of the forms in the database for the designer to select from.

Tips

It is especially important to be familiar with the available search builder condition options for the Application Development II exam.

Once the condition has been selected and the additional information provided, a selection formula is automatically created. This formula can be edited or modified if additional complexity is required.

Writing a Selection Formula

Selection formulas can also be written without using the search builder. This is beneficial if the selection formula requires complex functionality or multiple selection criteria. In the view design pane, select **Formula**. The default selection formula, **SELECT @ALL**, appears and the **Add Conditions** button is replaced by the **Fields & Functions...** button. This button provides a list of available fields and @functions for the designer to paste into the formula. Although no predefined conditions are available when writing the selection formula via @functions, the same functionality can be achieved. For example, to select all documents created with the Marketing form, the formula would be:

```
SELECT Form = "Marketing"
```

This formula can also become more complex. For example, if the designer wants all documents created with the Marketing form prior to today, the following formula would be used:

```
SELECT Form = "Marketing" & (@Created < @Today)
```

If the designer does not want to build the formula from scratch, the search builder can be used to create the basic formula, and additional complexity can be included by using @functions.

Form Formulas

Form formulas allow documents to be viewed with a particular form, regardless of the form used to create the document. Different forms can be displayed to the user, based on the results of the formula. For example, you might want to display one type of form for entering the data and another for reading the data. Since the form formula is evaluated at the view level, the form can differ based on the current view. Notes determines which form to display based on the following criteria:

1. If a form is stored in the document, that form is displayed regardless of a form formula.

2. If the form is not stored in the document, and a form formula exists for the view, the form formula is evaluated and the resulting form used.

3. If the form is not stored in the document and no form formula is identified, the form used to create the document is displayed. If that is not available, the default form of the database is shown.

The form formula must evaluate to the name of a form available in the database. For example, a form formula might look like this:

```
@If(@IsNewDoc;"New Topic";"Display Topic")
```

This formula states that if the document is a new document, then use the New Topic form, otherwise, use the Display Topic form.

Tips

For the Application Development II exam, it is important to understand the steps Notes uses to determine which form to display.

To create a form formula, select **View – Design** from the Notes menu. From the navigator pane, select **Design – Views** and select the view. On the Notes menu, select **Design – View Properties**. This opens the view properties infobox. Select the advanced tab (the hat icon) and press the **Formula Window** button. The design form formula dialog box appears as shown in Figure 7-2:

Figure 7-2
Form Formula
Dialog Box

```
┌─────────────────────────────────────────────────────────────┐
│ Design Form Formula                                      [X]  │
├─────────────────────────────────────────────────────────────┤
│  Form Formula:                                  ┌──────────┐  │
│                                                 │    OK    │  │
│                                                 ├──────────┤  │
│                                                 │  Cancel  │  │
│                                                 └──────────┘  │
│  ┌──────────────────────────────────────────────────────┐▲   │
│  │ @If(Status = "Archived";"ArchiveForm";Form)          ││   │
│  │                                                      ││   │
│  │                                                      ││   │
│  │                                                      ││▼   │
│  └──────────────────────────────────────────────────────┘    │
│     ┌────────────┐  ┌────────────┐  ┌────────────┐            │
│     │ Add @Func  │  │ Add Field  │  │  Zoom In   │            │
│     └────────────┘  └────────────┘  └────────────┘            │
└─────────────────────────────────────────────────────────────┘
```

Create the formula (which must evaluate to a form name), and press **OK**. When documents are opened from the view, the form formula is evaluated and the appropriate form displayed.

Sorting Documents in Views

Lotus Notes version 4.0 opened up a broad range of sorting options for designers. Designers now have the ability to place more functionality in the hands of the user, including sorting documents dynamically within the view and opening one view from another. These options can be set on a column-by-column basis.

Figure 7-3 illustrates the sorting tab in the column properties infobox.

Figure 7-3
Column Sorting Tab

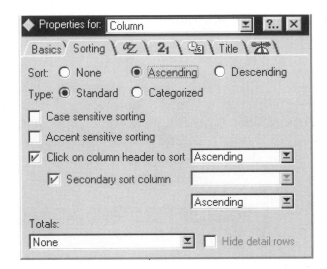

This tab allows the designer to sort, categorize and total documents based on the following selections:

- **Sort:** Documents can be sorted in three ways: **None, Ascending,** and **Descending**. The column defaults to **None**, which displays documents in the order they are added to the view. Documents can be sorted by one or many columns. If multiple columns are sorted, the sorting is evaluated from left to right.

- **Type:** If the column is sorted, the designer can select a sorting type. The type can be **Standard** (by default) or **Categorized**. Categorized columns group data together and can be expanded or collapsed.

- **Case sensitive sorting:** This option enables sorting based on case as well as any other attributes set in the column properties. By default, sorting is *not* case sensitive.

- **Accent sensitive sorting:** This option enables sorting based on accents as well as any other attributes set in the column properties.

- **Click on column header to sort:** Selecting this option allows users to sort the documents dynamically. Arrows will appear in the column header informing the user they can sort the column in **Ascending** (up arrow), **Descending** (down arrow), **Both** (up and down arrows are displayed), or **Change to a different view** (a curved arrow displays). If the designer selects the **Change to View** option, a view from the database must be selected.

In Figure 7-4, the first column allows the user to sort in both ascending and descending order. The second column allows the user to manually sort in ascending order. The third column allows the user to manually sort in descending order. The curved arrow in the fourth column signifies that by clicking on the column header, the user will be sent to a different view.

Figure 7-4

Manual Sorting Using Column Headers

Name	⬍	Company	▲	State	▼	Business	↗
Gaskill, Claire		Little Tykes		IL			

- **Secondary sort column:** If the designer selects **Ascending**, **Descending**, or **Both** in the "Click on column header to sort" option, a secondary sorting column can also be selected from the view. This refines the sorting in the user-sorted column. In the example above, the designer could set the secondary sort of the first column to be the third column rather than the second column, which would be the next sorted column by default. This secondary sorting only occurs when the user clicks on the column header to perform manual sorting.

These sorting options can be manipulated to force documents and their responses to appear in the desired order. One way to utilize sorting options is through hidden columns.

Notes

The Application Development II exam focuses on using the "Click on column header to sort" options and allowing users to manipulate views within the application to find information.

Hidden Columns

Adding *hidden columns* to a view allows document sorting based on a value which is not viewed by the user. For example, the designer might want to sort documents sequentially by month (January, February, March), rather than alphabetically. A hidden column could sort the documents based on the numeric value of the month. This column does not need to be shown to the user. The following formula would be used in the hidden column:

```
@If(Month = "January"; 1; Month = "February";2;Month =
"March";3; Month = "April"; 4; Month = "May"; 5; Month
= "June"; 6; Month = "July"; 7; Month = "August"; 8;
Month = "September"; 9; Month = "October"; 10;Month =
"November"; 11; Month = "December"; 12;"")
```

To create a hidden column, select **View – Design** from the Notes menu. In the navigator pane, select **Design – Views** and select the view. Double-click on the column header to present the column properties infobox. Click the **Hide column** option on the basics tab (shown in Figure 7-5).

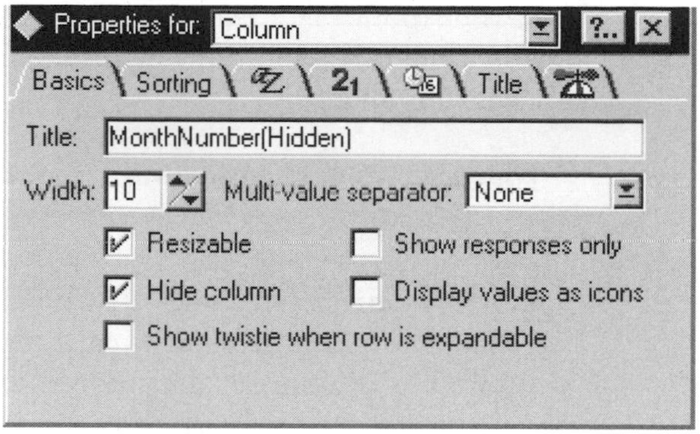

Figure 7-5
Hidden Column
Option

Finally, write the formula for the column in the design pane using a simple function, field, or formula.

Column Formulas & @Functions

Column formulas determine the contents of a column. The formula can be created using simple functions, a field name, or an @formula. Simple functions allow the designer to use common functionality without any programming. This includes information such as the document's creation date or information about attachments. The designer can also select from a list of field names. Only fields which can be displayed in the view are included in the list. Computed for display, rich text and encrypted fields cannot be used in views. If the designer writes a formula, a combination of field names, @functions, and operators are available. The formula can only use one data type. For example, to use the chapter number and chapter title in one column, the formula would be:

```
@Text(ChapterNum) + ". " + ChapterTitle
```

If dates or numbers are used by themselves (not within a formula), they do not need to be converted to text. To include static text in the column, place the text in quotes.

In the Application Development II exam, you will be asked to troubleshoot complex column formulas, as well as determine the results of a column formula.

There is a set of @functions specifically designed to be used with views. Two of the key @functions are listed below:

- **@AllChildren:** This @function is used in view selection and selective replication formulas. All response documents that match the parent documents are included in the view. However, only the immediate responses and no response-to-response documents will be included. This differs from @IsResponseDoc in that only responses to parent documents included in the view are selected or replicated.

Example:

```
SELECT selection formula | @AllChildren
```

- **@AllDescendents:** This @function is used in view selection and selective replication formulas. All response and response-to-response documents that match the parent documents included in the view. This differs from @IsResponseDoc in that only responses to parent documents included in the view are selected or replicated. It differs from @AllChildren in that *all* responses at any level are returned, rather than only the immediate responses.

Example:

```
SELECT selection formula | @AllDescendents
```

These are two of the @functions covered in the Application Development II exam. You should feel comfortable understanding how @functions work and how they are evaluated. See the @function table in Chapter 3—*Working with Fields and Formulas* for more information on @functions. See the *Lotus Notes Programmers Guide* for a complete description of all @functions.

Displaying Notes Icons in View Columns

Lotus Notes provides a set of 170 icons that can be displayed in columns. Figure 7-6 shows the available icons:

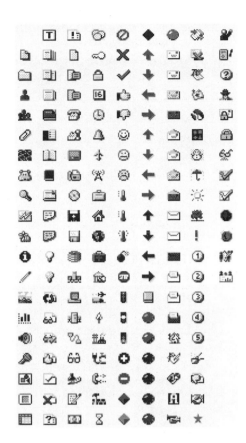

Figure 7-6

Available View
Icons

To display an icon, the column formula must evaluate to a number between one and 170. **Display values as icons** must be selected on the Basics tab of the View Properties. These icons are useful for providing graphical interpretations of information in the document. These icons can only be used within column formulas.

@PickList

@PickList cannot be used within the view; it displays the *contents* of a view from within a dialog box. This allows the user to select documents in a view format. The value of the column defined in the formula is returned as the result of the formula. @PickList can also display the Address Book in a dialog box format. This functionality allows the user to select people, groups, or servers from any available address book. When used this way, the function returns the people, groups, or servers selected.

Notes

@PickList is an extremely important concept for the Application Development II exam. It is important to understand the function's syntax as well as its use within an application.

The syntax below is used to present the user with a dialog box containing the specified view:

```
@PickList([Custom];server : file; view; title;prompt;
column )
```

As an example, this formula:

```
@PickList([Custom]; "" ; "1. All product ideas" ;
"Topic Selection" ; "Please select a topic from the
list below:" ;1)
```

would present the user with the dialog box in Figure 7-7 below:

Figure 7-7

Example of an
@PickList Dialog Box

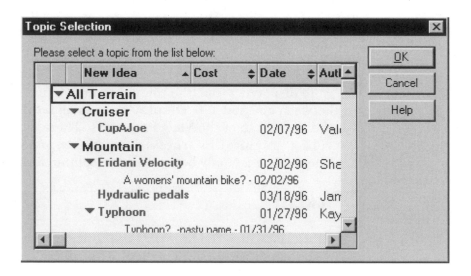

As you can see, the dialog box presents the view in its exact format, including column headers and manual sorting options. The Quick Search functionality can be utilized to locate the document by typing the first few characters.

The formula provides the information needed to specify the view and the text of the dialog box. Each parameter is described below:

- **[Custom]:** The [Custom] parameter indicates that a view, rather than an address book, will be displayed in the dialog box.

- **server : file:** To display a view dialog box, the designer must specify which database the view is located in. The server's name and the database's path and filename must be specified in quotes. To indicate the current database, use double quotes ("").

Notes

Unlike @DBLookup and @DBColumn formulas, the database's replica ID cannot be used instead of the server : file *parameter in @PickList! This is an important drawback of using @PickList in applications which will be replicated. Additional pros and cons to using @PickList are outlined at the end of this chapter.*

- **view:** The name of the view located in the specified database. The view name should appear in quotes. If the view is cascaded, two backslashes (\\) must be used in the formula.

Example:

```
@PickList([Custom]; "" ; "1. All product ideas\\By
Type" ; "Topic Selection" ; "Please select a topic
from the list below:" ;1)
```

- **title:** The window title that will display at the top of the dialog box. This text must be placed in quotes. In the example above, the window's title is "Topic Selection."

- **prompt:** The text which will prompt the user to select documents. For example: "Please select a topic from the list below:"

- **column:** The number listed in the formula is the column number (counting from left to right including all—even hidden—columns). The value listed in this column for the selected documents will be returned as the value of the formula. This number should *not* be in quotes.

If the designer wants to present the Address Book dialog box, a different syntax is used. The syntax below presents the user with the Address Book dialog box:

```
@PickList ([Name])
```

or

```
@PickList ([Name]:[Single])
```

This formula presents the user with the dialog box in Figure 7-8 below:

Figure 7-8

Example of an @PickList Address Book Dialog Box

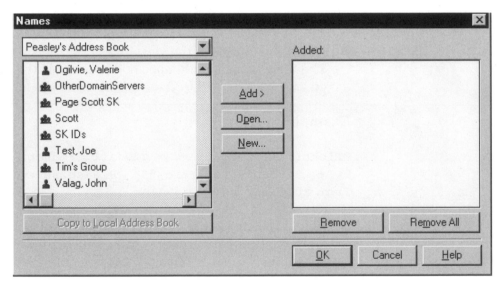

If the **[Single]** parameter is added to the formula, the user is only allowed to select one name from the Address Book dialog box. Figure 7-9 illustrates the Address Book dialog box that only allows one selection:

Figure 7-9

Example of an @PickList
Address Book Dialog Box
Allowing Only One Selection

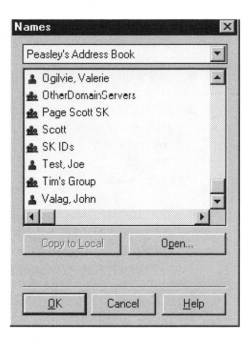

Name and Single are the only necessary parameters for the
Address Book dialog box prompt. These are described below:

- **[Name]:** This parameter indicates that the Address dialog box
  should be displayed rather than a view.

- **[Single]:** Indicates that only one name can be selected from
  the list. This is similar to deselecting the **Allow multi-values**
  option. The format of the dialog box reflects that only one name
  should be selected, as shown in Figures 7-8 and Figure 7-9.

Notes

*@PickList can only be used in buttons, manual and paste
agents, and form and view actions. @PickList cannot be used
in column formulas, selection formulas, mail and scheduled
agents, hide-when formulas, form formulas, or window titles.*

Although @PickList is similar to an @DBColumn or @DBLookup
formula, there are some important differences. @PickList provides
the following benefits over @DB formulas:

- @PickList is not limited by the 64K data return restriction as @DB formulas are.

- @PickList can perform the lookup faster than @DB formulas.

- @PickList contains the Quick Search functionality which allows the user to locate the document by typing the first few characters.

However, @PickList also has its drawbacks:

- The ReplicaID cannot be used to name the database in the @PickList([Custom]) formula. This causes problems when a database is replicated to many servers and the directory structure is not necessarily consistent.

- There is no NoCache option for @PickList. The lookup must be performed every time @PickList is executed. Although @Pick-List executes faster than @DB formulas, this could slow the application significantly if a large amount of data is returned every time.

The decision on which functionality to utilize within the application will depend on the particular situation.

Chapter 7 Sample Questions

Objective: Create views that use the search builder.

Kaylie is creating a view selection formula. She wants to use the search builder to build her formula, but she's not sure if she can do this. Which of the following options does she have?

A. Kaylie must write the selection formula using @functions

B. Kaylie could use the Search Builder to create a selection formula, but she can't edit the formula once it has been built

C. Kaylie could use the Search Builder, but a selection formula is not created

D. Kaylie could use the Search Builder to create a selection formula and she could edit that formula once it has been created

Answer: D

The Search Builder is a great way to learn about selection formulas. You can use the Search Builder to create the formula, then switch the View Selection option from **Easy** to **Formula** to see the formula Notes created.

Objective: Create views that use selection formulas.

Edwin wants to create a view that only contains documents which have "Approved" in the Status field. How should he build the selection formula?

A. By Field

B. By Form

C. By Form Used

D. A and B

Answer: D

In the Search Builder, the designer could select the **By Field** condition and select the Status field and add **Approved** to the *contains* value. The **By Form** option presents the designer with the form and allows the designer to place **Approved** into the Status field.

Objective: Create views which use form formulas.

Kelly created a document in the Regional Sales database with the New Order form. The default form in the database is Product. The form is stored in the document. The designer also created the following form formula: `@If( Type = "Order"; "New Order"; "Sale")`. The Type field on Kelly's document is Product. What form will be displayed when this document is opened in the database?

        A. New Order

        B. Product

        C. Type

        D. Sale

Answer: A

Notes determines the form to display the document based on whether the form is stored in the document, then on the form formula, which would result in "Sale", then on the form with which the document was created, then the default form. Since the form is stored in the document, that form is used to display the document.

Objective: Create views which use form formulas.

Steve has created a view for ABC Steel Company. The view contains a form formula. The database contains a default form and all of the documents in the view have the form stored in the document. Which of the following will determine which form is used to display the document?

A. The default form will be used

B. The form specified in the form formula will be used

C. The form stored in the document will be used

D. It will depend on the form formula

Answer: C
Notes determines which form to display based on three steps: if the form is stored in the document, that form is used. If a form formula exists for the view, the resulting form is used. Then the form the document was created with is used; if that can't be found, the default form of the database is displayed.

Objective: Create views that use column formulas.

Meredith creates the following column formula:

```
@PickList([Name]:[Single])
```

What value will this column formula return?

A. One name from the Address Book

B. All selected names from the Address Book

C. The Single column in the Name view

D. None of the above

Answer: D
@PickList cannot be used in a column formula. It can only be used in buttons, manual and paste agents, and form and view actions. @PickList cannot be used in column formulas, selection formulas, mail and scheduled agents, hide-when formulas, form formulas, or window titles. If this formula was used in the correct design element, it would display the Address Book dialog box, allowing only one name to be selected.

Objective: Create views that use view icons.

Isaac wants to show the status of a project in the view with a thumbs up or thumbs down icon. How can he accomplish this?

> A. Write a column formula which evaluates to an icon name
>
> B. Write a column formula which evaluates to a number
>
> C. Write a column formula which evaluates to the status field
>
> D. Select **Display value as icon** in the column properties

Answer: B and D
View icons are based on a numeric value between one and 170. The **Display value as icon** option must also be selected.

Objective: Create views that use hidden columns.

Dan organizes the menus for people who work overtime at the accounting firm. He has developed a database where people can select which items to order for dinner based on the day of the week. Currently, Dan's view is sorted and categorized by the day of the week alphabetically (Friday, Monday, Thursday, Tuesday, Wednesday). How can Dan reorganize the view so that the days of the week show up in order?

> A. Add an additional sorted column which is not categorized
>
> B. Write a formula which allows the user to sort the view dynamically
>
> C. Write a formula which assigns a number to each day of the week, and create a sorted hidden column off that value
>
> D. Write a formula which allows the user to specify what the current day of the week is and sort based on that information

Answer: C
If each day of the week is assigned a number in the column formula, the column can then be sorted in ascending order. This is not information the user should see, so a hidden column is created.

Objective: Use @PickList and @Prompt.

Jimmy is designing a database for his tax clients. He wants to allow his users to select their tax forms from a picklist which is based on a view. With which design elements can he not use the @PickList functionality?

        A. Buttons

        B. Mail Agents

        C. Paste Agents

        D. View Actions

Answer: B
@PickList can only be used in buttons, manual and paste agents, and form and view actions. @PickList cannot be used in column formulas, selection formulas, mail and scheduled agents, hide-when formulas, form formulas, or window titles.

Objective: Use @PickList and @Prompt.

Michael designed a button on his form which gives the user a picklist. However, it is not working. Here is the formula Michael is using:

```
@PickList ([YESNOCANCEL]; ""; "NoCache"; @DBName; "All By
Project Title"; "Please select a Project from the following
options"; "Project List"; 1)
```

Which formula will work correctly?

A. @PickList ([YESNOCANCEL]; ""; "All By Project Title"; "Please select a Project from the following options"; "Project List"; 1)

B. @PickList ([Custom]; @DBName; "All By Project Title"; "Project List"; "Please select a Project from the following options"; 1)

C. @PickList ([Custom]; ""; @DBName; "All By Project Title"; "Please select a Project from the following options"; "Project List"; ProjectTitle)

D. @PickList ([YESNOCANCEL];"NoCache"; "" ; "All By Project Title"; "Project List"; "Please select a Project from the following options"; ProjectTitle)

Answer: B

The correct syntax for @PickList is:

```
@PickList([Custom];server : file; view; title; prompt; column )
```

Note that @DBName can be used in the place of the server and filename, and a column number must be specified, or a field name will not work.

Objective: Use @PickList and @Prompt.

Why would a database designer use @PickList rather than @DBLookup or @DBColumn? (Select all that apply:)

A. @PickList allows the designer to specify a Replica ID, rather than the server and file name

B. @PickList avoids the 64K data return limit that @DBLookup and @DBColumn have

C. @DBLookup and @DBColumn don't take advantage of the Quick-Search functionality

D. Unlike @DBLookup and @DBColumn, @PickList does not have to execute the search everytime

Answer: B & C

@PickList does not allow the designer to specify a Replica ID. @PickList does not have a "NoCache" option and therefore must perform the search each time it is executed.

App. Dev. II

Chapter 8

Agents, Actions, & Design Templates

Notes functionality can be automated in several ways. Agents allow Notes tasks to be performed automatically on a manual or scheduled basis. Actions allow users to trigger processes. Design templates allow designers to automate the process of creating new database designs.

The Application Development II exam requires a more detailed understanding of these topics than the Application Development I exam. It is important to understand how these design elements are integrated into Notes applications. This chapter covers each of these topics.

Working with Agents

Agents automate all types of Notes processes, from simple tasks to complex document routing. They work within applications to support, enhance, or replace an existing manual or automated process. Several situations are suited to using Notes agents:

- Repeatable processes or events

- Processes triggered by a repeatable event

- Repeatable actions that are the result of a process

- Scheduled processes or tasks

- Manual processes that are too complex for the average user

To create a new agent, select **Create – Agent** from the Notes menu. The agent design window appears, as shown in Figure 8-1:

Figure 8-1
Agent Design
Window

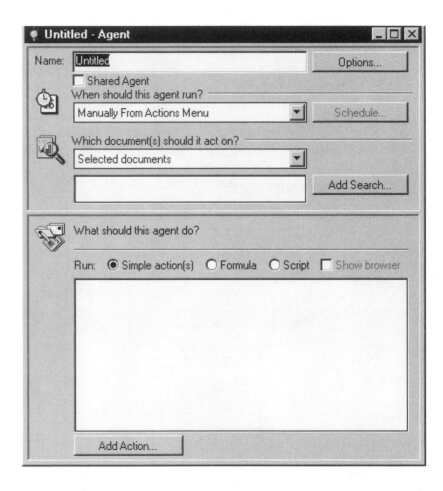

This window sets all design attributes for the agent including the name, schedule, document selection, and formula.

The agent's **name** should be descriptive and understandable. If users are allowed to run the agent manually, the name will be visible to them. The **Options** button provides three additional options for the agent (see Figure 8-2):

Figure 8-2
Agent Options
Window

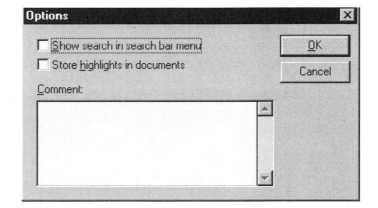

- **Show search in search bar menu:** This option allows users to view the agent's search query when they view the search bar for the database.

- **Store highlights in documents:** This option will display a red highlight around the search words after the agent has run.

- **Comment:** Comments can be added to provide an additional description of the agent. The first few words of the description will be displayed in the Agent List window below the agent's name.

The agent can be *shared* or *private*. If the agent is created as a private agent, it must be re-created in order to be shared with other users. The **Shared Agent** box is grayed out once the agent has been saved as private.

Traps

It is important to remember that once the agent is created as a private agent, it cannot be changed to shared without recreating the agent.

Notes

A shared agent is restricted by the access control rights of the last person who runs it or the last designer who edits the agent (in scheduled agents). For example, if the person running the agent has only author access to the database, only documents that person created will be modified by the agent. The agent cannot modify any other documents, because that person does not have access to those documents.

The agent requires three different types of information: a trigger, the group of documents on which to run, and the process the agent should perform.

Agent Triggers

Agents can be triggered by several different events. The agent designer selects the trigger in the **When should this agent run?** combo box. Different triggers allow the designer to specify which documents the agent affects. Three types of triggers are available: *manual triggers* (where a user activates the agent), *event driven triggers* (such as the receipt of mail, pasted documents, or new/modified documents in the database), and *schedule driven triggers*. The following agent triggers are available:

- **Manually From Actions Menu or Agent List:** If the agent is triggered manually, the designer has several options for determining the set of documents to run on, including:

  - All documents in the database

  - All new and modified documents since the agent was last run

  - All unread documents in the current view

  - Selected documents

- Run once (this option allows @Commands to be used in the agent formula)

The user then selects the agent from either the Actions menu option or the agent list.

Tips

If the agent designer selects **Manually from Agent List,** *the trigger will be displayed as* **Hidden** *in the Agent List window. This is because the agent will not be displayed in the Actions menu to the user. They will have to go to the Agent List window, or the designer can create an action button that calls the agent.*

- **If New Mail Has Arrived:** If an agent runs automatically when new mail arrives in the database, the agent will run on the newly received mail documents. Note that there are several @functions which will be ignored when documents are mailed into the database if they are included in the agent formula: @DBLookup, @DBColumn, @DBCommand, @MailSend, @Prompt, @Command, and @PostedCommand.

- **If Documents Have Been Created or Modified:** If an agent is set to run whenever documents are created or modified in the database, newly created or modified documents included in the search criteria of the agent will be affected.

- **If Documents Have Been Pasted:** This agent will affect any document which has been pasted since the last time the agent ran. Note that @Command and @PostedCommand functions in the agent formula will be ignored if this trigger is selected.

- **On Schedule Hourly, Daily, Weekly, Monthly, or Never:** Scheduled agents affect all documents in the database or all new and modified documents since last time the agent was run, depending on the designer's selection. Note that using a selection formula or search can refine this. Each schedule frequency has parameters which can be set to modify the schedule; these options are set by clicking the **Schedule** button. Each of the parameters are described below:

● **Hourly:** The schedule dialog box for hourly agents is shown in Figure 8-3:

Figure 8-3
Hourly Agent
Options

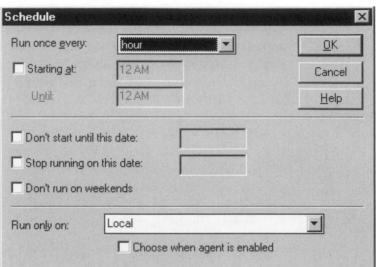

The designer can run an "hourly" agent once every 30 minutes, every hour, every 2 hours, every 4 hours, or every 8 hours. The starting and ending times of the agent can also be specified. By default, the agent runs at the specified interval, 24 hours a day. However, sometimes this is not necessary (if the agent only needs to run during business hours, for example). Specific dates can be selected for running the agent, as well as whether the agent runs on weekends. The server the agent should run on must also be selected.

Traps

By default, the current server is selected whenever the agent is modified. The server must be reselected if the design changes are not made on the same server as the agent.

The server can also be specified when the agent is enabled by selecting the **Choose when agent is enabled** option.

● **Daily:** The schedule dialog box for daily agents is shown in Figure 8-4:

Figure 8-4
Daily Agent
Options

Schedule	☒
Run once every day	

Starting at: `1 AM`

OK

Cancel

Help

☐ Don't start until this date:

☐ Stop running on this date:

☐ Don't run on weekends

Run only on: `Local` ▼

☐ Choose when agent is enabled

The designer can specify what time a daily agent is run. The designer can specify what date the agent starts and stops, as well as whether the agent runs on weekends. The server the agent should run on must also be selected.

Traps

By default, the current server is selected whenever the agent is modified. The server must be reselected if the design changes are not made on the same server as the agent.

The server can also be specified when the agent is enabled by selecting the **Choose when agent is enabled** option.

● **Weekly:** The schedule dialog box for weekly agents is shown in Figure 8-5:

Figure 8-5

Weekly Agent
Options

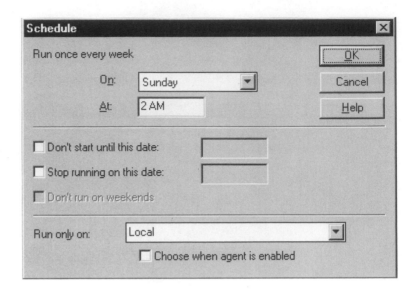

The agent can be run on any day of the week at any time. The beginning and ending dates can also be selected; however, the weekend option is grayed out since the day of the week is selected. The agent's server must also be selected.

Traps

By default, the current server is selected whenever the agent is modified. The server must be reselected if the design changes are not made on the same server as the agent.

The server can also be specified when the agent is enabled by selecting the **Choose when agent is enabled** option.

- **Monthly:** The schedule dialog box for monthly agents is the same as the weekly agent dialog box, except instead of selecting the day of the week, the day of the month is selected (by number).

- **Never:** The designer can also select **Never** as the scheduled frequency. There are no options for this selection. Designers might set this option when another agent will trigger an agent or none of the other triggers will meet the application's needs.

Selecting Documents

The search builder allows the designer to refine the list of documents the agent affects. To use the Search Builder, click on the **Add Search** button to bring up the Search Builder dialog box, shown in Figure 8-6:

Figure 8-6
Search Builder
Dialog Box

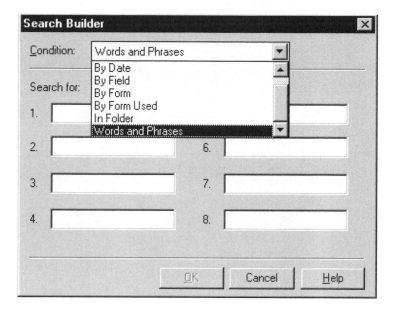

A list of options is provided from which the user can build the search. These options include:

- By Author

- By Date

- By Field

- By Form

- By Form Used

- In Folder

- Words and Phrases (default)

Each of these options require that additional conditions be provided. Click **OK** to exit the Search Builder dialog box. A formula must now be created to determine what action should be taken on the documents.

Agent Formulas

The agent design pane allows the designer to use simple actions, @formulas, or LotusScript to write the agent. Simple actions can be used to perform many of the common functions of agents, such as:

- Managing documents in databases and folders

- Managing read and unread marks

- Modifying fields

- Sending messages

- Sending newsletters

- Running other agents

- Archiving documents

Examples of these simple actions can be found in the "Using Actions/Agents in Applications" section of this chapter.

When an @formula is written to determine the functionality of the agent, the @function is considered a selection formula. The agent will run on the documents specified in the search builder and the documents selected within the @formula. The **SELECT** keyword should be used before the formula to define the set of documents. If a **SELECT** statement is not included in the @formula by the designer, Notes will automatically append **SELECT @All** to the formula.

When an @formula is used to build the agent's formula, Notes runs the entire formula on each document which meets the selection criteria before moving on to the next document. The designer must specify what the agent should do when it locates each document. Three options are available:

- Modify the document

- Create a new document

- Select the document

By default, the document is modified by the formula and saved with the new changes. However, there are some circumstances where the original copy of the document should be preserved and the changes made to a new copy. This instance would require that a new document be created. The designer might also want to use the formula to only select the documents which meet the selection criteria, but not make any changes. This is useful for testing the selection criteria before modifying the documents.

LotusScript can also be used for the agent's formula. LotusScript is not covered in the Application Development II exam.

Troubleshooting Agents

It is useful to be able to test and troubleshoot the agent before using it. Notes provides a set of tools to perform these operations. Agents can be tested in two ways: the agent can be run in test mode (which does not actually affect the documents), or a copy of the database can be created and the agent run on the test data.

Running an Agent in Test Mode

A test can be run on the agent in the database without affecting the documents. In the database, select **View – Agents** from the Notes menu. Select the agent and run **Actions – Test** from the menu. This will create a log which describes how many documents the agent would have been run on. This log can be reviewed and the agent modified, if necessary.

Copy the Database

To actually see the results of the agent on the data without affecting the production data, a copy of the database can be made. This copy should include a sample of the data in the actual database. Run the agent and review the documents to verify that the expected results occurred. The agent log can be reviewed to verify that the agent ran on the expected number of documents.

The Agent Log

The **Agent Log** is the primary tool available for troubleshooting agents. The log reports three key characteristics of the agent:

● Time the agent was last run

● The number of documents the agent ran against

● The action performed on the documents

Each agent creates a separate log, but the log only contains information about the most recent occurrence of the agent. The agent log writes over itself each time the agent is run.

To view an agent's log, select **View – Agents** from the Notes menu in the database. Highlight the agent from the list and select **Agent – Log** from the menu. Review the information and click **OK** to close the log. To modify the agent after reviewing the log or running a test, select the agent from the Agent List window and double-click on the agent to open and modify it. Figure 8-7 illustrates an agent log.

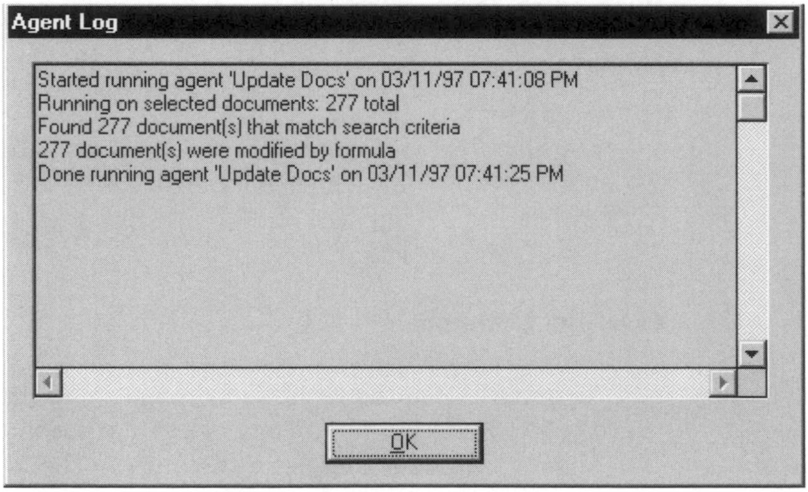

Figure 8-7
Agent Log
Dialog Box

```
Agent Log                                                    [X]

Started running agent 'Update Docs' on 03/11/97 07:41:08 PM
Running on selected documents: 277 total
Found 277 document(s) that match search criteria
277 document(s) were modified by formula
Done running agent 'Update Docs' on 03/11/97 07:41:25 PM



                        [    OK    ]
```

If an agent is not running as expected, there may be a problem with the agent's access on the server. The agent inherits the access level of the person running the agent (for manual agents) or the last person who updated the agent (for scheduled agents). For example, a person with Author access to the database can create a private agent which modifies documents in the database. However, regardless of the selection formula in the agent, only the documents which that person has access to will be modified.

The Notes Administrator can also control who can run agents on the server. In the Public Name and Address Book, the Server document contains a section for the Agent Manager. The *Agent Manager* is a server task that handles running the agents on the server. The Notes administrator has the ability to change fields within the Agent Manager section of the Server document. The administrator can specify three items:

- Who can run agents on the server

- The time interval in which agents can be run on the server

- How many agents can run on the server at one time

The server document and these items are important to check when agents are not running as expected.

Actions

Actions are useful for automating simple tasks within Lotus Notes. They are triggered by action buttons, hotspots, or from the **Action** menu. Unlike agents, actions cannot be scheduled. They are run manually by the user by one of the triggers. Actions can run agents that exist in the database by selecting the simple action **Run Agent** and naming the agent.

Action Buttons

Actions buttons can be associated with forms or views. They are available via the **Actions** menu item or on the **Action Bar** of the form or view. Notes provides a set of default actions on all forms and views. These actions include common form and view functionality. Use them to:

- Categorize the document

- Edit the document

- Send the document

- Move the document to a folder

- Forward the document

- Remove the document from a folder

The designer can also create new actions by selecting **Create – Action** on the menu. Action buttons can use simple actions, formulas, or script.

Action buttons have their own set of properties which can be set by the designer (See Figure 8-8):

Figure 8-8
Action Properties
InfoBox

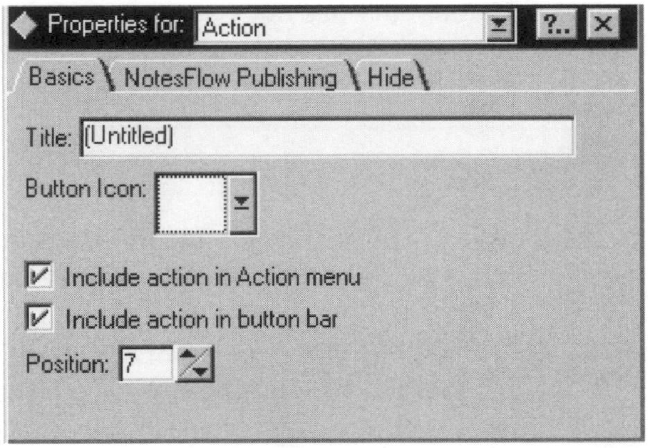

The title contains the text that will appear in the menu and on the button in the button bar. The button icon can be selected from the drop-down list; this provides a distinguishing graphic on the button. The designer has the option of displaying the action in the **Actions** menu or in the button bar. The position determines where the action is displayed in relation to other actions.

The action properties infobox also allows actions to be hidden, based on document events or hide-when formulas.

Actions can run simple actions, @formulas, or LotusScript. The Application Development II exam focuses on agents which run simple actions. Examples of the functionality most frequently described on the exam are located in the section "Using Agents/Actions in Applications," later in this chapter.

Hotspots

Hotspots come in different types, providing the designer with myriad options. Hotspots can link to another document, display text in a pop-up box, run a formula, or perform an action. Hotspots are added to the form by selecting **Create – Hotspot – *Hotspot Type***. Hotspots can be created on forms or in rich text fields on documents. The different types of hotspots are listed below:

- **Link Hotspot:** These are used to link a document, view, folder, or database. The user clicks on the text or graphic hotspot, and Notes switches them to the linked item. This functionality is similar to using a doclink, but instead of clicking on the Notes doclink icon the user clicks on the text or graphic hotspot.

- **Text Pop-Up:** When the user clicks on a text pop-up hotspot, text is displayed while the mouse is held down. This is not useful for large amounts of text, since the user cannot scroll through the information. The text is entered in the hotspot properties infobox. The normal text formatting options are available, including font, spacing, hiding, and style.

- **Button:** Buttons automate Notes actions. They are similar to buttons on the action bar, but they can be placed anywhere on the form (or in a rich text field of a document). Buttons can be programmed to run simple actions, formulas, or script. When the user clicks the button, the action, formula, or script runs.

- **Formula Pop-Up:** A formula pop-up works exactly like a text pop-up, except instead of the designer typing the text into the hotspot properties infobox, the design pane appears and the designer can add an action, formula, or script that evaluates to text.

- **Action Hotspot:** When the user clicks on an action hotspot, a Notes action is performed. The action can run a simple action, formula, or script.

Using Actions/Agents in Applications

Although it would be impossible for us to provide examples of all of the scenarios where actions and agents are utilized in applications, there are two key instances focused on in the exam: using actions to call agents, and creating a newsletter. The creators of the exam focus on using simple actions to perform these tasks, and they will be explained here. However, note that there are certainly other ways to design these tasks.

Writing an Action to Run an Agent

An agent can be run via an action from a form or view. The agent must exist in the database and the users must have access to the agent. To create the action:

1. Create the agent in the database and verify that users have access to run the agent.

2. Open the form or view from which you want to run the agent.

3. Create an action.

4. In the design pane of the action, select **Simple Action** and click on the **Add Action...** button.

5. Select **Run Agent** and enter the name of the agent you want to run from the action.

6. Save the action.

When the user clicks on the action button or selects the action from the **Action** menu, the agent will run. An agent log is created, even though the agent is run from the action.

For more complex processes, agents can be run from other agents. This allows the designer to mix the programming format. For example, one agent can use @formulas to perform certain actions, then it can call the @Command([ToolsRunMacro]; *"agent name"*) (or use the Run Agent simple action) to run another agent which uses LotusScript to modify the documents.

Create an Agent to Send a Newsletter

The Send Newsletter Summary simple action is new to version 4 of Lotus Notes. In some shape or form it will show up in your exam. A newsletter document can be mailed out to specified users which includes doclinks to documents selected by the agent. Summary information about the linked document can also be included in the document based on a view. To create an agent to send a newsletter:

1. Open the database which will contain the agent.

2. Select **Create – Agent...** from the Notes menu. (You must have appropriate access to the database in order to create an agent.)

3. Provide a name for the agent. If other users will be running the agent, select the **Shared** option. (Only users with Designer access or above can create shared agents.)

4. Select the trigger for the agent from the **When should the agent run?** list box.

5. Select the documents to be included in the newsletter from the **Which document(s) should the agent run on?** list box.

6. In the design pane, the Simple Actions option is selected by default. Click on the **Add Action...** button and select **Send Newsletter Summary** from the action options. The Edit Action dialog box will be presented, as shown in Figure 8-9:

Figure 8-9
Send Newsletter
Summary Dialog Box

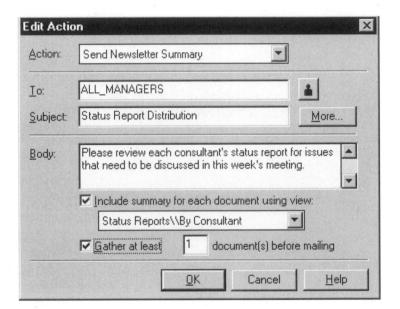

7. Complete the **To, Subject,** and **Body** fields. Click on the **More...** button to create formulas for any of the mail sending fields or the subject. To include a summary of the documents included in the newsletter, select the **Include summary for each document using view:** option and select the view.

8. To prevent the message from being sent when there are not more than a minimum number of documents, select the **Gather at least:** option and provide the minimum number of documents.

9. Save and close the agent. This agent can be run automatically on a scheduled basis, manually by the user via an action button, or from another agent.

These examples provide some insight to the types of information which will help you answer questions related to agents. For the Application Development II exam it is important to know the functionality available via agents and actions as we have described them here.

Using Design Templates

Agents and actions are not the only way to automate tasks within Lotus Notes; database design management can also be automated by using design templates. Templates allow designers to centralize the administration of database design changes.

A design template provides a source for design elements. Notes template files (files with a .NTF file extension) or Notes databases (.NSF files) can be used as design templates for other databases. When the designer makes a change to the template, these changes can be inherited by other databases. The server **DESIGN** task automatically updates databases from their corresponding template. The Notes administrator has the option of running the server **DESIGN** task on all servers, or running the task on one server and replicating the design changes.

To define a design template:

1. The database should have a .NTF file extension and be located in the default data directory.

2. Highlight the database icon on the Notes Workspace.

3. Select **Edit – Properties** from the Notes menu. The database properties infobox will appear.

4. On the **Design** tab, select the **Database is a template** option
   and provide a name for the template, as shown in Figure 8-10:

Figure 8-10
Specify Database
as a Template

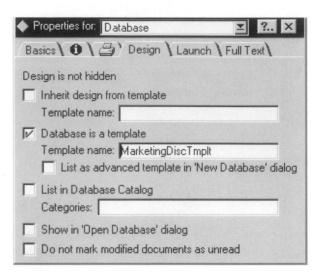

A database can inherit the entire design from a design template,
or only inherit individual elements. To inherit all design elements
from a template, select the **Inherit design from template** option
on the database properties **Design** tab. Indicate the name of the
template, as shown in Figure 8-11:

Figure 8-11
Specify Design
Template

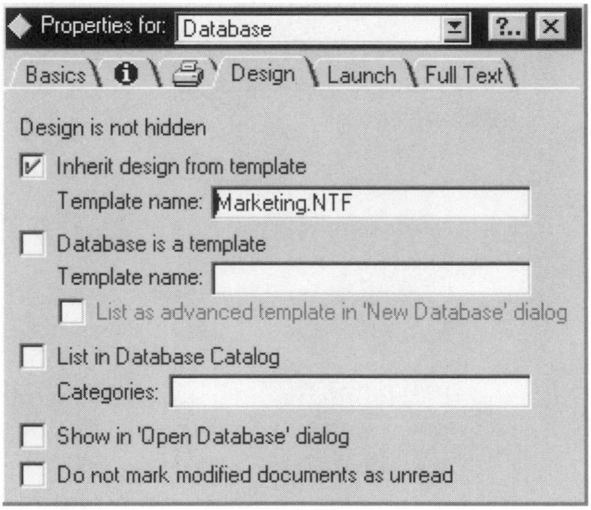

Specific design elements can also be inherited from a central design template, including shared fields, forms, subforms, agents, views, folders, and navigators. To specify a design template to inherit the design element from, follow these steps:

1. In the Folders pane of the database, select **Design – *Design Element***. Any of the design elements listed (except **Other**) can inherit their design from a template.

2. Select the specific design element and open its properties by selecting **Edit – Properties** from the Notes menu. The **Design Document** properties infobox appears.

3. Select the **Design** tab and provide the name of the design template to inherit from, as shown in Figure 8-12:

Figure 8-12
Design Document
Properties InfoBox

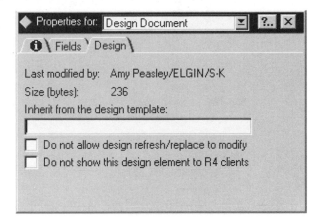

Updating the Design

If a database is based on a template, the design can be updated in two ways: refreshed or replaced.

Refreshing the Design

When the database's design is refreshed, any design changes made to the design template are inherited by the database. Any elements that are marked **Do not allow replace/refresh to update** in the Design Document properties (shown in Figure 8-8) will not be updated. This is an incremental update of the design of the database.

Design changes can be automatically distributed on a nightly basis via the **Design** server task, or manually by selecting **File – Database – Refresh Design**. **Inherit future design changes** must be selected in the document properties in order to update the design via the server task.

Replacing the Design

Replacing a database's design will indiscriminately replace all design elements of the database with those of the template. The template will overwrite any modifications made to the database. The design can be replaced by selecting **File – Database – Replace Design** from the Notes menu.

Notes

Replacing the design of the database does not overwrite certain design elements. The following items must be individually copied into the database:

- Any element marked **Do not allow replace/refresh to update** in the Design Document properties infobox (shown in Figure 8-8)

- The elements listed in the **Other** category: the **database icon**, the **About document**, and the **Using document**.

- Private agents

Chapter 8 Sample Questions

Objective: Write agents that run automatically/on schedule.

Steve wants to update documents automatically every 30 minutes. What should he do to accomplish this?

A. Create an action which runs every half hour

B. Create an agent which runs "On Schedule Hourly"

C. There is no way to update documents on a half-hour scheduled interval

Answer: B

Selecting the options button when **On Schedule Hourly** is selected as the trigger allows the designer to select 30 minutes as the interval. Actions cannot be scheduled.

Objective: Write agents that run automatically/on schedule.

Birke has created an action button that will run his agent to update documents. He does not want to display the agent in the action list. What is the best way to "hide" the agent from the users?

A. The **Manually from Agent List** option

B. Select **Hide Agent** in the Options dialog box

C. Use the **On Schedule Never** option

D. Use any **On Schedule** option and disable the agent

Answer: A

The **Manually from Agent List** option is the best selection here. The agent is still triggered manually, but the trigger is hidden. It will not be displayed in the Actions menu. There is no such option as **Hide Agent** in the Options dialog box. Answers C & D are feasible, but they are not a good solution to the problem.

App. Dev. II

Objective: Create forms which use automatic/scheduled actions.

Phil wants to automatically copy a document to an archive database when its status is completed. How can he perform this action without any user intervention?

A. Create an agent triggered when documents are modified which runs the **Copy to Database** simple action

B. Create a scheduled action which runs the **Archive** simple action

C. Create an agent which is triggered by the **Modify Field** action

D. Create an agent triggered when documents are modified which runs the **Archive** simple action

Answer: A

The agent should run only when documents are modified, rather than on a scheduled basis, in order to have the fastest response time. There is no such simple action called **Archive**. The document must use the **Copy to Database** action, an @formula, or LotusScript to move to another database.

Objective: Write agents that run automatically/on schedule.

Debbie has written an agent formula using @functions. She did not specify a search criteria using the Search Builder or within her formula. What will happen when she tries to save the agent?

A. An error will appear warning her that she must specify a selection formula

B. The agent will run on all documents in the database

C. The agent will not run on any documents in the database

D. SELECT @ALL will be appended to the formula

Answer: D

Notes automatically appends the SELECT @ALL statement to the formula if the designer uses @ functions and fails to specify a selection formula.

Objective: Create views which use automatic/scheduled actions.

Sumeet created an agent which automatically marks documents in his database unread if the user has not taken an action on them. What type of action did he use in his agent?

A. Mark Selected Documents Unread

B. Refresh Unread Marks

C. Mark Document Unread

D. Update Unread Marks

Answer: C

You should be familiar enough will the simple actions that you can identify valid options. The test creators like to throw out fake simple actions to confuse you. **Mark Document Unread** is the only valid action.

Objective: Write applications which use automatic/scheduled agents.

Leah wants to notify her department when certain documents have been posted in a database. She wants to automatically send a message which includes doclinks to the documents. Which action should Leah use?

A. Send a mail message action

B. Send a document summary action

C. Send a newsletter summary action

D. Publish a document action

Answer: C
The **Send a newsletter** action will be covered on the exam. You should have a basic understanding of how this and other actions function within an application. The other options are valid actions, but they do not meet the user's needs as described in the question.

Objective: Write agents that run manually.

Hilda's users are not very familiar with the Notes menu system. She wants to make it very easy for users to update a field on all of the documents in the database. What type of design element should she create?

> A. An action button which uses the **Run an Agent** simple action
>
> B. An agent object which automatically runs the agent when the user opens the document
>
> C. An action button which uses the **Modify a Field** simple action
>
> D. A or C

Answer: A
Actions can run agents. This is very useful when an action should affect multiple documents within the database. An action button that only runs a simple action will only affect one document in the database. Thus, C cannot be used, because the question requests that all documents in the database be changed.

Objective: Troubleshoot agents.

Lindsey created an agent which automatically sends a newsletter to users to run daily at 2 AM. None of the users are receiving the newsletter. Where can she look to see which documents the agent ran on at 2 AM?

A. Server Log

B. Database Log

C. Agent Log

D. Document Log

Answer: C

The Agent Log provides the time the agent was last run, the number of documents it ran against, and the action performed on the documents.

Objective: Troubleshoot agents.

Adam is manually running an agent which modifies all documents in the database. However, only certain documents are reflecting the change. When Megan runs the agent, different documents are getting modified. When Vicky runs the agent, all documents are modified. What could the problem be?

A. There is an error in the agent's formula

B. Adam and Megan do not have access to run agents on the server

C. Adam and Megan only have Author access to the database

D. Vicky is a designer of the database, so she is the only one who can run agents on it

Answer: C

Manual agents only have the same level of access as the person running them. The agent is running correctly for Adam and Megan on certain documents. Thus, there is probably not an error in the formula and they must have access to run the agent because it is running, just not correctly. Adam and Megan only have Author access to the database. The agent can only modify documents that Adam is the author of when Adam runs the agent. The agent can only modify documents that Megan is the author of when Megan runs the agent. Vicky must have at least Editor access to be able to modify all documents in the database, but she does not necessarily have designer access.

Objective: Troubleshoot agents.

Jamie is working on a server running a mission-critical application. He is concerned that a bug in an agent could bring down the server, so he would like to add some security at the server level regarding agents. What should Jamie ask the System Administrator to do?

A. Open the Server document and modify who can run agents on the server, what agents can run on the server, and how long an agent can run on the server

B. Open the Server document and modify who can run agents on the server, the time interval in which agents can be run on the server, and how many agents can run on the server at one time

C. Open the Agent Manager and modify who can run agents on the server, what agents can run on the server, and how long an agent can run on the server

D. Open the Agent Manager and modify the level of access required to run an agent on the server, the time interval in which agents can be run on the server, and how many agents can be run on the server at one time

Answer: B
The Agent Manager section of the Server document should be modified. (There is no such thing as an "Agent Manager" document.) The administrator can specify who can run agents on the server, the time interval in which agents can be run on the server, and how many agents can run on the server at one time.

Objective: Write applications that use manual agents.

Larry wants to run an agent on specific documents in the database. He wants to select documents which were created with the New Product form and contain Completed in the Status field. Which of the following options will select the correct documents? Select all that apply.

A. The **By Field** and **By Form** options in the agent's Search Builder

B. SELECT Status = Completed & Form = New Product

C. The **By Field** option in the agent's Search Builder and the SELECT Form = NewProduct selection formula

Answer: B & C

The documents can be selected by using the Search Builder, a selection formula, or a combination of the two. Answer A is incorrect because the **By Form Used** option would need to be selected rather than the **By Form** option to determine what form was used to create the document.

Objective: Write applications which use manual hotspots.

Charles wants to add some online help to his database. He has created several documents to guide users through some of the more complex functionality. He has a question mark graphic that he is adding to the areas where he thinks the users will become confused. How can he use this graphic to send the user to the specified Help document?

A. Make the graphic into an action button which launches the appropriate Help documents

B. Create a link hotspot which links to the appropriate Help document

C. Create a button which runs @Command([OpenHelp])

D. Create a text pop-up which shows the content of the help document

Answer: B

A link hotspot would work best in this situation. Link hotspots are easy to program and will automatically open the linked document without any additional programming. The other options would either not allow Charles to use his graphic, or would not actually take him to the help document.

Objective: Use design templates.

Which of the following design elements will be updated when the database's design is refreshed? Select all that apply.

        A. About and Using Documents

        B. Access Control List

        C. Shared Folders

        D. Private Views

Answer: C
Only the Folders will be updated. Refreshing/replacing the design does not update Help documents, the database icon, the ACL, private views or private folders, or full-text index settings. Note that although updating the design does not modify these design elements, it does not eliminate them either. Thus, users' private views and folders will not be deleted when then design is refreshed or replaced.

Objective: Use design templates.

Jacques updates the design of his database on a nightly basis automatically via the DESIGN task on the server. What is happening?

        A. The design of the database is being replaced with the design
           of the template

        B. The design of the database is being refreshed with the design
           of the template

        C. The design of the database is being replicated to the design
           of the database

        D. The design of the template is being replicated to the design
           of the design

Answer: B

When the DESIGN task is used to update the database from the template, the design is being refreshed. Only new changes since the last refresh are updated. Replacing the design overwrites the entire design of the database.

Objective: Use design templates to create applications.

Bogie wants to create several databases based on one design. He wants each of the databases to inherit specific design elements from the template without overwriting the design changes made to other elements that are specific to each database. How can Bogie accomplish this?

    A. Select the **Inherit Design from template** option in the database properties.

    B. In each design element which should be inherited, open the Design Document properties and provide the template name on the **Design** tab.

    C. When the database is created, select the template to inherit from and select **Inherit future design changes**.

    D. Select **File – Database – Refresh Design** to inherit design elements only.

Answer: B

The design elements must be specified individually. Otherwise, the entire database's design will be updated based on the template; this will overwrite elements which should *not* be based on the template.

Chapter 9

Securing Notes Applications

For the Application Development II exam, it is important to understand the design elements used to secure a Notes application. There are several layers of security available in Notes. The following list demonstrates the hierarchy of security from highest to lowest:

- Authentication

- Notes Server Access

- Notes Database Access

- Form & View Access

- Document Access (Reader and Author Fields)

- Field Access (Encryption Keys)

The user must have access to the first levels of security before accessing additional layers. Authentication is the first level of security when accessing a Notes server. If the Notes user ID and Server ID do not share a certificate in common (or a cross-certificate), then access is denied. Once successful authentication is accomplished, the next layer of security is access to the Notes server, which is assigned within the Notes Server document in the Public Name and Address book. The user must have access to the server in order to access a Notes database residing on a particular Notes server. Once access is granted to a Notes server, a user may begin accessing Notes applications stored on the server. Access to a database is controlled by the Access Control List for each individual database. Once a user has access to the database, form and view access lists control which forms and views a user can access. Reader and Author fields then control who can access a particular document within the database. Finally, field level encryption allows security to be placed on particular fields within documents. Other security features such as electronic signatures are also available within documents, and prevent a document from being printed, forwarded, or copied. User roles can also be used to refine a group of users' access within an application.

The Application Development II exam requires that the candidate understand security starting at the database level. You are not required to understand server access. This chapter covers the use of these security features within a Notes application. For more information about Notes security for System Administration, see Chapter 14—*Notes Infrastructure Security*.

Access Control Lists

The highest level of security covered in the Application Development II exam is the Access Control List (ACL), which allows users to access the database. The ACL determines the following three things:

- **Who can access the database:** If users, servers, and groups are not included in the ACL of the database, their access will be based on the level of access given to the **-Default-** group.

- **What functions each person or group can perform**: Each user or group is given a level of access allowing them to perform certain functions within the database, such as reading, authoring, editing, designing, or managing. These access levels are described in detail in the next section.

- **Each person's roles:** Roles can be set up which include certain individuals and groups listed in the ACL. Roles are used to refine access levels within the database. Roles are covered in more detail in the "Using Roles" section.

To view the ACL for the database, select **File – Database – Access Control** from the menu. The Access Control List dialog box appears as shown in Figure 9-1.

App. Dev. II

Figure 9-1
Database ACL
Dialog Box

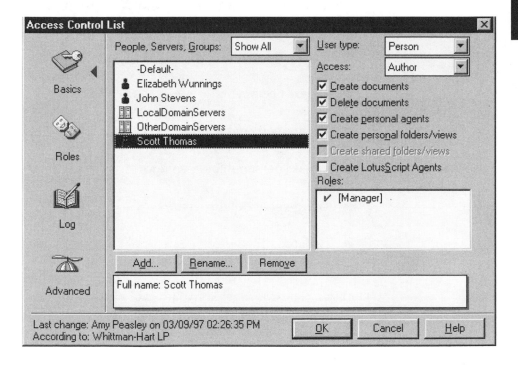

The ACL dialog box Basics pane allows the manager of the database to add, rename or remove people or groups from the Access Control List. The **-Default-** group controls access for all users.

Designer access is automatically given to the Default group on creation of the database. Set the Default access level to **No Access** to restrict who can open the database. The Default group cannot be removed or renamed.

To add a user or group to the ACL of the database, click the **Add...** button. A prompt will appear, allowing the manager to type a name or select from the Name and Address Book. A user with Manager access may also manually type in a group or user name.

Access Levels

The manager of a Notes application can select from seven different levels of access to grant to users and/or groups. Each level contains options, which can be selected or deselected based on the level:

- Create documents

- Delete documents

- Create personal agents

- Create personal folders/views

- Create shared folder/views

- Create LotusScript agents

Depending on the access level, only certain choices can be changed. These are listed in the level descriptions below:

- **Manager:** Users with Manager access can do things allowed by no other access level, such as modify ACL settings, modify replication settings, encrypt a database for local security, and delete the database. Managers can also perform all tasks allowed by other access levels. Only the **Delete documents** option can be changed. All other options are selected and cannot be deselected as shown in Figure 9-2.

Figure 9-2
Manager Options

- **Designer:** Users with Designer access can modify all design elements, including fields, forms, views, agents, the database icon, and About and Using documents. Designers can create full text indexes and perform all tasks allowed by lower access levels. All options are predetermined, except for **Delete documents** and **Create LotusScript agents.** See Figure 9-3.

Figure 9-3
Designer Options

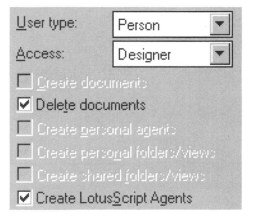

- **Editor:** Users with Editor access (Figure 9-4) can create documents and edit all documents in the database. Editors can create documents by default, but every other option can be modified, including **Create shared folders/views**.

Figure 9-4
Editor Options

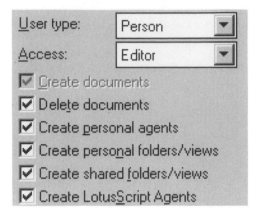

- **Author:** Users with Author access can create documents and edit only documents they create. Authors can also edit documents created by others if listed in an Authors data type field on the document. Give users Author access rather than Editor access to reduce Replication and Save Conflicts. As shown in Figure 9-5 below, author access can be modified for any of the options other than **Create shared folders/views**.

Figure 9-5
Author Options

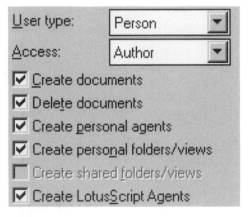

- **Reader:** Users with Reader access can read existing documents in a database, but cannot create or edit documents. Readers do not have the **Create, Delete,** or **Create shared folders/views** options, as shown in Figure 9-6:

Figure 9-6
Reader Options

● **Depositor:** Users with Depositor access can create documents, but cannot read any documents in the database, even documents they create (Figure 9-7). This type of access is useful for mail-in databases such as surveys. Depositors only have the **Create documents** option selected, and no other options can be modified.

Figure 9-7
Depositor Options

● **No Access:** Users with No Access cannot access the database. They cannot even add the icon for the database to their workspace. No options can be selected for users without access to a database.

Using Roles

Roles allow the application designer to group together users who should have access to specific design elements within the database. Roles are specified at the database level in the Access Control List. These roles can then be used in place of individual names in design elements such as form and view access lists, authors and readers fields, and sections. This eases the burden of maintaining lists of individual names. Other advantages to using roles in an application include:

- Roles allow application designers to centralize security. Access to a design element can be changed by including or excluding an individual from the role at the ACL level, rather than modifying the list of users in every field and access list. This also avoids the need to update all of the documents every time a security change is made.

- Roles provide group control to managers who might not have access rights to create a group in the Public Name and Address book.

- Since roles are listed in the ACL dialog box, a manager is more likely to remember to include a user in the correct roles when modifying the ACL. If the manager was required to review all design elements, this would be much more difficult to maintain.

- Roles are easily included in formulas. They are represented as text strings in brackets ("[Product_Managers]").

Roles are created in the Access Control List dialog box. Select **File – Database – Access Control...** to view this, as shown in Figure 9-8.

Figure 9-8

Access Control
List Dialog Box

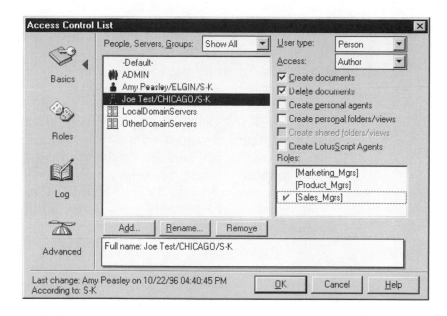

The roles are listed in the **Roles:** box on the lower right-hand corner of the dialog box. The checkmark indicates that the selected user or group is included in that role. Only users, servers, or groups listed in the ACL of the database can be included in a role.

To add, rename, or remove a role, select the **Roles** box on the left side. Figure 9-9 illustrates the dialog box used to modify roles:

Figure 9-9

Modifying Roles

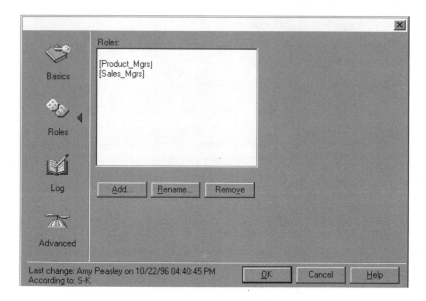

This dialog box allows the database manager to add, rename, or remove a role. Up to 75 roles can be included in a database. The role name can be up to 15 characters in length.

To control access to a design element, use the @UserRoles function. This function requires no paraments and returns a list of the roles the user is included in. @UserRoles can be used within other formulas to take action based on a user's level of access. For example, the formula **@IsMember("[Product_Mgrs]";@UserRoles)** could be used in a hide-when formula for a button. This would hide the button if the Product_Mgrs role was not included in the list of the user's roles.

Notes

@UserRoles does have some caveats. It cannot be used in column, selection, mail agent, or scheduled agent formulas. Also, the Enforce Access Control List on all replicas option must be selected on the Advanced tab of the ACL dialog box in order to use @UserRoles on a local database. If this option is not selected, the function returns an empty list.

Form and View Access Lists

Access can also be controlled at the form and view level by access lists set in the properties of each form and view. The names are selected out of those listed in the ACL of the database.

View Access List

The view access list is set on the Security tab of the View Properties infobox. To open the infobox, open the view in design mode. Select **Design – View Properties** to open the properties infobox. Click on the Security tab (the key icon) as shown in Figure 9-10.

Figure 9-10

View Security Tab

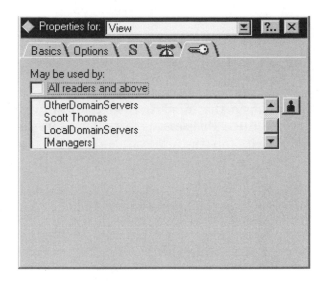

By default, the **All readers and above** option is selected. This allows any user with Reader or above access in the ACL of the database to see the view. To only allow specific users, groups, servers, or roles access to the view, deselect **All readers and above** and select the desired names from the list. Click the name again to remove it from the list. The blue Person button on the right hand side of the list allows users to be added to the list from the Public Name and Address Book. However, a user must have access to the database through the ACL to get to the view, even if that person's name is listed in the view access list.

Notes

View access lists should not be used as the only means of security. Users can still create private views to display and edit the data.

Notes

The LocalDomainServers group or equivalent should be included in the selected list if a view access list is utilized. Otherwise, the view may not replicate correctly.

Form Access Lists

Form access lists are very similar to view access lists. Form access lists are set on the Security tab of the form properties infobox. To open the infobox, open the form in design mode. Select **Design – Form Properties** to open the properties infobox. Click on the Security tab (the key icon), as shown in Figure 9-11.

Figure 9-11
Form Security Tab

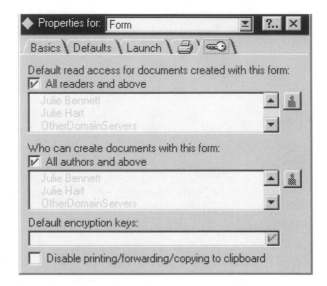

On the form properties Security tab, you can see that there are two types of access control lists: *read access* and *create access*.

● **Default read access for documents created with this form:** This access list allows the selected users to read documents created with this form. By default, this is set to **All readers and above**, allowing anyone to view the documents.

When the **All readers and above** option is deselected, a $Readers reserved field is automatically created on the form. When determining whether a user has access to the document, Notes will search all fields of Readers data type and the $Readers field if it exists. Thus, if a $Readers field exists, and a user is included in either type of access list, they will be able to read the document. The user does not have to be listed in both places. If the **All readers and above** option is selected (thus no $Readers field exists), only the names listed in the Readers data type field will have access to the document.

- **Who can create documents with this form:** This access list determines who can create and edit documents with this form. This is set to **All authors and above** by default. The form access list cannot override the database ACL. Users must have at least Author access to create a document, even if they are listed in the form create access list. Only users within this list will see the form in the Create menu option.

Notes

Users with Editor access or above who are listed in the read access list can still edit documents even if they are not listed in the form create access list. However, if the user is not listed in the read access list, the person cannot read the document, regardless of their access level in the Access Control List.

Select the names, groups, servers, or roles from the access lists based on the ACL of the database to allow the user to read or create documents with this form. Click on the name again to deselect it.

Notes

If users can read documents, but not create documents with the form, they can still edit the document if they have Author or above access in the ACL.

Readers and Authors Fields

Readers and Authors fields control access at a document level. These are editable or computed fields which result in a list of names. Only the names listed in these fields will have access to the information in the document. Readers and Authors fields allow designers to refine the ACL of the database, but not override it. The Application Development II exam requires a detailed understanding of Readers and Authors fields.

Readers Fields

A Readers field in a document determines who can read it. A Readers field is a text list of names of users, servers, groups, or roles in a field of Readers data type. Use a Readers field to allow access on a document-by-document basis. If an individual is not listed in the Readers list, they cannot even see the document in the view. However, if the view is categorized on more than one column, they can see the information in the categorized columns.

It is important to understand how Readers fields work with the other forms of access within the database. If a user has at least Reader access to the database, the following points hold true:

● If a document contains a Readers field and the user is included in the list, the user can read the document.

● If a document contains a Readers field, but the user is not included in the list, the user will not be able to read the document, regardless of the user's level of access in the ACL.

● If a document contains multiple Readers fields, and the user is included in *any* of the lists, the user can read the document.

● If a read access list is used in the form (the **All readers and above** option is deselected in the form or document properties), and a Readers field is included in the document, and the user is included in *either* list, the user can read the document.

● If a Readers field is added to the document but left blank, no restrictions are placed on the document. It is as though no Readers field existed on the document. However, as soon as a name is included in the field, only that person will be able to access the document.

● In order to replicate a document containing a Readers (or $Readers) field, the server must be included in the list. Thus, the server group LocalDomainServers (or a similar group) should always be included in the Readers list of a replicated document. If the server is not included in the list, the server cannot "see" the document and it will not be replicated to other servers.

- If a Readers field and Authors field are both included in the document, and a name appears in the Authors list but not in the Readers list, the user still has reader access to the document. The fact that a user can edit the document automatically allows them to read the document. Authors fields automatically give reader access to the users included in the list.

To create a Readers field to control access on a document-by-document basis, open the form in design mode and add a field. Select **Readers** as the data type. The list of readers can be created in several ways:

- Manually entering names, groups, servers, or roles into the formula for the field.

- Using a formula to compute the list of names. Note that the formula must evaluate to a valid list of names or the data will be inaccessible.

- The user (usually the document author) can populate names.

If the user selects the names, the following options are available for populating the list:

- **None:** This is the only option in two instances: if the field is computed, or if the field is located within a layout region. If the field is computed, the designer is relying on a formula to populate the list of names. In a layout region, none of the other options are available.

- **Use Address dialog for choices:** This option allows the names to be selected from the Personal or Public Name and Address Book dialog prompt.

- **Use view dialog for choices:** The user is prompted with a view from which to select documents. This is the same functionality available within keywords.

Select the **Allow multi-values** option in the Field properties to include more than one name in the list of readers.

Notes

To use Readers fields on a local copy of a database, the Enforce a consistent access control list across all replicas *option should be selected on the Advanced tab of the ACL. Remember that if this option is selected, all replicating servers must have manager access to the database or replication will not occur.*

Authors Fields

Authors fields allow users to edit documents they didn't create, without giving them Editor access. This is especially useful in workflow-type applications where editing capability needs to shift from person to person as the document moves through the workflow.

An Authors field is a text list of names of users, servers, groups, or roles in a field of Authors data type. Use an Authors field to allow editing access on a document-by-document basis.

It is important to understand how Authors fields interact with other access control features within the database. The following points are important to understand when using Authors fields:

- Regardless of whether an Authors field exists on a document, users with Editor or above access in the ACL can edit the document and users with Reader access or below cannot edit the document. The ACL overrides the Authors list for all access levels other than Author.

- The Authors field contains a list of *potential* editors for the document. The internal $UpdatedBy field stores the list of users who have actually modified the document. When a user clicks on an Authors field, the contents of the $UpdatedBy field are displayed, not the list of names in the Authors field. This is an important distinction for the Application Development II exam.

- A document can contain multiple Authors fields, but the user need only be listed in one of the fields to edit the entire document.

- If an Authors field is added to the document but left blank (or the field is editable and all the names are removed), then only a user with Editor or above access in the ACL of the database can edit the document.

- If a Readers field and Authors field are both included in the document, and a name appears in the Authors list but not in the Readers list, the user still has reader access to the document. The fact that a user can edit the document automatically allows him to read the document. Authors fields automatically give reader access to the users included in the list.

To create an Authors field to control access on a document-by-document basis, open the form in design mode and add a field. Select **Authors** as the data type. The list of authors can be created in several ways (these are the same options available for a Readers data type field):

- Manually entering names, groups, servers, or roles into the formula for the field.

- Using a formula to compute the list of names. Note that the formula must evaluate to a valid list of names or the data will be inaccessible.

- The user (usually the document author) can populate names.

If the user selects the names, the following options are available for populating the list:

- **None:** This is the only option in two instances: if the field is computed, or if the field is located within a layout region. If the field is computed, the designer is relying on a formula to populate the list of names. In a layout region, none of the other options are available.

- **Use Address dialog for choices:** This option allows the names to be selected from the Personal or Public Name and Address Book dialog prompt.

- **Use view dialog for choices:** The user is prompted with a view from which to select documents. This is the same functionality available within keywords.

Select the **Allow multi-values** option in the Field properties to include more than one name in the list of authors.

Notes

To use Authors fields on a local copy of a database, the Enforce a consistent access control list across all replicas *option should be selected on the Advanced tab of the ACL. Remember that if this option is selected, all replicating servers must have manager access to the database or replication will not occur.*

Encryption

Encryption is the most secure method of controlling access to information within a Notes database. Every Notes ID contains a public and private key used to encrypt documents and mail messages. The Notes ID may also contain encryption keys the user creates or receives in order to control access to data within fields. There are a few differences between encrypting documents in a database and mail encryption, and it is important to understand both types of encryption for the Application Development II exam. For more information on encryption, see Chapter 14—*Notes Infrastructure Security*.

Document Encryption

The encryption key must be added to a user's Notes ID to access the data stored in an encrypted field. To encrypt a field within a document, four steps are required: encrypting the field, creating the encryption key, applying the key, and distributing the key to users.

1. **Make the field encryptable.** You must do this in order to encrypt a document through field encryption. This field can be any data type. However, note that in an encrypted rich text field, OLE objects are only visible to users who hold the encryption key. Attachments are accessible to all users who can read the document, regardless of whether or not they hold the key.

   To create an encryptable field, open the field properties infobox and select the Options tab. In the Security options list box, select **Enable encryption for this field**. See Figure 9-12 for an illustration:

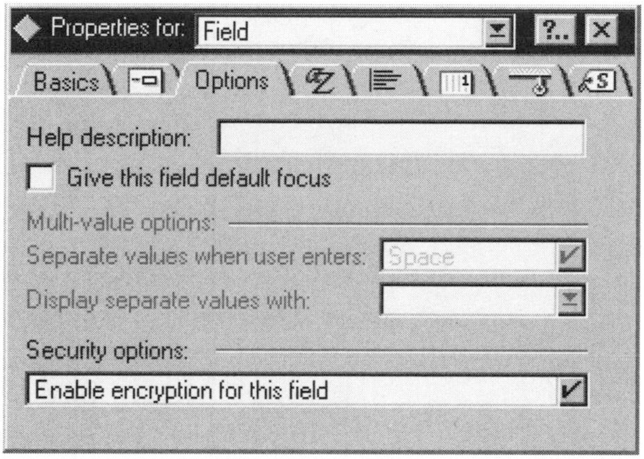

Figure 9-12

Making a Field
Encryptable

   Note that this is only the first step. The key must be applied in order for the field to actually be encrypted.

2. **Create the Encryption Key.** The encryption key must be created before it can be applied to the field. Encryption keys are created, stored, and validated through the user's Notes ID. Once the key is created, it must be distributed to the desired users.

   To create the encryption key, select **Tools – User ID** from the Notes menu. The User ID dialog box (Figure 9-13) will appear. Select **Encryption** from the left side of the dialog box. This dialog box shows the current encryption keys associated with the user's ID and allows the user to create a new key, delete a key, mail a key to another user, export a key, or import a key.

Figure 9-13

User ID
Dialog Box

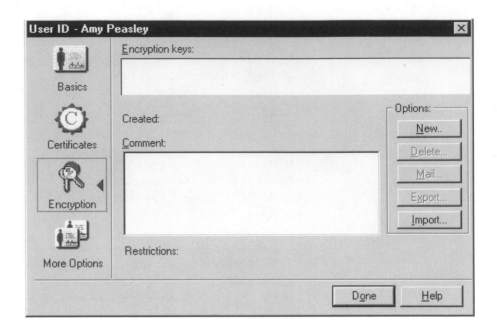

Click on the **New...** button to create the key. The **Add Encryption Key** dialog box will be presented. Enter a unique name for the key and provide a description to distinguish between keys.

3. **Apply the key.** Three options are available for applying an encryption key to a form or document: forced, optional, or manual encryption.

● **Forced Encryption:** This is done by the designer. An encryption key is associated with the form on the security tab in the form properties infobox. An encryption key is selected in the **Default encryption key** list box as shown in Figure 9-14:

Figure 9-14

Applying an
Encryption Key
to a Form

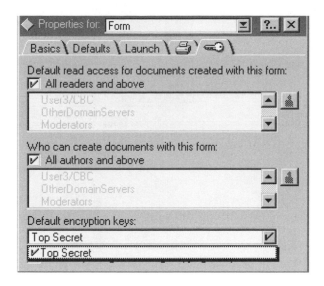

● **Optional Encryption:** Designers can also create a reserved Notes field named **SecretEncryptionKeys**. The field must be of data type text or keywords and must evaluate to the name of an encryption key. The name can be derived using a formula, or as a keywords selection using the key name as the synonym.

For example, the following formula determines which encryption key will be used based on the value of a field where Phase1 and Phase2 are encryption keys:

```
@If(PhaseLevel = "1"; "Phase1"; "Phase2")
```

To utilize a keywords selection, the field properties would be set as shown in Figure 9-15:

Figure 9-15

Using Keywords to
Apply Encryption Keys

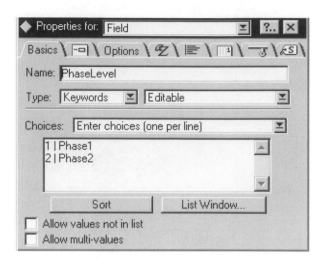

Note that encryption key names are case sensitive.

● **Manual Encryption:** Authors and editors can also encrypt documents. By selecting the document in the view and selecting **Edit – Properties...** in the Notes menu, the document properties infobox shown in Figure 9-16 will appear. Click on the Security tab and select an encryption key from list. This requires that the user distribute the encryption key.

Figure 9-16

Document Properties
Dialog Box

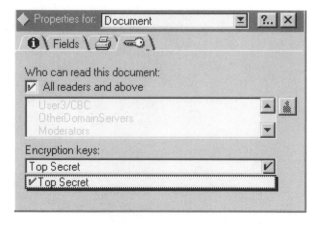

Multiple keys can be applied to documents to encrypt fields. However, you cannot associate one key to one field and another key to another field. Once a user has access to the document through one key, the user can perform all actions allowed by their level of document access.

4. **Distribute the Encryption Keys to user:** To access an encrypted document, users must have the encryption key inserted into their Notes ID. Two forms of distribution are available: Notes mail and exporting to a file.

● **Using Notes Mail to Distribute Encryption Keys:** In the User ID dialog box shown in Figure 9-13, one of the options is to **Mail...** the encryption key. When the user clicks on this button, the following dialog box shown in Figure 9-17 appears:

Figure 9-17
Mail Encryption Key
Dialog Box

This will send a Notes mail message to the users listed in the **To:** option. The subject of the mail message is listed in the **Subject:** box. This informs users of the name of the key and how to accept it.

● **Using a file to distribute Encryption Keys:** A **.KEY** file can be created to distribute the encryption key to other users. By selecting the **Export...** button from the User ID dialog box (shown in Figure 9-13), you are prompted to add a password to the file as illustrated in Figure 9-18:

Figure 9-18

Encryption Key
Export Dialog Box

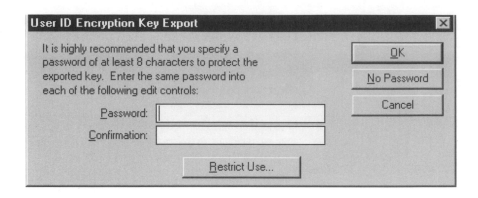

By selecting the **Restrict Use...** button, you can prevent the key from being forwarded. This should be done unless another user will be responsible for distributing the key. This .KEY file can then be distributed to other users.

To receive a key, the user will select the **Import...** button from the User ID dialog box.

Before the keys are distributed, it is important to realize what users will be able to do once they have the key. If a user has Author access to the document, she will be able to disable encryption from documents she created. If a user has Editor access or higher, he can disable encryption from any document, regardless of whether or not he created it. Thus, if a user has at least Editor access to the database and holds the encryption key, that person can unencrypt any information contained in the document.

Mail Encryption

Notes mail utilizes the user's public and private keys to allow and prevent access to mail messages. When the user's ID is registered, the public key is stored within the user's ID file and the Public Name and Address Book. The private key is stored in the user's Notes ID and is used to decrypt the information when it is received.

There are three ways to encrypt mail in Notes:

- **Encrypt incoming mail:** This option prevents unauthorized users from accessing your mail messages when they reach your server. The messages cannot be read by administrative access or via the server. This option is set in the Person document in the Public Name and Address Book.

- **Encrypt outgoing mail:** This option encrypts mail that you send to other users. The message cannot be accessed at any point in the delivery process. Encryption can be set on any outgoing message by selecting the **Encrypt** option in the Mail Send dialog box. This can also be the default setting on every mail message by selecting the **Encrypt Mail** option in the mail setup options, or with a **NOTES.INI** file setting. Designers can also force encrypting of all outgoing mail by creating a field named Encrypt on the mailed document and setting the value equal to 1. This will encrypt the message regardless of any other settings. This can only be done for outgoing messages, not incoming or saved messages.

- **Encrypt saved mail:** This prevents access to messages stored in your mail database by the system administrator or anyone who has access to the server. This option is set by selecting **Tools – Setup – Mail – Encrypt Saved Mail** from the Notes menu.

Notes

To encrypt a document which will be mailed and stored in a database, both document and mail encryption must be enabled. Two fields must be added to the form: SecretEncryptionKeys and Encrypt. Setting the SecretEncryptionKeys field to the value of the encryption key to be used to encrypt the document secures the document stored in the database. Setting the Encrypt field to "1" forces encryption of the mailed document.

Additional Security Features

There are two additional security features you need to know about: electronic signatures and how to prevent users from printing, forwarding, or copying information on a form. These are discussed in the following section.

Electronic Signatures

Electronic signatures place a stamp on the document which assures the reader that the signer was the last person to modify the document. The signature is attached to a field or section by combining the data in the field or section with the user's private key from their Notes ID. Signatures can be attached to documents through sign-enabled fields, or to sections within the document.

To apply a signature to a section or document, open the form in design mode by selecting **View – Design** from the menu. In the navigation pane, select **Design – Forms** and select the form. Create a field, or click on an existing field. Select **Design – Field Properties...** from the menu to open the field properties infobox. On the Options tab, select **Sign if mailed or saved** from the Security options combo box as show in Figure 9-19 below:

Figure 9-19

Signing a Field

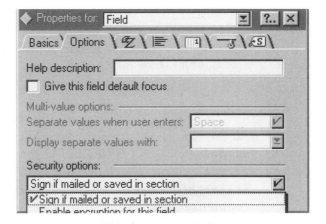

Any field on a form can be enabled for signing. To sign a section, enable signing on any field within the section. However, predefined mail fields (i.e., SendTo, CopyTo) should not be enabled for signing as they can be updated during mail routing. Notes will see that the document has been modified and re-sign the field with the server information rather than the sender's information.

Signing a field signs the entire document. However, multiple signatures can be attached to a document by signing sections. This is useful within workflow applications where multiple users need to sign a document. To sign a section, enable signing for any field within the section. This field will be signed every time an editor of that section saves the document. Note that the editor does not have to modify a field *within* the section for the section to be signed. Any time any possible editor of the section modifies any part of the document, the section's signature is updated. Thus, in a workflow application, the document contains several sections which can only be edited by one signer each. As each approver/reviewer edits the document, their signature is attached to the section, providing a history of electronic signatures.

If a field enabled for signing is located within a section, the signature is attached when the document is *saved*. If the field enabled for signing is located outside of a section, the signature is attached when the document is *mailed*.

Preventing Printing/Forwarding/Copying

It is possible to prevent users from printing, forwarding, or copying information on a form. This is beneficial any time designers want to restrict the mass distribution of sensitive information. However, it is important to note that the information can still be copied using a screen capture application; thus, it should not be considered a true security feature.

This option is available on the Form Properties security tab. This tab is accessed by opening the form in design mode, selecting **Design – Form Properties...** from the menu, and clicking on the Security tab (the key icon). Figure 9-20 illustrates this tab.

Figure 9-20

Preventing Printing/
Forwarding/Copying

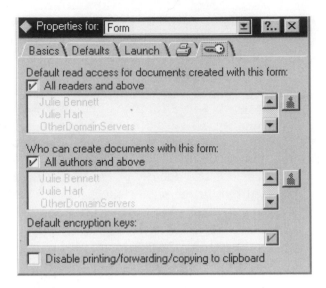

The security features detailed in this chapter provide an overview of the features necessary for the Application Development II exam. For additional information on security in application development, see the *Lotus Notes Programmers Guide*.

Chapter 9 Sample Questions

Objective: Using Notes Security.

Bernie is setting up the initial security on his Lotus Notes application. What is the hierarchy of security he must remember when planning his application? Select the correct hierarchy (from highest to lowest):

> A. Authentication, Notes Database Access, Document Access, Form Access, Field Access
>
> B. File Server Access, Notes Server Access, Authentication Notes Database Access, Field Access, Document Access
>
> C. Field Access, Document Access, Database Access, File Server Access
>
> D. Authentication, Notes Server Access, Database Access, Form & View Access, Document Access, Field Access

Answer: D
Authentication is the first level of security which functions at the Notes ID level. Document access relates to Reader and Author fields, which control who can create, edit and view documents. Field level access is controlled by encryption keys.

Objective: Control database access through access control lists.

Which item listed below is not determined by the Access Control List?

> A. Who can access the database
>
> B. What functions each person or group can perform
>
> C. The database's encryption keys
>
> D. Each person's roles

Answer: C
Encryption keys are not controlled through the database's Access Control List.

Objective: Control database access through access control lists.

Kelly wants to allow the Default access level to perform three functions:
Create documents, create personal agents, and create LotusScript agents, but not delete documents. What is the minimum level of access that is required in order to perform these actions?

        A. Reader

        B. Author

        C. Editor

        D. Designer

Answer: B
At the Author level of access, the manager can allow (or prevent) the user to create or delete documents, create personal agents, create personal folders/views, and create LotusScript agents.

Objective: Control database access through access control lists.

Gary clicks on a button in a Notes mail message. This button brings up a volleyball survey in the Chicago Sports Club database. Gary completes and saves the survey, but cannot view it in the database. What level of security does Gary have to the Chicago Sports Club database?

        A. Author

        B. Reader

        C. Depositor

        D. No Access

Answer: C
The Depositor level of access allows users to create documents, but not read documents in the database—even documents the user creates.

App. Dev. II

Objective: Control database access through access control lists.

Steve wants to allow his managers to create shared folders and views which everyone can utilize. What is the minimum level of access he must give to his managers?

A. Author

B. Editor

C. Designer

D. Manager

Answer: B

At the Editor level, the **Create shared folders/views** option is available.

Objective: Control database access through access control lists.

Dan wants to allow some of the users in the database to see a particular view. He doesn't have access to create a group in the Public Name and Address Book. How, as a manager of the database, can he allow a group of users to access a view?

A. Create a role in the database, add the users to the role, and give the role access to the view

B. Create a group in his private Name and Address Book

C. Create a role in the public Name and Address Book

D. Create a role in the database, give the role manager access to the database

Answer: A

Roles allow users to be grouped together to allow access to certain design elements. This is useful when you don't want to add a group to the public Name and Address Book.

Objective: Control database access through access control lists.

Theresa is considering using a role in her database. Which of the following is *not* true about using roles in a database?

       A. Centralized security

       B. Roles can't be used in formulas

       C. Roles give group control to managers who cannot create groups in the Public Name and Address Book

       D. Managers don't have to remember to change the role in all design elements when a user is added or removed from the role

Answer: B
Roles can be used in formulas by placing the role name in brackets.

Objective: Troubleshooting data access.

Heidi is a mobile user. She has replicated the database locally so she can do her work without being connected to the network. Heidi is a member of the "Admin" role, which gives her access to certain views and documents in the database. However, when she is running locally, she can no longer see the views, buttons aren't appearing and other strange things are happening. What created the problem?

       A. Heidi's ID is not functional when she is remote

       B. Heidi used a selective replication forumla which didn't replicate some of the views and buttons that Heidi usually sees

       C. The manager of the database did not select **Enforce a consistent access control list across all replicas** in the ACL of the database

       D. LocalDomainServers was included in the role

Answer: C
In order to utilize roles in a locally replicated database, the **Enforce a consistent access control list across all replicas** option must be selected on the Advanced tab of the ACL.

Objective: Control database/document access through form/view access lists.

Jordan wants to allow only the users included in the Managers role to create documents with the Admin form. How can Jordan accomplish this without using Author fields?

A. Access Control List

B. Author Access

C. View Access Lists

D. Form Access lists

Answer: D
Form access lists allow designers to control who can create documents with a form without modifying Authors fields at the document level.

Objective: Control form printing/forwarding/copying.

The Public Affairs department has some sensitive information contained in documents within their database. They want to prevent users from forwarding these documents and distributing them to unauthorized individuals. How could this be accomplished?

A. Create hide-when formulas for the entire form

B. Select the **Disable printing/forwarding/copying to the clipboard** option in the document properties

C. Select the **Disable printing/forwarding/copying to the clipboard** option in the form properties

D. Select the **Disable printing/forwarding/copying** option in the view properties

Answer: C
Disable printing/forwarding/copying to the clipboard is a form attribute available on the security tab in the form properties infobox.

Objective: Control document access through Reader fields.

Jennifer is included in a document's $Readers field, but she is not included in the list of names in the Readers data type field. Jennifer has Author access to the database in the ACL. Can Jennifer read the document?

    A. Yes, because Author access in the ACL overrides the all Readers fields in the document

    B. Yes, because she is listed in the read access list

    C. No, because the Readers data type field overrides all other types of access

    D. No, because Jennifer must be listed in both the $Readers and Readers data type fields to have access to the document

Answer: B

Three different keys were necessary to understand this question. First, you must understand that a read access list automatically generates a $Readers internal field on the document. Thus, stating that Jennifer is listed in the read access list is the same as saying that she is listed in the $Readers field. Second, you must remember that if a user is listed in either the read access list *or* any of the fields of Readers data type, she can read the document. Third, Reader access lists and Readers fields refine the ACL in that if these security elements are utilized, the user's access level (Reader or above) doesn't matter.

Objective: Control document access through Reader fields.

Bernie has included an editable field of Readers data type in his form. The field is located in a layout region. What are Bernie's options for displaying the choices? Select all that apply.

    A. None

    B. Use the access control list dialog for choices

    C. Use address dialog for choices

    D. Use view dialog for choices

Answer: A

In a layout region, the user must manually enter all options. None of the dialog prompts can be utilized. If the field was *not* in a layout region, all of the options would be available.

Objective: Control document access through Author fields.

Isabelle wants to allow users within a role to add information to certain documents in the database after they are created. However, these users only have Author access to the database. How can Isabelle allow users within a role to edit documents they didn't create without changing their access level in the database? Select all that apply.

    A. Include the role in the form edit access list

    B. Include each person in the role individually in the form edit access list

    C. Include the role in a field of Authors data type

    D. Include the role in a field of Readers data type

Answer: C

Authors fields allow names, groups, servers, and roles to be added to a text list which allows them to edit the document. This only affects users with Author access in the ACL of the database. There is no such element as a form edit access list.

Objective: Control document access through Reader fields.

Marty is included in the Authors field on the document. However, he is not included in the Readers field. No internal $Readers field exists on the document. Marty has Author access to the database in the ACL. Can Marty read the document?

    A. Yes, because if a user is included in an Authors field which allows editing the document, the user can automatically read the document

    B. No, because he is not included in the Readers field

C. Yes, because he has Author access to the database and the ACL overrides the other access control elements

D. No, because if a document contains a Readers field it must also contain a $Readers field; the document is not functional

Answer: A

If a user can edit the document, the user can read the document. By being included in the Authors field, Marty is automatically given read access to the document without being included in the Readers field.

Objective: Control document access through Reader fields.

Wendy is the author of a document which contains an editable field of Readers data type. By default, the Managers role is included in this field. Wendy deletes this value and saves the document. Who can read this document now?

A. No one

B. Everyone with at least Reader access to the database

C. Only Wendy

D. Any user with at least Editor access to the database

Answer: B

Anyone with at least Reader access to the database can read the document. An empty Readers field is equivalent to not including a Readers field on the document at all. However, as soon as someone edits the document and places a name in the Readers field, only the listed readers will be able to read the document.

Objective: Troubleshooting data access.

Brent opens a categorized view in a database. When he clicks on a category, the twistie changes to the down position, but no rows appear. What has happened?

A. Parent documents have been deleted and the orphaned documents are showing in the view, but they cannot be accessed without a parent document

B. The database has become corrupt, a new copy must be created

C. No documents are included under that category

D. Brent does not have read access to the documents included in the category

Answer: D

If a user is prevented from reading a document by a read access list or Readers field, the document cannot be seen in the view. However, if the view is categorized, the category will be displayed, although none of the documents under the category can be seen.

Objective: Troubleshooting access.

Dany is working out of her home office. She replicates a database locally and starts using it. She should be able to create new document by using a **Create New Product** button in the view. However, she cannot see this button. Joseph, the database designer, sees that she is included in the role which allows her to view the button via an @UserRoles hide formula. Why can't Dany see the button?

A. Dany only has reader access to the database so she can't create documents

B. The @UserRoles formula cannot be used on a local machine

C. Roles are not replicated locally

D. Joseph forgot to set the **Enforce a consistent ACL on all replicas** setting

Answer: D

The **Enforce a consistent ACL on all replicas** setting must be selected in order to allow local machines to use an @UserRoles formula. Otherwise, an empty string is returned.

Objective: Control field access through encryption.

Sean has created a database to monitor projects and consultants. He wants to track each consultant's rate, but he only wants certain people to have access to this sensitive information. On the same form, he has another field which tracks the consultant's salary. He wants a different group of people to have access to this information. He does not want the people who can access the salary information to see the rate information. He creates two encrypted fields with two different keys and distributes the only the salary key to the salary people and only the rate key to the rate people. What information will a user with the salary key be able to see on the document?

    A. The document and the salary information, but not the rate information

    B. The document and the rate information, but not the salary information

    C. Nothing, the user must have both keys to access the information in the encrypted fields

    D. Everything in the document in all encrypted fields

Answer: D
Multiple encryption keys can be used on a document, but if a user has any of the encryption keys, the user can see all information in all encrypted fields.

Objective: Control access through encryption.

Big Brother Company wants to monitor every mail message that is sent out by the users in the company. They want to prevent the users from encrypting outgoing messages. How could this be accomplished at the database level?

    A. By setting each user's user ID setting to not encrypt sent mail

    B. By adding a computed SecretEncryptionKeys field to the memo form in the mail template

C. By adding a key in the mail router to decrypt all sent mail

D. By adding a computed Encrypt field to the memo form
   In the mail template and setting the value to 0

Answer: D

The Encrypt field is used for mail encryption. By computing the field's value, users could not change it. This value overrides any other settings.

Objective: Control access through encryption.

Karlana has created an encryption key for documents related to users' time sheets. She wants to distribute the key to specific managers who can review these documents. Which of the following ways can be used to distribute the encryption key to the users?

A. Exporting a **.KEY** file and distributing it to users

B. Copying the key to a diskette and handing the diskette
   out to all users

C. Mailing the encryption key from the UserID dialog box

D. Creating a Notes mail message and selecting
   Mail – Encryption Key

Answer: A & C

Encryption keys can be distributed using Notes Mail (from the User ID dialog box) or by exporting the **.KEY** file.

Objective: Understanding electronic signatures.

Danielle wants to attach the electronic signature of each approver of the document. There are, at most, three approvers per document. How can she do this?

App. Dev. II

A. Documents can only have one electronic signature

B. She creates a field and selects **Sign if mailed or saved**; each signature will be appended

C. Danielle must create three sections, each of which can be signed

D. Danielle must sign-enable the form which will allow all editors to sign it

Answer: C

Multiple signatures can only be added to a document by using sections. A signature can be attached to each section.

System

Administration I

10

Notes Infrastructure Planning and Design

With this chapter, we begin to cover the key competencies associated with the System Administration I exam. Throughout the coverage of System Administration, topics are presented and described with the assumption that the reader has a basic understanding of Lotus Notes administration and configuration. For the novice Notes administrator, some topics may require additional research to understand the concept. In fact, some topics necessary for successful administration of a Notes network may not be covered at all. Instead, the focus of these sections is to help prepare the reader for the System Administration exams.

Topics covered within this chapter include designing a replication strategy using both single and multiple replicators. We will also look at designing a Notes mail routing topology and how Notes named networks affect the design. For Notes clients, the replicator page is a new addition to version 4 of Lotus Notes. This replicator page is another important concept to understand for the exam. Finally, within this chapter we will look at the very important concept of hierarchical naming and how to configure a structure for a Notes environment.

Designing a Notes Replication Architecture

Replication is simply the exchange of data between two Notes servers or a Notes server and a client. This action occurs between databases in common, in either a bidirectional or one-way mode. The Lotus replication engine automatically synchronizes data between like Notes databases, so that the end result after a replication event is two identical Lotus Notes databases containing the same information. On a Notes server, the replication engine is a program that runs on the server. For Notes replication to occur between two machines, the machines must share a protocol in common that is enabled within Notes.

The replication server task starts automatically on a Notes server upon startup via the **NOTES.INI** file. The entry is shown as follows:

```
ServerTasks=Replica,...
```

Notes servers and clients replicate databases by what is termed a *replica ID*, not by database title or file name. Each database has its own unique replica ID number. It can be compared to the concept that every person in America is identified by his or her social security number, not his or her name. In fact, to Notes at both the file system and database name levels, there can be duplicate names. It is the replica ID number that matters to Notes; that is, what gets looked up by a Notes server or client when replication commences. Notes will replicate all like databases based on like replica IDs between servers and/or clients. This includes all databases that exist in the data directory of Notes as defined in the **NOTES.INI** file, as well as in any directory/database links. If any database does not exist within the data directory or one of its subdirectories or links, the Notes server or client will not replicate the database.

Figure 10-1 illustrates the database properties infobox, where the replica ID can be found on a Notes database:

1. Click **File – Database – Properties**.

2. Then click the **Information** tab.

Figure 10-1

Notes Database
Replica ID Information

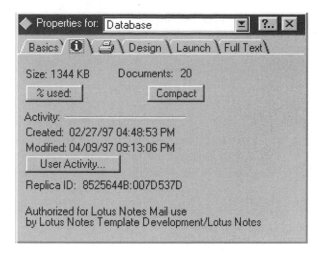

When a replication process begins between two servers, the initiating server first builds a list of replica IDs of its databases. The receiving server then also builds a list of replica IDs (independent of database titles and filenames). If any like matches exist, the servers then determine if documents have been changed or added. Any documents that have been changed are then identified and the date and time of creation ascertained. The initiating server first *pulls* any data from the second Notes server. Then the initiating server *pushes* its data to the receiving server (assuming default replication settings and proper security access). This is why only the initiating server will have entries in its Notes log for replication events (again, assuming defaults for replication are in place).

With release 4 of Lotus Notes, replication now occurs at the field level of Notes databases rather than the document level. This feature is automatically used for version 4 Notes servers and clients. Prior to release 4 of Lotus Notes, every new or edited document within a database was replicated in full to all replica databases throughout the Notes infrastructure; this produced a lot of unneeded overhead. For example, let us take a large existing document within a Notes application containing many fields. If a person were to edit just one field of the document, without field level replication enabled, the entire document (all fields including the ones that were not edited) would be replicated to all other Notes replica databases. However, if the machines were both running Notes version 4, only the field that was edited would be replicated between the replica databases, the other fields within the document would be skipped. As one can imagine, field-level replication can greatly reduce network traffic and replication times.

Notes

In order to take advantage of field level replication, the two replicating machines must both be running at least version 4.0 of Lotus Notes. If one of the servers or clients is running an earlier version, field level replication will not be used.

If a new document is ever added to a Notes database, it is added to all replica copies within the Notes infrastructure at the next scheduled replication event, assuming proper security rights. Replication of existing documents to other replicas is based upon sequence numbers and dates. For example, if a document exists in location A and location B, and a user edits a field in the application in location B, location B's change will replicate to location A and reflect the edit. This is because the sequence number of the field that was edited was incremented by one. The sequence number for the document containing the edited field will also increment by 1. To view the sequence number of a document, open the document and select **File – Document Properties** from the Notes menu. The sequence number appears within the document ID number following the letters **SN** (Sequence Number). The sequence number for a document can be found as shown in Figure 10-2:

Figure 10-2
Document
Sequence Number

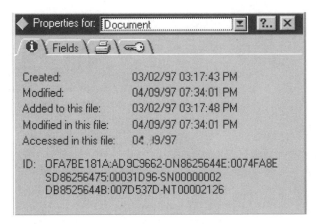

To view the sequence number of a field, open the document and select **File – Document Properties** from the Notes menu. Click the **Fields** tab and highlight the field you would like to view. The sequence number appears in the data box following the **Seq Num** entry. See Figure 10-3.

Figure 10-3
Field Sequence
Number

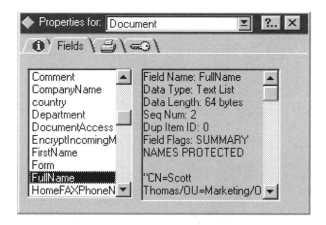

Notes

In order for replication to occur between two Notes machines within the same Notes domain and same organization certification hierarchy, the Notes servers must be allowed access to each other based on the Access server *field within each Notes machine's server documents. Also, all Notes database applications to be replicated must allow each server proper access in the ACL of the databases.*

Replication is determined at the database level by the following factors:

- ACL (Access Control List)

- Replication Settings

- Replica ID

- Replication History

Replication is determined at the document level by the following factors:

- Unique Document Identifier
- Last Modification Date and/or Time
- Document Sequence Number

Replication is determined at the field level by the following factor:

- Field Sequence Number

The following lists some advantages to using replication:

- Decreased network traffic, as Notes user traffic is limited to a local Notes server
- Automatic backup of the Notes applications, as they exist on multiple servers
- Increased access to applications, as more servers can handle more users

The following lists which types of Notes applications to replicate:

- Notes applications that are used by other Notes servers and Notes administrators within the company. This includes the public Name and Address book, the database catalog, template files, and the Administration Requests database.
- All Notes applications that need to be accessed by other Notes users in remote locations. Application types may include discussion databases, policies databases, workflow applications, and human resource applications, to name a few.
- Any Notes application that needs to be accessed by remote users that may not have connectivity all the time to a Notes server. A sales Notes application is a good example of this.

Replication Structures

When more than one Notes server exists within an organization, you will need to set up a replication structure between Notes servers even if you do not have any Notes applications created. This is because the public Name and Address book for your organization must replicate in order to contain all administration updates. Administration is only done to one public Name and Address book within your Notes infrastructure. Replication then carries those changes to other Notes servers.

There are three major models of replication between Notes servers, including the peer-to-peer architecture, hierarchical architecture, and hub-and-spoke-architecture. The sections below define and explain each architecture.

Tips

For the System Administration I exam, you should understand all three of these types of replication strategies. Pay particular attention to the hub-and-spoke architecture.

Peer-to-Peer Model

A peer-to-peer replication architecture is used for smaller Notes environments. In this type of architecture, all Notes servers replicate with one another. Figure 10-4 depicts such a replication architecture:

Figure 10-4
Peer-to-Peer
Replication Model

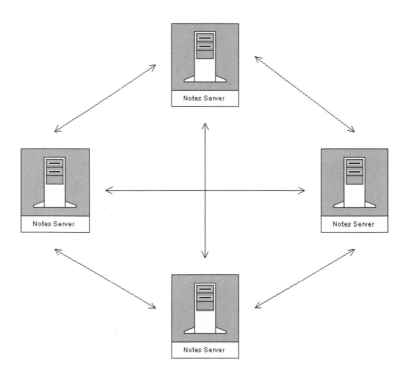

You should consider using a peer-to-peer replication architecture only if the total number of servers within the Notes domain is less than six. If the environment contains more than six Notes servers, or if the environment is anticipated to grow past this number of Notes servers, another replication architecture is recommended. For example, under the peer-to-peer architecture, six Notes servers would require 15 replication connection records within the public Name and Address book to connect all Notes servers with one another. The equation to use to figure the number of connection documents is $n*(n-1)/2$ where n is the total number of servers.

Peer-to-peer replication is a relatively inefficient means of distributing data, especially as the total number of Notes servers grows. Peer-to-peer replication architecture does offer more reliable replication, as all servers replicate with one another. However, the administrative overhead and complexity outweighs such an approach for larger Notes environments.

Hierarchical or Binary Tree Model

This type of replication architecture is arranged in a pyramid structure with a top-level Notes server replicating with servers below. Those child Notes servers then are responsible for replicating with their children, and so on. Such an architecture is depicted in Figure 10-5:

Figure 10-5
Binary Tree
Replication Model

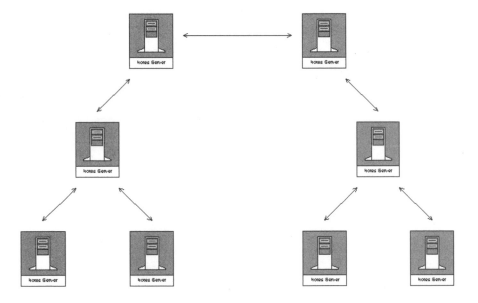

This type of replication architecture is a more efficient means of distributing data than the peer-to-peer model; however, it is not as efficient as a hub-and-spoke architecture. The main fault with this type of architecture is that if one server fails in replication, all others fall behind. Organizations that are spread internationally may want to consider such an architecture where distances and prices concerning those connections are an issue.

Hub-and-Spoke

The hub-and-spoke replication architecture is the most popular replication architecture, especially for larger Notes installations, as it offers the most efficient means of distributing data. With this type of design, there is a central Notes server or a combination of servers (hubs), responsible for replicating to outer Notes servers (spokes). The hub(s) are responsible for calling all spoke servers and distributing data to the Notes servers. Such an architecture is shown in Figure 10-6:

Figure 10-6
Hub-and-Spoke
Replication Model

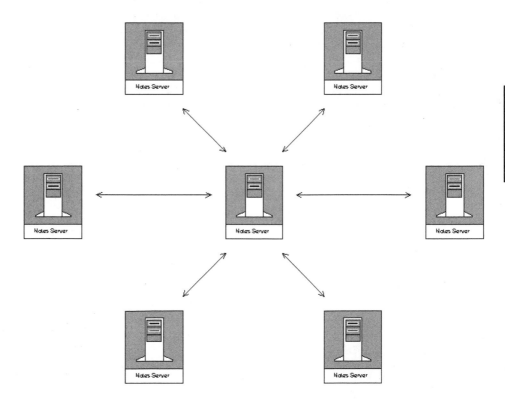

This type of replication model centralizes Notes administration as all connection records will be from the hub(s) to spokes, and all replication events will appear within the hub Notes logs as the hub(s) Notes server will initiate the replication event. If your environment is running multiple protocols, the hub Notes servers can be configured so that it will run multiple protocols. It can then replicate with Notes servers running those protocols, acting like a "bridge" between the two environments.

Tips

A hybrid hub-and-spoke and hierarchical model can be used in organizations with regional servers. These regional servers would then act as top-level servers replicating to child servers. This method can be effectively used to maintain consistent and timely replication between hubs and spokes, while providing local efficiencies.

Replication has made it possible for all users, both in the office and remotely connected, to effectively and efficiently share information regardless of location or time zones. Replication also makes it possible for people to share information without the need to access a central database.

Replication Direction

Replication within Lotus Notes is one-way. In order for two-way replication to occur, another one-way process must be initiated between the two Lotus Notes machines. Each one-way replication process may be configured to guarantee a bidirectional replication, as discussed below.

Within a replication connection document, you may specify which server sends and/or receives documents. Connection records are explained in Chapter 11—*Notes Server Installation and Setup*. This is accomplished within the **Replication Type** field within the connection document within the public Name and Address book. The choices are **Pull-Push**, **Pull-Pull**, **Push-Only**, and **Pull-Only**. Specifying a different replication type does not affect the replication process in terms of how the program works; it only affects in which direction replication occurs and which server does the work.

Notes

These four types of replication should be thoroughly understood by the user, as the exam will test on these types of replication settings.

- **Pull-Push:** This is the default setting within Notes. With this type of replication, changes are distributed to both Notes servers, with the initiating server first pulling the changes from the target server. Then, the initiating server pushes any changes to the target Notes server. The replicator program on the initiating Notes server does all the work of replication, and all data concerning the replication event is only recorded in the initiating Notes server's log file. The replicator program on the target Notes server is not run in this type of replication.

- **Pull-Pull:** This type of replication is also a two-way distribution of data to both Notes servers. This model distributes the workload of replication where each Notes server's replicator program is run. Each Notes server pulls data from one another, so both replication programs on each server are running.

- **Push-Only:** This type of replication is a one-way process, where the initiating Notes server pushes changes to the target Notes server only. No updates are added to the initiating Notes server in any Notes application. Only the target Notes server receives updates to Notes applications.

- **Pull-Only:** This type of replication is a one-way process where the initiating Notes server only pulls changes to itself from the target Notes server. No updates are added to the target Notes server in any Notes application. Only the initiating Notes server receives updates to Notes applications.

Notes

The Pull-Only and Push-Only replication types can be used in combination to pull during one time interval and then push during another. This would be used in combination with pull *and* push *connection records in the Name and Address book. This type of replication scheme could be used in a hub-and-spoke scenario to allow all hub servers to gather new and/or modified documents and then push all changes out to servers, thus guaranteeing that all replica copies of databases were updated within a given replication cycle.*

It should be understood that in a pull replication situation the replicator server task performs the following tasks:

● Reads from the target Notes server's application(s)

● Writes to its own Notes application(s)

Within a reverse scenario (push situation), the opposite is true. In both cases, all replication is controlled by the Access Control Lists of the individual Notes applications on both servers.

Multiple Replicators

With the release of Notes 4.0, a Notes server is now able to support multiple replication tasks to service multiple spoke Notes servers at once. This gives the administrator the ability to replicate with more Notes servers and to broaden the infrastructure's daily replication window.

To enable multiple replicators on a Notes server, add the following setting to the Notes server's **NOTES.INI** file:

```
REPLICATORS = number
```

where *number* is the number of replicators to run on the Notes server.

This setting may also be configured from a configuration document within the public Name and Address book.

If the setting is added in either manner to the **NOTES.INI** file as explained above, the Notes server must be restarted for the change to take place.

If you wish to have an additional replicator running immediately without having to restart the Notes server, you may run it from the console or remote console of the Notes server by entering the following command:

```
load replica
```

The maximum number of replicators that may be run on a single Notes server is ten. Factors that should be considered when running multiple replicator server tasks include:

- The Notes server's hardware specifications

- The Notes servers function (e.g. Hub Server)

- The Replicator server tasks is an intensive process

Notes Application Replication and Save Conflicts

Replication conflicts occur in Notes databases when two or more users edit and save changes to the same document in the same Notes application on *different* Notes servers. When the next scheduled replication occurs, Notes flags the document as a replication conflict.

A save conflict is the same as a replication conflict, except the action happens on the same server. Two or more users edit the same document in the same Notes database on the *same* server.

There are a number of ways to handle save and replication conflicts. First, when designing the application, this problem should be kept in mind. For large, intensive applications where people need to modify the same document in the same database, Notes is probably *not* a good solution. Granting users author access to a Notes database will eliminate this problem, as users will only be able to edit their own documents.

Lotus has helped resolve these problems in version 4.0 and higher of Lotus Notes with a process called *merging conflicts*. The merging conflicts process must be enabled by the designer of the database. The setting can be found by entering the design of a form of a database and then selecting **Form Properties**. At the bottom right-hand corner of the Basic tab is a check box where this option can be selected (see Figure 10-7).

Figure 10-7

Database Merge
Conflicts Setting

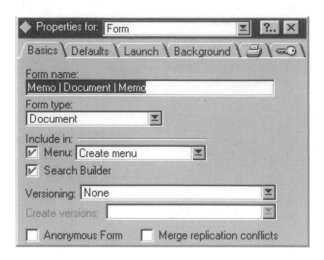

Without merging conflicts, when a person edits the same document as someone else either on the same server or on a different server, a replication or save conflict is flagged. With merging conflicts enabled on the form(s) within the database, a replication or save conflict may not necessarily occur using the above scenario. If a person edits a particular document and another person edits the same document either on the same or on a different server, and the fields edited are different, then Notes will merge the two documents together as one document without flagging a replication or save conflict. However, if the document edited and saved has a change done to the same field, then a replication or save conflict will still occur.

It must be noted, however, that if this feature is turned on, it may actually make some documents incorrect in what type of data is expected. Take for example a Notes application where merge conflicts is enabled, and the application has two fields: *user* and *location*. One user edits a document and changes the user's name. Another person edits the same document at the same time and changes the location. With merge conflicts on, the document now has a new user's name with another new location, making the document incorrect. Great care and planning must be considered before enabling this feature.

Most organizations give responsibility to the Notes database manager to scan for replication and save conflicts. If there is an occurrence, the database manager decides which document should be the "winner."

Many times, this involves cutting and pasting information from one document to another; then the manager deletes the old document.

Designing a Notes Named Network

A Lotus Notes named network definition groups servers that share a common network protocol on the same physical LAN. Lotus Notes servers that exist on different LAN segments separated by a router should be housed on a different Lotus Notes named network. All Notes servers on the same Notes network appear in a user's server list when a Notes client performs a **File – Database – Open**.

A Notes named network is configured in the Public Name and Address book within each server document. A single Notes server may belong to multiple Lotus Notes named networks if the Notes server has multiple network cards attached to different physical segments, or if a single network card is running multiple protocols. COM ports are not associated with Lotus Notes named networks, and therefore are not defined within a Notes server document for Notes named networks.

Figure 10-8 shows an example of the configuration of a Lotus Notes named network within a server document in the public Name and Address book:

Figure 10-8

Lotus Notes
Named Network
Configuration

▼ **Network Configuration**

Port	Notes Network	Net Address	Enabled	
⌈TCPIP⌋	⌈Chicago-TCPIP⌋	⌈192.2.2.2⌋	● ENABLED	○ DISABLED
⌈SPX⌋	⌈Chicago-SPX⌋	⌈Chicago-Notes01⌋	● ENABLED	○ DISABLED
⌈ ⌋	⌈ ⌋	⌈Chicago-Notes01⌋	○ ENABLED	● DISABLED
⌈ ⌋	⌈ ⌋	⌈Chicago-Notes01⌋	○ ENABLED	● DISABLED
⌈ ⌋	⌈ ⌋	⌈Chicago-Notes01⌋	○ ENABLED	● DISABLED

As can be seen within Figure 10-8, SPX and TCP/IP are running on the Notes server. Each protocol therefore needs to be established within its own Notes network. It is helpful to give a Notes named network a descriptive name. Naming by location and protocol are usually the preferred method.

An important point to understand about Notes named networks is that Notes servers within the same Notes named network do not need mail connection records between them. The Notes mail router knows the existence of other Notes servers, and e-mail is instantly delivered to Notes servers on the same Notes network. Also, as stated before, Notes servers grouped in the same named Notes network will all appear in the server lists when Notes users perform a **File – Database – Open**.

With this point understood, it is possible by design to include Notes servers sharing the same protocol on a WAN within the same Notes network, assuming the network connections are capable of handling external connectivity. To illustrate, if ACME has three Notes servers all running TCP/IP located in NY, Chicago, and Los Angeles within a WAN environment, the administrator could set up the Notes named network to include all three servers. In this scenario, no mail connection records would be necessary between the servers, only replication connection records. Electronic mail would be delivered between the servers automatically. All three Notes servers would appear within server lists for users in all three locations, enabling them to connect to other servers (assuming proper security standards).

This design, however, especially for slower WAN links, is not desired. The preferred method in the above scenario would be to create three separate Notes named networks.

Traps

By design, mail connection records between servers on the same Notes Network are not needed. They only add confusion and complexity to connection records within public Name and Address books, as well as overhead to mail routing between those servers.

To further illustrate Lotus Notes named networks, let us look at Figure 10-9, depicting five different Lotus Notes named networks all within a single Lotus Notes domain.

Figure 10-9

Lotus Notes Named
Network Example

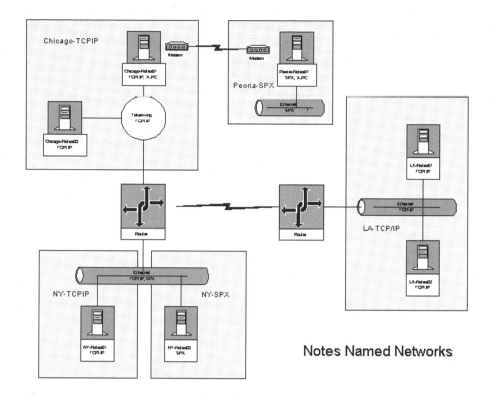

Notes Named Networks

Within the Chicago location, both Notes servers are on the same token ring, running the same protocol (TCP/IP). Therefore, these two servers are grouped on the same Lotus Notes named network and only need a replication connection record between them. An e-mail connection record is not necessary.

The NY location however is configured in two separate Notes named networks, even though the two Notes servers reside on the same ethernet segment. This is because the two Notes servers are running separate protocols. For this reason, the two servers will not be able to replicate or route mail between them. Replication and mail routing will have to be accomplished through a remote Notes server. This is obviously not an ideal design situation. The Notes administrator should configure one of the Notes servers with an additional protocol shared by the other Notes server to avoid routing and replicating through a remote Notes server.

Sys. Admin. 1

Tips *For the exam, the definition of a Notes named network should be understood with the comprehension of how Notes servers are grouped within a Notes named network. For example, you should know how it is determined when Notes servers should be grouped within the same Notes named network.*

Tips *A Notes named network should not be confused with a Notes domain. A Notes named network groups servers by location and protocols. A Notes domain groups users and servers within a public Name and Address book (see Chapter 13 for a discussion on Notes domains).*

Designing a Notes E-Mail Architecture

With the release of Notes version 4.0, a variety of mail protocols and platforms are now supported. Notes mail, along with SMTP, cc:Mail, and X.400 are all supported within a Notes mail infrastructure. Gateways (MTAs or *Message Transfer Agents*) enable Notes mail users to exchange mail with any SMTP, cc:Mail, or X.400 mail system.

If the Notes mail client is used, you get one of the industry-leading products in terms of security, incorporating digital signatures and encryption using RSA's encryption algorithm. Unlike many other e-mail systems, Notes mail provides each user with a separate file for his or her mail repository. A mail database for a user is simply another Notes database application. This means that all the security and functionality measures incorporated into a Notes database are also part of a user's mail file. This includes forms, views, ACL, encryption, full-text indexes, rich-text fields including file attachments, and replication, to name a few items that can be exploited.

Like replication connection records between Notes servers, you must create mail connection records between Notes servers in order to route Notes mail. (Connection records are explained in Chapter 11—*Notes Server Installation and Setup.*) The structure should follow the same replication structure that is defined for replication of Notes databases. This includes either a peer-to-peer, binary tree, or hub- and-spoke architecture. Mail connection records may be a part of a replication record where both mail routing and replication are enabled within a single connection record. However, unlike replication records where only the calling Notes server needs a replication connection record, mail connection records are necessary for each Notes server to provide mail routing in both directions.

Tips

For Notes servers on different Notes named networks, mail connection records within the public Name and Address book are necessary for both Notes servers to provide two-way mail routing between them. To route Notes mail to and from Notes servers A and B, one Notes mail connection record routes mail from A to B, and a separate mail connection record routes mail from B to A.

Tips

Although replication connection records are necessary between Notes servers in the same Notes named network, mail connection records are not needed. Notes mail is automatically transferred to Notes servers on the same Notes named network, and mail connection records only causes increased complexity in the design of the architecture. They represent unneeded overhead to the public Name and Address book.

The Notes mail router on every Notes server is responsible for routing mail from the sender to the receiver's Notes mail database. This may include multiple Notes server hops until the message is finally delivered.

Tips

The maximum number of Notes mail server hops a message may take is 25. This is to prevent an undeliverable mail message within a routing loop from creating a Notes mail flood.

Notes Mail Routing

Same Notes Server

The Notes mail router on each server uses the public Name and Address book (**NAMES.NSF**) and the router mail box (**MAIL.BOX**) to determine the destination of the Notes mail message. When a sender addresses a Notes mail message to a recipient, the following happens:

If the recipient exists on the same Notes server as the sender, the router automatically moves the Notes mail message from the router mailbox and places the message into the receiver's Notes mail database. See Figure 10-10.

Figure 10-10
Notes Mail
Routing—Same
Notes Server

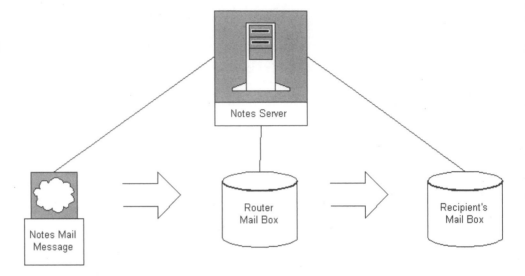

Same Notes Named Network

If the recipient exists on another Notes server and the target Notes server is within the same Notes named network, the message is automatically transferred from the sender's Notes server's router mailbox to the target Notes server's router mailbox. The router server task on that Notes server then moves the message from the **MAIL.BOX** database (router mailbox) to the recipient's Notes mail database. Note that no mail connection records between the Notes servers are necessary for this routing to occur. See Figure 10-11.

Figure 10-11
Notes Mail
Routing—Same
Notes Network,
Different Notes
Server

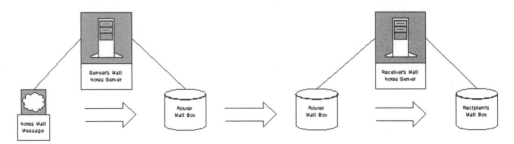

Different Notes Named Network

If the recipient exists on another Notes server, and the target Notes server is on a different Notes named network, the sender's mail server looks for a mail connection record to the target Notes server. If one exists, the message is automatically transferred to the target Notes server's router mail box (**MAIL.BOX** Notes database) from the sender's Notes server's mailbox. The router server task on that Notes server then moves the message from the mailbox database to the recipient's Notes mail database, as in Figure 10-12.

Figure 10-12
Notes Mail Routing— Different Notes Server

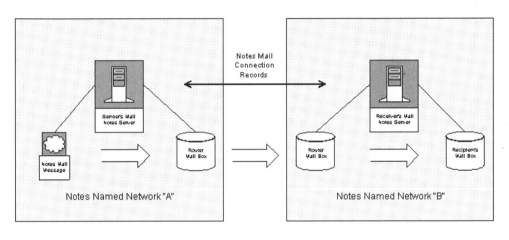

Notes Named Network "A"   Notes Named Network "B"

Non-Direct Mail Connection

If the recipient exists on another Notes server that does *not* have a direct mail connection record to the target Notes server, the message is transferred to each Notes server's router mail box along the path until the message reaches the recipient's Notes server's mailbox. The router server task on that Notes server then moves the message from the mailbox application database to the recipient's Notes mail application database.

Sys. Admin. I

Figure 10-13

Notes Mail
Routing—
Multiple Notes
Server Hops

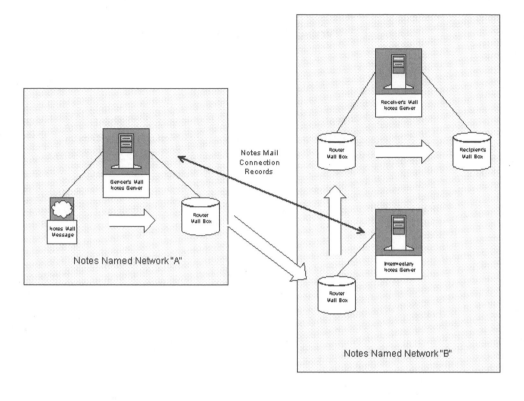

Tips

If multiple mail routing paths exist to a target Notes server, the mail router routes a mail message based on the least-cost route per connection record as set in the routing cost field of each mail connection document.

As with replication, a Notes administrator may force a Notes server to deliver any pending Notes mail immediately, including low priority mail, by typing the following command from the Notes server console or remote Notes server console:

```
route servername
```

where *servername* is the name of the destination Notes server.

You should enter the fully distinguished name of the Notes server. If there are any spaces within the server name, the fully distinguished server name should be encompassed within quotes, e.g. "Chicago Notes01/ACME."

If you wish to shut down the mail router on a Notes server, you may do so by typing the following command from the Notes server console or remote Notes server console:

```
tell router quit
```

If you wish to start it again, type the following command:

```
load router
```

Tips

For the examination, a basic understanding of how Notes mail routes in each of these scenarios is necessary.

Using Notes Workstation Replicator Page

Continuing with our discussion of replication and mail routing, release 4 and higher of the Lotus Notes client now supports a new predefined tab within a Notes user's workspace. This new page is known as the *replicator page* and its tab is labeled as such.

Figure 10-14 shows what this page looks like:

Figure 10-14

Sample
Workstation
Replicator
Page

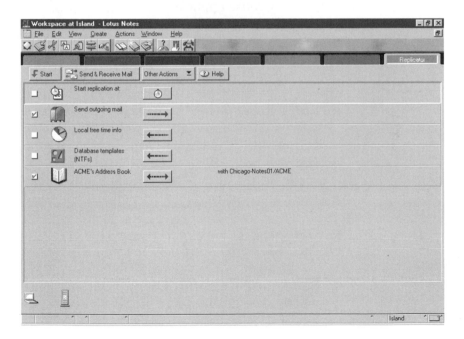

Within this page, the following entries can be found:

- **Start Button:** This button will initiate replication and send mail, assuming check boxes are checked next to each entry. Replication and/or mail entries are processed in the order they are shown on the page. The order may be changed by dragging and dropping each entry to the position desired.

- **Send & Receive Mail Button:** By pressing this button, only mail will be sent and received to the user's Notes mail application.

- **Other Actions Button:** This button has four selections:

  A. **Replicate High Priority databases:** By selecting this entry, only Notes applications designated as High Priority will be replicated.

  B. **Replicate with Server:** By selecting this entry, you may initiate replication with the target Notes server.

  C. **Replicate Selected Databases:** By selecting this entry, only those application(s) selected (highlighted) on the replicator page will be replicated.

  D. **Send Outgoing Mail:** This selection will send any outgoing mail messages.

- **Start Replication At Entry:** This entry on the replication page is used to configure the replication schedule for the workstation which is stored within the user's personal name and address book. With this selection enabled, replication may occur on the user's workstation automatically, without any user intervention.

- **Database Template Entry:** This entry is used to replicate database templates from the target Notes server.

- **Send Outgoing Mail Entry:** This entry is used to determine whether or not to deliver mail messages to the target Notes server.

- **Replica Database(s) Entries:** Any replica copies of database(s) on the user's local workstation will appear on this page. For each entry, a user may determine how replication is handled. If a box is not checked, replication will not occur for that application. By pressing the arrow, the direction (send and/or receive documents) and target server may be selected.

- **Call Entry:** Use this entry to determine which server to call for remote workstations using modems.

- **Hangup Entry:** Use this entry to hangup a remote connection.

Notes

Each box must be checked next to each entry for that action to happen when the Start button is pressed. In other words, if two databases are checked along with the Send Outgoing Mail entry, but a third database entry is unchecked, this third database will not replicate once the Start button is pressed.

Notes

A red explanation point will appear within each entry for those Notes applications that are High Priority.

Tips

For the exam, an understanding on how to configure this page is necessary. For example, the candidate should know how to configure this page to replicate selective databases with a target Notes server, along with how to route mail to a Notes server. Each button's function should also be understood.

Designing a Notes Hierarchical Naming Structure

Hierarchical naming closely follows x.500 naming standards, and can be compared to Novell's NDS naming format in Novell version 4.x environments. Unlike flat user and server ID files, a hierarchically created ID file may only contain one hierarchical certificate ("stamp").

Tips

This is an important point for the examination. A hierarchical ID file may only have **one** *hierarchical certificate. It may contain several flat certificates, however.*

Since the release of version 3 of Lotus Notes, hierarchical naming is the default naming standard for registering Notes users and servers. Flat user and server names are still supported, but must be created separately. Most organizations have converted or are in the process of converting from flat certifiers, user, and server names to the default hierarchical naming standard. With the release of version 4 of Lotus Notes, built-in conversion utilities exist to automate much of the conversion process.

Figure 10-15 shows what a hierarchical tree looks like:

Figure 10-15
Sample Hierarchical
Naming Tree

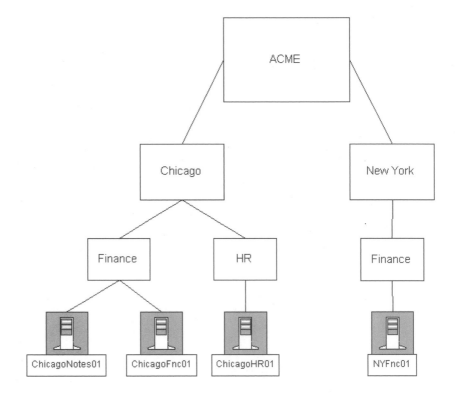

Hierarchical naming has the following advantages over flat naming standards:

- **Reduction of duplicate server and user names.** This especially holds true for larger companies where two or more users have the same name. Because of the format of a hierarchical name, users and servers may share the same common name, as long as they have different organizational units within their fully qualified name.

- **More specific security entries.** Although not inherently designed to improve security, fully distinguished names provide a higher level of security by enabling administrators to enter fully qualified names in database access control lists and server access lists. In a flat naming structure, a user from within or outside the company has a higher probability of using an ID with the same name of another person to fraudulently access a Notes application or server.

- **Faster user and server authentication.** By design, in order for two IDs to authenticate (either Notes server to server or Notes server to Notes client), the IDs must have a certificate in common. Hierarchical IDs can only contain one certificate and require cross-certificates in order to authenticate outside of its hierarchy. In a flat naming scheme, a user or server ID may contain multiple certificates in order to authenticate. As more flat certifiers are added to an ID file, the authentication process slows.

- **Decentralization of registering new users and servers.** In a flat naming environment, a single Notes administrator does most of the registering of new users and servers. With hierarchical naming, organizational unit certifiers may be distributed to local offices, where a local administrator may handle certification of local users and servers at that specific office.

- **Use of the administration process.** The administration process that runs on Notes version 4 servers will only recognize hierarchical users and servers.

Hierarchical Names are used within the following Notes locations:

- Notes Server console commands

- ACL's (Access Control Lists)

- Reader Name Fields

- Author Name Fields

- Group Entries

- Mail-In Databases

- Server Access Fields

- Person Records

Lotus Notes uses the following structure for hierarchical naming:

`CN/OU/OU/OU/OU/O/C`

where:

`CN = Common Name`

`OU = Organizational Unit (can be up to four levels deep)`

`O = Organization`

`C = Country Code (optional)`

For example:

`CN=Scott Thomas/OU=Marketing/OU=Chicago/O=ACME/C=US`

`CN=Chicago-Notes01/O=ACME/C=US`

As you can see from this naming structure, users and servers can have the same name as long as the OU format is different. In other words, another user named Scott Thomas could exist in the Finance group in Chicago as well as in the Marketing group, and Notes would treat each user as unique. The second Scott's fully distinguished name would be:

```
CN=Scott Thomas/OU=Finance/OU=Chicago/O=ACME/C=US
```

Each of the above layers of a hierarchical name will now be explained.

Country Code

The two-letter country code is optional in terms of the hierarchical naming scheme. All country codes are defined by the CCITT. It is recommended for use only if your company has locations outside the country of the installed base. It is also used to distinguish one company from another in the event a company of the same name exists in a different country. The country code will appear on all e-mail messages and is necessary in all documents in terms of naming. In other words, when a user receives an e-mail message from another user, the country code (US in our example) will appear appended at the end of his or her name.

Organization

The organization is the top level of the hierarchy and is required for all Notes server and user ID files. The organization name appears on all server and user names, including e-mails, unless otherwise specified by Notes applications designers. The organization certifer name is usually the name of the company. In our example, the organization would be ACME. The length of the organization name may be from 3 to 64 characters. The Organization (O) is created when the first Notes server is created and is saved on the first Notes server with a file name of CERT.ID. The registration of the organization certifier is also recorded in the public Name and Address book of the Notes server. With this certifier file, Notes users and servers may be created, as well as additional Organizational Units (OUs), explained in the following section. It is one of the most important files in a Notes infrastructure and should be password protected and maintained only by one or two Notes administrators.

Sys. Admin. I

Another Organizational certifier file may be created after the first Notes server is created, but proper planning must be considered in performing this task. An example where a Notes administrator may create a new Organizational certifier would be an instance where a company was changing its name. The administrator would then have to recertify all user and server Notes ID files. Another example would be when the administrator wishes to connect to another set of Notes servers, perhaps for external connectivity to another third-party Notes network.

Organizational Units

Organizational Units are optional and are used to further distinguish a user or server within an company. OUs appear directly underneath an Organization or another Organizational Unit in the naming hierarchy. They usually represent a division or geographical location within a company.

You may have up to 4 such division levels (OUs), however, we recommend that you implement no more than 2 or 3 layers. Each Organizational Unit may be up to 32 characters in length. You may, however, have as many OUs as you wish at a given level (such as in our example, as many city locations at the first level as you wish). For example:

```
CN=Scott Thomas/OU=Marketing/OU=NewYork/O=ACME/C=US

CN=Scott Thomas/OU=Marketing/OU=Chicago/O=ACME/C=US

CN=Scott Thomas/OU=Marketing/OU=Dallas/O=ACME/C=US
```

The more levels you use, the more administration is likely to be involved. If users in our example transfer divisions from Chicago to Dallas, the person must be re-certified. If the organization did not have any OUs defined, as in `CN=Scott Thomas/O=ACME/C=US`, the user would not have to be recertified.

The use of OU certifiers can help ease the burden of administration especially when creating new users. For example, if administration of ACME is done from the Chicago office, the OU certifier file of `/OU=Marketing/OU=NewYork/O=ACME/C=US` could be sent to New

York, and the local Notes administrator in that location could be responsible for certifying and creating new users. This would reduce the burden of the central Chicago Notes IS staff.

When registering Notes servers, it is recommended that in environments where organizational units are used, proper consideration be attended to when determining where to place the server. Many times, multiple departments will be accessing a Notes server. Let us take a look again at our examples at ACME:

User:

`CN=Scott Thomas/OU=Marketing/OU=Chicago/O=ACME/C=US`

Server:

`CN=Chicago-Notes01/O=ACME/C=US`

The ACME Notes administration team decided to place the Notes server under the `/ACME` certifier. The Notes server could be placed anywhere in the hierarchy, but to keep things simple and to avoid confusion, this where the ACME teams decided to place all Notes servers within the company. Different departments and geographic locations of ACME will be accessing the Notes server. Because of this, it does not make sense to place the server at the department level, such as `/Marketing/Chicago/ACME`. This leads to confusion for other departments that may be using the Notes server.

Actual placement of the Notes server in the hierarchy of a company's fully distinguished naming scheme is not important in terms of performance. However, whichever level is decided upon by your Notes administration team should be followed to provide consistency and avoid confusion both to the Notes administration team and Notes user community.

Tips

If you are considering using Organizational Units in your hierarchical naming scheme, keep the number of levels to a minimum. A single Organizational Unit usually suffices for most organizations. Two Organizational Units is usually the recommended maximum number of levels.

"Fake" Organizational Units

"Fake" Organizational Units are used in the event that two people have the *same* name at the *same* level of the hierarchy. In our example, two users named Scott Thomas exist within the same hierarchy:

```
CN=Scott Thomas/OU=Marketing/OU=Chicago/O=ACME/C=US
```

In such an event, a "Fake" organizational unit could be used to distinguish this person from the other Scott Thomas. This OU would be counted as another level in the hierarchy. The "fake" level would not be used for security checks within the Notes security model, though. An example might look something like this for the two users named Scott Thomas:

```
CN=Scott Thomas/Manager/OU=Marketing/OU=Chicago
/O=ACME/C=US

CN=Scott Thomas/Operations/OU=Marketing/OU=Chicago
/O=ACME/C=US
```

The "fake" organizational unit provides a way for all Notes users to easily distinguish between the two users.

Instead of incorporating a fake organizational unit most companies simply use the user's middle initial. This method of the middle initial proves less confusing and simplifies the naming format.

Common Name

The common name (CN) represents a Notes user or server name. It may be up to 80 characters in length depending on what protocol is used. Different protocols support different common name lengths. The common name of an ID can be compared to the format a Flat user or server ID would have.

Normally, for company installations that are not too large, only a CN (Common Name) and an O (Organization) are used. Adding additional OUs puts further administration burden and complexity on the environment and usually are not necessary.

For larger Notes installations, one or two organizational units are necessary to provide detail of a user's location and/or department, as well as avoiding the possibility of duplicate user names. If OUs are going to be used, it is recommended that it only go one or two levels deep. Most of the time, one OU is the preferred level of complexity within a hierarchical naming scheme.

Each level in the fully distinguished naming scheme except the Common Name and Country Code is represented as a certifier ID File. In other words, the O level is a certifier ID file, and for each OU, they too represent separate certifier ID files. These are some of the most important files in the Notes environment and must be password protected, stored securely, and accessed only by a handful of Notes administrators.

Traps

If an authorized user were to get hold of an Organization or Organizational Unit certifier ID file, he or she could create any new or existing Notes user or server and gain access to Notes applications and servers within the Notes infrastructure.

Let us look again at out examples of a fully distinguished Notes user and server.

```
CN=Scott Thomas/OU=Marketing/OU=Chicago/O=ACME/C=US

CN=Chicago-Notes01/O=ACME/C=US
```

In this example, Marketing and Chicago both represent Organizational Units. Each Organizational Unit is a certifier ID file. The Organization /ACME is also a certifier ID file.

Chronologically, the /ACME certifier was created first. This was done when the first Notes server of the company was created. It was saved on this Notes server as the file name **CERT.ID**. The Notes administrators at ACME then decided the first level organizational units for the Notes network will be geographically based. From the /ACME certifier, the OU certifier /CHICAGO was created by the Notes administrator from his Notes workstation. Other second level OU certifiers could also be created from the /ACME certifier to represent other geographic location.

From the /Chicago certifier OU, the Notes administrator of ACME created the /Marketing OU certifier. Any number of 3rd level OU certifiers could be created from the /Chicago OU certifier to represent different departments within the company at each location. Take note that if the Notes administrator of ACME could have created a /Marketing OU certifier from a /NewYork/ACME certifier, this would be a separate file from the /Marketing/Chicago/ACME certifier.

Finally, in our example, the user Scott Thomas was created from the /Marketing OU certifier. Any number of users or servers could be created from the /Marketing OU certifier ID file. As stated before, another Scott Thomas could exist as long as the ID file is created with different OU certifier.

As with our Notes server example above, it is also important to point out that Notes users necessarily don't have to be created off of the second level OU certifier. A server or user could have been created from the first level OU certifier or even from the O certifier itself. Such examples would be:

```
CN=Scott Thomas/OU=Chicago/O=ACME/C=US
```

or

```
CN=Scott Thomas/O=ACME/C=US
```

Tips

Although possible, the registering of Notes users in the high levels of a hierarchical naming scheme is not recommended. If a procedure is set by the Notes administration team to register users and servers at the same level of hierarchy, then it should be followed to avoid confusion.

As mentioned before, in order for a hierarchical Notes user ID and server ID to authenticate, they must share a certificate in common or obtain a cross-certificate. (Cross-certification is explained in

Chapter 16— *Advanced Notes Infrastructure Security,* and is covered within the System Administration II material.) In ACME's case, all server and user IDs share a common certificate ancestor of /ACME. Because of this, all ID files within the company are able to authenticate with one another.

Lotus Notes will automatically enter the current naming hierarchy for users and servers if it is left off. For example, if a user types in the following:

```
Scott Thomas
```

Lotus Notes will automatically expand the name to:

```
Scott Thomas/Marketing/ACME
```

Asterisks may also be used to refer to certain hierarchies in order to address mail and control security access to servers and applications. For example:

```
*/Marketing/ACME
```

This entry may be used to grant or deny access to all users with the /Marketing/ACME naming hierarchy.

Tips

For the System Administration I exam, the candidate should understand how to build a simple hierarchical naming structure and know the definition of each component (Common Name, Organization Unit, Organization, and Country Code). Also, it should be understood where and how hierarchical naming is used within Notes (Access Control Lists, duplicate user names, and administration process, to name a few).

Chapter 10 Sample Questions

Objective: Designing Notes Replication Architectures.

Corey, a Notes administrator at ACME Corporation, is trying to replicate a Notes application between two Notes servers. Replication, however, is not occurring between the databases. Which items should he check?

A. He should make sure the database titles are the same on each Notes server

B. He should make sure the Notes application is located within the same directory on each Notes server

C. He should make sure the Notes application has the same replica ID on each Notes server

D. He should make sure the ACL on each application on each server allows each server the proper access rights

E. He should make sure the filenames are the same on each Notes server

F. He should make sure the replication settings on each application are correct on each Notes server

Answer: C, D, and F

Replication will occur based upon access rights, replication settings, replication history, and the replica ID of a database. The location and filename of a Notes application does not matter as long as the application exists within the Notes server's data directory or a subdirectory relative to the data directory.

Objective: Designing Notes Replication Architectures.

Corey's Notes application exists on two Notes servers that are successfully replicating. Within a single document on one of the Notes servers, a user edits a field within the application. What will happen during the next scheduled replication?

      A. The entire document will be replicated to the other Notes server, thus synchronizing the databases

      B. The entire database (all documents) will replicate regardless of whether or not there are any modifications in order to keep the applications synchronized

      C. Only the modified field within the modified document will replicate with the other Notes server

      D. Nothing; replication only occurs when a new document is added to a Notes application

Answer: C
With version 4 Notes servers, field level replication is automatically incorporated. This means that only modified fields within a Notes application will replicate between Notes servers. However, if a version 3 Notes server is replicating with a version 4 Notes server, the entire document will replicate.

Objective: Designing Notes Replication Architectures.

Which of the following is true about replication on a Notes server?

      A. Replication must be started by an administrator

      B. The Replication server task starts automatically upon Notes server startup as configured within the ServerTasks line in the server's **NOTES.INI** file

C. The name of the server task within the NOTES.INI file is "replicator"

D. The name of the server task within the NOTES.INI file is "replica"

Answer: B and D
The replication server task is automatically configured to start up per the ServerTasks line in the server's **NOTES.INI** file. The name of the task is called "replica".

Objective: Designing Notes Replication Architectures.

What types of Notes applications should be replicated to remote Notes servers?

A. Databases that need real-time access by users

B. Databases that are needed by remote servers and administrators

C. Databases that are used by all Notes users at all locations

D. An application that is only accessed locally by a few users

Answer: B and C
Administrators should replicate those applications that are used company-wide by Notes users to reduce network traffic and increase performance for users located in other offices. Also, applications that are needed by other Notes servers (e.g. public Name and Address book) and those applications needed by other administrators should be replicated. Databases that are needed in real-time and databases that are not needed in remote locations should not be replicated to remote offices.

Objective: Designing Replication Structures.

Genet is designing a replication structure to support a large number of Notes servers (over 100) throughout the country. She wants a few central servers to distribute data, and administration to be handled in a central location. What type of replication structure should she consider?

A. Hub-and-Spoke

B. Hierarchical

C. Peer-to-Peer

D. Meshed

Answer: A

A hub-and-spoke replication environment would best serve her Notes infrastructure. A hub-and-spoke environment would offer centralized administration and would provide an efficient means of distributing data. A peer-to-peer design would be much too complex for the number of servers in Genet's environment.

Objective: Replication Direction.

Bill and Brad wish to have their Notes servers within their environment perform the equal load for replication on each Notes server. They wish to configure this using only a single connection document. What type of replication model should they configure their Notes servers for?

A. Pull-Pull

B. Pull-Push

C. Pull Only

D. Push Only

Answer: A

With a Pull-Pull configuration, each Notes server will run its replicator server task and pull any new changes to its Notes application(s). Within the Pull-Push model, only the calling server's replicator task will run.

Objective: Replication Direction.

Which is true of "pull" replication?

> A. The initiating server writes to its own applications
>
> B. The target server reads from the initiating server's applications
>
> C. The initiating server reads from the target server's applications
>
> D. The target server reads from the initiating server's applications

Answer: A and C

A pull replication from an initiating server reads from the target server and writes to its own Notes applications.

Objective: Multiple Replicators.

Wayne has a central hub server in a hub-and-spoke environment, however, it is not keeping up with replication with its spoke Notes servers. He has sufficient bandwidth and hardware to enable multiple replicators on the hub Notes server. How can he configure his hub Notes server to support multiple replicators?

> A. Create a server configuration document within the public Name and Address book using the REPLICATORS setting
>
> B. Edit the **NOTES.INI** file of the Notes server and add setting for multiple replicators manually
>
> C. Type **load replica** from the Notes server console
>
> D. Nothing. When Notes senses that replication is failing, it will automatically launch another replicator task

Answer: A, B, and C

Multiple replicators may be enabled by creating a server configuration document, modifying the server's **NOTES.INI** file, or manually loading another replicator task from the Notes server console.

Objective: Replication Conflicts.

Chad is working in Chicago and edits a document within the ACME tracking Notes application. He changes the status field. Jenny in Peoria edits the same document within the same Notes applications. She also edits the status field. The Notes application designer has merge conflicts enabled. What will be the result the next time replication occurs between the Chicago and Peoria Notes servers?

> A. Replication will occur as normal because merge conflicts is enabled so the result will be no replication conflicts
>
> B. Chad's document will win as he edited it first
>
> C. A replication conflict will occur
>
> D. Nothing. Replication conflicts no longer occur in version 4 of Lotus Notes

Answer: C

Even though the Notes application designer has enabled merge conflicts on the application, a replication conflict will be flagged. This is because the same field on the same document was edited. However, if different fields of the same document were edited, a replication conflict would *not* have been flagged, assuming the application designer has the merge conflicts option enabled.

Objective: Notes Named Networks.

Susie is designing her Notes network and her Notes servers will be running multiple protocols in multiple locations. She will have 3 Notes servers; NY-Notes running TCP/IP, Chicago-Notes01 running TCP/IP and SPX, and Chicago-Notes02 running the SPX protocol. What is the ideal Notes Network naming standard she should follow?

> A. She should set up three separate Notes named networks
>
> B. She should set up two separate Notes named networks

C. She should configure one Notes named network for all Notes servers

D. None of the above

Answer: A

The ideal configuration is to set up three Notes named networks. In Chicago, there will be two separate protocols, so each protocol will be in a separate Notes named network. The Chicago-Notes01 Notes server will be a member of both Notes named networks in Chicago. The NY-Notes server will be a member of the third Notes named network. Servers separated by a router should be placed in separate Notes named networks.

Tips

Remember, Notes servers within the same Notes named network will appear in server lists (File – Database – Open). Also, Notes servers within the same Notes named network do not need connection records between them to route mail—only a replication connection record.

Objective: Designing an E-Mail Architecture.

The Notes mail router uses which of the following to route Notes mail?

A. **MAIL.BOX**

B. Person Record in the public Name and Address book

C. Connection Record in the public Name and Address book

D. Hub-and-Spoke Record in the public Name and Address book

Answer: A, B and C

The Notes mail router on Notes servers uses the **MAIL.BOX** database (Mail router application), the person record, connection record, domain records, server records, group records, and server records within the public Name and Address book to route Notes mail. There is no such thing as a "hub-and-spoke record" within the public Name and Address book.

Objective: Designing an E-Mail Architecture.

Louise has just configured a replication architecture for her Notes network. Now she is focusing on the Notes mail architecture. What items should she consider?

    A. If she has a hub-and-spoke architecture for replication, she must use a peer-to-peer strategy for Notes mail routing

    B. If she has a peer-to-peer architecture for replication, she must use a hub-and-spoke strategy for Notes mail routing

    C. Normally for a Notes network, whichever replication architecture is designed for the environment, a Notes mail architecture also uses as well

    D. Nothing needs to be considered, Notes mail routing is automatic

Answer: C
Normally for Notes mail routing, the same architecture used for replication is also used for Notes mail routing. Answer D is somewhat correct in that for Notes servers within the same Notes named network, nothing needs to be configured as Notes mail routing is automatic for those servers on the same Notes named network.

Objective: Designing an E-Mail Architecture.

Pete, who exists on a Notes mail server in Chicago, is sending a Notes mail message to Dylnne, who exists on a Notes mail server in Pittsburgh. Mail connection records exist between Chicago and an intermediary Notes server in Indianapolis. Another mail connection record exists between Indianapolis and Pittsburgh. How does Notes determine how to deliver the message from Pete to Dylnne?

    A. The Chicago Notes server looks up Dylnne's Notes mail location and automatically delivers it to the Pittsburgh mail router (**MAIL.BOX**)

B. The Chicago Notes server determines Dylnne exists upon the Pittsburgh server and determines the least cost path to route the e-mail message to the Pittsburgh. The message then traverses to the Indianapolis router application. The Indianapolis router then transfers the message to the Pittsburgh mail router application. From there, the Pittsburgh router moves the message to Dylnne's mail application.

C. The Chicago Notes server determines Dylnne exists upon the Pittsburgh server and determines the least cost path to route the e-mail message to the Pittsburgh. The message then traverses to the Indianapolis router application. The Indianapolis Notes server then connects to the Pittsburgh Notes server and delivers the message directly to Dylnne's mail application.

D. The message cannot be delivered because a direct connection does not exist between the Chicago and Pittsburgh Notes server

Answer: B

In this scenario, the Chicago Notes server will determine the location of Dylnne's mail file based on her person record. The Chicago Notes server will then determine the least cost route to the Pittsburgh Notes server based upon connection records and deliver the message from its router mail application to the Indianapolis router mail application. The Indianapolis mail router application then will determine the route to the Pittsburgh Notes server, connect to the target server, and deliver the message to the Pittsburgh router mail application. From there, the Pittsburgh router mail application will look within Dylnne's person record in the public Name and Address book and deliver the message within her mail application.

Objective: Using the Notes Workstation Replicator Page.

Kristine wants to replicate all her local Notes applications with her home Notes server. She also wants to send her outgoing mail messages she has composed. What is the easiest way for her to accomplish this?

A. Highlight every local Notes application on her desktop and replicate them manually.

B. Enter the replicator page on her Notes desktop and check the box next to **Send Outgoing Mail** and check the boxes of all local Notes applications. Then she should click the **Start** button.

C. She should click the **Send and Receive Mail** button.

D. She should double click each entry on her replicator workspace page that she wishes to replicate.

Answer: B

The easiest way is to use the replicator page and check the boxes for all replica Notes applications and send outgoing mail. Then the user clicks the **Start** button. If a schedule is configured, the Start button does not need to be clicked as replication and mail routing will commence at the next scheduled replication.

Objective: Designing a Notes Hierarchical Naming Structure.

Debbie is the Notes administrator for the ACME corporation and is designing a hierarchical naming structure for her Notes environment. She has several hundred people located within her New York office. She also has several hundred people in her Los Angeles and Chicago branches. What is the ideal hierarchical naming structure within her environment?

A. Create an Organization certifier, /ACME, and place all users under this single hierarchy

B. Create three Organization certifiers, /New York, /Los Angeles, and /Chicago and place the users under the proper certifier

C. Create an Organization certifier, /ACME, and then create three Organization Unit certifiers, /New York, /Los Angeles, and /Chicago from the /ACME Organization certifier. Users then can be created from the appropriate Organizational Unit certifier

D. Notes does not support hierarchical naming

Sys. Admin. I

Answer: C
Although A and B are possible, they are not the best solutions. If all users are placed under the /ACME certifier, the possibility exists that duplicate user names will arise. Also, answer A does not give users the ability to quickly determine the location of the user from his or her name. Answer B is possible, but cross-certification within the Notes infrastructure would be necessary and is not a recommended approach.

Objective: Designing a Notes Hierarchical Naming Structure.

Lee is assigning access rights to a Notes application. Within the ACL of the database, he assigns the following entry with reader rights:

`*/Marketing/ACME`

Which of the following are true?

A. All users created with the `/ACME` Organization certifier will have reader access to the Notes application

B. All users created with the `/Marketing/ACME` Organization Unit certifier will have reader access to the Notes application

C. All users created with the `/Sales/ACME` Organizational Unit certifier will have reader access to the Notes application

D. Wildcards cannot be used with hierarchical names to assign database security rights

E. All users created with the `/Chicago/Marketing/ACME` Organization Unit certifier will have reader access to the Notes application

Answer: B and E
Wildcard entries can be used within the ACL of a Notes application. Rights are granted at the level of hierarchy and lower. For this reason, any user or server listed at the Marketing level or lower will be granted reader access to the Notes application.

Objective: Designing a Notes Hierarchical Naming Structure.

Two potential Notes users named Amy Peasley exist within the New York office and the Chicago office of the ACME Corporation. The ACME Notes administrator has created two separate Organizational Unit certifiers under an ACME organization certifier. What is the most efficient way the administrator should register the users to avoid duplicate names?

  A. Register both Amys with the `ACME` organization certifier.

  B. Register both Amys with the `ACME` organization certifier using the middle initials of each user.

  C. Register one Amy with the `Chicago` organizational unit certifier and the other with the `New York` organizational unit certifier.

Answer: C

Although answer B will work, it is not the most efficient. One of the advantages of hierarchical naming is the fact that it reduces the chances of duplicate names. In our scenario, each user with the name of Amy Peasley may exist within different branches of the hierarchical naming tree. Notes will treat each user (`Amy Peasley/Chicago/ACME` and `Amy Peasley/NY/ACME`) as different users.

Sys. Admin.

11

Notes Server Installation and Setup

Within this chapter, we will be reviewing those points necessary to understand when installing and configuring a Notes server. Certainly all points are not inclusive; only those points related to the System Administration I exam will be covered. You should not expect to gain all knowledge necessary to configure and install a Notes server from this chapter.

Specific topics include the installation of Notes server and client software, as well as a discussion on the three different Notes license types. Also discussed is configuring scheduled replication and electronic mail along with Notes' shared message store. In terms of connectivity, we will focus on topics related to configuring and tracing ports, including Notes passthru services. Finally, we will look at the very important topic of creating new certifier, user, and server ID files.

Installation of Notes Server Software

The installation of the first Notes server within a Notes infrastructure is usually a one time occurrence. From that point forward, only additional Notes servers will ever be added to your corporate Notes domain. One of the major points that differs from additional Notes server installations is the fact the certifier ID is created during the first Notes server installation. It is with this certifier ID file that additional Notes servers, certifiers, and users will be created. Certifier ID files are covered later in this chapter.

You may install the Notes server directly from the Notes CD or from a shared directory on a network drive where the Notes installation files have been copied. Multiple platforms are supported, including Windows NT, Novell, UNIX, OS/2, and Windows 95.

The default directories for a Notes server installation include:

`\NOTES`

From this directory, the following subdirectories are created by default:

```
\NOTES
        \DATA
                \MODEMS
                \WIN
                \DBCS
                \VDKHOME
```

This directory structure for Notes servers and clients is an important point. Questions on the System Administration I exam focus heavily on this structure.

If you are going to reinstall a Notes server, you should make a backup of the following files first:

- **NOTES.INI**

- **DESKTOP.DSK**

- **CERT.ID**

- **SERVER.ID**

- **USER.ID files**

- **NAMES.NSF**

- **LOG.NSF**

Tips

This list should be memorized, as questions relating to these specific files will be found on the examination.

Configure New Notes Server (Create First Server and Certifier ID Files)

All necessary Notes files should now be copied to the hard drive of the Notes server. Follow these steps to install a Notes server:

1. Start the Notes user interface. This is the Notes client workstation on the Notes server machine itself.

2. The Notes server setup screen (Figure 11-1) will appear. Click on the **The first Lotus Notes server in your organization** option and then click **OK**.

Tips

If this is an additional Notes server within your organization, then click **An additional Lotus Notes server in your organization.** *In this case, some of the following procedures will be slightly different. Also, the Notes server ID for an additional Notes server must be created before setting up the Notes server.*

Figure 11-1
Lotus Notes Server
Setup Screen

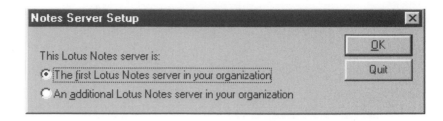

3.   The First Server Setup screen (Figure 11-2) appears:

Figure 11-2
Lotus Notes First
Server Setup Screen

The following fields should be configured:

●   **Server Name:**   Enter the name of the Notes server.

●   **Organization name:**   Enter the name of the organization. This will be the name of the top-level hierarchy in a fully distinguished name. The company's Organizational level certifier will be created from this name.

●   **Administrator's last name:**   Enter the last name of the Notes administrator.

- **First name:** Enter the first name of the Notes administrator.

- **MI:** If middle initials are going to be used, enter the middle initial of the Notes administrator.

- **Administration password:** Enter the password for the Notes administrator's user ID file and certifier ID file. This Notes administrator's ID file will be created from the entries in the **last name**, **first name**, and **MI** fields.

- **Network type:** Enter the network protocol that will be used on this Notes server. Additional protocols may be added once the server is installed.

- **Serial port:** Enter the serial port, if any, that this Notes server will be using. Additional serial ports may be installed once the server is installed.

- **Modem type:** Enter the modem type attached to the serial port.

4. Once the above fields are set, click the **Advanced Options** button. The screen shown in Figure 11-3 appears:

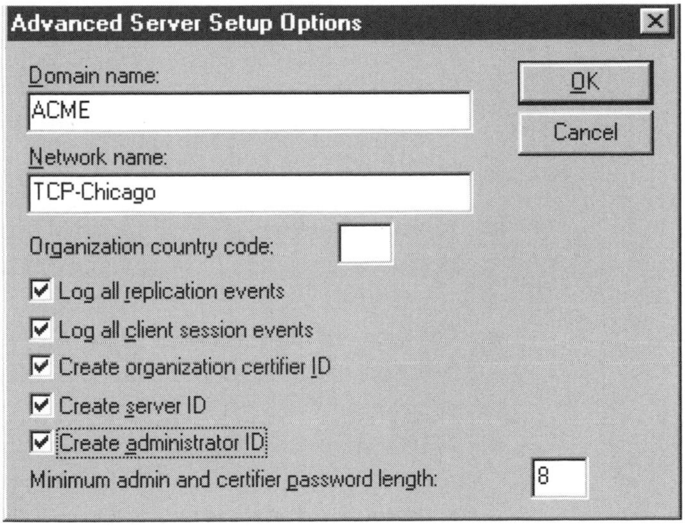

Figure 11-3
Lotus Notes Advanced
Server Setup Options

The following fields should be configured:

- **Domain name:** Enter the domain of the Notes server. This is usually the company's name and normally matches the name of the organization certifier.

- **Network name:** This is the name of the Notes named network the Notes server will belong to.

- **Organization country code:** This is an optional field that represents the country code for a hierarchically named server. Most companies do not use this field.

- **Log all replication events:** This check box will enable all replication events to be logged to the Notes log on the Notes server. This option may be turned on or off later, if desired, once the server has been configured. We recommend that you enable this option to assist in any troubleshooting you may need to perform.

- **Log all client sessions events:** This check box will enable all Notes client sessions to be logged to the Notes log on the Notes server. This option may be turned on or off later, if desired, once the server has been configured. You should enable this option to assist in any troubleshooting you may need to perform.

- **Create organization certifier ID:** Click this box so that the company's organizational certifier ID file is created. This box should be checked.

- **Create server ID:** Click this box so that the Notes server's ID file is created. This box should be checked.

- **Create administrator ID:** Click this box so that the Notes administrator's ID file is created. This box should be checked.

- **Minimum admin and certifier password length:** Enter the minimum number of characters for the password length of the Notes administrator's ID file and certifier ID file.

Sys. Admin. I

5. Once all the above fields are configured, click **OK**. The Notes server (**SERVER.ID**), certifier (**CERT.ID**), and Notes administrator's (**USER.ID**) ID files will be created and will be registered in the public Name and Address Book.

6. You will be prompted with the time zone screen. Select the proper time zone and Daylight Savings time option and click **OK**.

The first Notes server is now configured and ready to be run. When this first Notes server first starts, the following databases are created:

- **LOG.NSF** (Notes Server Log)

- **MAIL.BOX** (Notes router box)

Tips

For the examination, the exact settings do not need to be known for setting up a Notes server; however, the overall process should be understood.

Installation of Notes Client Software

Like a Notes server installation, a Notes client installation may be performed directly from the Notes CD or from a shared network directory.

Before installing Notes on a workstation, the user should first be created from the Notes administrator's workstation on the Notes user's home Notes server. The new ID file may be stored within the public Name and Address book or on a floppy or shared network drive.

There are now three different types of Notes client licenses. Following is a description of each type.

Lotus Notes License

This is the full-featured Notes license type. It enables users to perform all of the Notes functionality including server and user administration, Notes application development, and all end-user functions including Notes application and mail usage.

Lotus Notes Desktop License

The Lotus Notes Desktop license gives users the same functionality as the Lotus Notes license, minus the administration tools and Notes database application development functionality. Users are able to access and use all Notes applications, including custom Notes applications. The license can easily be upgraded to the full-featured Notes license should the need arise.

Lotus Notes Mail License

The Notes mail client license enables users to use Notes e-mail, which also includes all the functionality of group scheduling and calendaring. Users with this license type are unable to access any custom Notes applications or perform any Notes administration tasks. Like the Notes desktop license, users can be easily upgraded to the desktop or full-featured Lotus Notes license if the need arises. A Lotus Mail license is permitted to access Notes databases created from the following Notes templates:

- **ALOG4.NTF**
- **CATALOG.NTF**
- **DBLIB4.NTF**
- **MAILBOX.NTF**
- **PERNAMES.NTF**
- **PUBNAMES.NTF**
- **WEB.NTF**
- **DISCUSS4.NTF**

- **DOCLIB4.NTF**

- **DOCLIBM4.NTF**

- **JOURNAL.NTF**

Tips

For the examination, pay attention to what each client type may access—especially what the Notes Mail license is permitted to access.

With version 4 of Lotus Notes, the **DESKTOP.DSK** can now be compacted from the Workspace Properties page. The **CACHE.DSK** file stores users' unread marks for server Notes applications.

Lotus Notes Client Location Documents

Location documents are new for Notes 4 users. These documents may be configured within each Notes user's personal name and address book. Locations may be set to configure the user's ports based upon location. For instance, a travel location document may be established where only the COM port is active. Another location document may be created where only the network port is active. The following location documents are created automatically upon a Notes workstation installation:

- HOME (Modem)

- INTERNET

- ISLAND (Disconnected)

- OFFICE (Network)

- TRAVEL (Modem)

Notes

A port will not be available within a location document unless the port is activated within the user's preferences (File – User Preferences – Ports).

Sys. Admin. I

Configuring Shared Mail

With version 4, Notes administrators may configure Notes servers to utilize a shared Notes database to store users' mail. Simply speaking, Notes can be configured to store electronic mail messages in a single Notes database for messages intended for multiple recipients.

The shared Notes mail database is sometimes called the **single copy object store** (SCOS) and is the repository Notes database where all users access a multiple-recipient mail message. Users may still perform the same functionality as if the Notes mail message existed within their own Notes mail database. The Notes mail server running shared mail transparently to all shared mail users performs these actions. The shared mail server keeps track of all shared mail messages and automatically deletes unneeded shared mail messages once all users have marked that message for deletion.

Tips

The shared mail topic is the single most important topic on the System Administration I exam. It is very important that you understand the concept of shared mail and how it works in all scenarios. This includes all three settings (0, 1, and 2) as well as how shared mail works for remote Notes users.

A Notes mail message can be divided into two parts; the summary and non-summary data. The summary data includes all header information including the **TO**, **CC**, **BCC**, **SUBJECT**, and **FROM** fields of an e-mail message. The non-summary data is the body of the text, including all file attachments.

If shared mail is enabled on a Notes server, the mail router splits the message, only delivering the summary data to recipients. All non-summary data is delivered to the shared Notes mail application. Then when a Notes user opens a Notes mail message when connected to the network, the message is displayed from the shared application database transparently to the user. If the user decides to delete a message that is being shared, only the summary information is deleted from the user's personal Notes mail database. For remote users that are replicating their mail databases, all data (including summary and non-summary information) is replicated to their remote machines.

In terms of security, the shared Notes mail database is encrypted so that only the server ID file that created the shared application may access it. The ACL of the database is set so that only the server ID can access the application as a server, meaning that only the server process may access the file; the user interface on the server machine will not be allowed access. The shared application does not contain any views and none may be added. The shared mail application cannot be added to any user's desktop.

Tips

If you allow users to encrypt incoming and outgoing mail that is bound for a shared Notes application database, the message will not be stored within the shared application. Instead, it is stored in each user's personal mail files. Only unencrypted mail messages can be stored within a shared mail database.

When shared mail is installed on a Notes mail server, two Notes databases are created. The first is called **MAILOBJ.NSF** which is a database link that points to the actual shared Notes mail application. This is the default name used by the shared mail process and will exist within the data directory of the shared mail Notes server. It is created automatically once shared mail is enabled. The second Notes application that is created is the actual shared Notes mail database. The Notes mail server will also create this once the Notes administrator enables shared mail.

To install shared mail on a Notes mail server, type the following command from the Notes server console:

```
tell router use shared mail database
```

where *shared mail database* is the name of the Notes database that will store users' mail messages. A descriptive name such as **USERMAIL.NSF** is recommended. Notes will automatically create the database link **MAILOBJ.NSF** and the shared Notes mail application **USERMAIL.NSF**.

Sys. Admin. I

Tips

*For the examination, Lotus uses **MAILOBJ.NSF** for the database link name and **MAILOBJ1.NSF** (**USERMAIL.NSF** in our illustration) for the actual database store. These names can be confusing on the examination, so it is important to keep them straight.*

There are two different ways to configure shared mail on a Notes server. The first method of shared mail uses the **NOTES.INI** setting of **Shared_Mail=1.** This type of shared mail only routes mail to the shared Notes mail application if the message is destined for two or more recipients. Initially, the Notes mail router places the message within the receiver's personal mail file. If the message is intended for two or more people, the message is written to the shared Notes mail database (**USERMAIL.NSF**), and the message for the first recipient is removed from his or her mail file in favor of the shared Notes mail store. If a Notes mail message is only sent to one person, the shared message store is not used. Figures 11-4 and 11-5 depict these scenarios:

Figure 11-4
Shared_Mail=1,
One Receiver

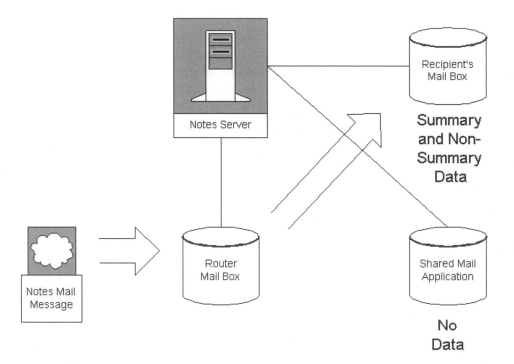

Figure 11-5
Shared_Mail=1,
Multiple Recipients

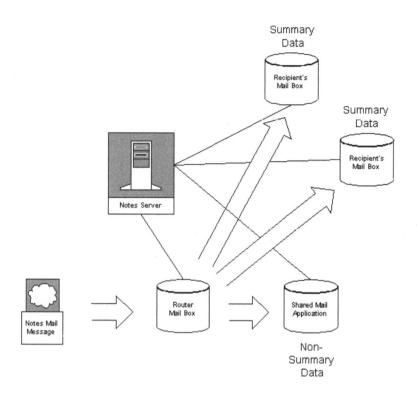

The second method to configure shared mail uses the **NOTES.INI** setting of **Shared_Mail=2**. This is the default setting when shared mail is first installed on a Notes mail server. This type of configuration will use the shared mail message store regardless of the number of intended recipients. Even if the recipient is not on the mail server, the message is written to the message store. The message is then removed once the mail router determines a recipient is not on the mail server. Figure 11-5 shows the method the Notes mail router will use to deliver all mail to users, even if there is only one recipient.

Tips

For Notes servers that will be housing shared Notes mail as well as being involved in multiple mail transfers to other Notes mail servers, this is not the ideal setting. The setting Shared_Mail=1 would be more efficient.

After all users delete the summary information for a mail message in their personal mail databases, the Notes server process "Object

Collect" removes the message from the shared Notes mail database application. This task runs every morning at 2 AM. The process can also be run manually from the Notes server console by typing the following line:

```
load Object Collect USERMAIL.NSF
```

If you wish to link a mail file that has messages that are not included in the shared mail Notes database, type the following line:

```
load object link STHOMAS.NSF USERMAIL.NSF
```

This will link Scott Thomas' mail file to the shared mail message store and move all non-summary data to this database.

If you wish to remove a user's mail from the shared message store back into the user's personal mail file, type the following command from the Notes server console:

```
load object unlink STHOMAS.NSF
```

This will unlink the user's mail file and move all non-summary data back into the user's mail file.

Traps

If you specify the shared Notes mail application file name instead of the user's name, all user mail files will unlink.

Statistics concerning shared mail can be gathered by typing the following line from the Notes server console:

```
show stat Object
```

To disable shared mail, set the **NOTES.INI** variable **Shared_Mail** equal to 0.

The following points concerning when the message store is not used, as well as remote user topics with the message store, are very important points on the System Administration I exam.

Tips

The main reason for using shared mail is to save significant disk space on the Notes server. However, under the following situations, duplicate copies of a mail message will exist:

● A user edits a mail message

● A user saves a mail message

● A user encrypts incoming mail

● A user makes a replica copy of a mail file

Under the above circumstances, the shared message store will not be used for the user performing any of these actions (summary and non-summary data will be stored within the user's mail file).

For mobile users, replica copies of their mail files will have summary and non-summary data both stored upon their local machine's mail file (object store is inaccessible from the Notes server while mobile). Mobile users may opt not to save sent mail, and rather cc: themselves to maximize disk space. This is due to the fact the mail router is responsible for splitting a mail message into summary and non-summary data. If a user simply saves a mail message, the mail router will never touch the mail message. If a user cc:'s himself, the message will be split by the mail router and be delivered to the message store.

Sys. Admin. I

Again, we are stressing the importance of the points discussed in the above section for shared mail. Although rarely used in corporate environments, the topic of shared mail is a major focus of the System Administration I examination.

Tips

Configuring Replication and E-Mail

Continuing with our discussion on replication and electronic mail topologies from Chapter 10, we will now look at methods of configuring and scheduling replication and electronic messaging. In order to configure replication, a Notes administrator must configure connection records in the public Name and Address book. Settings such as times to replicate, frequency of replication, and priorities of databases are set in the records (high, medium, low). Creating a connection record within the public Name and Address book is explained in Chapter 13—*The Name and Address Book Structure.*

Tips

Unlike mail connection records, replication connection records are only needed for one Notes server. The initiating Notes server will pull and push all documents, as replication is a two way process (assuming default replication configurations). Once a replication connection record is created on a Notes server, you will not have to create another connection record for the target Notes server.

A Notes administrator or Notes database manager may specify three possible priority settings for a Notes database. These settings are HIGH, MEDIUM, and LOW. Connection records for replication can be set to replicate all types or a subset of each type of application. In other words, a connection record that replicates every hour could be created to only replicate HIGH priority databases with a target Notes server. Still another connection record with the same target Notes server could be created to only replicate MEDIUM and LOW databases once or twice a day.

Within a Notes connection record, this setting is established with the **Replicate databases of:** field of the connection document as shown in Figure 11-6:

Figure 11-6

Replication Fields Within
a Connection Record

Routing and Replication	
Tasks:	⌐Replication⌐▼
Replicate databases of:	⌐Low & Medium & High⌐▼ priority
Replication Type:	⌐Pull Push⌐▼
Files/Directories to Replicate:	⌐⌐ (all if none specified)
Replication Time Limit:	⌐⌐ minutes

On a Notes database, the priority can be set by entering the replication settings of the Notes database as shown in Figure 11-7:

Figure 11-7

Notes Database
Priority Setting

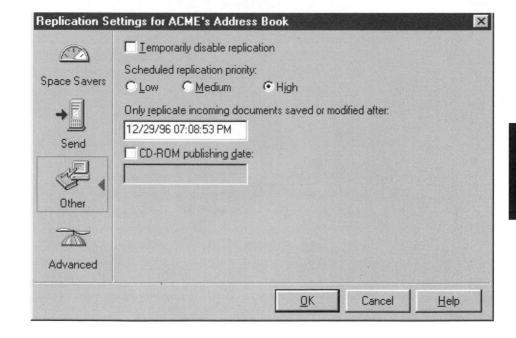

This is accomplished as follows:

1. Highlight the Notes database icon and click **File – Database –
   Properties**.

2. Click the **Replication Settings** button.

3. Click the **Other** icon.

4. The replication priority for the Notes application can be set.

Scheduling

Lotus Notes enables you to schedule replication at a specific time(s) each day or to specify a range of times with a repeat interval. Scheduling times is handled within the **Scheduled Connection** section of the Notes connection record within the public Name and Address book. This section is shown in Figure 11-8:

Figure 11-8

Notes Connection Record Replication Schedule

Scheduled Connection	
Schedule:	⌐ENABLED⌐▼
Call at times:	⌐08:00 AM - 10:00 PM⌐ each day
Repeat interval of:	⌐60⌐ minutes
Days of week:	⌐Sun, Mon, Tue, Wed, Thu, Fri, Sat⌐▼

There are four different types of schedules that may be established: one specific time, a list of times, time range with a repeat interval, and time range without a repeat interval.

- **One specific time:** To replicate with a target server at one specific time each day, enter that time within the **Call at times** field. Do not populate the **Repeat interval of** field with a value. The initiating Notes server will then call once each day at this time. If there is a failure, the initiating Notes server will retry for one hour. If a connection still is not established after this hour, replication will not be retried until the next day.

This type of connection is usually used to replicate Notes applications of LOW priority.

- **A list of times:** This type of connection will replicate with the target Notes server at the times entered within the **Call at times** field of the Notes connection document. For example, to replicate at 8:00 am, 12:00 pm, and 4:00 pm each day, you would enter those three separate times within the **Call at times** field. No value should be entered within the **Repeat interval of** field. If the connection fails, the target Notes server will continue to try to connect for up to one hour. If after an hour the connection still has not been established, replication will not commence until the next time scheduled within the **Call at times** field.

This type of schedule is usually used to replicate Notes applications of MEDIUM and/or LOW priority.

- **Time range with a repeat interval:** With this type of schedule, the initiating Notes server will replicate with the target Notes server for a specified time range repeating every certain number of minutes. For example, you may wish to have your Notes server replicate with a target Notes server from 8:00 am to 10:00 pm every two hours. For this type of configuration you should enter the times, **8:00 am–10:00 pm** within the **Call at times** field and **120** minutes within the **Repeat interval of** field.

If the first replication attempt is unsuccessful, the initiating Notes server will continue attempting until the end of the specified time range or at the next time of repetition.

This type of connection record is usually used to replicate databases of HIGH priority.

- **Time range without a repeat interval:** With this type of schedule, the initiating Notes server will replicate with the target Notes server once, commencing at the beginning of the specified time range. If the scheduled replication is successful, replication will not occur until the next day. However, if the attempt is unsuccessful, the initiating Notes server will retry continuously throughout the time range. For this type of configuration you should enter the schedule within the **Call at times** field and leave the **Repeat interval of** field blank.

If the first replication attempt is unsuccessful, the initiating Notes server will continue attempting until the end of the specified time range; however, the time between each call attempt will increase. This type of connection record is usually used to replicate databases of LOW or MEDIUM priority.

Tips

If mail routing is going to be enabled within the connection record as well as replication, issues surrounding routing mail should be considered. It may be necessary to create a separate connection record for e-mail and another connection record for replication to the target Notes server, depending on your organization. It should also be noted that e-mail that is destined for the target server is delivered during the replication cycle, regardless of the mail settings within the connection record.

The **Days of the week** field can also be set to schedule replication only during certain days of the week. It may be valuable to create two connection records for replication to a target Notes server, where one record is for Monday–Friday and the other connection record is for Saturday and Sunday.

When establishing connection records within a hub-and-spoke replication architecture, you may wish to stagger connection records from the hub to spoke servers with a call range of times without a repeat interval. This will make it so that a hub Notes server does not try to replicate with multiple spoke servers at the same time (assuming only one replicator is enabled on the hub server). Also, using this staggered approach reduces the likelihood a Notes server will be skipped as the call range is increased. For example, the hub Notes server may be set to replicate with Notes spoke server A at 8:00 AM–10:00 AM, spoke B at 9:00 AM–11:00 AM, and spoke C at 10:00 AM–12:00 pm. With this type of scheduling, each Notes server is guaranteed at least an hour of replication time. In the event of failure, there will also be a retry period of two hours to each spoke Notes server.

Tips

If your company is spread throughout different time zones, you should replicate with spoke Notes servers within a later time zone first. This will ensure that people see more timely data before people residing in earlier time zones. As an example, in the United States, you would replicate with servers in the Eastern Time zone before those in the Pacific Time zone.

Tips

For the examination, scheduling and priority types should be understood. In terms of scheduling, each type of scheduling (repeat intervals, a single call, and a range of calls) should be studied.

Port Settings

Within the Port screen of User Preferences, several options are available to the Notes user and administrator. Ports need to be configured on both the Notes server and workstation. The Notes server must be down in order to add ports. Also, each active port needs to be configured within the Notes server document for that particular Notes server (see Chapter 13, within the "Server Record" section for the exact location).

To reference the Port User Preferences screen, click **File – Tools – User Preferences – Ports**

The screen shown in Figure 11-9 appears:

Figure 11-9

User Preferences
for Notes Ports

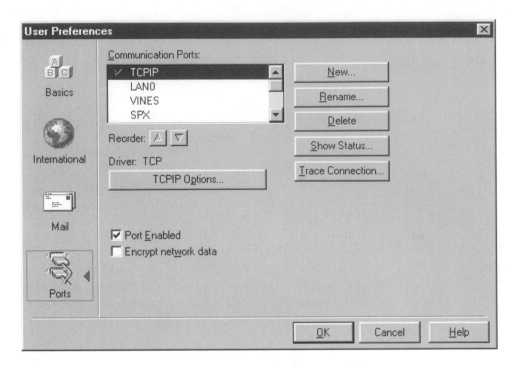

- **Port Reorder:** This button will reorder the port drivers listed within the ports communication box. To reorder the ports on a Notes server or client, highlight the first desired protocol and then click the Up Arrow of the reorder port button, as shown in Figure 11-9. Continue to click the Up arrow until the desired protocol appears in the order you wish Notes servers and clients to connect. In other words, a Notes server with a listing of TCPIP then SPX (assuming both ports are enabled) will connect with other Notes servers first using TCPIP and then SPX, if TCP/IP fails.

This procedure will also reorder the port listing order in the **NOTES.INI** file of the machine. In prior releases of Lotus Notes, the port order needed to be configured through the **NOTES.INI** file or directly on the Notes server console by using the **SET CONFIG** command.

This setting is only valid on machines where more than one port driver is enabled for use.

● **New Port:** The new port will enable a user to add a new port to the Notes server or client. The screen shown in Figure 11-10 appears after the **New** button is clicked:

Figure 11-10
New Notes
Port Configuration

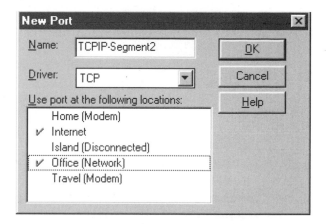

The user then should fill in the name of the port. This can be any name the user wishes. It should be descriptive, with naming associating to the driver that will be used. In other words, the name of the port should not be "SPX-Ring5" if the port will be using the TCP/IP driver.

In the driver box, select the driver for Notes to use.

In the **Use Port at the following locations** box, select the locations you wish to have use this port driver. They will appear within the location forms of the name and address book of that machine.

It should be noted that for the COM ports, the number at the end of the name should directly coincide with the actual COM port used. For example, PORT NAME COM1 should use COM1 of the operating system.

For new network ports on Notes servers, the port should also be added to the server record of the Notes server (for Notes named networks). COM ports do not need to be added to the server record.

Sys. Admin. 1

● **Rename Port:** As stated earlier in the "New Port" section, the name of a port is for descriptive purposes only. The driver selected for the port is the factor that decides what protocol Lotus Notes will use.

By clicking the **Rename** button of the Port User Preferences screen, the user can rename the port. Again, it does not affect what type of protocol Notes will use.

● **Delete Port:** The delete port does simply what its name says: it removes the port from the Notes server or client.

Tips

For Notes servers, once a port is deleted, the corresponding port should be removed from any server and connection records of the public Name and Address book for that particular server. Also, for the first Notes server that is installed, you will need to add the port to the server record of the public Name and Address book within the port name field.

● **Show Status:** The **Show Status** button shows the status of the highlighted, active port. Network statistics for the port driver will be provided as shown in Figure 11-11, a sample screen of TCP/IP:

Figure 11-11
Notes Port Status

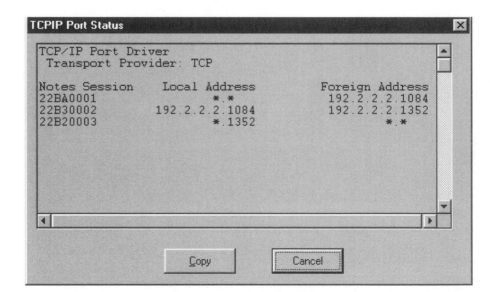

Note that for TCP/IP, the local and foreign TCP/IP addresses are shown with the port number of the application appended. As mentioned before, Notes uses TCP/IP port number 1352, unless otherwise configured within the **SERVICES** file of the operating system.

Tips

For the examination, the candidate should understand how to set up and configure a port within Notes. Each configuration detail should also be understood (port reorder and rename port, to name a few).

Tracing Connections

Notes users and administrators can trace network connections to ensure they are working properly. This is done by clicking: **File – Tools – User Preferences – Ports**. Then click **Trace Connection** while highlighting the protocol you wish to trace.

The screen shown in Figure 11-12 appears:

Figure 11-12
Tracing Port
Connections

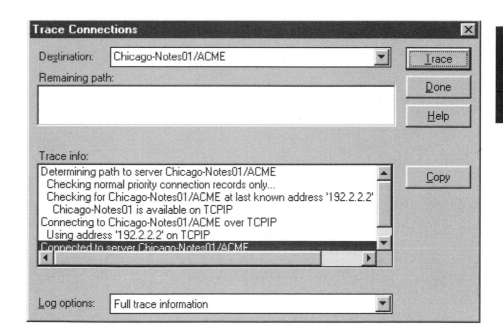

There are 5 log options to choose from:

- **Nothing:** No information will be logged to the user screen, even if there are errors.

- **Errors Only:** Once **Trace** is clicked, only error messages that the Notes server or client encounters will be reported to the user.

- **Summary progress information:** This setting will not only report errors like the Errors Only setting, but will also report to the user all major comments in connecting to the target Notes server.

- **Detailed progress information:** This is the default setting for tracing a connection. It will report all information that the summary progress information setting will report, with additional information concerning the connection process.

- **Full trace information:** This setting will return very detailed information concerning the entire process of connecting to the target Notes server.

Tracing a connection is very helpful in determining problematic connections. All ports that are enabled on the server or client will be traced and returned until a successful connection is accomplished. If a failure occurs, this will also be reported to the user. Network traces can be done from a Notes workstation to any Notes server where there is physical network connectivity or a modem connection. Notes network traces are *not* limited to servers within a Notes named network or Notes domain.

Configuring Notes Passthru

New with version 4.0 of Lotus Notes is a feature called *Notes passthru*. This feature enables Notes users to dial into a Notes server and not only access that Notes server, but also traverse other network and modem ports to access other Notes servers, thus providing

Sys. Admin. I

a central dial-in point to the entire Notes infrastructure (assuming proper security rights are granted). Only Notes resources are accessible using this procedure; other NT and Novell file and print services will not be accessible.

Passthru may also be used to provide connectivity between two Notes machines where no common protocol is available. The passthru server then acts as a protocol gateway between the source and destination server. In other words, if Server A is running SPX, Server B is running SPX and TCP/IP, and Server C is running TCP/IP, Server A and C may communicate via Server B using passthru.

In order for passthru to work for dial-in purposes, the Notes administrator must install analog or digital modems on a Notes server. Also, the administrator must configure the proper fields on the passthru Notes server's—and any destination Notes server's—server document within the public Name and Address book to allow client passthru access. These fields include:

- **Access this server through Passthru:** This field allows users, groups, and servers to access this server as a passthru destination. If this field is left blank, then *no* users or servers can access this Notes server as a passthru destination.

- **Passthru route through:** This field should be populated with users, servers, or groups you wish to access the Notes server for passthru to another Notes server destination. If this field is left blank, then *no* user or server will be able to use this Notes server as a passthru server.

- **Passthru cause calling:** This field designates which servers, groups, or users may force the Notes server to call or contact another server and act as an intermediary (passthru) contact to another Notes server. If this field is left blank, then *no* destinations may be called.

- **Passthru destinations allowed:** This field lists all destination Notes servers that are allowed. If this field is left blank, then *all* Notes servers are possible destinations via passthru.

Sys. Admin. I

Traps

By default, NO ACCESS is allowed to passthru Notes servers and to connect to destination servers via passthru Notes servers. The restrictions must be configured within the server documents of the respective Notes servers.

Tips

It is extremely important to understand the default settings for these four fields for the examination.

On the client machine, connection record(s) needs to be configured in order to access a Notes server through a passthru Notes server.

The following are advantages for using Notes passthru:

● A passthru Notes server allows a client the ability to only have to dial into a single Notes server and then access other Notes servers via the passthru Notes server.

● A passthru Notes server enables other Notes servers and clients to connect to it and access other Notes servers where a protocol in common is not present between the source and destination Notes machines. The passthru Notes server acts as a "stepping stone."

● A passthru Notes server can ease the load upon a network modem pool, as modems may be added to a dedicated passthru Notes server.

It should be noted that there are limitations to passthru:

● The hard coded limit is 10 hop counts for passthru. The practical limit is four and typically only one or two hops are ever used.

● A version 3 Notes server cannot act as a passthru Notes server but can be the ultimate destination Notes server.

Remote LAN Service

Microsoft's Remote Access Server provides remote node connectivity for users through standard analog lines, ISDN, x.25, and SNA connections. Shiva products also provide this type connectivity. When an RAS client dials in and establishes a PPP connection, the remote operating system (Windows NT or Windows 95) becomes a node on that network segment, as if it were connected on the LAN in the office. Throughput obviously will be limited to the speed of the modem; however, all resources, including file and print (Novell and NT file servers) as well as Notes Servers, are accessible. Lotus Notes version 4.0 and higher supports RAS connections directly so that Notes can automatically launch a RAS connection from Windows 95 or Windows NT.

Nothing needs to be done on the Notes server to support this functionality. However, on the network where the Notes server exists, a Windows NT RAS server or Shiva remote dial-in product must be installed. The RAS server will handle all connectivity issues with the remote client, and enable the remote PC to become another node on the network in order to connect to the target Notes server with the proper network protocol.

Lotus Notes currently supports the use of either Microsoft's LAN service (RAS) or AppleTalk Remote Access (ARA) on the machine doing the calling. The Microsoft RAS server and client provide connectivity through a PPP (Point to Point Protocol) connection. Within a PPP connection, the protocols the Notes servers are running (TCP/IP, SPX, etc.) are encapsulated within the PPP protocol. The RAS service can use either a standard analog modem or an ISDN device. These devices are configured within the Windows NT or Windows 95 RAS service. As far as the Notes servers are concerned, they are communicating via the network protocol, such as TCP/IP, as if the two machines were on the same LAN or WAN.

Converting User's E-Mail Files

The **Convert** server utility can be used to upgrade Notes mail databases from Notes version 3 to version 4 format. The utility will run

Sys. Admin. I

on every document in the user's Notes mail database application. Read and unread marks will be unaffected, and the file format of the database will not be changed. To run the utility, type the following command on the Notes server command prompt:

```
load convert database name
```

where *database name* is the filename of the user's Notes mail database application. You may use wildcards to convert more than one user's mail file, such as:

```
load convert mail\*.nsf
```

Read and unread marks are unaffected and the database file format is unchanged.

Database Libraries

A *database library* is a collection of databases that are associated with a division within a company. The Notes databases are configured so that members within the division or group can access the databases within the library. Once a database library is created on a Notes server, you may publish a database within the library. To do so, follow these steps:

1. Highlight the Notes application and click **File – Database – Publish.**

2. Select the library to add the application from the library list.

3. Type in an abstract and description and save the document.

It should be noted that multiple libraries can exist on a single Notes server. A library may be created per each group or division within your company to house the applications that will be used within that group. For example, one library Notes database can exist for the Marketing group and another for the Sales group. Each library will contain those applications used by each group.

A user can access a library and choose to browse a database, add the icon to the Notes workspace, and/or open the database.

Registering New Notes Users, Certifiers, and Servers

Notes ID files are one of the most important items within a Notes infrastructure. Without these files, a Notes user or server cannot operate. There are three types of Notes ID files: server, user, and certifier ID files. A certifier ID file is used to create new Notes user and server ID files. A certifier ID file is also used to certify existing server, user, or certifier files of other organizations to allow authentication to your Notes environment. The following sections explain the procedures of how to create new ID files.

A Notes ID file has the following security features:

- **Anti-Spoofing:** The login panel for Notes uses graphical elements displayed in random order each time a key is pressed. This makes it difficult for a hacker to write a background program to appear to a user as a legitimate login screen.

- **Retry-Delay:** If a password is incorrectly entered, Notes pauses before another entry is allowed. Each time a mistake is made, the pause increases in time.

- **Multiple Passwords:** You are now able to assign multiple passwords to ID files in version 4 of Lotus Notes. This is especially helpful for certifier ID files, where it can be implemented so that at least 2 people must enter a separate password for the ID file in order to create a new user, server, or organizational unit certifier. Subsets may also be set in that only a specific number of the total passwords assigned are needed to access the ID file. For example, you could set the ACME certifier to require three separate passwords for the ID file, but only two of the three passwords are needed to access the ID file. In this manner, no one person is assigned complete authority of an ID file, especially in the case of certifier ID files.

To assign multiple passwords to a user, server, or certifier ID file, follow these procedures:

1. Click **File – Tools – Server Administration**.

2. Click the **Certifiers** icon and click **Edit Multiple Passwords**.

3. Select the ID file to assign the passwords to. The screen shown in Figure 11-13 appears:

Figure 11-13
Multiple Passwords
Dialog Box

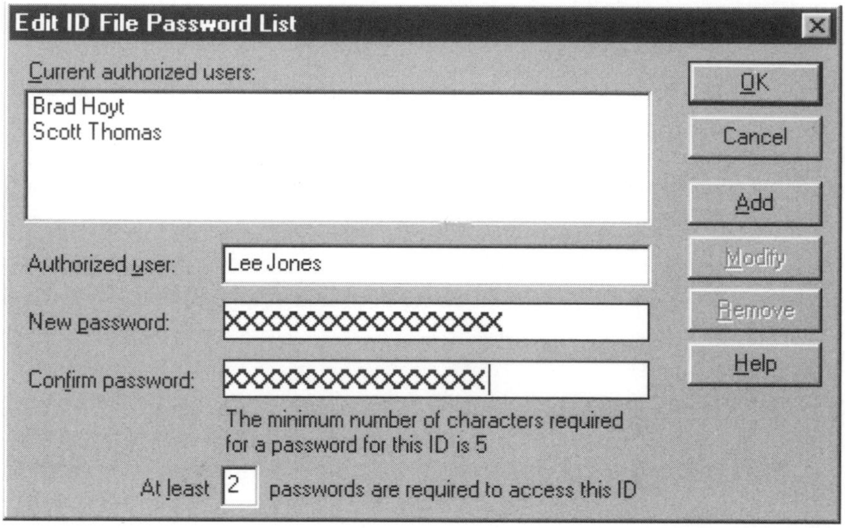

4. Within the **Authorized user** field, enter one of the user names.

5. Enter the password for that user in the **New password** field.

6. Retype the password in the **Confirm password** field.

7. Click **Add**.

8. Other users need to repeat steps 4–7.

9. Enter the number of passwords required to access this ID file.

Creating User ID Files

A Notes user ID file consists of six components, including:

- **User Name:** This is the name of the Notes user.

- **Notes License Number:** This is the license number assuring the ID is a legitimate North American or International ID file. It cannot be changed once created.

- **Public and Private Keys:** These keys are used for various security measures, such as authenticating with a Notes server. During authentication, a challenge-response sequence is initiated between the Notes client and Notes server. Every Notes user's public key within a single domain is also stored within the public Name and Address book. It is with this public key that a challenge is composed that only the User ID file with the appropriate private key may unlock. If not completed properly, authentication with the Notes server is not completed. This public-private key authentication is based upon public key cryptography licensed from RSA.

- **Encryption Keys:** If any Notes administrator or Notes developer creates an encryption key to encrypt certain fields within a Notes application, the encryption keys are stored within the user's ID file.

- **Certificate(s):** An ID file must contain at least one certificate. For hierarchical user ID files, an ID file may only contain one hierarchical certificate. Cross-certification is needed to access other hierarchical organizations. However, an ID file may contain several flat certificates.

- **Password:** The password for a user ID is stored within the ID file as well. It is not stored on the Notes server.

The Notes user ID file for the Notes administrator is automatically created when the first Notes server within your company is set up. In order to set up additional users on Notes, you must first register those new Notes users. The person registering new users must have at least AUTHOR access with the UserCreator role assigned in the public Name and Address book.

Sys. Admin. I

Registering a new person will create a person document within the public Name and Address book, create the user's ID file, and create the user's mail file (if so desired). To register new Notes client users, follow these steps:

1. From the Notes administrator's Notes user workstation, click **File – Tools – Server Administration**.

2. Click the **People** icon, and choose **Register Person**. Click **Yes** to indicate you have purchased the required Notes ID license for the person.

3. Type in the password for the Notes certifier ID.

4. The Register Person dialog box, shown in Figure 11-14, appears:

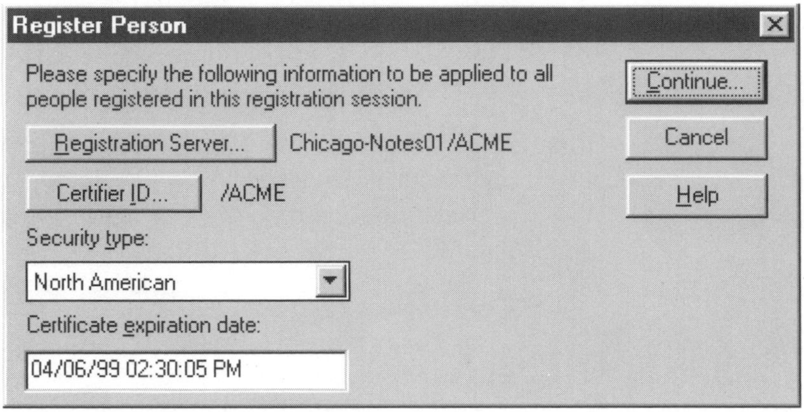

Figure 11-14
Register Person
Dialog Box

The following options need to be configured:

- **Registration Server:** Select the Notes server in which to register the Notes user(s).

- **Certifier ID:** Select the certifier ID file to register the person. If a hierarchical certificate is used, this is the level in the tree at which the user will be registered.

- **Security type:** Select either the North American or International ID file type.

- **Certificate expiration date:** Select the expiration date of the certificate for the user ID file(s). The default is 2 years.

5. Click **Continue** when finished.

6. The user name specifics for registering a person will appear in the Basics dialog box; shown in Figure 11-15

Figure 11-15
User Name Basics
Dialog Box

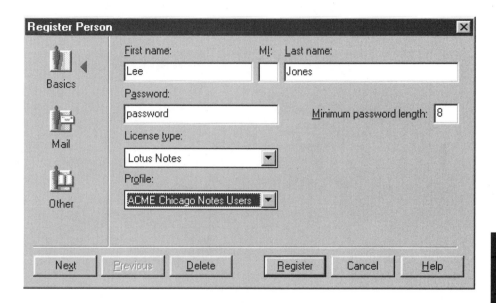

The following fields should be configured:

- **First, MI, and Last name:** Enter the user's first and last name.

- **Password:** Enter the password for the user. It may be changed by the user once his or her Notes desktop is configured. The password is case sensitive.

- **License Type:** Select the Notes license type for the user. This would be Lotus Notes, Lotus Notes Desktop, or Lotus Notes Mail.

● **Profile:** Enter the profile, if any, for the user. The profile can be configured by the Notes administrator so that when a Notes user is first created, some of the user's information is automatically set.

● **Minimum password length:** Enter the minimum character length for the Notes user's password. We recommend that you use a minimum password length of 8. A Notes password cannot be cleared if a length is set.

7. Click the **Mail** icon. The Mail dialog box will appear, as shown in Figure 11-16:

Figure 11-16
User Name Mail
Dialog Box

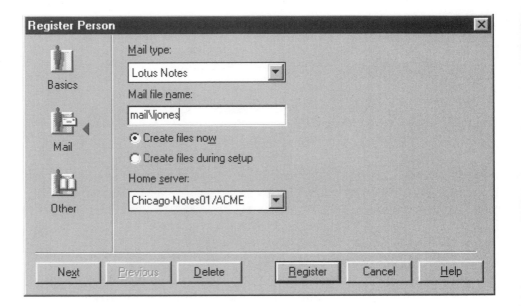

The following fields should be configured:

● **Mail type:** Elect the user's appropriate e-mail program, or none for no mail or for mail not dependent on a Notes server.

● **Mail file name:** Enter the path relative to the Notes data directory and filename of the user's mail file.

● **Create files...:** Select whether or not to create the user's mail file now or when the user is set up.

- **Home Server:** Enter the name of the server that will store the user's mail file.

8. Click the **Other** icon. The Other dialog box, shown in Figure 11-17, appears:

Figure 11-17
User Name Other
Dialog Box

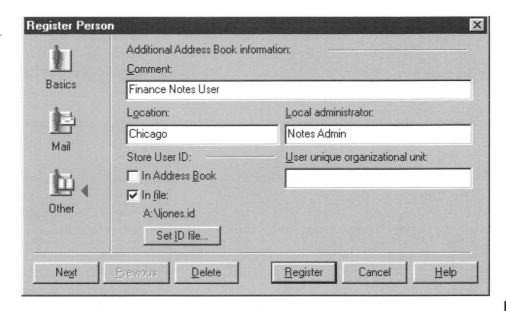

The following fields should be configured:

- **Comment:** (Optional) Enter a comment about the Notes user.

- **Location:** (Optional) Enter a location for the user.

- **Store User ID:** Select whether or not to store the User's ID file in the public Name and Address book and/or on a floppy or network drive.

If the ID file is stored within the public Name and Address book, and the user has AUTHOR access to the public Name and Address book (default), then the ID file will be removed from his or her person record and copied to the desktop of the machine where Notes is installed.

If you choose to create the ID file to a floppy or network drive, click the **Set ID File** button to change the target location of the file if necessary.

- **Local administrator:** (Optional) Enter the local administrator's name.

- **User unique organizational unit:** (Optional) Enter a unique organizational unit for users within the same Notes hierarchy with the same user name. This field is rarely used, in favor of using a middle initial to distinguish users with the same name in the same hierarchy.

9. (Optional) Click **Next** to continue to register other Notes users and repeat the above steps for these users.

10.   Click **Register** when you are ready to register the user(s).

You may also register persons from a text file. To do so, you must first create a text file with the following format:

```
Lastname;Firstname;MiddleInitial;organizationalunit;
password;Idfiledirectory;IDfilename;homeservername;
mailfiledirecotry;mailfilename;location;commenct;
forwarding address;profile name; local administrator
```

The file should contain one user per line.

Once the file is created:

1. Click **File – Tools – Server Administration.**

2. Click the **People** icon and select **Register From File.**

3. Follow the onscreen instructions.

Tips

For the examination, you should understand how to create new Notes users from both the System Administration console and from a text file.

Creating Server ID Files

Like a Notes user ID, a Notes server ID file consists of up to six components, including:

- **Server Name:** This is the name of the Notes server.

- **Notes License Number:** This is the license number assuring the ID is a legitimate North American or International ID file. It cannot be changed once created.

- **Public and Private Keys:** These keys are used for various security measures, such as authenticating with a Notes server. During authentication, a challenge-response sequence is initiated between the Notes client and Notes server or between two Notes servers. Every Notes user's and server's public key within a single domain is also stored within the public Name and Address book. It is with this public key that a challenge is composed in that only the user or server ID file with the appropriate private key may unlock. If not completed properly, authentication with the target Notes server or user is not completed. This public-private key authentication is based upon and licensed from RSA.

- **Encryption Keys:** If any Notes administrator or Notes developer creates an encryption key to encrypt certain fields within a Notes application, the encryption keys are stored within the user's ID file.

- **Certificate(s):** An ID file must contain at least one certificate. For hierarchical server ID files, an ID file may only contain one hierarchical certificate. Cross-certification is needed to access other hierarchical organizations. However, an ID file may contain several flat certificates.

- **Password:** The password for a server ID is stored within the ID file as well. It is not stored within the public Name and Address book on the Notes server.

Sys.Admin. I

The Notes server ID file for the first Notes server is automatically created when the first Notes server within your company is created. In order to set up additional Notes servers within your company, you must first register those new Notes servers. When you register a new Notes server, a server record in the public Name and Address book will be created, a Notes server ID file will be created, and the new Notes server will be added to the group, **LocalDomainServers**. The person creating a new Notes server must have at least AUTHOR access to the public Name and Address book with the ServerCreater role assigned.

To register a new Notes server, follow these procedures:

1. Click **File – Tools – Server Administration.**

2. Click the **Servers** icon and select **Register Server.**

3. Click **Yes** once you have agreed you have purchased the necessary Notes server license for the new Notes server.

4. Type in the password for the certifier ID file and click **OK.**

5. The registration server dialog box, shown in Figure 11-18 will appear:

Figure 11-18
Register Notes Server
Dialog Box

The following fields should be configured:

- **Registration Server:** Select the Notes server in which to register the Notes server.

- **Certifier ID:** Select the certifier ID file to register the server. If a hierarchical certifier is used, this is the level in the tree where the server will be registered.

- **Security type:** Select either the North American or International ID file type.

- **Certificate expiration date:** Select the expiration date of the certificate for the server ID file. The default is 100 years.

6. Click **Continue** when finished.

7. The Register Server Basics dialog box will appear, as shown in Figure 11-19:

Figure 11-19
Register Server
Name Basics
Dialog Box

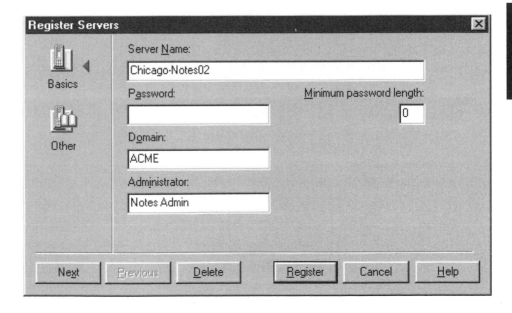

The following fields should be configured:

- **Server Name:** Enter the name of the new Notes server.

- **Password:** Enter the password for the Notes server. The password is case sensitive.

- **Domain:** Enter the Notes domain in which the new Notes server will exist.

- **Administrator:** Enter the Notes name or group that will administer the Notes server.

- **Minimum password length:** Enter the minimum character length of the password for the new Notes server ID file.

8. Click the **Other** icon. The Register Server Other dialog box, shown in Figure 11-20, appears:

Figure 11-20
Register Server Name Other Dialog Box

The following fields should be configured:

● **Server Title:** Enter the title of the new Notes server. This should be a descriptive title that will appear in the server record of the domain Name and Address book.

● **Network:** Enter the Notes named network that this new Notes server will belong in.

● **Local administrator:** Enter the Notes name or group that will administer this Notes server.

● **Store Server ID file:** Select whether or not to store the new server's ID file in the public Name and Address book and/or on a floppy or network drive.

If the server ID file is stored within the public Name and Address book, the ID file will be removed from the server record and copied to the machine when the new Notes server is configured.

If you choose to create the ID file to a floppy or network drive, click the **Set ID File** button to change the target location of the file if necessary.

9. (Optional) Click **Next** to continue to register other Notes servers and complete steps 5–8 for these servers.

10. Once you are finished, click **Register** to register the new Notes server(s).

Creating Certifier ID Files

A certifier ID file is used to create new servers and users. For hierarchical ID files, a certifier ID file can also be used to create organizational unit certifiers, as well as to certify other companies' ID files (cross-certification).

From this definition, you can see the importance of the certifier ID file. Only administrators should have access to this file.

Sys. Admin. I

Organization Certifiers

The top level certifier (Organization Certifier [o]) for a company is automatically created when the first Notes server is created. Normally, you will never need to create another top level organization-certifier for your company, unless you are creating one to set up an external Notes firewall domain. To create an organization certifier, follow these procedures:

1. Click **File – Tools – Server Administration.**

2. Click the **Certifiers** icon and choose **Register Organization**.

3. The Register Organization Certifier screen appears, as shown in Figure 11-21:

Figure 11-21
Register Organization
Certifier Dialog Box

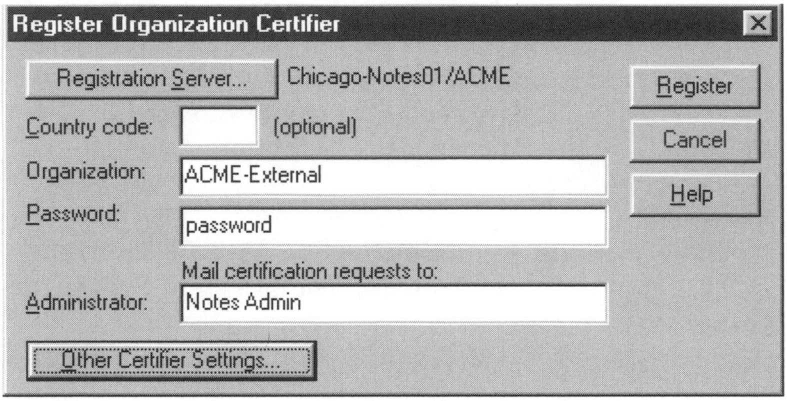

The following fields should be configured:

● **Registration Server:** Click the button to change the Notes server in which to register the organization certifier.

● **Country Code:** (Optional) Enter the Country Code, if desired, for the organization certifier. Most companies do not use country codes.

● **Organization:** Enter the name of the organization certifier.

- **Password:** Enter the password for the organization certifier. This field is case sensitive.

- **Administrator:** Enter the name of the administrator who will handle recertification requests. All requests that are handled through e-mail will be mailed to this user or group.

4. Click the **Other Certifier Settings** button. The Other Certifier Settings dialog box will appear (Figure 11-22):

Figure 11-22
Other Organization
Certifier Settings
Dialog Box

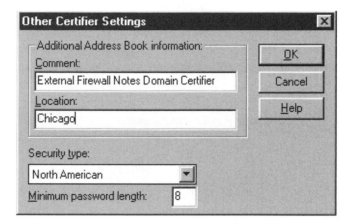

The following fields should be configured:

- **Comment:** (Optional) Enter a comment about the organization certifier.

- **Location:** (Optional) Enter a location for the organization certifier.

- **Security type:** Choose either the North American or International license type for the certifier.

- **Minimum password length:** Enter the minimum number of characters for the password for the certifier.

5. When finished, click **OK** to return to the first screen and then click **Register**. You will be prompted where to store the new organization certifier ID file.

Organizational Unit Certifiers

For larger companies, you may wish to create organizational unit certifiers to further break down your naming structure hierarchy. Normally, companies do this by department or geographic location. For example:

Scott Thomas/Chicago/ACME

Lee Jones/NY/ACME

or

Amy Peasley/Finance/ACME

Joe User/HR/ACME

or

Scott Thomas/Finance/Chicago/ACME

Amy Peasley/HR/Chicago/ACME

Organization Unit certifiers may be created from organization certifiers or from other organizational unit certifiers, creating a hierarchy up to four levels deep.

To create an organization unit (OU) certifier, follow these procedures:

1. Click **File – Tools – Server Administration.**

2. Click the **Certifiers** icon and choose **Register Organization Unit**. Enter the password for the previous certifier if prompted.

3. The Register Organization Unit Certifier screen will appear (See Figure 11-23):

Figure 11-23

Organization Unit
Certifier Settings
Dialog Box

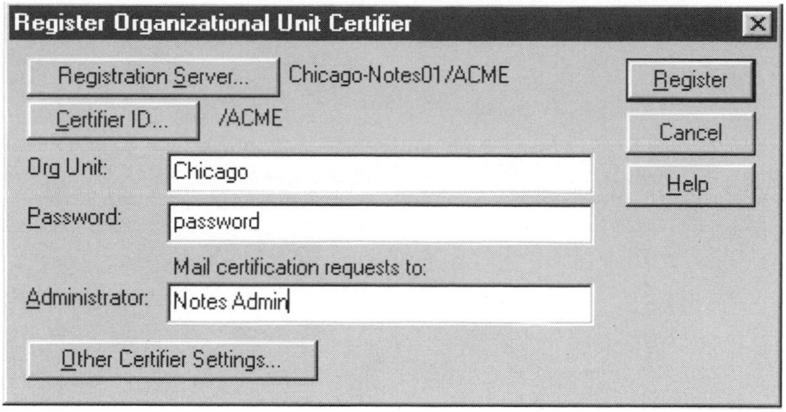

The following fields should be configured:

● **Registration Server:** Click the button to change the Notes server in which to register the organization unit certifier.

● **Certifier ID:** Click the Certifier ID button to change the certifier ID file to register the new organizational unit certifier. The certifier ID file will be the parent of the new organizational unit, and the level in the tree at which the new organizational unit certifier will appear.

● **Organization Unit:** Enter the name of the organization unit certifier.

● **Password:** Enter the password for the organization certifier. This field is case sensitive.

● **Administrator:** Enter the name of the administrator or group who will handle recertification requests. All requests that are handled through e-mail will be mailed to this user or group.

4. Click the **Other Certifier Settings** button and the Other Certifier Settings dialog box will appear, as shown in Figure 11-24:

Figure 11-24
Other Organization
Unit Certifier Settings
Dialog Box

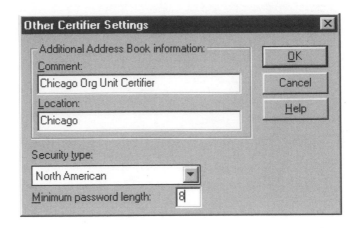

Figure 11-24
Other Organization
Unit Certifier Settings
Dialog Box

The following fields should be configured:

● **Comment** (Optional): Enter a comment about the organization unit certifier.

● **Location** (Optional): Enter a location for the organization unit certifier.

● **Security Type:** Choose either the North American or International license type for the certifier.

● **Minimum password length:** Enter the minimum number of characters for the password for the certifier.

5. Click **OK** to return to the previous screen and **Register** to register the new organizational unit certifier ID file. You will be prompted to enter the filename and path for the new organizational unit certifier ID file.

Chapter 11 Sample Questions

Objective: Installing Notes Server Software.

Kristine is installing the first Notes server within her organization. What are the files that are created before starting the Notes server?

      A. **CERT.ID** (Organization Certifier File)

      B. **SERVER.ID**

      C. The administrator's ID file

      D. User ID files

      E. **NAMES.NSF**

      F. Organizational Unit Certifier Files

Answer: A, B, C, and E.
When you configure your first Notes server within your organization, the server (**SERVER.ID**), certifier (**CERT.ID**), and administrator ID (**USER.ID**) files are created. Also created is the public Name and Address book (**NAMES.NSF**). After the first server is created, the administrator may then create additional Notes servers, organization unit certifiers, and new Notes users.

Objective: Installing Notes Server Software.

What files should you back up if you are going to reinstall a Notes server?

      A. **NOTES.INI, DESKTOP.DSK, CERT.ID, SERVER.ID, USER.IDs, NAMES.NSF, LOG.NSF**

      B. **NOTES.INI, CERT.ID, NAMES.NSF, SERVER.ID**

      C. **NOTES.INI, DESKTOP.DSK, CERT.ID, SERVER.ID, LOG.NSF**

      D. **NAMES.NSF, CERT.ID, LOG.NSF**

Answer: A

In order to retain all your original settings and configurations all files listed in answer A should be backed up in case of problems.

Objective: Installing Notes Server Software.

What databases are automatically created when the first Notes server is started?

> A. **NAMES.NSF**
>
> B. **MAIL.BOX**
>
> C. **CERTLOG.NSF**
>
> D. **LOG.NSF**

Answer: B and D

The mail router box (**MAIL.BOX**) and Notes server log (**LOG.NSF**) are automatically created whenever a Notes server starts if they do not currently exist. The **NAMES.NSF** database (public Name and Address book) is created when the first Notes server is config-ured. The certification log database must be manually created by the Notes administrator.

Objective: Installing Notes Server Software.

The modem files for a Notes machine are stored within which directory by default?

> A. **\NOTES**
>
> B. **\NOTES\MODEMS**
>
> C. **\NOTES\DATA**
>
> D. **\NOTES\DATA\MODEMS**

Answer: D

Modem files for Lotus Notes are stored within the **\MODEMS** subdirectory relative to the Notes data directory by default. However, upon Notes installation, the user may choose an alternate location.

Objective: Installing Notes Client Software.

Jeanine is developing a discussion Notes database from scratch without using any Notes templates to track sales calls. Which types of Notes client licenses will be able to access her application?

> A. Lotus Notes
>
> B. Lotus Notes Desktop
>
> C. Lotus Notes Mail

Answer: A and B
Lotus Notes Mail licenses may only access Notes mail applications and any applications inheriting their designs from Lotus-approved templates.

Objective: Installing Notes Client Software.

Wayne is a mobile Notes user and is tired of having to manually reconfigure his Notes workstation every time he moves from office to remote locations. What can he do to ease the administration of this process?

> A. Nothing, that is one of the drawbacks of remote computing with Lotus Notes
>
> B. Create and configure location documents within his personal Name and Address book where each document is configured per his location
>
> C. He can have his Notes administrator create and configure location documents within the public Name and Address book where each document is configured per his location
>
> D. He can edit his person document and configure location types based upon his location

Answer: B
Wayne can configure location documents within his personal Name and Address book. Each document may contain information such as dialing rules and phone numbers, as well as port and server settings.

Objective: Configuring Shared Mail.

Shared mail is split by the Notes mail router into summary and non-summary data. Which statements are true concerning summary and non-summary data with Shared_Mail=2?

> A. Summary data contains the message body of a Notes mail message including attachments; non-summary data contains any information within the **TO**, **CC**, **BCC**, **SUBJECT**, and **FROM** fields.

> B. Non-Summary data contains the message body of a Notes mail message including attachments. Summary data contains any information within the **TO**, **CC**, **BCC**, **SUBJECT**, and **FROM** fields.

> C. Summary data is stored in the shared message store; non-summary data is stored within the user's mail file.

> D. Non-Summary data is stored in the shared message store; summary data is stored within the user's mail file.

Answer: B and D
Non-summary data (body of a message) is stored within the shared message store and summary data (message headers) are stored within user's personal mail files.

Objective: Configuring Shared Mail.

Which file stores the non-summary data for shared mail messages?

> A. **MAIL.BOX**

> B. **LOG.NSF**

C. **MAILOBJ.NSF**

D. The shared Notes mail application as named by the Notes administrator.

Answer: D
When the Notes administrator initially configures shared mail, he names the shared mail application. The file, **MAILOBJ.NSF**, is automatically created and only is a database link that tracks which of the databases is the active object store database.

Objective: Configuring Shared Mail.

The Notes administrator has shared mail configured on a Notes server with the setting of "Shared_Mail=1." Kristine sends a Notes mail message to Corey, both of whom reside on the shared Notes mail server. What will happen?

A. The message will reside in the shared message store

B. The message will reside in Corey's server mail file

C. The message will reside in both Corey's server mail file and the shared message store

Answer B
With "Shared_Mail=1," only mail bound for multiple recipients will use the shared message store. If "Shared_Mail=2" were used, then the above scenario would use the shared message store.

Objective: Configuring Shared Mail.

Which of the following actions will cause the shared message store not to be used?

A. Editing a message, saving a message, locally encrypting a message, making a replica of a mail database

B. Saving a message, locally encrypting a message, making a replica of a mail database, deleting a message

C. Locally encrypting a message, deleting a message, and making a replica of a mail database

D. Saving a message, locally encrypting a message, making a replica of a mail database, and receiving a new message

Answer: A

If a message is edited and saved, then the message is removed from the shared message store. Since the Notes mail router is responsible for splitting a mail message, saving a document will not be mailed and therefore will not use the shared message store. If encryption is used for incoming mail, the Notes mail router cannot use the shared message store. The making of a replica copy of a Notes application will copy those messages from the shared message store.

Objective: Configuring Shared Mail.

Hurley is a remote user. He composes a Notes mail message bound for multiple users on his home Notes server which is configured with "Shared_Mail=2." He mails the message and saves it to his local replica copy of his mail file. He then replicates with his Notes server. What will happen?

A. The mail message will use the shared message store for all recipients, and the saved document will use the shared message store in both the local copy and the server copy

B. The mail message will use the shared message store for all recipients, but the saved document will not use the shared message store in either the local copy or the server copy

C. The mail message will use the shared message store for all recipients, but the saved document will not use the shared message store in the local copy, However, the server copy will use the shared message store

D. The shared message store will be used for the mailed message as well as the saved document in the local and server mail files

Answer: B

Objective: Configuring Shared Mail.

Wayne, a Notes administrator, just received Steve's Notes mail file. Steve was a Notes user in another branch of the company and his mail file is not a part of Wayne's Notes server. Wayne is using shared mail and would like to add Steve's mail file to the shared message store. How can he accomplish this?

> A. Copy Steve's mail file to the Notes server; the shared mail process will automatically add the mail file to the shared mail store at 2:00 AM when the object task runs
>
> B. Make a replica copy of Steve's mail file to the Notes server; the shared mail process will automatically add the mail file to the shared mail store at 2:00 AM when the object task runs
>
> C. Make a copy of the mail file on the Notes server and type **load object link <Steve's mail file name> <shared message store file name>**
>
> D. Make a copy of the mail file on the Notes server and type **load share <Steve's mail file name> <shared message store file name>**

Answer: C
The "object link" server console command will link a mail file(s) to the shared message store.

Objective: Configuring Shared Mail.

The shared message store on Wayne's Notes server has become quite large containing numerous mail messages that are no longer needed, as they have been deleted by users. How can Wayne remove the unneeded non-summary documents from the shared message store?

A. Let the server task collect automatically remove the old documents when it runs at 2:00 AM.

B. Type in **load object collect <*shared mail application name*>** from the server console.

C. The shared message store does not need to be maintained

D. Type in shared mail; remove old docs from the server console

Answer: A and B

The server task collect runs on Notes servers with shared mail enabled every evening. Also, the task may be run manually from the Notes server console by typing **load object collect <*shared mail application name*>**.

Objective: Configuring Replication and E-Mail.

Brad is configuring replication between two of his Notes servers. He would like the two Notes servers to replicate daily during business hours every 2 hours. How should he configure the connection document?

A. Do nothing: this is the default setting that is automatically configured when a Notes server is installed

B. Open the public Name and Address book and create a new connection record with Notes server A calling Notes server B. Within the **Call at times** field, enter the range **8:00am–6:00pm**. Within the **Schedule** field, enter **120** minutes

C. Open the public Name and Address book and create a new server record with Notes server A calling Notes server B. Within the **Call at times** field enter the range **8:00am–6:00pm**. Within the **Repeat interval of** field enter **120** minutes

D. Open the public Name and Address book and create a new connection record with Notes server A calling Notes server B. Within the **Call at times** field, enter the range **8:00am–6:00pm**. Within the **Repeat interval of** field, enter **120** minutes

Answer: D

Connection records are used to establish replication. The **Call at times** field establishes the call times and the **Repeat interval of** field establishes how often the Notes server should repeat this replication within the time range specified in the **Call at times** field.

Objective: Configuring Replication and E-Mail.

Corey is configuring his Notes mail architecture in order to route mail between Notes servers. He has two Notes servers running the same protocol on the same physical LAN segment (same Notes named network). How should he configure the mail connection records between the Notes servers?

> A. Create a new mail connection record from Notes server A to Notes server B
>
> B. Create a new mail connection record from Notes server A to Notes server B, and a new mail connection record from Notes server B to Notes server A
>
> C. Do not create any mail connection records
>
> D. Edit the server document and edit the mail connection fields of each Notes server

Answer: C

For Notes servers on the same Notes named network, mail connection records are not necessary. Only when Notes servers are on different Notes named networks are connection records needed. Also when using mail connection records, mail connection records are needed in both directions—unlike replication records, where they are only needed in one direction.

Objective: Configuring Replication and E-Mail.

Debbie has several Notes applications within her Notes infrastructure but only needs to replicate a few of the applications throughout the day. All others can replicate once a day. How can she accomplish this?

A. She cannot, notes replicates all databases in common between two machines based upon the replication ID of the applications

B. She can assign the applications that need to be replicated several times a day a priority of HIGH, then create a separate replication connection record to replicate only HIGH priority databases several times a day

C. She can run multiple replicator tasks—one to replicate high priority databases and the other to replicate normal and low priority databases

Answer: B
Databases tagged as high priority can be used to replicate databases more often than other databases of lower priority. This is done by configuring each database and then creating a corresponding replication connection record.

Objective: Configuring Ports.

Wayne wishes to configure his Notes server that is running TCP/IP and SPX so that TCP/IP is the first protocol used to connect to target Notes servers. How can he accomplish this?

A. Edit the server document so that TCP/IP is listed before SPX

B. Click the **Reorder** button so that TCP/IP is listed first within the Communication Ports dialog box

C. Do nothing, TCP/IP is always used first to connect to other Notes servers

D. Assign a priority of 1 to TCP/IP and 2 to SPX within the Communications Ports dialog box

Answer B
The port **Reorder** button is used to order the ports in which they try to connect with other Notes servers.

Objective: Configuring Ports.

Amy is having trouble connecting with another Notes server. What tool within Notes can she use to troubleshoot connectivity problems?

> A. The **Trace Connection** utility found within the User Preferences dialog box
>
> B. There are no connectivity tools within Notes
>
> C. The protocol analyzer found within the User Preferences dialog box

Answer: A

The trace connection utility can be used to test connectivity problems between two Notes machines.

Objective: Configure Notes Passthru.

Chad is running a Notes workstation only configured for dial-up access (running the X.PC protocol). Within his company, there are two Notes servers, server A and server B. Server A is only running the TCP/IP protocol. Server B has a dial-up modem and the server is configured with the X.PC and TCP/IP protocol. Chad needs to connect to Notes server A. How can he do this?

> A. Chad cannot connect to server A as they do not share a protocol in common
>
> B. Chad can establish a telnet session with Notes server A to gain access
>
> C. Chad can connect to Notes server B as a passthru Notes server to then connect to Notes server A

Answer: C
Notes servers can be configured as passthru Notes servers so other Notes servers and clients may connect through them to connect to other Notes servers. This is helpful for remote clients so that only one server is needed in order to connect to multiple Notes servers. Also, passthru Notes servers may be configured with multiple protocols so that they act as "gateways." This way, the calling and destination servers may communicate even though they do not share a protocol in common.

Objective: Configure Notes Passthru.

In order for a calling Notes machine to connect to another Notes server via a passthru Notes server, what fields must be configured within the server record of each Notes server?

A. **Access this server through Passthru, Passthru route through, Passthru cause calling, Passthru destinations allowed**, all on the passthru Notes server record

B. Only the **Access this server through Passthru** and **Passthru route through** fields on the passthru Notes server record

C. Only the **Passthru route through** and **Passthru cause calling** fields on the passthru Notes server record.

D. Only the **Passthru route through, Passthru cause calling**, and **Passthru destinations allowed** fields of the passthru Notes server record

E. **Access this server through Passthru** on the destination Notes server record, **Passthru route through, Passthru cause calling, Passthru destinations allowed** on the passthru Notes server record

Answer E
The **Access this server through Passthru** field on the destination Notes server record must be configured. If it is left blank, no users or servers will be able to reach it via a passthru Notes server. The **Passthru route through, Passthru cause calling**, and the **Passthru destinations allowed** fields on the passthru Notes server record should be configured.

Objective: Configuring Remote LAN Service.

Remote LAN services has the following advantages when used within a Notes environment:

> A. Access to Notes servers
>
> B. Access to network file and print services
>
> C. There are no advantages when using LAN services
>
> D. Use of network modem pools

Answer: A, B, and D

Lotus Notes can be configured to use Remote LAN services, such as Microsoft's RAS, in order to connect to a LAN through a modem. Using remote LAN services enables the machine to become just like a network node—as if they were directly connected to the LAN.

Objective: Converting E-Mail Files.

When running the convert server task on a Notes server, the following actions are performed on users' mail files:

> A. The mail database file format is changed
>
> B. Read and unread marks are unaffected
>
> C. The mail file will be upgraded from version 3 to
>   version 4 format

Answer: B and C

The convert server utility will upgrade the mail file from version 3 to version 4 and not affect read and unread marks. The mail file format, however, will not change. You need to run the server task "compact" in order to convert the file format from version 3 to 4.

Objective: Using Database Libraries.

Amy wishes to create a database library so that all members in her sales group know what Notes applications they should be using. How can Amy add Notes applications to the database library?

        A. Do nothing, the catalog server task automatically add Notes applications to the database library every evening

        B. Highlight the Notes application and click **File – Database – Publish**

        C. From the Notes server console, type **load library** *<Notes application filename>*

Answer: B
Publishing Notes applications to a Notes library is a manual process that must be done to each Notes application. Multiple library Notes applications may exist upon a single Notes server.

Objective: Registering Notes servers, certifiers, and users.

Genet wishes to register new Notes users. What items must be in place for Genet to register new Notes users?

        A. Genet must have proper access rights to the public Name and Address book

        B. Genet must have a copy of the certifier ID file

        C. Genet must be connected to a file server such as Novell or Windows NT

Answer: A and B
In order to register a new person, the Notes administrator must have proper access rights to the public Name and Address book (AUTHOR with the role CreateUser granted). The administrator must also have a copy of the certifier ID file.

Objective: Registering Notes Servers, Certifiers, and Users.

The ACME corporation wants have at least two people present whenever a new Notes server is registered within their organization. How can ACME prevent a single user from gaining access to the corporate certifier ID file and registering a new Notes server?

A. Assign multiple passwords to the certifier ID file and require at least two different passwords be entered before the file is unlocked

B. Nothing can be done, proper care must be used to guard a certifier ID file

C. Assign multiple passwords to the certifier ID file and require at least one password to be entered before the file is unlocked

Answer: A

Multiple passwords may be assigned to any ID file including a user, server, or certifier ID file. Also, a required number of successful passwords may be assigned so that more than one person is required in order to unlock a file.

Objective: Registering Notes Servers, Certifiers, and Users.

Debbie wishes to create a new first level organizational unit certifier for a new branch office. What items need to be in place to accomplish this task?

A. She needs the organization certifier

B. She needs the proper access rights to the public Name and Address book

C. She needs a copy of the new branch's server ID file

D. She should use the administration panel of her Notes workstation

Answer: A, B, and D

In order to create a new first level organizational unit certifier, you need the top level organization certifier ID file. From this certifier ID file, you may create the new organizational unit certifier. You also need AUTHOR access to public Name and Address book with the NetCreator role granted. The creation of certifier ID files is done from a Notes workstation using the administration panel (**File – Tools – Server Administration**).

Chapter 12

Notes Server Administration

This chapter focuses on those issues surrounding administering a Notes server. Like previous System Administration chapters, not all administration procedures are covered. Instead, we are covering only those points related to the System Administration I exam.

The administration topics covered in this chapter include forcing replication and electronic message routing, as well as sending mail traces. We also look at creating new replica databases and controlling replication with replication formulas. With version 4 of Lotus Notes, we will look at monitoring and troubleshooting the Notes server console, including remote console. New with version 4 are several options available using the system administration control panel and the administration process (adminp), including renaming and recertifying users. Finally, we will focus on database administration issues, including fixing corrupt applications and setting database quotas.

Forcing Replication

At times, it may be necessary for a Notes administrator to force an unscheduled replication between Notes servers. For example, users in two different locations may need to have more recent data within a Notes application, and waiting for the next scheduled replication may not suffice.

A Notes administrator may force an unscheduled replication with a target Notes server (e.g. Chicago-Notes01/ACME) by typing in the following command from the Notes server console or from a Notes remote server console:

```
Replicate Chicago-Notes01/ACME

Push Chicago-Notes01/ACME

Pull Chicago-Notes01/ACME
```

The fully distinguished Notes server name should be used following the command. The **replicate** command will initiate replication in a two-way direction between Notes servers. The **push** command is a one-way command that will only push changes to the target Notes server. The **pull** command is a one-way command that will only pull changes from the target Notes server.

If the command with server name is followed by a database name, only that database will be replicated. The complete path relative to the initiating Notes server's data directory must be entered. For example:

```
Replicate Chicago-Notes01/ACME admin\discuss.nsf
```

This command will only replicate the database **discuss.nsf** with Notes server Chicago-Notes01. If the push command is used, the **discuss.nsf** database on Chicago-Notes01 will only receive changes.

Within version 4 of Lotus Notes, other mechanisms exist to initiate a replication event. These include:

- From the Server Console (as explained above)

- From a Replication Connection document (scheduled replication—by definition, not really a forced event)

- From the Replicator Workpage (as discussed in Chapter 10—*Notes Infrastructure Planning and Design)*

- From a Stacked Icon from the Notes Workspace

- From the Notes client menu (**File – Replication – Replicate**)

Tips

For the examination, it should be understood how replication can occur, focusing especially on an unscheduled, forced replication event from the server console or remote server console for a single database, as shown in the above section.

Forcing E-Mail Routing

Like replication, a Notes administrator may force a Notes server to deliver any pending Notes mail immediately, including low priority mail, by typing the following command from the Notes server console or remote Notes server console:

```
route servername
```

Where *servername* is the name of the destination Notes server. You should enter the fully distinguished name of the Notes server. If there are any spaces within the server name, the fully distinguished server name should be encompassed within quotes, e.g.

```
route "Chicago Notes01/ACME."
```

An example where this command may be used is where Notes mail is scheduled to only route when five messages are pending, and a user needs a pending message routed immediately as the waiting queue has not yet reached the threshold of five. If, for example, three messages were pending, forcing a route would cause the destination Notes server to be called, and all three messages would be routed.

If you wish to shut down the mail router on a Notes server, you may do so by typing the following command from the Notes server console or remote Notes server console:

```
tell router quit
```

If you wish to start it again, type the following command:

```
load router
```

Sending Mail Traces

If the Notes administrator is experiencing problems sending Notes mail from one Notes server to another, a Mail Trace may be run to troubleshoot any potential routing problems. When using this utility, a trace report will be returned by every Notes version 4 server or higher between the sending and receiving Notes servers. This utility can be compared to the TCP/IP trace route (tracert) utility. To run a mail trace between two Notes servers, perform the following steps:

1. Click **File – Tools – Server Administration.**

2. Click the **Mail** icon and click **Send Mail Trace**. The screen shown in Figure 12-1 appears:

Figure 12-1
Mail Trace
Dialog Box

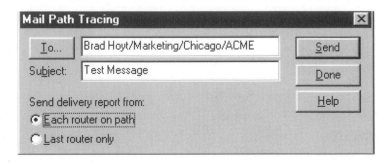

3. Within the **To** field, enter the recipient on the target Notes server. You may press the **To** button to search the public Name and Address book if the user is within the same Notes domain.

4. Select the delivery report option from the radio buttons. Select **Each router on path** to receive a mail trace report back from every Notes server between the sender and receiver Notes mail server. Select **Last router only** to only receive a mail trace report from the receiving Notes mail server.

5. Click **Send**.

For the examination, the candidate should be familiar with sending mail traces to Notes users within a multiple Notes domain configuration.

Tips

Creating Replica Databases

Deploying new replica databases within a Notes infrastructure should always be performed from the Notes administrator's desktop machine. By default, a new replica of a Notes application may not be created by any Notes user from a Notes workstation. The field **Create new replica databases** within the Notes server document controls who may create new replicas of Notes databases on the Notes server.

In order to create a new replica, follow these steps:

1. Highlight the database and click **File – Replication – New Replica**.

2. The New Replica dialog box will appear as shown:

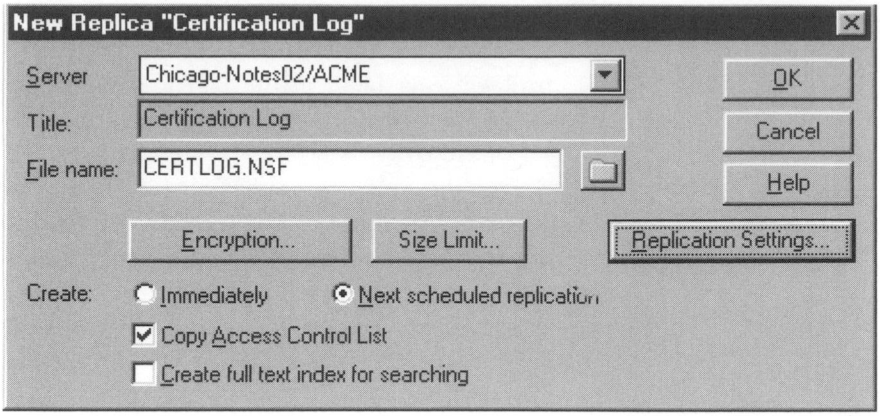

Figure 12-2

Create a New
Replica Database

The following fields should be configured:

- **Server:** Enter the destination Notes server for the new replica copy of the Notes application.

- **File Name:** Enter the destination file name and directory (if necessary) on the target Notes server. The database will appear in the data directory of the target Notes server, or in a subdirectory relative to the data directory.

- **Create:** Select whether to create the replica copy immediately or during the next scheduled replication by selecting the appropriate radio button.

- **Copy Access Control List:** Select whether or not to replicate the ACL as it is set in the current replica copy. If you do not select to replicate the ACL, LocalDomainServers, OtherDomainServers, the administration server, and yourself will appear with Manager access. The default access will be set to Designer. The database manager could set other default access control attributes that would then be in effect.

- **Create full text index for searching:** This checkbox will create a full text index of the database on the target Notes server. You may create a full text index later if you decide not to create one at this time.

- **Encryption:** Press the **Encryption** button if you wish to encrypt the database.

- **Size Limit:** Press the **Size Limit** button if you wish to change the absolute size the database may reach. Once the database is created, the setting may not be changed.

- **Replication Settings:** Press the **Replication Settings** button to change any of the replication settings of the database, such as configuring a selective replication formula.

Tips

For the examination, it should be known that the database creator must exist within the **Create New Replica Databases** *field of the Notes server document. By default, this field allows* **no** *users to create new replica databases. However, by default, any Notes user can create a new, non-replica Notes application as controlled by the server field* **Create New Databases.** *For details on these two fields within the Notes server document, see Chapter 13—The Name and Address Book (Domain) Structure.*

Sys. Admin. I

Controlling Notes Servers from the Server and Remote Server Consoles

You may issue a series of commands to control the server from the Notes server console. Many have already been listed, including, push, pull, replicate, and route. Others include:

- Set configuration (to set **NOTES.INI** variables)

- Show configuration

- Broadcast (to send a message to user[s])

- Exit or quit (to stop the Notes server)

- Drop (to drop a user from the server)

- Load (to load a program)

- Set secure (to secure the Notes server console)

- Show Statistics (to show Notes server statistics)

To access the remote server console from a Notes workstation, click **File – Tools – Server Administration**. Click the **Console** icon. Within the **Server** field, select the Notes server to monitor.

To send a command to the Notes server, simply enter the command in the **Server Console Command** field, then click **Send**.

Tips

For the examination, you should know how to perform server commands from the server console and from the remote console. Exact commands that need to be memorized may vary, but attention should be paid to the most used, such as **replicate, route** *and* **load.**

Listed below are all of the server console commands available with Notes version 4. For the examination, not all of them need to be memorized; however, a basic understanding is necessary.

Table 12.1

Notes Server
Console Commands

Command	Definition	Example
Broadcast	Sends a message to Notes user(s) logged onto the server.	`BROADCAST "Server is coming down"`
Drop	Drops user(s) logged onto the server.	`DROP "Jim Carlson" or DROP ALL`
Exit or Quit	Downs the Notes Server	`QUIT`
Help	Lists all server console commands available	`HELP`
Load	Runs a Notes server program or add-on.	`LOAD REPLICA`
Pull	Initiates a one-way replication from the target Notes server to the initiating Notes server.	`PULL CHICAGO-NOTES01 /ACME`
Push	Initiates a one-way replication to a target Notes server from the initiating Notes server.	`PUSH CHICAGO-NOTES01 /ACME`
Replicate	Performs a two-way replication to and from the initiating Notes server to and from the target Notes server.	`REPLICATE CHICAGO-NOTES01 /ACME`
Route	Route any pending Notes mail messages to the target Notes server.	`ROUTE CHICAGO-NOTES01/ACME`
Set Configuration	Sets Notes configuration variables for the Notes server. Also writes the variable and value to the server's **NOTES.INI** file.	`SET CONFIGURE DOMAIN=ACME`
Set Secure	Secures the Notes server console so that a password must be entered in order to run the following console commands: LOAD, TELL, SET CONFIGURATION, EXIT and QUIT	`SET SECURE password`
Set Statistics	Resets statistic(s) to a value of zero.	`SET STATISTICS MAIL.ROUTED`
Show Configuration	Show the value of a Notes server configuration variable.	`SHOW CONFIGURATION DOMAIN` (e.g. will show ACME if DOMAIN is set to ACME)
Show Directory	Will display all databases and templates within directories and directory links associated with the Notes server's data directory.	`SHOW DIRECTORY`
Show Diskspace	Will show the amount of free disk space for the target drive.	`SHOW DISKSPACE C`
Show Memory	Will show the free amount of available memory for the Notes server.	`SHOW MEMORY`

Sys. Admin. I

Table 12.1

Notes Server
Console Commands
(cont'd..)

Command	Definition	Example
Show Performance	Enables or disables showing the performance statistics for the Notes server. This includes the number of users and transactions per minute.	`SHOW PERFORMANCE`
Show Port	Show information for the specified Notes port.	`SHOW PORT SPX`
Show Schedule	Shows the next scheduled server program (e.g. replication, mail routing, program document, etc.)	`SHOW SCHEDULE` or `SHOW SCHEDULE program` (e.g. `SHOW SCHEDULE REPLICATION`)
Show Server	Show information pertaining to the Notes server (e.g. server up time, peak transactions, etc.)	`SHOW SERVER`
Show Statistics	Shows all Notes server statistics. All server statistics available may be found within the **EVENTS4.NSF** database on a Notes server.	`SHOW STATISTICS` or `SHOW STATISTICS name`
Show Tasks	Shows all the Notes server tasks running on the Notes server.	`SHOW TASKS`
Show Users	Shows all users logged into the Notes server.	`SHOW USERS`
Tell	Sends a command to the Notes server task.	`TELL REPLICA QUIT`

Creating Replication Formulas

A Notes administrator or database manager may configure a Notes application so that only a subset of the database replicates to a target Notes server or client workstation. For example, a Notes application could replicate documents to or from a target machine based upon date, user name, specific fields, or document type. This can be done by selecting the views or fields desired, or by creating a formula to select the desired documents.

To configure a selective replication formula, follow these procedures:

1. Highlight the desired Notes database application and click **File – Database – Properties**.

2. Click the **Replication Settings** button, then click the **Advanced** icon. The screen shown in Figure 12-3 appears:

Figure 12-3
Creating Selective
Replication Settings

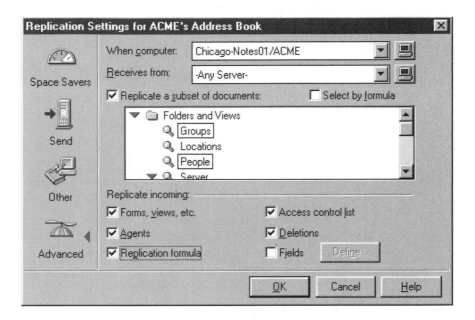

3. You may now select only the documents listed in the views by clicking the desired view(s), or you may create a formula to select the desired documents by clicking the **Select by formula** radio button.

4. Fill in the source and target Notes machines in the respective fields.

5. Select the incoming items to replicate by checking any desired radio buttons as listed in the **Replicate incoming** section. This includes any fields desired by using the **Fields** checkbox.

Renaming and Re-Certifying Users and Servers

On occasion, you may need to rename or recertify both users and servers. This section illustrates the necessary procedures.

Renaming User Names

To change a user's common name, perform the following steps:

1. Make sure all Notes servers have been converted to hierarchical named servers.

2. Open the public Name and Address book within the People view.

3. Select the user(s) that you wish to convert.

4. Click **Actions – Rename Person.**

5. Click **Change Common Name**. You may instead click **Request Move to New Certifier** if you wish to move the user to a different level or position within your hierarchical tree.

6. Select the hierarchical certifier that was originally used to create the person and enter the password.

7. For a name change, enter the new user name and click **Rename**. For a move to a new certifier, enter the new certifier name and click **Submit Request**.

8. Once Notes processes the request, click **OK**.

To move users to a different certifier, these additional steps must be followed:

1. Open the Administrations Request database and enter the Name Move Requests View.

2. Click **Actions – Complete Move** for the selected entries.

3. Select the new certifier ID file for the user(s) and enter the password.

4. Click **Certify**.

Notes users may also request a name change manually from their own Notes workstation by performing the following steps (this assumes that Notes mail is being used):

1. Click **File – Tools – User ID**. Enter the password and click **OK**.

2. Click the **More Options** icon.

3. Click the **Request New Name** button.

4. The user then enters the new common name and clicks **OK**.

5. The user then enters the Notes administrators name within the **To** field and clicks **Send**.

Once the Notes administrator receives the name request change, he or she should perform the following steps:

1. Open the e-mail message containing the name request change.

2. Click **Actions – Certify Attached ID File**.

3. Select the certifier ID file that *originally* was used to create the user and enter its password.

4. Change any of the desired settings (expiration date, password length, registration server) and then click **Certify**.

5. Confirm the name change and click **OK**.

6. An e-mail message will appear sending the ID file back to the user. Click **Send**.

7. The Notes administrator must now manually change any ACL settings of any database to reflect these changes, including the user's mail file.

The user now must perform these final actions:

1. Open the new e-mail message with the name change request.

2. Click **Actions – Accept Certificate**.

The user's name is now changed.

Recertifying ID Files

With release 4 of Lotus Notes, users and servers can be automatically recertified through the administration process. To recertify a Notes ID file:

1. Click **File – Tools – Server Administration**.

2. Click the **People** icon and choose the People view.

3. Highlight the user(s) you wish to recertify.

4. Click **Actions – Recertify Person**.

5. Select the certifier ID file that was used to originally create the person(s) and enter its password.

6. Click **Certify** once all settings are accepted (e.g. expiration date).

A Notes user may request recertification manually through Notes mail by performing the following steps:

1. From his or her workstation, the Notes user clicks **File – Tools – User ID**.

2. Click the **Certificates** icon.

3. Enter the name of the Notes administrator in the **To** field of the e-mail message.

4. Click **Send** and then **Done**.

Once the Notes administrator receives the recertification request, he or she needs to:

1. Open the e-mail message and click **Actions – Certify Attached ID File**. Select the certifier ID file to use and enter its password.

2. Click **Certify** and then **Send** once all settings are accepted (expiration date, password length, registration server).

The user then needs to perform the following steps:

1. Open the e-mail message and choose **Actions – Accept Certificate**.

2. Enter the password and click **OK**.

The user is now recertified.

Configuring and Using the Administration Process

New with version 4 of Lotus Notes is the Notes administration process (adminp server task). It is a significant addition designed to save the Notes administrator time by automating many of the Notes administration tasks. These include:

- Delete user, server, and group documents from the public Name and Address book

- Recertify Notes ID files

- Rename users and servers

- Create and delete users' mail files

- Create replicas of Notes applications

- Move databases to and from a cluster server

- Add and remove servers from a Notes cluster

- Enable password checking during authentication

- Remove user names from ACL, reader, and author name fields of Notes applications

- Convert users and servers from a flat to a hierarchical naming standard

Tips

The Notes administration process will only perform most of these tasks only if you use a hierarchical ID naming structure for your Notes infrastructure.

The administration process automatically initiates when a Notes server is started. However, before a Notes administrator can take full advantage of the tool, proper configurations of the process must be set and ACL access must be assigned to the proper administrators on each Notes database. The administration process task (named **adminp** on a Notes server) must interact with the public Name and Address book, all Notes databases that have an administration server set, the administration requests Notes database, and the certification log Notes database. Notes administrators must also have the proper ACL access to these Notes databases.

Tips

For the examination, it is important to understand how the administration process (adminp) works for a Notes server. Not all details we are explaining are completely necessary to learn for the test. Concentrate on its advantages, how the process works, and how it is triggered.

Setting the Administration Server for the Public Name and Address Book

The first step you need to perform is to assign an administration server for your public Name and Address book. This is performed as follows:

1. Shut down the Notes server process on the Notes server that will be the administration server for the public Name and Address book.

2. Start the Notes user interface on the Notes server (Notes client program).

3. Check to see if a wildcard replica of the Administration Requests (**ADMIN4.NSF**) database is already on the server. If so, delete the database. The Administration Requests database is a wildcard replica if it does not appear in the list of databases when you choose **File – Database – Open**.

4. Open the public Name and Address book locally on the Notes server (**File – Database – Open**). Select **Local** for the server, and **NAMES.NSF** for the filename.

5. Now click, **File – Database – Access Control**.

6. Click the **Advanced** icon.

7. The page shown in Figure 12-4 appears:

Figure 12-4

Administration Server Setting for Public Name and Address Book

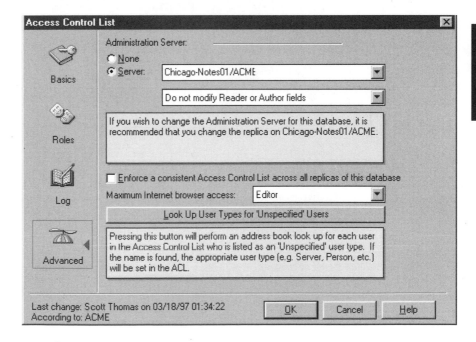

8. Within the administration server fields, enter the Notes server name to administer the public Name and Address book.

9. Make sure that a Notes certification log exists. If not, you will need to create a Notes certification log on the Notes server (see the "Certification Log" section within this chapter for details).

10. Shut down the Notes user interface and restart the Notes server.

Traps

It is important to note that the administration process for the public Name and Address book is an intensive process. For smaller Notes installations, the administration Notes server for the public Name and Address book can be the same Notes server that houses the Notes applications for that company. For larger installations, the process may become too much of a burden for the server, and a dedicated server may be needed whose only job is to perform administration requests.

By default, the administration process uses three threads to process administration requests. If you have multiple processors installed on your machine and would like to improve performance of the administration process, you may increase the number of threads. This setting is configured within the server document of the Notes server (see Chapter 13 for the exact configuration). Once this field is modified, the administration process on the Notes server must be shut down and restarted to take effect.

Once this task is completed, the Notes server will create the administration requests database (**ADMIN4.NSF**). It is within this database that all administration requests will post. Actual requests are not entered in this database, they are initiated from buttons within the public Name and Address book. This Notes application only houses requests where the **adminp** server task then carriers out the request. Every Notes server within your domain will have a replica copy of this Notes application. The administration Notes server automatically creates these replicas.

Tips

The Notes administrator should monitor the administration requests database daily for any errors that may occur and to track all requests that are being performed by the administration process.

Configuring Proper ACL Access to Perform Administration Procedures

Once the above tasks are completed, you now must configure ACL settings on the public Name and Address book, the administration requests database, and the Notes certification log. Most administration tasks that are performed within the public Name and Address book require at least Author access (with Create documents enabled) to the administration requests database. Unless changed by the Notes administrator, this is the default access of the database. Some tasks, such as renaming users in a different hierarchy and deleting users' mail files, require at least EDITOR access (with Delete documents enabled) to the administration requests database. Servers within your domain will need access rights to the administration requests database as well. As with most Notes applications, the LocalDomainServers group should have Manager level access.

The Notes certification log requires that users performing administration tasks have at least Author access (with Create documents enabled).

Setting the Administration Server for Notes Database Applications

In order for the administration process to modify ACL settings for a Notes application within your domain, you must set an administration server for each Notes application. To perform this action on one or more Notes applications:

1. Click **File – Tools – Server Administration**.

Sys. Admin. I

2. Click the **Database Tools** icon. The screen shown in Figure 12-5 appears:

Figure 12-5

Administration Server Settings for Notes Applications

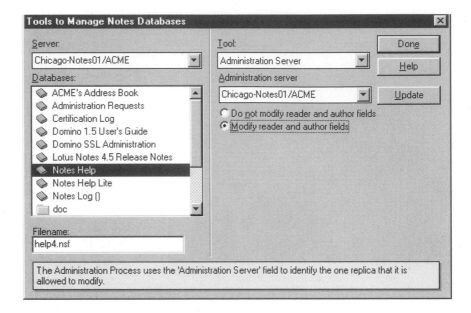

3. Within the **Server** box, select the Notes server you wish to use to access the Notes applications.

4. Within the **Tool** box, select **Administration Server**.

5. Within the **Databases** box, select the database(s) for which you wish to set the administration server.

6. Within the **Administration Server** box, select the Notes server that will be the administration server for the Notes database(s).

7. If you wish to have the administration process update Reader and Author name fields for the Notes application(s), select **Modify reader and author fields**.

8. Click **Update**.

As explained earlier in the section on configuring the administration server for the public Name and Address book, the administration server for a single database may be viewed or set by clicking the **Advanced** icon within the database's ACL settings as well as through the **Server Administration** console. If a key icon appears next to any server entry within the ACL of any database application, this specifies the ACL entry as the administration server.

You only need to set the administration server once per database replica. If a Notes database exists on multiple Notes servers and is a replicating database, once you set the administration server on the Notes database, the setting will be passed through replication to all replica copies on all Notes servers.

Scheduling the Administration Process

As explained in Chapter 13 within the "Server Document" section, scheduling of the administration process can be set. Please refer to that chapter for details.

Table 12.2 does not need to be memorized for the examination, but it should be read to understand that not all administration requests occur at the same time.

The timing of requests depends on the type of administration that is set. Table 12.2 lists the available requests and at what point they are executed.

Table 12.2

Administration
Request Timings

Request	Timing
Create Mail File	Immediate
Initiate Rename in Address Book	Per **interval** field set in server record
Rename Person in Address Book	Per **interval** field set in server record
Rename in Access Control List	Per **interval** field set in server record
Rename in Person Documents	Per the **execute once a day...** field set in server record
Rename in Reader/Author Fields	Per the **Start Executing...** fields set in the server record
Move Person's Name in Hierarchy	Performed by Notes administrator
Delete Obsolete Change Requests	Per the **execute once a day...** field set in server record
Re-certify Person in Address Book	Per **interval** field set in server record
Re-certify Server in Address Book	Per **interval** field set in server record
Delete in Address Book	Per **interval** field set in server record
Delete in Person Documents	Per the **execute once a day...** field set in server record
Delete in ACL	Per **interval** field set in server record
Delete in Reader/Author Fields	Per the **Start Executing...** fields set in the server record
Get Information for Deletion	Immediate
Approve File for Deletion	Done by Notes administrator
Request File Deletion	Immediate
Delete Mail File	Per **interval** field set in server record
Delete Unlinked Mail File	Per **interval between purging mail...** field set in server record
Resource Add	Immediate
Resource Delete	Immediate
Approve Resource Delete	Done by Notes administrator
Set Master Address Book	Per **interval** field set in server record
Set Password Information	Per **interval** field set in server record
Change User Password in Address Book	Immediate
Check Access for New Replica Creation	Immediate
Create Replica	Immediate
Add Server to Cluster	Immediate
Remove Server from Cluster	Immediate

Table 12.2

Administration
Request Timings
(cont'd.)

Request	Timing
Check Access for Move Replica Creation	Immediate
Move Replica	Immediate
Monitor Replica Stub	Per **interval** field set in server record
Delete Original Replica After Move	Per **interval** field set in server record
Copy Servers' Certified Public Key	Per **interval** field set in server record
Place Server's Notes Build Number in Server Record	Per **interval** field set in server record

Notes

Again, for the exam, you will not need to know all of the above settings, but it is a good idea to know that **adminp** *settings may be modified.*

The Notes administrator can tell which databases on a Notes server have the administration server set per database. To do so, type the following at the Notes server console:

```
tell adminp show databases
```

You may also override any scheduled settings for the administration process and force an immediate execution by typing the following at the Notes server console:

```
tell adminp process request
```

where *request* is one of the following settings:

- **Interval:** This setting initiates all immediate and interval based requests.

- **Daily:** This setting processes all new and modified administration requests to update person documents within the public Name and Address book.

- **Delayed:** This setting processes all requests that are scheduled per the **start executing...** setting.

- **Time:** This setting processes all requests that are based on the **delete unlinked mail...** setting.

- **All:** This processes all requests of all types except those based on **delete unlinked mail...** setting.

Using the Notes Server Administration Panel

New with release 4 of Lotus Notes is the Notes server administration panel, shown in Figure 12-6:

Figure 12-6
Notes Server
Administration
Panel

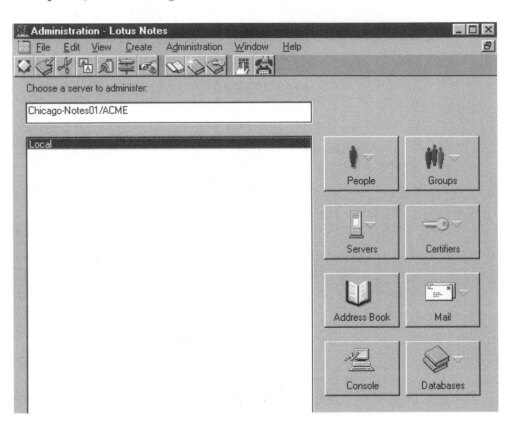

From this panel, the following buttons and features are available:

- **People:** People View: Register Person, Register from File

- **Groups:** Groups View, Create Group

- **Servers:** Servers View, Configure Server, Register Server, Log Analysis

- **Certifiers:** Certify ID File, Cross Certify ID File, Cross Certify Key, Edit Multiple Passwords, Open Certification Log, Register Organizational Unit, Register Organization, Register Non-Hierarchical

- **Address Book:** Opens an Address Book

- **Mail:** Opens Outgoing Mailbox, Sends Mail Trace

- **Console:** Starts the Remote Console

- **Database:** Opens Log, Opens Catalog, Opens Statistics, Opens Administrator Requests, Configure Statistics Reporting, Database Analysis, Database Compact, Database Full Text, Database Quotas, Database Administration Server

Tips

For the examination, it should be understood what administration tasks can be performed from the panel.

Configuring Notes Application Quotas and Database Limits

With version 4.0 and higher of Lotus Notes, the absolute size a database may grow to is 4 gigabytes (up from 1 gigabyte). The default size upon creation of an application is still set to 1 gigabyte. The maximum size of a database may not be changed once it is created; a new copy or a new replica must be made in order to change the maximum size. Figure 12-7 shows the absolute size settings dialog box for a Notes application:

Figure 12-7

Notes Database
Absolute Size Settings

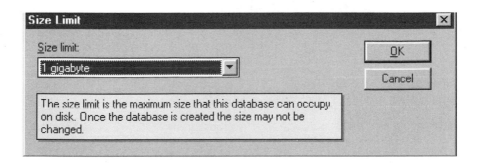

Sys. Admin. I

Quotas may now also be set with version 4.0 and higher of Lotus Notes. Warnings are sent to the log, console, and administrators when the size of the application reaches the quota size. This is beneficial when using Notes mail to prevent people from letting their mail files become too large. Quotas enable mail files to continue to receive e-mail once the quota is reached, but prevents users from adding any more documents. Alerts may be set to administrators when a database reaches a specified size. See Figure 12-8.

Figure 12-8
Notes Database
Quota Settings

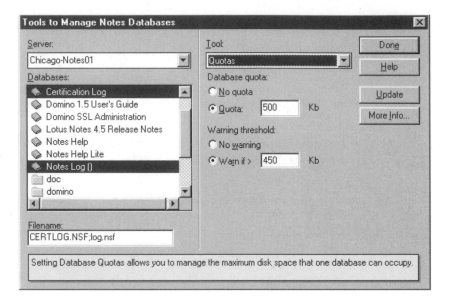

To create or adjust the quota for a Notes application:

1. Click **File – Tools – Server Administration**.

2. Click the **Database** icon.

3. Select **Database Quotas**.

4. Select the database from the **Databases** list box.

5. Within the **Quota** field, enter the quota for the application.

6. Within the **Warning Threshold** field, enter the threshold-warning amount for the application.

7. Click **Done**.

Monitoring Notes Servers

The Lotus Notes logs of each server represent the complete audit trail in terms of each server's actions. The Notes log is created automatically the first time a Notes server is run. Replication, mail routing, database size and usage, phone calls, and all events and errors are recorded within this database. Every morning and periodically throughout the day, the Notes administrator(s) should scan the Notes logs on each Notes server for any errors or inconsistencies that may be cause for concern.

The Notes log may be opened by simply performing a **File – Database – Open** on the specified Notes server, and then highlighting the selection and clicking **Open**.

You may also open the Notes log on a Notes server as follows:

1. Click **File – Tools – Server Administration.**

2. Select the appropriate Notes server.

3. Click the **Database** icon.

4. Click **Open Log**.

Corrupted Notes Databases

At times, a Notes database may contain corrupted documents, views, and/or folders. Corruption of a Notes database is usually caused by the improper shutdown of a Notes server (server crash, power failure, not shutting down the Notes server before shutting down the machine), improper database access through a Notes API program, or accessing a Notes application directly through the file system by two or more users or servers, thus by-passing a Notes server.

The Notes server program **FIXUP** can be used to attempt to repair damaged databases. It can be run from the Notes server console on any unopened Notes applications. The following command should be issued from the server console:

Sys. Admin. I

```
load fixup mail\sthomas
```

For applications that are opened, the Notes server should be shut down and the **fixup** program can be run on a Notes database from the command prompt against the database. Take note though: depending on the platform, the proper prefix for the program must be used. For example, to run **fixup** on the public Name and Address book on a Windows NT server, shut down the Notes server and open a command prompt, then type the following from the Notes directory:

```
nfixup data\names.nsf arguments
```

Arguments include:

- **-L** Reports all events to the Notes log. Without this option, only databases with problems are reported.

- **-V** This option prevents fixup from running on Notes application views.

- **-N** This option prevents fixup from purging corrupted documents from the Notes application.

Troubleshooting Notes Error Messages

Table 12.3 lists all Notes error messages that can be received by a Notes client and/or a Notes server. Types include:

- Mail = E-Mail

- Comm = Communication

- Security = Notes Security

- Server = Notes Server

- Replica = Notes Replication

- Misc = Miscellaneous

Tips

Like previous tables within this chapter, it is not necessary to memorize all contents of the table, but several questions on the examination will list an error message and the candidate will have to answer the question that best describes why the error message is being received. We cover every error message and provide a description of each message to help the candidate prepare for questions on the exam relating to troubleshooting.

Table 12.3

Notes Error
Messages

Error Message	Type	Description
A duplicate recipient was specified and will be ignored.	Mail	A user is listed twice within a Name and Addres Book or appears within multiple cascaded Name and Address Books.
A NetWare DLL could not be found.	Comm	If Novell's SPX protocol is being used for Notes, some DLLs cannot be found.
A NetWare library could not be loaded because a function is missing from the DLL.	Comm	If Novell's SPX protocol is being used for Notes, some DLLs cannot be found.
A passthru message was received without the necessary context.	Security	Passthru is not configured properly.
A path to the server could not be determined from the Connection records in the Name and Address Book.	Security	Connectivity via Notes to a Notes server is not possible via the network or modem.
A port with that name already exists.	Comm	A port already exists in Notes with that name.
A transient network error or network adapter failure has truncated a message from a client. If it recurs, run the appropriate adapter diagnostics.	Server	This occurs when a network card is malfunctioning or is improperly configured.
Access control is set in <Destination Server database> to not replicate forms or views from <Source Server database>.	Replica	This is a normal message when the ACL of the target database is set to designer.
Access control is set in <Destination Server database> to not replicate forms, views or edits from <Source Server database>.	Replica	This is a normal message when the ACL of the target database is set to author.
Access control is set in <Destination Server Pathname> to not allow replication from <Source Server Pathname>.	Replica	This is a normal message when the ACL of the target database is set to NO ACCESS.
Access to data denied.	Resource	This is a normal message received when access is not permitted to a resource such as a directory link.
Activity logging enabled for <Database Name>.	Misc	This is a normal message when activity logging is enabled for a database under Database Properties.
Added connection to server <Server Name> to catalog.	Misc	When a connection record is added within the public Name and Address Book, it is also added to the database catalog.

Table 12.3

Notes Error

Messages (cont'd.)

Error Message	Type	Description
Added database <Database Name> to catalog.	Misc	This is a normal message stating a database is added to the catalog when the server task **catalog** is run.
Added database <Database Name> to Cluster Database Directory.	Server	This is a normal message when Notes clustering is enabled.
Additional ports may not be enabled while the server is running.	Comm	A port (modem or network) may not be added while the Notes server is running.
AMgr: Agent <Agent Name>, cannot convert next run time to text	Server	The server cannot interpret the text data as data type time.
AMgr: Another Agent Manager detected on the system, only one allowed.	Server	Within the Agent Restrictions section of the Name and Address Book, the setting is only set to one allowable agent.
An unexpected authentication message was received.	Security	An error has occurred during authentication.
Another system is using the same server name as this system.	Comm	You have brought up a Notes server that is already using that server name.
AppleTalk is currently enabled on this port.	Resource	AppleTalk protocol is installed.
AppleTalk is not installed on this system.	Comm	The Notes AppleTalk driver is trying to load, but the machine's OS/2 does not have AppleTalk enabled.
At least one network port requires the Notes Server to be restricted to a single process, and that process has exceeded the maximum number of threads.	Server	The maximum number of allowable threads have been exceeded on a network port.
Attachment has been modified or corrupted since signed!	Misc	A digital signature has been corrupted or compromised.
Attempted encryption operation is not allowed outside of North America.	Security	An International version of Notes is trying to perform an encryption option only allowed by North American versions.
Beginning consistency check of databases.	Server	This is a normal message once a Notes server starts.
Building list of databases to replicate with <Server Name>.	Replica	This is a normal message once a Notes server begins a replication event.

Table 12.3

Notes Error

Messages (cont'd.)

Error Message	Type	Description
Call has finished.	Comm	This is a normal message once an analog Notes connection is finished.
Call in progress...	Comm	This is a normal message while an analog Notes connection is running.
Call timer expired.	Comm	This message is displayed once the call timer setting within the port setup of Notes has been reached.
Can't perform this operation on running task.	Server	An attempt to run a process or program is not able to run on the target Notes server.
Can not find the user or public key information in the Name and Address Book.	Misc	The public key of the Notes server or user cannot be found within the server or person record of the public Name and Address book.
Cannot access or create the ID file.	Security	Access to a Notes ID file has failed.
Cannot add the encryption key to your ID file. A key with that name already exists.	Security	An encryption key must have a unique name.
Cannot allocate database object—database would exceed its disk quota.	Misc	If a database quota has been set, the threshold will not be allowed.
Cannot create database—the specified filename is a directory.	Misc	A database name cannot be the same as a directory name.
Cannot create thread.	Resource	Usually signifies server overload. Additional hardware may be necessary.
Cannot do that to an NSF that may be in use.	Misc	An operation is trying to be performed on a database that is in use by another process on a Notes server.
Cannot find event types database <DB Name>.	Misc	The **EVENTS4.NSF** database cannot be located. It may need to be created.
Cannot locate required login information.	Comm	A login problem was encountered, such as in Microsoft's RAS.
Cannot read file.	Resource	A file cannot be read. It may not exist.
Cannot store document; database has too many unique field names. Please ask your administrator to compact the database.	Misc	This may happen to the mail router database (**MAIL.BOX**). The server task **compact** will clear the deletion stubs.

Sys. Admin. I

Table 12.3

Notes Error
Messages (cont'd.)

Error Message	Type	Description
Cannot support multiple processes using Notes in this environment.	Resource	Some environments will not support multiple processes (such as Windows 3.1).
Cannot write or create file (file or disk is read-only).	Resource	The floppy disk is write-protected.
Cannot write to file (possibly it is READ-ONLY or the disk is out of space or not ready).	Resource	The disk drive may be full. Files may need to be deleted, the **compact** server task run, or additional drive space may need to be added.
Cataloger was unable to open database <Database Name>.	Misc	The cataloger server task was unable to open the target database.
Cleared replication history in <Destination Database>.	Replica	A user with manager access to a Notes database has cleared the replication history of the database.
Clearing modem's DTR.	Comm	This is a normal message when an analog Notes connection terminates.
Command or option is not recognized.	Server	A server console command was issued that is not supported or recognized by Notes.
Communications port hardware is not configured or enabled.	Resource	A Notes COM port driver is enabled but is not enabled on the operating system of the machine.
Communications port hardware not present or in use by another device.	Comm	A COM port on the machine is not available or is in use by another program.
Compacting database <Database Name> (<Database Title>).	Server	The server task **compact** is running on a Notes database.
Compaction of the database was stopped prematurely because another user modified it while it was being compacted.	Misc	If a user is within a Notes application while the server task **compact** is being run, the task will terminate. Make sure no users are using an application before the task is run.
Copied access control list into <Destination Database> from <Source Database>.	Replica	When two servers replicate a database with manager access, the ACL will also replicate.
Could not detect carrier or dial-tone; or phone was busy or did not answer.	Comm	A normal message for Notes analog users and servers where a dial tone is not present.
Could not establish dialog with remote system.	Comm	A common error where the two analog Notes machines cannot handshake correctly. The most likely cause is an incorrect modem MDM file on one of the machines.

Table 12.3

Notes Error

Messages (cont'd.)

Error Message	Type	Description
Could not locate server document for <'Server Name'> in Stats & Events Types Config DB.	Server	Within the **EVENTS4.NSF** database, a server is not configured.
Could not open the ID file.	Security	The target ID file could not be opened.
Created database catalog: <Catalog Pathname>.	Misc	This message is shown when a database catalog is created, usually by the catalog server task.
Created database Cluster Database Directory: <Cluster Directory Name>.	Server	Message displayed when a Notes cluster is created.
Data Directory cannot be accessed. Check the path given in the DIRECTORY= line in your NOTES.INI file.	Server	The Notes data directory cannot be located on the machine.
Database already contains a document with this ID (UNID).	Misc	Every document within a Notes application is associated with a Notes ID number. A document is trying to be created or replicated to a database with that number.
Database has been corrupted and can't be repaired; cannot open.	Misc	A database is corrupted. **Fixup** or **Updall** may be able to repair it.
Database is corrupt—cannot allocate space.	Misc	A database is corrupted. **Fixup** or **Updall** may be able to repair it.
Database is currently being indexed by another process.	Server	A second index task is trying to run against a database.
Database is not full-text indexed.	Server	A full text search was trying to be performed against a database. Create a full text index.
Database object has been deleted.	Misc	A document is trying to be accessed that was already deleted.
Device or unit number already in use.	Comm	A device number for a protocol is already in use. Common for NetBIOS.
Directory does not exist.	Misc	A nonexistent directory was trying to be accessed.
Disconnected from Server.	Comm	A user or server was disconnected from the target Notes server.
Disk or network error (reading swap file)—cannot continue.	Resource	For OS/2 users, the swap file could not be read.
Document attachment is invalid.	Misc	A file attachment type that is not supported by Notes was specified.

Sys. Admin. I

Table 12.3

Notes Error
Messages (cont'd.)

Error Message	Type	Description
Document has been modified or corrupted since signed! (data).	Misc	The document has been modified or compromised since it was sent by the original sender.
Document has been modified or corrupted since signed! (signature).	Misc	The document has been modified or compromised since it was sent by the original sender.
Document is not signed.	Misc	The document does not contain a digital signature.
Drive is not ready.	Resource	The floppy disk is not being read properly.
Driver already in use.	Comm	A Notes driver is already being used.
Driver could not allocate memory for communications buffers.	Comm	The driver, usually a COM driver, does not have enough communication buffers allocated for use.
Entry not found in index or view's index not built.	Misc	The view should be built or rebuilt. This can be done using the **updall** server task.
Error attempting to load or run <Program Name> : <Additional Error Information>.	Server	An error occurred while trying to invoke a Notes server program.
Error Compacting database <Database Name>.	Server	An error was encountered while trying to compact a database.
Error fixing view <View ID> in <Database Name>.	Server	The server task **updall** encountered an error while trying to update a view.
Error fixing views in <Database Name>.	Server	The server task **updall** encountered an error while trying to update a view.
Error full text indexing document NT<Note ID> in database <Database Name>.	Server	An error occurred while trying to full-text index a database.
Error full text indexing <Database Name>.	Server	An error occurred while trying to full-text index a database.
Error getting list of AppleTalk Zones.	Comm	An error when AppleTalk cannot correctly communicate on an AppleTalk network.
Error handling possible update conflict in <Destination Database>.	Replica	A possible replication problem was encountered.
Error in Acquire or Connect Script; check the log file, Miscellaneous Events view, for further information.	Comm	An acquire or connect script error has occurred.

Table 12.3
Notes Error
Messages (cont'd.)

Error Message	Type	Description
Error looking up name in Name & Address Book (names.nsf).	Misc	An error has occurred looking up a user's name within the Name and Address Book.
Error opening modem command file.	Comm	A modem MDM file could not be opened.
Exceeded maximum folder count in database.	Misc	The maximum count of 256 folders for a database has been exceeded.
Exceeded maximum limit of 300MB of shared memory.	Resource	The maximum limit for shared memory has been exceeded.
Exchanging Read Marks between <Destination Database> and <Source Database>.	Replica	The Notes server and client are exchanging read marks between database(s).
Field is too large (15K) or View's column & selection formulas are too large.	Misc	A field or view's contents contain too much data.
Field names must be 250 characters or less.	Misc	A field name within a Notes form may only be 250 characters or less in length.
File already exists.	Resource	A database is trying to be created within a filename that already exists.
File does not exist.	Resource	A database is trying to be accessed with a filename that does not exist.
File is in use by another program.	Resource	A file is trying to be accessed that is already being used by another program.
File is not an object store. Rename it so that the router can create an object store with that name.	Mail	The shared mail object store is not configured properly.
File name too long or invalid file name syntax.	Resource	The filename being used is too long.
File not found or not a Notes database.	Misc	A file is trying to be opened by Notes and is not in standard Notes database format.
File object is truncated—file may have been damaged.	Misc	File is damaged. If it is a Notes application, the server task **fixup** can be run to try to repair it.
File truncated—file may have been damaged.	Resource	File is damaged. If it is a Notes application, the server task **fixup** can be run to try to repair it.

Table 12.3

Notes Error
Messages (cont'd.)

Error Message	Type	Description
Finished compacting <Database Name>, <KBytes> bytes recovered (<Percent Saved>).	Server	This message tells that the server task **compact** has finished running and reports the amount of space recovered.
Finished replication with server <Server Name>.	Replica	This messages alerts that replication has finished with the target Notes server.
Finished updating usage statistics.	Misc	This message alerts that the statistics server task has completed.
Finished updating views in <Database Name>.	Server	This message alerts that the index server task has completed updating database views.
Folder directory is corrupt. Please run Fixup to repair it.	Misc	File is damaged. The server task **fixup** can be run to try to repair it.
Folder has no free space but should have.	Misc	File may be damaged. The server task **fixup** can be run to try to repair it.
Folder is corrupt. Please run Fixup to repair it.	Misc	File is damaged. The server task **fixup** can be run to try to repair it.
Folder replication not supported by remote server.	Misc	Target Notes server does not support folder replication. Usually a v3 target Notes server.
Form has been deleted.	Misc	The Notes database form has been deleted that the document is using.
Formula Error.	Misc	The document, view, field, or agent formula contains an error.
Full text directory links must contain a valid directory name.	Server	The full text index is configured improperly.
Full text error from Topic; see log for more information.	Server	The full text index may contain an error(s).
Full text index not found for this database.	Server	The database has been full text indexed, but the actual index cannot be located.
Full text indexing documents in <Database Name>.	Server	The full text index is being built.
Groups cannot be nested more than 20 levels deep.	Mail	Groups nesting error encountered.
Groups cannot be nested more than 6 levels deep when mailing.	Mail	Groups nesting error encountered.
Help Section cannot be located.	Misc	The help section of a Notes application cannot be located.

Table 12.3

Notes Error
Messages (cont'd.)

Error Message	Type	Description
ID's certificate is invalid.	Security	An ID file's certificate is invalid.
ID file cannot be created.	Security	An ID file cannot be created.
ID file not found in Name & Address Book.	Misc	A Notes workstation is being configured for setup with the option of obtaining the ID file from the public Name and Address book. The ID file, however, does not exist.
Idle.	Replica	A server task is running but idle.
In the [386Enh] section, add: NetHeapSize=<Desired Heap Size>.	Server	For Windows 3.1 users, the NetHeapSize needs to be increased.
Incorrect console security password.	Server	A console password has been set on the Notes server, but has been incorrectly entered.
Index corrupted—will be rebuilt automatically when database is closed or server is restarted.	Misc	A database index is corrupted. Can be manually rebuilt using the **updall** server task from the server console.
Initializing.	Replica	Replication server task is initializing replication with a target Notes server.
Insufficient arguments. Enter 'HELP' for the correct syntax.	Server	A server console command was entered without the appropriate arguments.
Insufficient disk space.	Resource	Not enough disk space is available on the Notes machine. Run **compact** Notes server task, delete files, or add disk space.
Insufficient memory—a Notes memory pool is full.	Misc	A Notes memory pool has been exhausted. Increase the pool.
Internal error in network operating system.	Comm	An error occurred within the OS network driver.
Internal error in Notes NetWare port driver.	Comm	The Notes SPX network driver reported an error.
Internal error in Notes TCP port driver.	Comm	The Notes TCP network driver reported an error.
Mail Conversion Utility failed.	Mail	The **mail convert** server program failed.
Mail submitted for delivery. (1 Person/Group).	Mail	A Notes mail message was transferred for 1 user.
Mail submitted for delivery. (<Number of> People/Groups).	Mail	A Notes mail message was transferred for **x** users.

Sys. Admin. 1

Error Message	Type	Description
Mailconv: Categories to folder conversion failed on <Database Name>.	Mail	The **mail convert** server program failed.
Mailconv: Design replacement failed on <Database Name>.	Mail	The **mail convert** server program failed.
Mailconv: Failed to build a list of mail files in <Database Name>.	Mail	The **mail convert** server program failed.
Mailconv: Failed to build a list of mail files in <View Name>:View.	Mail	The **mail convert** server program failed.
Mailconv: Failed to open database <Database Name>.	Mail	The **mail convert** server program failed.
Mailconv: Failed to open template file <File Name>.	Mail	The **mail convert** server program failed.
Mailconv: Failed to open textfile <File Name>.	Mail	The **mail convert** server program failed.
Mailconv: Invalid Option.	Mail	The **mail convert** server program failed.
Mailconv: Missing file name.	Mail	The **mail convert** server program failed.
Mailconv: No database found that matches <Database Name>.	Mail	The **mail convert** server program failed.
Mailconv: Skipping database <Database Name>:Template does not match the specified old template name.	Mail	The **mail convert** server program failed.
Mailconv: When using the -d option you must specify old and new templates.	Mail	The **mail convert** server program failed.
Make call to server.	Comm	For analog Notes users, asks to make call to target Notes server.
Maximum hop count exceeded. Message probably in a routing loop.	Mail	Mail message "ping-ponging" between Notes servers. Maximum hop count is 25.
Modem command file contains an illegal character sequence.	Comm	Modem MDM file contains an illegal AT command.
Modem command file variable is not recognized.	Comm	Modem MDM file contains an illegal AT variable.
Modem could not detect dial tone.	Comm	Modem could not detect dial tone.
Modem lost carrier.	Comm	The modem lost the connection to the target Notes server.

Table 12.3

Notes Error
Messages (cont'd.)

Error Message	Type	Description
Name and Address database contains no Connection document for that server.	Comm	The Notes server is trying to connect to a target Notes server, but does not have a connection record within the public Name and Address book.
Name & Address Book contains a Connection entry with no schedule information.	Comm	The connection record does not have any scheduling information with the target Notes server.
Name & Address Book database (names.nsf) does not exist.	Misc	The Notes machine does not have a Name and Address Book. One must exist in order to operate.
Name & Address database does not contain a server entry for this server.	Server	The Notes server cannot start unless an entry within the public Name and Address book exists for the Notes server. See Chapters 6 and 7.
NETBIOS not loaded or not running.	Comm	The NetBIOS protocol is not configured.
NETBIOS unit number specified in NOTES.INI is too large.	Comm	The NetBIOS unit number is not configured.
NetWare AppleTalk is not installed or could not be initialized.	Comm	The AppleTalk protocol is not configured.
NetWare IPX is not installed or could not be initialized.	Comm	The IPX protocol is not configured.
NetWare IPX/SPX could not be initialized: Insufficient conventional memory. Try loading fewer DOS device drivers or TSRs.	Comm	The IPX protocol is not configured properly on the machine.
NetWare IPX/SPX could not be initialized: No IPX/SPX control blocks (ECBs) available.	Comm	The IPX protocol is not configured properly on the machine.
NetWare IPX/SPX could not be initialized: Packet size is too large.	Comm	The IPX protocol is not configured properly on the machine
NetWare IPX/SPX error: Lock failed, possibly due to insufficient memory.	Comm	The IPX protocol is not configured properly on the machine.
NetWare is not started or the netware.drv Windows driver is not installed.	Comm	The IPX protocol is not configured properly on the machine.
NetWare service advertising (SAP) failed to start.	Comm	On Windows NT, the SAP agent is required.
NetWare SPX is not installed or could not be initialized.	Comm	The SPX protocol is not configured.
Network adapter not installed or not functioning.	Comm	The network card is malfunctioning or is not installed.

Sys.Admin.1

Table 12.3

Notes Error

Messages (cont'd.)

Error Message	Type	Description
Network adapter not working; check cable.	Comm	The network card may not be functioning or the cable may be loose.
Network adapter too busy to handle request.	Comm	The network card may be too busy.
Network authentication message is too short.	Security	A possible network authentication occurred.
Network driver has not been initialized.	Comm	The network driver on the OS has not initialized.
Network error due to transient network condition or hardware failure.	Comm	A network error occurred.
Network error: message has been corrupted.	Security	A Notes document or message has been corrupted due to a network error.
Network error: message has incorrect sequence number.	Comm	A network packet was received out of sequence order.
Network not started.	Comm	The networking software on the OS has not yet been started.
Network operation did not complete in a reasonable amount of time; please retry.	Comm	The network is timing out. Due to an unreachable network/server or an overloaded network/server.
Network operation was canceled.	Comm	The network operation was canceled, usually due to a person pressing **Ctrl-Break** on the keyboard.
Network traffic is being encrypted at the server's request...	Security	All data with the target Notes server is encrypted over the network with the Notes port settings.
New mail has been delivered to you!	Mail	A new mail message has been delivered to the user's mail database.
Newly disabled ports will remain active until the program is restarted.	Comm	The network port will remain active until the Notes program is restarted.
No certificates in common.	Security	Two user ID files do not have a certificate in common.
No databases to replicate on that server.	Replica	The target Notes server does not have any replica databases in common to replicate.
No documents were deleted.	Misc	A request to delete documents was made, but none were deleted.

Table 12.3

Notes Error

Messages (cont'd.)

Error Message	Type	Description
No mail sent.	Mail	A request to send mail was made, but no mail was sent.
No Name & Address Book database found.	Mail	A search was made for a Name and Address Book, but none was found.
No route found to domain <Domain Name> from server <Server Name> via server <Server Name>. Check Server, Connection and Domain documents in Name & Address Book.	Mail	A Notes mail message was sent to a specified Notes domain, but the target Notes server did not have any connection records pertaining to that domain.
No route found to domain <Domain Name> from server <Server Name>. Check Server, Connection and Domain documents in Name & Address Book.	Mail	A Notes mail message was sent to a specified Notes domain, but the home mail server did not have any connection records pertaining to that domain.
No such port known.	Comm	A request to access a Notes port driver was initiated, but no such port is configured within Notes.
None of the selected databases has a replica on the server.	Replica	A request to replicate a specific database was initiated, but the target Notes server does not have a database with the same replica ID on the server.
Not authorized to open destination database.	Replica	A request to open a target Notes database was denied. The database ACL is set to not allow access.
Not authorized to open source database.	Replica	A request to open a target Notes database was denied. The database ACL is set to not allow access.
Not replicating <Destination Server database> (not authorized to read <Source Server database>).	Replica	The ACL of the target Notes application is set not to allow replication to the initiating Notes server.
Notes requires a newer NetWare OS/2 Requester, v1.3f (NSD4) or later.	Comm	Notes requires the latest network drivers.
Notes requires a newer NetWare OS/2 Requester, v2.0b or later.	Comm	Notes requires the latest network drivers.
Notes requires newer NetWare SPX.SYS and SPDAEMON.EXE files, v3.0b or later.	Comm	Notes requires the latest network drivers.

Sys. Admin. I

Table 12.3

Notes Error
Messages (cont'd.)

Error Message	Type	Description
Notes requires newer NetWare SPX.SYS and SPDAEMON.EXE files, v3.0g (July 23, 1992) or later.	Comm	Notes requires the latest network drivers.
Notes requires System 7.0 or later.	Resource	Notes requires at least System 7.0.
One or more of the source document's attachment are missing. Run Fixup to delete the document in the source database.	Misc	Document may be corrupted. Run the server task **fixup**.
Partially replicated <Destination Server database> (due to previously reported error).	Replica	A replication error has occurred.
Passthru connect to remote server failed.	Security	A passthru connection failed.
Passthru function codes is not recognized.	Security	A passthru connection failed.
Periodic full text indexer—Error full text indexing <Database Name>.	Server	An error occurred on the full text index of a database.
Periodic full text indexer error.	Server	An error occurred on the full text index of a database.
Periodic full text indexer not started—need to specify HOURLY, DAILY, WEEKLY program argument.	Server	Full text index settings not configured.
Periodic macro agent—Error opening macro <Macro Name> in <Database Name>.	Server	An error occurred opening a Notes agent.
Periodic macro agent—Error opening running <Macro Name> in <Database Name>.	Server	An error occurred opening a Notes agent.
Periodic macro agent—Error opening <Database Name>.	Server	An error occurred opening a Notes agent.
Periodic macro agent—Error searching <Database Name> for macros.	Server	An error occurred opening a Notes agent.
Port specified in Connection document in Address Book (to reach that server) is not configured on this system.	Comm	The Notes port is not configured within the server document.
Program shutdown in progress.	Comm	Notes program is shutting down.
Recipient's Name & Address Book entry does not specify a mail file.	Mail	The person record for the recipient must be configured to specify a mail file.

Table 12.3

Notes Error

Messages (cont'd.)

Error Message	Type	Description
Remote user's identity is fraudulent.	Security	Under the security section of the server document, check public keys is enabled and the ID file is assumed fraudulent.
Remote user failed authentication.	Security	The user failed to authenticate with the Notes server.
Removed database <Database Name> from catalog.	Misc	The catalog server task removed a database from the Notes catalog.
Removed database <Database Name> from Cluster Database Directory.	Server	The **adminp** server task removed a database from a Notes cluster.
Replicating files with <Server Name>.	Replica	The Notes machine is replicating with the target Notes server.
Replicating <Destination Database> from <Source Database>.	Replica	The Notes machine is replicating with the target Notes server.
Replication can not proceed because can not maintain uniform access control list on replicas.	Replica	The Notes database has **Enforce Consistent ACL Across all Replicas** enabled.
Replication history in <Destination Server database> is corrupted and cannot be repaired. Please make a new replica copy of the database.	Replica	The replication history is corrupted in the Note database.
Replication history is corrupted. Use File Database Copy (Replica) to clear the history.	Replica	The replication history is corrupted in the Note database.
Replication is disabled for this database.	Replica	Replication has been disabled for the database.
Replication is disabled for <Database Name>.	Replica	Replication has been disabled for the database.
Replicator added <number of> document(s) to <Destination Database> from <Source Database>.	Replica	Replication has finished and is reporting all document replicated.
Replicator deleted duplicate document in <Database Name>.	Replica	The Notes replicator task found duplicate documents and deleted the duplicate.
Replicator deleted <number of> document(s) in <Destination Database> from <Source Database>.	Replica	The replicator task is reporting the number of deleted documents for the recent replication event.
Replicator unable to build list of local databases—insufficient memory in pool.	Replica	The memory pool on the Notes server does not have enough resources to spawn a replication event.

Table 12.3

Notes Error

Messages (cont'd.)

Error Message	Type	Description
Replicator updated <number of> document(s) in <Destination Database> from <Source Database>.	Replica	The replicator task is reporting the number of updated documents for the recent replication event.
Requesting system's ID is the same as the server's ID. You cannot use the same ID on two systems.	Server	You have tried to access a Notes server with the same ID file that is running the current Notes server.
Router task not running.	Server	The Notes mail router task is not running on the Notes server.
Router: Beginning mailbox file compaction.	Mail	The Notes mail router mail box (**MAIL.BOX**) is being compacted.
Router: Completed mailbox file compaction.	Mail	The Notes mail router mail box (**MAIL.BOX**) was compacted.
Router: Connection from server <Server Name> not used; Server not found in Address Book.	Mail	A connection document to a Notes server within the same domain was found to a nonexistent Notes server.
Router: Error opening Name & Address Book <Database Name>.	Mail	The public Name and Address book could not be opened.
Router: Error reading public key for <Server Name> from the Name & Address Book.	Mail	The server key within the server document could not be read.
Router: Error searching mailbox file <Database Name>.	Mail	The Notes server mail router database (**MAIL.BOX**) could not be opened.
Router: Mailbox file <Database Name> is corrupt.	Mail	The Notes server mail router database (**MAIL.BOX**) is corrupted. Either delete it and the Notes server will recreate upon startup, or try to run **fixup**.
Router: No messages transferred to <Server Name>.	Mail	No mail messages were transferred to the target Notes server.
Router: Transferred <Message Count> messages to <Server Name>.	Mail	The Notes mail router is specifying the number of mail messages transferred.
Router: Unable to compact mailbox file <Database Name>.	Mail	The **compact** server task is unable to compact the mail router mailbox while it is open.
Router: Unable to find view <View Name> in Address Book.	Mail	The mail router is looking for a specific view within the Name and Address Book and cannot locate it.

Table 12.3

Notes Error
Messages (cont'd.)

Error Message	Type	Description
Router: Unable to open mailbox file <Database Name>.	Mail	The Notes mail router is trying to deliver mail to a target Notes server; however, the server is not responding or accepting deliveries
Server is not a cluster member.	Replica	The Notes server is not a member of a Notes cluster.
Template file does not exist.	Server	The designer server task is trying to update the design of a database based on a Notes template that cannot be located.
The full text index needs to be rebuilt.	Server	The full text index may be corrupt and needs to be rebuilt.
The Notes server is not a known TCP/IP host.	Comm	The Notes server name cannot be resolved into a TCP/IP address. Check the connection record, local HOST file on the server, or DNS.
The remote TCP/IP host is not running the Notes server, or the server is busy.	Comm	The remote server cannot be reached via the TCP/IP network. Check network connectivity and make sure the target Notes server is running.
The server's Address Book does not contain any cross certificates capable of authenticating you.	Security	Authentication is not allowed.
The specified ID file may only be used inside of North America.	Security	A North American ID file is trying to be used with an International version of Notes.
This recipient's public key could not be found in the Address book.	Mail	Check the person document of the recipient.
Unable to fixup database <Database Name>.	Server	The **fixup** server task was unable to fixup the database.
Unable to replicate with server <Server Name>.	Replica	The Notes server was unable to replicate with the target Notes server.
Unable to replicate <Database Name>.	Replica	The Notes server was unable to replicate the database with the target Notes server.
WARNING: Both <Template File> and <Template File> claim to be Design Template '<Template Name>'.	Misc	A database and a template both claim to be the template for a database. Under database properties, deselect one database within design properties.

Table 12.3

Notes Error

Messages (cont'd.)

Error Message	Type	Description
Wrong Password. (Passwords are case sensitive—be sure to use correct upper and lower case.)	Security	An incorrect password was entered for a Notes ID file.
You are not authorized to access that database.	Misc	The ACL of a database is set not to allow access.
You are not authorized to create new databases on this server.	Misc	The field within the server document of the Notes server is set to not allow you access to create new databases.
You are not authorized to create new replica databases on this server.	Misc	The field within the server document of the Notes server is set to not allow you access to create new databases.
You are not authorized to delete that database.	Misc	You need manager ACL access to a database in order to delete a database.
You are not authorized to perform that operation.	Misc	The proper security equivalencies have not been granted to perform that function.
You are not authorized to use the remote console on this server.	Server	You are not listed as an administrator for the Notes server within the Notes server document.
You are not authorized to use the server.	Server	You are not allowed access to the Notes server within the Restrictions section of the server document.
Your certificate has expired.	Security	Your certificate has expired and you must be recertified.

Tips

Again, for the exam, it is not necessary to know all of the above Notes error messages. However, questions based on these messages will appear.

Chapter 12 Sample Questions

Objective: Forcing Replication.

Bill is a Notes administrator for two Notes servers. A discussion database on the remote office Notes server in New York has an addition that needs to be added to the replica copy on his home server; it cannot wait for the next scheduled replication. What is the most efficient way for Bill to update the discussion database on his home Notes server?

      A. `Replicate NY-Notes01/ACME`

      B. `Pull NY-Notes01/ACME`

      C. `Pull NY-Notes01/ACME discuss.nsf`

      D. `Push NY-Notes01/ACME discuss.nsf`

Answer: C
The `replicate` command will pull and push changes so that all replica copies of applications are synchronized. The `push` command will only push updates to the target Notes server. The `pull` command will only pull changes to the initiating Notes server. If `replicate`, `push`, or `pull` is followed with a database name, only that database will be replicated.

Objective: E-Mail Routing.

Susie is having problems sending mail messages to another Notes recipient in another company (another Notes domain). Notes mail connection records exist between the two companyies' mail servers, but Notes mail is not routing. How can she troubleshoot this problem?

      A. Send a mail trace from her Notes workstation that will report any errors as well as return routing information for each Notes server hop the mail message takes

B. She cannot send a mail trace because the target Notes server is not within her Notes domain

C. Susie cannot send a mail trace because the target Notes server is not located on her physical LAN segment

D. There are no mail tools available within Notes

Answer: A

The mail trace utility can be used from a Notes workstation to trace mail routing problems. It can be used to trace mail routes between any two Notes servers. Any Notes version 4 server within the path will report tracing information.

Objective: E-Mail Routing.

Corey, a Notes administrator, needs to route pending Notes mail messages from his server, CHICAGO-NOTES01 to another Notes server, NY-NOTES01, on another Notes network. The next scheduled mail routing event is not for another hour and the mail pending threshold value is set at 10. How can he immediately route any pending messages on his Notes server to the target Notes server, NY-NOTES01?

A. Mail cannot be forced to route; it will only route during scheduled connections

B. He can type `ROUTE NY-NOTES01` from the Notes server console

C. He can type `ROUTE CHICAGO-NOTES01` from the Notes server console

D. He can type `MAIL NY-NOTES01` from the Notes server console

Answer: B

The server console command **route** can be used to route immediately any pending Notes mail messages to a target Notes server.

Objective: Creating Replica Databases.

Louise is a Notes administrator who wishes to create a replica copy of a Notes database located on her home server on another Notes server located in a remote office. How can she perform this operation?

> A. Highlight the Notes database on her Notes desktop, select **File – Database – New Copy**, then fill in the target Notes server information within the dialog box, and click **OK** to create the new copy
>
> B. Highlight the Notes database on her Notes desktop, click **File – Replication – New Replica**, fill in the target Notes server information within the dialog box, and click **OK** to create the new copy
>
> C. Highlight the Notes database on her Notes desktop, click **File – Database – Publish**, fill in the target Notes server information within the dialog box, and click **OK** to create the new copy.

Answer: B
Notes tracks Notes databases by replica ID numbers, not by filename or title. Simply making a new copy of a database will not create a replica copy of the Notes database, and the new copy will not replicate.

Objective: Creating Replica Databases.

Jenny is having trouble replicating a Notes application between two Notes servers. Which of the following statements could cause her replication problems?

> A. Jenny created a new replica of the application on the target Notes server
>
> B. Jenny created a new copy of the application on the target Notes server

Sys. Admin. I

C. Jenny named the new replica of the application with a different file-name on the target Notes server

D. Jenny placed the new replica of the application within a different directory on the target Notes server

Answer: B

Notes replicates databases by replica ID number, not by database title, filename, or location. If Jenny makes a copy of the database (**File – Database – New Copy**), then the application will *not* replicate between Notes servers (the new copy will have a different replica ID number). New replicas must be created by using the **File – Replica – New Replica** options.

Objective: Server and Remote Server Consoles.

Wayne is teaching Dan how to check server statistics from the Notes server console using the remote Notes server console of his Notes workstation. How can Dan accomplish this?

A. Click **File – Tools – Server Administration** and then click the **Console** icon; within the server console command field enter **report statistics** and click **Send**

B. Click **File – Tools – Server Administration** and then click the **Console** icon; within the server console command field enter **show statistics** and click **Send**

C. Statistics can only be gathered from the server console itself

D. Click **File – Tools – Server Administration** and then click the **Server** icon; within the server console command field enter **report statistics** and click **Send**

Answer: B

The remote server console can be used in the same manner as if you are at the Notes server console itself. The command to gather statistics on the Notes server is **show statistics**.

Objective: Creating Replication Formulas.

Replication formulas can be created to replicate based on which of the following?

> A. Field
>
> B. View
>
> C. Server
>
> D. TCP/IP address

Answer: A, B, and C
Replication formulas can be created within a Notes database to replicate only a subset of documents based upon a predefined formula or element of the Notes database.

Objective: Renaming Notes Users.

Brad needs to rename a Notes user who has just been married. What is the most efficient means of renaming a Notes user?

> A. Recreate the Notes user and modify all groups and database ACLs to reflect the name change
>
> B. From the Notes server console, type **load rename *<person name>*;** the person's name will be changed on all groups and database application ACLs
>
> C. Using the administration process, highlight the user's name within the public Name and Address book and click **Actions – Rename Person**; all groups and Notes application ACLs will be changed, assuming the administration server has been properly set

Answer: C
If the administration process is properly configured on the Notes server and on all Notes applications, it can be used to automatically rename a user.

Objective: Recertifying Notes Users.

Jim wishes to recertify some Notes users, as their certificates are ready to expire. How can he accomplish this task?

> A. Recreate the Notes users and send them their new Notes ID files
>
> B. From the Notes server administration panel on his Notes workstation, highlight the users' names and click **Actions – Recertify Person**
>
> C. He needs to visit each workstation and recertify each ID file
>
> D. From within the certifier log, highlight the users' names and recertify them from the certification button

Answer: B
Using the administration process, a Notes administrator may automatically recertify Notes users.

Objective: Configuring the Notes Administration Process.

What functions can be performed using the Administration Process?

> A. Delete user, servers, and group documents from the public Name and Address book
>
> B. Recertify and Rename Notes ID files
>
> C. Create and delete users' mail files
>
> D. Remove user names from ACL
>
> E. Convert users and servers from a flat to a hierarchical naming standard

Answer: A, B, C, D, and E
All listed functions may be performed by using the Notes administration process.

Objective: Configuring the Notes Administration Process.

Tom just deleted a Notes user from the public Name and Address book, but that user still appears within some ACL listings of the company's Notes databases. Why did the administration process not remove the user names from the ACLs of the Notes databases?

A. The administration process cannot perform this function

B. The Notes databases do not have an administration server set

C. Tom forgot to select **remove ACL entries** when he deleted the users from the public Name and Address book.

D. The Notes databases have Tom listed as Manager access.

Answer: B
Within each Notes database, the database manager or administrator must set the Notes administration server in order to take advantage of the administration process.

Objective: Using the Notes Server Administration Panel.

What functions may be performed from the Notes Server administration panel?

A. Register a person from a file

B. Create a new group

C. Configure a Notes server

D. Edit multiple passwords

E. Add a new network port

F. Set database quotas

Answer: A, B, C, D, and F

All listed functions except Answer: E may be performed from the Notes server administration panel. New network ports are added from the User Preferences dialog box.

Objective: Configuring Notes application Quotas and Limits.

Chad wishes to set a size limit on his Notes user's mail files so that they may only reach 10 megabytes in size, but does not want to prevent his users from receiving new e-mail messages if the 10 megabyte size limit is reached. What should Chad do?

A. When Chad creates a new user's Notes mail file, he should set the absolute limit to 10 megabytes

B. From the Notes server administration panel, Chad can select absolute database limits and set the application to 10 megabytes

C. Limits cannot be set on user's mail files

D. From the Notes server administration panel, Chad can select database quotas from the database pop-up menu and set the application to 10 megabytes

Answer: D

Absolute limits can only be set to a Notes application when it is first created. Absolute limits are also limited to 1, 2, 3, and 4 gigabyte settings, and represent the maximum size the application may reach in size. Quotas may be set and changed on a Notes application whenever a Notes administrator wishes. Quotas are used to control application sizes.

Objective: Monitoring Notes Servers.

Pete wishes to monitor replication and mail routing events on his Notes server. How can he easily accomplish this?

A. Establish a remote Notes server console session and watch the console for replication and e-mail events

B. Enter each Notes application he wishes to monitor and check for new documents

C. Monitor the Notes log application on the Notes server and monitor replication and e-mail events

D. Monitor the public Name and Address book on the Notes server and monitor replication and e-mail events

Answer: C

The Notes log on each Notes server can be used to monitor all Notes server activity, including initiated replication events and e-mail events.

Objective: Corrupted Notes Applications.

How can a corrupted view within a Notes application be fixed?

A. Create a new replica of the application, and cut and paste the corrupted view from the old database to the new one.

B. Run the **fixup** server program against the corrupted application.

C. Run the **compact** server program against the corrupted application.

D. Run **updall** server program against the corrupted application.

Answer: B

The **fixup** Notes server application will attempt to fix corrupted Notes documents, forms, and views within a Notes application. The **compact** server program will take "white space" out of a Notes application. The **updall** server program updates a Notes application's view indices.

13

The Name and Address Book (Domain) Structure

This chapter covers each of the forms within the Notes Name and Address book. For the System Administration I exam, you will not have to know each form with great detail; however, you should know the names of all forms and have a basic concept of its function. Some fields are very important within each type of document; we will point these important fields out within this chapter. You should also know how to create each document.

Tips

For the exam, particular attention should be paid to creating connection records (especially passthru), as well as security fields within the server document (especially passthru). Also, as stated before, you should know how to create each type of document and the function of each within Notes.

Public Name and Address Book—Notes Domain

A Lotus Notes *domain* is defined as a collection of users, servers, and groups that share a common name and address book within a Notes environment. A Notes domain can encompass servers and users on the same as well as different physical networks.

The Lotus Notes infrastructure within a company must be designed to replicate this common Name and Address book to all Notes servers within the organization. This same replica copy must exist on every server within the company's Notes network. Any changes made to this database should then be replicated to all other Notes servers to keep the configuration of all components the same. It is also responsible for basic security and management of all users and servers. Although it is possible to have multiple domains (multiple Name and Address books) within a company, it is recommended that a company only use one Name and Address, book as it is much easier to control the functions of servers and users, and the security of each.

The public Name and Address book for a Notes infrastructure is the heart of the network. All Notes servers, users, groups, and other configuration items are added and maintained within this Notes database. For this reason, proper security measures need to be put into place to prevent unauthorized access. Normally, all administration of the public Name and Address book is handled centrally by a select few people to avoid confusion. As pointed out before, it is important that these select few Notes administrators only make additions or modifications to the public Name and Address book on one Notes server, preferably a Notes hub server. The additions and modifications then will be replicated to all other Notes servers within the infrastructure through scheduled replication events.

There are two types of address books within Lotus Notes. The first is the public Name and Address book, which is based upon the template **PUBNAMES.NTF**. The second is the personal Name and Address book, which exists on each user's Notes workstation and is based upon the template **PERNAMES.NTF**. The remainder of this chapter shows each form within the *public* Name and Address book.

Sys. Admin. I

Group Record

The group form contains listings of servers, users, and/or other groups. They are used for mailing purposes, ACLs in Notes applications, and server access (see Figure 13-1).

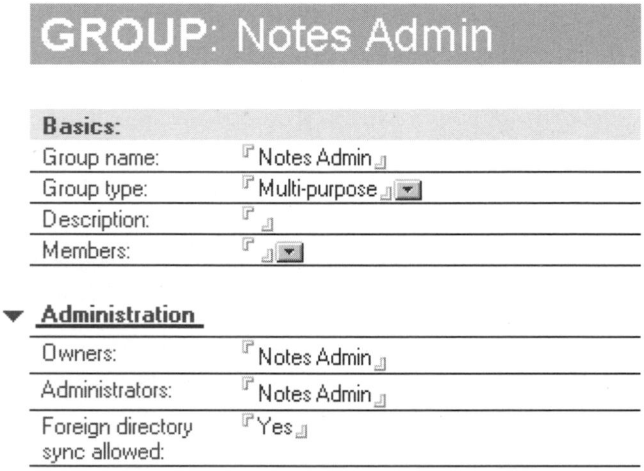

Figure 13-1
Group Record

GROUP: Notes Admin

Basics:

Group name:	Notes Admin
Group type:	Multi-purpose
Description:	
Members:	

▼ **Administration**

Owners:	Notes Admin
Administrators:	Notes Admin
Foreign directory sync allowed:	Yes

This form can be created by opening the Name and Address book and selecting **Create – Group** from the Notes menu.

- **Group Name:** Within this field, you should type in the name of the group as it will appear for ACL access and/or e-mail listings.

- **Group Type:** The type of group should be either Multi-Purpose, Access Control List Only, Mail Only, or Deny List Only.

  - **Multi-Purpose:** use for access control and mailing lists.

  - **Access Control List:** use for server and database access control.

- **Mail Only:** use for e-mail mailing lists.

- **Deny List Only:** use to deny access to servers and databases.

- **Description:** This field is for descriptive purposes only and provides no functionality in terms of Notes server processes. It appears within the Group view of the public Name and Address book.

- **Members:** This is the field where user, servers, and other group names appear. A user's fully distinguished name or common name may be used. The pull-down button may be used to search the public Name and Address book and select any members to be added to the group.

- **Owners:** The owner(s) of the group is responsible for maintaining and editing the group document. It is this field that the Author level ACL access is assumed. In other words, if a user or group has Author access to the public Name and Address book, and appears within a group document within this field, the user or group listed will be able to modify the document.

- **Administrators:** This field also enables any users or groups listed with the ability to edit the entire group document. This is usually reserved for administrators of the Notes infrastructure.

Location Record

This form (Figure 13-2) gives the ability to mobile users to store different configurations for their Notes workstation.

Figure 13-2

Location
Record

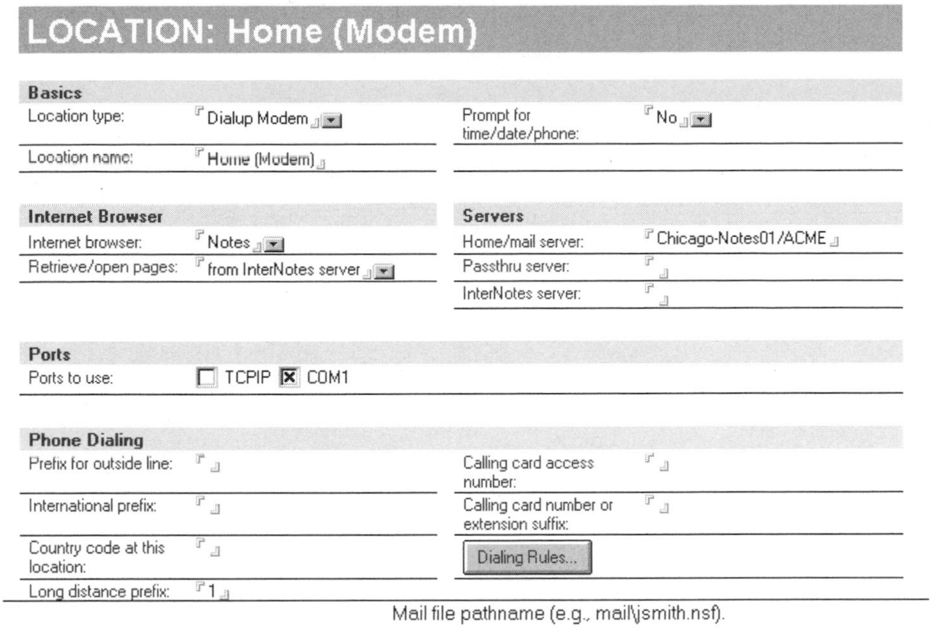

LOCATION: Home (Modem)

Basics

Location type:	Dialup Modem ▼	Prompt for time/date/phone:	No ▼
Location name:	Home (Modem)		

Internet Browser

		Servers	
Internet browser:	Notes ▼	Home/mail server:	Chicago-Notes01/ACME
Retrieve/open pages:	from InterNotes server ▼	Passthru server:	
		InterNotes server:	

Ports

Ports to use: ☐ TCPIP ☒ COM1

Phone Dialing

Prefix for outside line:		Calling card access number:	
International prefix:		Calling card number or extension suffix:	
Country code at this location:		[Dialing Rules...]	
Long distance prefix:	1		

Mail file pathname (e.g., mail\jsmith.nsf).

This form can be created by opening the Name and Address book and selecting **Create – Location** from the Notes menu.

- **Location Name:** The name of the location.

- **Location Type:** Specifies the type of connection to the Notes server. Choices include **Local Area Network, Dialup Modem, Both Dialup and Local Area Network,** and **No Connection.**

- **Ports to use:** Check the port(s) this location will use. The ports have to be enabled on the Notes workstation's preferences for them to appear within the document (**File – Tools – User Preferences – Ports**).

- **Local time zone:** The time zone for the Notes workstation.

- **Prompt for time/date/zone:** This determines whether or not the user will be prompted for the time and phone information each time Notes is started.

Sys. Admin. I

- **Home/mail server:** Specifies the user's home mail Notes server.

- **Passthru server:** Specifies the user's passthru Notes server if one will be used.

- **InterNotes server:** Specifies the user's InterNotes server, if one will be used.

- **Phone Dialing Section:** Specifies the dialing parameters and numbers to connect to the Notes server.

- **Mail File Location:** Specifies the location of the user's mail file (local machine or Notes server).

- **Mail File:** Specifies the filename of the user's mail file.

- **Mail Domain:** This specifies the Notes mail domain for the user.

- **Recipient Name Type-Ahead:** This specifies what type of lookahead feature will be used. Choices include **Disabled**, **Personal Address Book Only**, and **Personal then Public Address Book**.

- **Recipient Name Lookup:** Determines when the lookahead feature will stop. Choices include **Stop after first match** and **Exhaustively check all Address Books**.

- **Transfer outgoing mail if ... messages pending:** This setting will force Notes to call the Notes server and deliver pending mail messages based upon this number. The default is 5 mail messages pending.

- **Schedule:** This determines whether scheduled replication is disabled or enabled.

- **Replicate daily between:** This field is the time(s) the Notes machine will replicate. The default is 8AM to 10PM.

- **Repeat every:** If a range of times is used to replicate, a repeat interval in minutes may be used. The default is 60 minutes.

- **Days of week:** Specifies the days of the week this replication schedule will use.

- **Daylight saving time:** Specifies whether or not to observe daylight savings time at this location.

- **Only for user:** Specifies the name of the Notes user(s) that may use this location document.

- **Owners:** The owner(s) of the location document is responsible for maintaining and editing the group document. It is at this field that the Author level ACL access is assumed. In other words, if a user or group has Author access to the public Name and Address book, and appears within a group document within this field, the user or group listed will be able to modify the document.

- **Administrators:** This field also enables any users or groups listed the ability to edit the entire group document. This is usually reserved for administrators of the Notes infrastructure.

Person Record

The person record (Figure 13-3) is used to identify Notes users and is used by Notes for mail file locations, ACL access to Notes applications, and to provide user information within a Notes domain.

Figure 13-3

Person Record

Name	
First name:	Scott
Middle initial:	
Last name:	Thomas
User name:	Scott Thomas/Marketing/Chicago/ACME Scott Thomas, slt
Short name and/or Internet address:	sthomas
HTTP password:	(355E98E7C7B59BD810ED845AD0FD2FC4)

Mail	
Mail system:	Notes
Domain:	ACME
Mail server:	Chicago-Notes01/Chicago/ACME
Mail file:	mail\sthomas
Forwarding address:	

Work	
Title:	Groupware Manager
Company:	ACME
Department:	IT
Location:	Chicago
Manager:	
Office phone:	312-555-555
FAX phone:	
Cell phone:	
Assistant:	

Home	
Street address:	
City:	
State/province:	
Zip/postal code:	
Country:	
Home phone:	
FAX phone:	
Spouse:	
Children:	

Notes automatically creates a person record for each Notes user you create. This form can also be manually created by opening the public Name and Address book and selecting **Create – Person** from the Notes menu.

- **First Name:** This is the first name of the Notes user. The field is filled upon user creation and should never be changed within this document.

- **Middle Initial:** Like the First Name field, this field is filled upon user creation and also should never be modified from within this Notes document. Normally, most administrators never use this field unless there are two people within the company with the same name.

- **Last Name:** Again, this field is filled at user creation and should not be modified from within this record.

- **User Name:** This field is also filled upon user creation and will contain the user's fully distinguished name followed by another entry of the user's common name. The entry containing the user's fully distinguished name is where all ACL resolutions for Notes database and server access is performed. For this reason, it is essential that this first entry within the field *never* be changed. If it is changed, users will not be able to access any Notes applications or servers.

  Any other entries following this first entry are assumed aliases of that person. Any name can follow this initial entry. All aliases will only be used for e-mail resolutions. All aliases will not be used for ACL access to Notes applications and Notes server access. Alias entries should be entered followed by commas. When the document is saved, the field will be parsed and the commas removed.

- **Short name and/or Internet address:** The short name is commonly used by foreign e-mail systems, such as PROFS, or the Internet, using products such as the Lotus SMTP MTA. This field is also filled at user creation and shouldn't be modified by users. Administrators may need to modify this field if an external mail system needs to access this field and two users within the Notes infrastructure both have the same short name.

- **Mail System:** This field is where the mail system is determined. Selections include **Notes mail**, **cc:Mail**, **Internet mail (SMTP)**, **X.400 mail**, **Other**, and **None**. Notes mail is the default selection. The cc:Mail, Internet mail, and X.400 mail systems require that the appropriate add-ons be installed within the Notes infrastructure. The cc:Mail and SMTP (Internet Mail) MTA's (Message Transfer Agents) are free of charge from Lotus. The X.400 MTA is an additional product that must be purchased separately and installed within the Notes network.

  If this entry is changed to a value other than Notes mail, then many of the following described fields will not appear within a person record, or the names of the fields may be different.

- **Domain:** The domain field is filled upon creation of the Notes user assuming Notes mail is used. This field contains the domain name the Notes user belongs to. The Notes administration team creates the domain name when the Notes network is first architected. A Notes user should not modify this field.

- **Mail Server:** For Notes mail users, this signifies the Notes mail user's home mail server where his or her mail database application resides. The field is filled initially when the Notes mail user is created. It is from this field that the Notes mail router decides how to route mail to the correct Notes mail server. This field should never be modified unless by a knowledgeable Notes administrator; incorrect information will result in undeliverable mail.

- **Mail File:** The Notes mail file field within the Notes person record is filled upon creation of the Notes mail user. The field directs the Notes mail router on a Notes server where to deliver a Notes mail message. The contents should contain the path of a Notes user's mail file, starting from where the Notes data directory exists on the Notes server. In other words, if the Notes server code is installed in the directory "c:\notes\data," then this is assumed to be the root directory. Most mail files then are stored in "c:\notes\data\mail" so the entry for a user would be "mail\sthomas". The ".nsf" extension is assumed and is not needed. This field should never be modified unless by a Notes administrator; incorrect information will result in undeliverable mail.

- **Forwarding Address:** This field is by default left blank and should only be used in the event a user wishes to have his or her mail forwarded to another e-mail address. It should be noted that if this field is filled, e-mail will not be delivered to the user's Notes mail address. Users many times fill this field when they are going to be in a location where Notes mail is inaccessible, but they have an external Internet account where they can access mail. When they return, the field is then cleared.

- **Work and Home Information** Sections: These sections are for informational purposes only. A Notes user can fill these fields in a manner they wish.

- **Comment:** This field is for descriptive purposes only and can be modified and filled by either the Notes administrator or Notes user.

- **Encrypt incoming mail:** This field instructs the Notes mail router to encrypt all incoming mail to the specified Notes mail user. If this selection is set to **yes**, only the recipient will be able to read his or her mail messages in the respective Notes mail file. Not even a Notes administrator with Manager access to the user's Notes mail file—or even from the Notes server itself—will be able to read the encrypted mail.

- **Other X.400 address:** This field is used to resolve other X.400 addresses that a user may have if an X.400 e-mail system is being used within the organization.

- The **Public Keys** Section of the Notes person record contains the certified public key of the Notes user and is in hexadecimal format. This field should never be modified, unless intentionally by a Notes administrator. Modification of this field will corrupt the private/public key relationship for the Notes user. Encrypting mail will no longer operate correctly.

- **Owners:** This field signifies who may modify this document with Author ACL access. In most cases, this is the name of the person themselves.

- **Administrators:** This field enables any users or groups listed with the ability to edit the entire person record. This is usually reserved for administrators of the Notes infrastructure. It should be noted that this field is irrelevant if a potential modifier has Editor access or higher to the public Name and Address book, or if a user or group other then the owner of the document has Author access with the UserModifier Role granted.

- **Notes Client License:** This field is used to signify what type of Notes license the Notes user is utilizing: Notes mail, Notes Desktop, or a full Notes license.

- **Setup profile:** This field is used when a Notes user is set up for the first time. The administrator upon user creation populates it.

- **Foreign directory sync allowed:** This field is responsible for allowing synchronization of the person record information to other foreign mail and directories. Such an example would be to cc:Mail environments.

Server Record

The server form (Figure 13-4) provides information about each Notes server, including configuration, location, network configuration, security, and any MTA's (Message Transfer Agents) that are used.

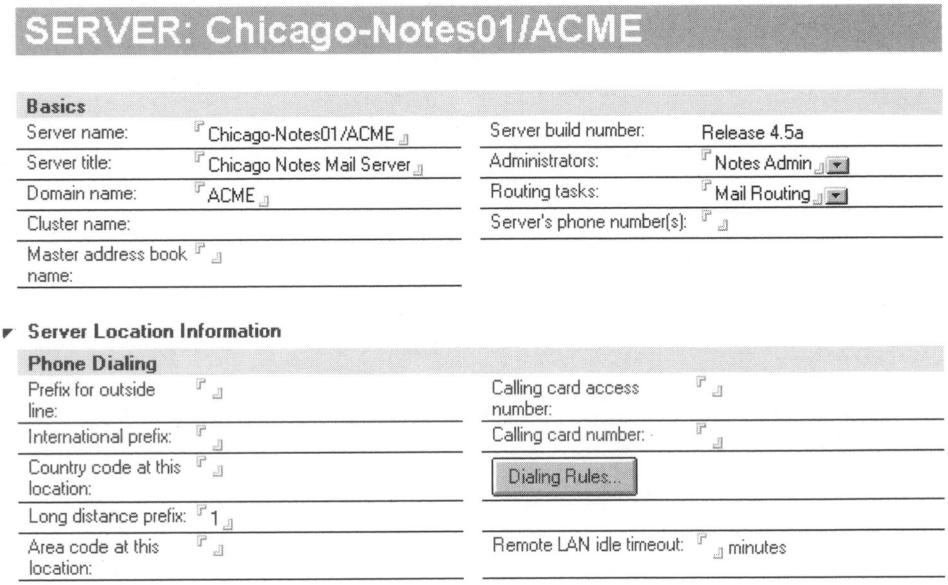

Figure 13-4
Server Record

A server document is automatically created when a Notes server is registered.

- **Server name:** This field is populated when the Notes administrator creates a new server within the organization. This field usually should never be modified.

- **Server title:** This field is for descriptive purposes only and does not have any operational purposes for the Notes server.

- **Domain name:** This field is filled upon the creation of the Notes server. The field is normally never modified, unless the Notes server is moved from one Notes domain to another.

- **Server build number:** This calculated field is populated by the administration process running on the Notes server.

- **Administrators:** This field should be populated with the Notes administrators in charge of administering the server. It gives the proper authority to manage the Notes server and provides access to items such as remote console.

- **Routing tasks:** This field specifies the type of e-mail routing that will be performed on the Notes server. Choices include **Mail Routing**, **X.400 Routing**, **SMTP Mail Routing**, and **cc:Mail routing**.

- **Server's phone number(s):** If the Notes server will be permitting dial-in access to the Notes server itself, then the administrators should enter those dial-in numbers. The field is for descriptive purposes only.

- **Phone Information:** These fields contain dialing rules and phone information for this server to use.

- **Remote LAN idle timeout:** Enter a number in minutes to force the Notes server to hang up the line in the event of inactivity.

- **Local time zone:** Populate this field with the proper time zone.

- **Daylight savings time:** Specify whether or not daylight savings time is observed at this location.

- **Mail server:** Enter the Notes mail server. This field is important if the Notes server will be e-mailing documents.

- **Passthru server:** If this Notes server will be using another server to pass through access to other Notes servers, enter the name of that Notes passthru server.

- **InterNotes server:** If this Notes server will be using an InterNotes server, enter the name of that Notes server.

- **Port:** All the enabled network ports of the Notes server need to be entered within the Ports fields. COM ports do not need to be entered.

- **Notes Network:** This field should contain the name of the Notes named network the server and port belong to. All Notes servers that share the same common protocol and exist within the same LAN should be included within the same Notes named network.

Tips

For the examination, memorize the Notes Network field and how it relates to configuring Notes named networks.

- **Net Address:** This should be the address of the Notes server's network port. For IP networks, this should be the IP address or the DNS entry of the server.

- **Enabled/Disabled:** This field signifies whether the port is enabled or disabled.

- **Compare public keys:** This field will compare the public key of the user ID with the entry of the user's public key in the public Name and Address book during authentication. If they do not match, access will not be granted. This field protects against the prospect of a fake user ID.

- **Allow anonymous Notes connections:** Enabling this field will enable all Notes ID files to authenticate with the Notes servers, regardless of certificates held.

- **Only allow access to users in N&A book:** When set to **Yes**, this field will only allow users with person records in the public Name and Address book to access the Notes server. Note, however, that with this field set to **Yes,** other Notes servers will not be able to access the Notes server unless it is listed in the Access Server field or is a member of a group within the Access Server field.

- **Access server:** This field contains those users, servers, and groups that are allowed access to the Notes server. If this field is left blank, then **all** Notes users, servers, and groups will be allowed access.

- **Not access server:** Enter servers, groups, or users that you wish to deny access to the Notes servers. It is beneficial to populate a group such as *Deny Access* with users who have left the company and then to place this Notes group within this field.

- **Create new databases:** Only place users or groups you wish to grant the ability to create new Notes database applications on the server. If the field is left blank, then **all** Notes users will be able to create new Notes database applications.

- **Create replica databases:** Place users or groups you wish to be able to create new replica Notes applications within this field. If this field is left blank, **no one** will be able to create new replica database applications unless done at the Notes server interface.

Traps

For the exam, know the consequences of leaving the **Create new databases** *and* **Create replica databases** *fields blank, as they have different settings.*

- **Access this server through Passthru:** This field allows users, groups, and servers to access this server as a passthru destination. If this field is left blank, then **no** users or groups can access this Notes server as a passthru destination.

- **Passthru route through:** This field should be populated with users, servers, or groups you wish to access the Notes server for passthru to another Notes server destination. If this field is left blank, then **no** user or server will be able to use this Notes server as a passthru server.

- **Passthru cause calling:** This field designates which servers, groups, or users may force the Notes server to "call" or contact another server and act as an intermediary (passthru) contact to another Notes server. If this field is left blank, then **no** destinations are allowed to be called.

- **Passthru destinations allowed:** This field lists all destination Notes servers that are allowed. If this field is left blank, then **all** Notes servers are possible destinations via passthru.

Tips

For the examination, the candidate should know the defaults of all four above passthru fields, and the effects of modifying the fields for passthru access.

- **Run personal agents:** This field designates which people and groups are allowed to run personal agents on a Notes server. If this field is left blank, all people and groups are allowed to run personal agents.

- **Run restricted LotusScript agents:** This field signifies those users and groups that are able to run restricted LotusScript agents. If this field is left blank, no one is allowed to run restricted LotusScript agents.

- **Run unrestricted LotusScript agents:** This field signifies those users and groups that are able to run unrestricted LotusScript agents. If this field is left blank, no one is allowed to run unrestricted LotusScript agents.

- **Refresh agent cache:** This field contains the time the Agent Manager's agent cache will be updated.

Daytime and Nighttime Parameters

The agent manager can be configured to run differently during the day and in the evening. Each section (daytime and nighttime) has the following fields:

- **Start time:** This field contains the time of day or night to start agent executions.

- **End time:** This field contains the time of day to end agent executions.

- **Max concurrent agents:** This field contains the maximum number of agents that may be run at any given time. It should be noted that only one agent can run on a Notes database at a time. However, other agents can run on other Notes databases at the same time. Multiple agents will consume resources that could be used by other Notes processes, so care should be taken when increasing this value.

- **Max LotusScript execution time:** This field contains the maximum number of minutes a LotusScript agent is able to run. If the agent has not completed in the allotted time, the agent will not be permitted to complete. If the value is set too high, it could consume too many resources, so care should also be taken when setting this value.

- **Max % busy before delay:** This field represents the maximum amount of time in percentage that a server may spend running an agent.

Administration Process

The following fields within the server document control the administration process on the specific Notes server:

- **Maximum number of threads:** This field controls how many threads the administration process will use on the specified Notes server. This value normally should not be increased unless the Notes server is running on a SMP machine with large amounts of RAM.

- **Interval:** This field signifies how often the administration process will carry out administration requests.

- **Execute once a day requests at:** This field contains the time of day the administration process will update person documents in the public Name and Address book.

- **Interval between purging mail file...:** This field details the number of days the Object Collect task waits until it runs against users' mail files that use shared mail and when the users' mail files are deleted.

- **Start executing on:** This field signifies on what day(s) of the week delayed requests are carried out on the Notes server.

- **Start executing at:** This field details what time of day delayed requests are carried out.

- **Owner:** This field is the owner of the document and represents those people with only Author access to the public Name and Address book who are able to edit the document. Users or groups with Editor or higher access or with Author access and the ServerModifier Role may still edit the document, however, without existing in this field.

- **Administrators:** This field should be filled with any Notes administrators or groups in charge of administrating this document.

- **Certified Public Key:** This field contains the certified public key of the Notes server. The field should never be modified, unless on purpose by a knowledgeable Notes administrator.

- **Change request:** The administration process of a Notes server uses this field if a change is requested on the Notes server. The contents of the field expire after 21 days unless otherwise set by the **Name_Change_Expiration_Days** setting in the **NOTES.INI** file.

Certifier Record

There are two types of certifier forms: one is for internal certifiers registered within your Notes domain and the other lists cross-certificates that you may have with other organizations. See Figure 13-5.

Figure 13-5
Certifier Record

CERTIFIER:/Chicago/ACME

Basics
Certifier type:	Notes Certifier
Certifier name:	/Chicago/ACME
Issued by:	/ACME
Certified public key:	XXXX

Contact
Company:	
Department:	
Location:	
Office phone:	
Comment:	

E-Mail
Notes mail server:	
Notes mail filename:	
Other mail address:	Scott Thomas/Marketing/Chicago/ACME

▼ **Administration**
Owners:	Scott Thomas/Marketing/Chicago/ACME
Administrators:	Notes Admin
Change request:	XXXX

A certifier document is created automatically when you create a new certifier or cross-certify another organization.

- **Certifier type:** This computed field is populated when either a certifier ID or cross-certificate is created by a Notes administrator. The field entry is either a certifier or cross-certificate entry.

- **Certifier name:** This field is the distinguished name of the certifier. It is filled upon creation of the certifier ID. It should not be modified except by a knowledgeable Notes administrator.

- **Issued by:** This field is also filled upon creation and contains the higher level of the fully distinguished name that created the certifier. In other words, it is the father of this hierarchical ID in a x.500 format.

- **Certifier public key:** This is the public key of the certifier ID and should never be modified except by a knowledgeable Notes administrator.

- **Contact Info:** The fields within this section have no functionality in terms of operating a Notes infrastructure. The fields are only for informational purposes.

- **Notes mail server:** When a user or server ID's certificate expires, a user may use Notes mail to send a request to renew the certificate. Within this field, a Notes administrator may place a mail server where these requests would reside.

- **Notes mail filename:** This field is used to direct certificate requests to the appropriate file on the mail server to reside.

- **Other mail address:** Instead of using the Notes mail filename and Notes mail server fields, a Notes administrator may place a person's name within the **Other mail address** field to receive certificate requests.

- **Owners:** This field is the owner of the document and represents those people with only Author access to the public Name and Address book who are able to edit the document. Users or groups with Editor or higher access or with Author access and the NetModifier Role may still edit the document, however, without existing in this field.

- **Administrators:** This field should be filled with any Notes administrators or groups in charge of administrating this document. The entire document can be edited by these people and/or groups.

- **Change Request:** This field should contain the Notes administrator's public key in charge of handling certificate requests. The field is only pertinent if encryption is going to be used for Notes mail certificate requests to the recipient listed within the **E-mail** section of this document.

Server Configuration Record

The Notes server configuration record (Figure 13-6) enables Notes administrators to modify the **NOTES.INI** file of the Notes server from the public Name and Address book.

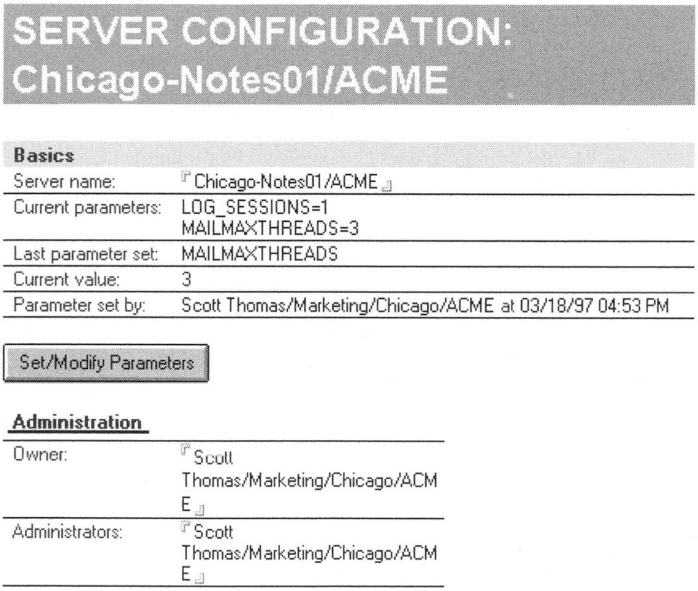

Figure 13-6
Configuration
Record

```
SERVER CONFIGURATION:
Chicago-Notes01/ACME
```

Basics

Server name:	⌐Chicago-Notes01/ACME ⌐
Current parameters:	LOG_SESSIONS=1
	MAILMAXTHREADS=3
Last parameter set:	MAILMAXTHREADS
Current value:	3
Parameter set by:	Scott Thomas/Marketing/Chicago/ACME at 03/18/97 04:53 PM

[Set/Modify Parameters]

▼ **Administration**

Owner:	⌐Scott Thomas/Marketing/Chicago/ACME ⌐
Administrators:	⌐Scott Thomas/Marketing/Chicago/ACME ⌐

This form can be created by opening the Name and Address Book and selecting **Create – Server – Configuration** from the Notes menu.

- **Server name:** This field represents which server(s) the parameters within the current document will be applied to. An asterisk (*) means that all Notes servers within the domain will be affected by the configuration settings. A group of servers may also be listed within the field.

Sys. Admin. I

● **Current parameters:** This field shows any settings that have been set within the configuration document. The included button within the document can be used to populate the field with the appropriate settings.

● **Last parameter set:** This field lists the last parameter that was set within the configuration document.

● **Current value:** Shows the current value of the last parameter set.

● **Parameter set by:** Shows the person that last set a configuration setting within the document.

● **Set/Modify Parameters** Button: This button can be used within the document while in edit mode to add or change configuration settings for a particular Notes server or group of Notes servers.

● **Owner:** This field is the owner of the document and represents those people with only Author access to the public Name and Address book who are able to edit the document. Users or groups with Editor or higher access or with Author access and the NetModifier Role may still edit the document, however, without existing in this field.

● **Administrator:** This field should be filled with any Notes administrators or groups in charge of administrating this document.

Table 13.1 shows configuration settings that are available via the configuration documents.

Table 13.1

Notes Configuration
Variables

NOTES.INI Variable	Description
ADMINPINTERVAL	This setting determines the interval in which the administration process on a Notes server looks for any administration requests to perform.
ADMINPMODIFYPERSONDOCUMENTSAT	This setting determines when the person documents will be modified within the public Name and Address book by the administration process.
AMGR_DOCUPDATEAGENTMININTERVAL	This value determines the minimum amount of time between the executions of the same document update triggered agent.
AMGR_DOCUPDATEEVENTDELAY	This setting determines the delay time at which the Agent Manager schedules a document update triggered agent after a document update event.
AMGR_NEWMAILAGENTMININTERVAL	The minimum amount of time in minutes between the execution of the same new mail triggered agent.
AMGR_NEWMAILEVENTDELAY	The setting represents the time in minutes that Agent Manager schedules a new mail triggered agent after a new mail message is delivered.
AMGR_WEEKENDAYS	This setting represents values for the **Don't run on Weekends** checkbox option in the **Agent Run on Schedule** Options box.
DEFAULT_INDEX_LIFETIME_DAYS	This value set the time in days before the view index for Notes applications are discarded. The default setting is 45 days.
LOG_AGENTMANAGER	This setting specifies whether or not agent executions are logged to Notes server Notes log file.
LOG_MAILROUTING	This setting represents the level of reporting to the Notes log file of a Notes server for mail events.
LOG_REPLICATION	This value specifies whether or not replication events are logged to the Notes server's log file.
LOG_SESSIONS	This value specifies whether or not users' sessions (users access a Notes server) are logged to the Notes log file.
LOG_TASKS	This value specifies whether or not information is displayed and logged when a Notes server polls configuration documents and server records.
LOG_VIEW_EVENTS	This value species whether or not information is logged to the Notes log and to the console when Notes applications' views are rebuilt.
MAIL_LOG_TO_MISCEVENTS	This setting specifies whether or not all mail router events are logged to the Notes log under the Miscellaneous view instead of the Mail Routing Events view.
MAILDISABLEPRIORITY	This setting will force the mail router on the Notes server to ignore Notes mail message priorities.
MAILLOWPRIORITY	This value sets the time that LOW priority mail messages will be delivered.
MAILMAXTHREADS	This value can be set to determine the number of mail threads a Notes server will use to route mail to other Notes servers.

Sys. Admin. I

Table 13.1

Notes Configuration
Variables (cont'd.)

NOTES.INI Variable	Description
MAILTIMEOUT	This value is used to determine the number of days the Notes mail router will hold undelivered mail until it is sent back to the sender.
MEMORY_QUOTA	This variable is used only on OS/2 servers and is responsible for the maximum amount of virtual memory the Notes server may use.
NAME_CHANGE_EXPIRATION_DAYS	This value sets the number of days a change request may remain active.
NETWARENDSNAME	This value sets the NetWare Directory Services Object Name for the Notes server to known within a NDS tree. This setting is used with the SPX driver in Novell 4.1 environments.
NO_FORCE_ACTIVITY_LOGGING	This variable setting is used to control activity logging for each Notes application.
NSF_BUFFER_POOL_SIZE	Notes views that are in use are kept within the NSF buffer pool. The size of this variable is automatically determined upon server startup. Once this value is changed, a Notes server restart is necessary.
NWNDSPASSWORD	This value is intended to automatically log a Notes server into a Novell NDS tree, and is intended for unattended operations.
NWNDSUSERID	This value sets the user name to use in order to log into a Novell NDS tree.
PHONELOG	This value determines whether or not phone calls are logged to the Notes log file.
REPL_ERROR_TOLERANCE	This setting determines the number of accepted replication errors of the same type between a Notes application before replication is terminated.
REPL_PUSH_RETRIES	This setting determines the number of times a push replication will be tried by the calling Notes server.
REPLICATORS	This setting determines the number of replication server tasks that will run on a Notes server.
REPORTUSEMAIL	This setting determines whether or not the Notes mail router will be used to pass Notes server statistics to another server.
SERVER_MAXSESSIONS	This setting is used to determine the number of maximum sessions that will be supported on the Notes server. Once this value is reached, the user or server that is the least recently connected will be dropped.
SERVER_SESSION_TIMEOUT	This setting determines the maximum number of minutes a user or server can remain idle before the connection is dropped.
SERVER_SHOW_PERFORMANCE	This setting will show on the Notes server console the number of users and transaction each minute.
SERVERPULLREPLIACTION	This setting forces the Notes server to use Pull-Pull replication, and will override any connection documents within the public Name and Address book.
SHARED_MAIL	This setting determines whether or not the Notes server will use shared mail for Notes mail users.

Table 13.1
Notes Configuration
Variables (cont'd.)

NOTES.INI Variable	Description
SHOW_TASK_DETAILS	This setting determines whether or not the name of the current transaction is displayed with the session message.
SWAPPATH	This value is used with OS/2 servers and sets the location of the swapper file.
UPDATE_NO_FULLTEXT	This setting is used to determine whether or not the creation of full text indexes are allowed on the Notes server.
UPDATE_SUPPRESION_LIMIT	This setting will override the UPDATE_SUPPRESSION_TIME setting if the specified number of duplicate requests to update indexes and views are received.
UPDATE_SUPPRESSION_TIME	This setting specifies the delay time between Notes application view updates and full text index updates.
UPDATERS	This setting specifies the number of indexer processes that may run simultaneously on a Notes server.

Server Connection Record

Connection records (Figure 13-7) are used to defined connections between two Notes servers or a Notes client and a Notes server. These include Local Area Network, Dialup Modem, passthru, remote LAN services, SMTP, and cc:Mail connections to a Notes server.

Figure 13-7
Connection
Record

SERVER CONNECTION

Basics

Connection type:	Local Area Network	Usage priority:	Normal
Source server:	Chicago-Notes01/ACME	Destination server:	Chicago-Notes02/ACME
Source domain:	ACME	Destination domain:	ACME
Use the port(s):	TCPIP	Optional network address:	192.22.554.36

Choose ports

Scheduled Connection

Schedule:	ENABLED
Call at times:	08:00 AM - 10:00 PM each day
Repeat interval of:	60 minutes
Days of week:	Sun, Mon, Tue, Wed, Thu, Fri, Sat

Routing and Replication

Tasks:	Replication, Mail Routing
Route at once if:	1 messages pending
Routing cost:	1
Replicate databases of:	Low & Medium & High priority
Replication Type:	Pull Push
Files/Directories to Replicate:	(all if none specified)
Replication Time Limit:	minutes

Sys. Admin. I

This form can be created by opening the Name and Address Book and selecting **Create – Server – Connection** from the Notes menu.

- **Connection type:** Select which type of server connection record you wish to use to connect to the target server. Choices include **Local Area Network**, **Dialup Modem**, **Passthru Server**, **Remote LAN Service**, **X.25**, **SMTP**, **X.400**, **cc:Mail**, and **SNA**.

- **Source server:** Select the source Notes server that will be initiating the replication or e-mail connection.

- **Source domain:** Select the domain of the Notes server that is initiating the replication or e-mail connection.

- **Use the port(s):** Select the port(s) that the initiating Notes server will use. The initiating and target Notes server must be running at least one protocol in common in order to transfer e-mail or replicate Notes applications. If this field is left blank when Local Area Network is selected within the connection document, then Notes will use all available information, including all enabled ports and all enabled and disabled connections records, to try to make a connection to the target server.

- **Choose ports** Button: The **Choose ports** button will let you select the network ports available on the Notes server. Once you select the ports desired, the selections will populate into the Use the port(s) field.

- **Usage priority:** If the Normal selection is set, then Notes will use this connection document. If the Low setting is set, then Notes will look at this connection record last.

- **Destination server:** Select the target Notes server that the initiating Notes server will be replicating and/or routing e-mail to.

- **Destination domain:** Enter the destination domain of the target Notes server.

- **Optional network address:** Enter the optional network address of the target Notes server. For TCP/IP networks, this is the IP address or host name of the target Notes server.

- **Schedule:** The schedule field is used to enable or disable the connection document.

- **Call at times:** The **Call at times** field lists the times the initiating Notes server will replicate with the target Notes server. This field does not affect when a Notes server will route e-mail. Replication must appear in the task field of this connection document for this field to operate.

- **Repeat interval of:** Enter the interval for the replication event to repeat in minutes.

- **Days of week:** Enter the days of the week you wish the replication schedule to operate.

- **Tasks:** Enter the task(s) this connection record will be performing, including replication and/or any e-mail routing.

- **Route at once if:** This field tells Notes how often to force a call or connection to route e-mail. If this number is set to a number such as five, then Notes will not route e-mail to the target Notes server until five e-mail messages exist within the router mail box or until the next scheduled replication. This excludes servers on the same Notes named network.

- **Routing cost:** This is the relative cost of the connection that the Notes servers use to determine the best path for Notes to connect. This number can have values in the range of 1–10 and should not be modified unless there is a specific reason.

- **Replicate databases of XXX Priority:** Notes database applications can be set to a priority of High, Medium, or Low. This field within the connection record specifies what databases, based on priority, the connection record will replicate. Each database in a Notes network can have a priority assigned to it by administrators or designers.

- **Replication type:** This specifies in what manner and direction the initiating Notes server will replicate. The replication types are **push-pull**, **pull-pull**, **pull-push**, and **push-push**.

- **Files/Directories to replicate:** If this field is left empty, all replica databases in common will be replicated assuming proper ACL access. If this field contains entries, then only those Notes applications will be replicated by this connection record.

- **Replication Time Limit:** This is the time limit that a scheduled replication may use. If the limit is surpassed, replication for the connection will be halted.

- **Comments:** This field is for informational purposes only.

- **Owners:** This field lists the owner of the document and represents those people with only Author access to the public Name and Address book who are able to edit the document. Users or groups with Editor or higher access or with Author access and the NetModifier Role may still edit the document, however, without existing in this field.

- **Administrators:** This field should be filled with any Notes administrators or groups in charge of administrating this document.

Server Domain Record

A domain record (Figure 13-8) is used to define a domain other than the one for your Notes infrastructure. This record can be used to route mail to another Notes domain, as well as preventing mail from specific Notes domains.

Figure 13-8

Domain
Record

DOMAIN

Basics

Domain type:	Foreign Domain
Foreign domain name:	Pager
Domain description:	Pager Gateway Domain

Mail

Gateway server name:	Chicago-Notes01/ACME
Gateway mail file name:	pager

Calendar

Calendar server name:	Chicago-Notes01
Calendar system:	Organizer 2.x

Administration

Owners:	Scott Thomas/Marketing/Chicago/ACME
Administrators:	Notes Admin

Restrictions

Allow mail only from domains:	ACME
Deny mail from domains:	

This form can be created by opening the Name and Address Book and selecting **Create – Server – Domain** from the Notes menu.

- **Domain type:** This setting specifies which type of domain the record will be. Choices for domains include: **foreign**, **non-adjacent**, **adjacent**, **foreign x.400**, **foreign SMTP**, **foreign cc:Mail**, and **Global**. Foreign domains are used for gateway add-ons. Non-adjacent and adjacent domain records are used to control access for e-mailing to other domains. Also, a non-adjacent domain record directs Notes mail to the appropriate target domain without users knowing the intermediary domain. Foreign cc:Mail, SMTP, and Global domains control other e-mail functions.

- **Foreign domain name:** This field contains the name of the foreign domain.

- **Domain description:** This field is for informational purposes and describes the domain record.

- **Gateway server name:** This field contains the name of the Notes server where the server gateway product is installed.

- **Gateway mail file name:** This field contains the name of the gateway's mailbox database file.

- **Owners:** This field lists the owner of the document and represents those people with only Author access to the public Name and Address book who are able to edit the document. Users or groups with Editor or higher access or with Author access and the NetModifier Role may still edit the document, however, without existing in this field.

- **Administrators:** This field should be filled with any Notes administrators or groups in charge of administrating this document.

- **Allow mail only from domains:** This field will only allow e-mail from the specified domain(s). An example for populating this field would be the case where a pager gateway existed and external users should not be allowed to use the gateway, tying up the resource and thus costing the company more money.

- **Deny mail from domains:** Similar to **Allow mail only from domains**, this field restricts who may mail documents to the domain.

Mail-In Database Record

This type of record (Figure 13-9) is used so that mail messages may be delivered to a Notes database. See Chapter 5—*Workflow Applications & Form Design,* for more information about using mail-in databases in application design.

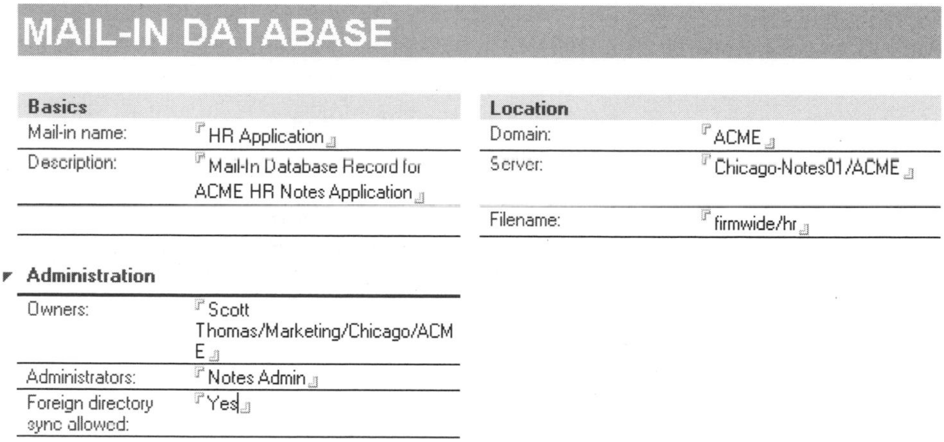

Figure 13-9

Mail-In Database
Record

MAIL-IN DATABASE

Basics

Mail-in name:	HR Application
Description:	Mail-In Database Record for ACME HR Notes Application

Location

Domain:	ACME
Server:	Chicago-Notes01/ACME
Filename:	firmwide/hr

▼ **Administration**

Owners:	Scott Thomas/Marketing/Chicago/ACME
Administrators:	Notes Admin
Foreign directory sync allowed:	Yes

This form can be created by opening the Name and Address Book and selecting **Create – Mail-In Database** from the Notes menu.

- **Mail-in name:** This is the name that will be used to direct Notes mail to the Notes database application. Within a Notes e-mail memo, this is the name that will be placed by users in the **TO** field.

- **Description:** This is for informational purposes only and should describe the purpose of the Mail-in database record.

- **Owners:** This field lists the owner of the document and represents those people with only Author access to the public Name and Address book who are able to edit the document. Users or groups with Editor or higher access or with Author access and the NetModifier Role may still edit the document, however, without existing in this field.

- **Administrators:** This field should be filled with any Notes administrators or groups in charge of administrating this document.

- **Foreign directory sync allowed:** This field is responsible for allowing synchronization of the record to other foreign mail and directories. Such an example would be to cc:Mail environments.

Sys.Admin. I

- **Domain:** Enter the domain where the Notes Mail-In database application exists.

- **Server:** Enter the Notes server where the Notes Mail-in database application exists.

- **Filename:** This field contains the file location on the Notes server where the Notes Mail-in database application resides. The filename is always relative to the Notes data directory.

Program Record

The program record (Figure 13-10) is used to run scheduled programs on a Notes server.

Figure 13-10
Notes Program
Record

PROGRAM: ncompact.exe

Basics		Schedule	
Program name:	ncompact.exe	Enabled/disabled:	ENABLED
Command line:		Run at times:	11:00 PM each day
Server to run on:	Chicago-Notes01/ACME	Repeat interval of:	0 minutes
Comments:	Notes Compaction Program	Days of week:	Sun, Mon, Tue, Wed, Thu, Fri, Sat

Administration	
Owners:	Scott Thomas/Marketing/Chicago/ACME
Administrators:	Notes Admin

This form can be created by opening the Name and Address Book and selecting **Create – Server Program** from the Notes menu.

- **Program name:** This field contains the name of the actual program to run on the Notes server. It should be noted that if the program is a Notes server program, that program will have a prefix to it. For instance, the Notes server program **compact.exe**, if run on a Windows NT server, will be named **ncompact.exe** and must be entered as **ncompact.exe** within the program name field of a program document.

- **Command line:** If any commands are needed to execute the program, they should be entered within this field.

- **Server to run on:** This field should contain the Notes server(s) that the program will run on.

- **Comments:** This field is for descriptive purposes only and will not have any affect upon how a program runs on a Notes server.

- **Owners:** This field lists the owner of the document and represents those people with only Author access to the public Name and Address book who are able to edit the document. Users or groups with Editor or higher access or with Author access and the NetModifier Role may still edit the document, however, without existing in this field.

- **Administrators:** This field should be filled with any Notes administrators or groups in charge of administrating this document.

- **Enabled/disabled:** This field determines whether or not the program is **DISABLED** or **ENABLED**. The third setting, **STARTUP ONLY**, will only run the program when the Notes server is first started.

- **Run at times:** This field specifies the time of day the program will run.

- **Repeat interval of:** The repeat interval field specifies how often the program will repeat. A value of zero will only run once.

- **Days of week:** The days of week field specifies on what days of the week this program will run.

Setup Profile Record

The setup profile record (Figure 13-11) is used to automatically configure new Notes user workstations. Settings that may be used include initial passthru Notes server, InterNotes server, and remote connections.

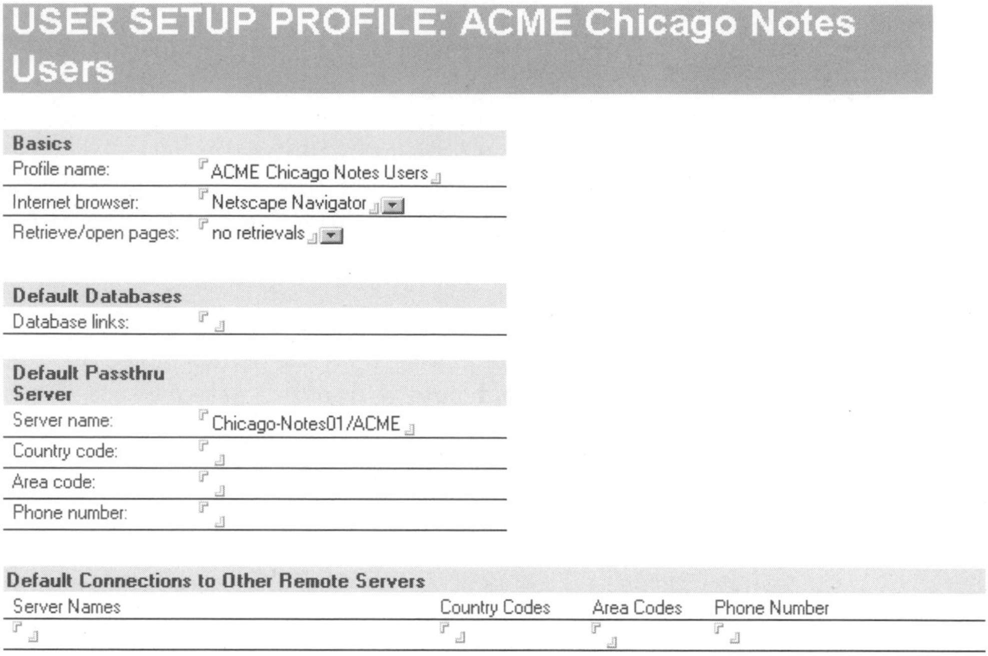

Figure 13-11

Notes Setup
Profile Record

USER SETUP PROFILE: ACME Chicago Notes Users

Basics

Profile name:	ACME Chicago Notes Users
Internet browser:	Netscape Navigator
Retrieve/open pages:	no retrievals

Default Databases

Database links:	

Default Passthru Server

Server name:	Chicago-Notes01/ACME
Country code:	
Area code:	
Phone number:	

Default Connections to Other Remote Servers

Server Names	Country Codes	Area Codes	Phone Number

This form can be created by opening the Name and Address Book and selecting **Create – Server – Setup Profile** from the Notes menu.

- **Profile name:** Enter the name of the profile for descriptive purposes.

- **InterNotes Server:** The name of the Notes server to use for the user's InterNotes server.

- **Server name:** Within this field you may place the Notes server name you wish users to use for Notes passthru operation.

- **Country code/Area code/Phone number:** Within these fields you may place the phone number of the Notes server performing passthru.

- **Server Names:** Within this field, place Notes server(s) name(s) of other Notes servers to which you wish to have connection records.

- **Country codes/Area Codes/Phone Number:** Within this field you may enter the phone number(s) of the other Notes servers.

- **Owners:** This field lists the owner of the document and represents those people with only Author access to the public Name and Address book who are able to edit the document. Users or groups with Editor or higher access or with Author access and the NetModifier Role may still edit the document, however, without existing in this field.

- **Administrators:** This field should be filled with any Notes administrators or groups in charge of administrating this document.

Upgrade Message Record

With version 4.0 and higher of Lotus Notes, Notes administrators may now upgrade Notes clients to newer versions through Notes mail. The Notes mail message includes two buttons, the first of which shuts down the user's Notes client and performs an upgrade to the person's Notes client from a shared directory on a file server on the network. The second button then performs an upgrade to the Notes user's mail file.

Before an upgrade message may be sent out, the Notes administrator must perform the following steps:

1. Copy the Notes source install directory from the Lotus Notes CD to a shared directory upon a file server that all Notes users will have access to. For Windows 95 and Windows NT client machines, the directory on the Notes CD that should be copied is **\W32INTEL\INSTALL**. Copy all other Notes client platforms that are necessary for each operating system supported in your organization. For example, if your company has Windows and Macintosh machines that will be running the Notes client, you would want to create two separate directories for each platform. On a Windows NT file server, the following directories should be created:

Sys. Admin. I

```
\\ACME01\APPS\Notes\WIN32
```

```
\\ACME01\APPS\Notes\Mac
```

2. Grant users the correct access rights in the Windows NT directory so that they may read and execute the files within the above directories.

Once these tasks are completed, a Notes administrator may now send a Notes mail message to Notes users in order to perform a Notes client upgrade to their machines. To do this the Notes administrator should perform the following tasks:

1. Open the public Name and Address book using the Notes view **MAIL USERS.**

2. Within this view, select the Notes user(s) that you wish to upgrade.

3. Once all Notes users are selected, click the **Send Upgrade Notifications** button. The screen shown in Figure 13-12 will appear:

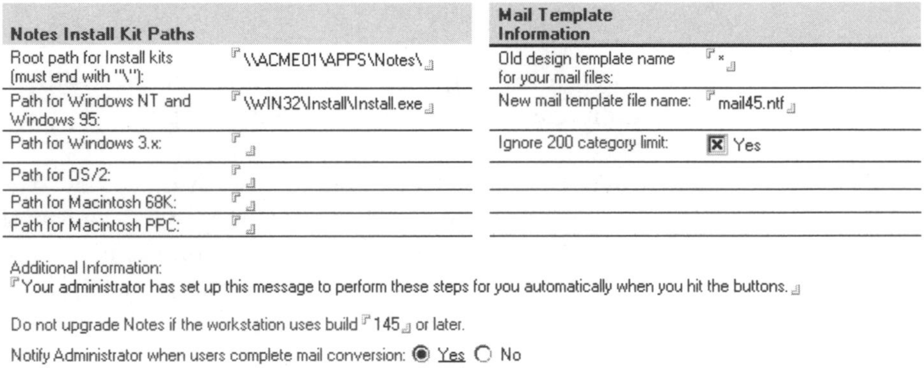

Figure 13-12
Notes Mail Upgrade
Notification

Notes Install Kit Paths		Mail Template Information	
Root path for Install kits (must end with "\"):	\\ACME01\APPS\Notes\	Old design template name for your mail files:	x
Path for Windows NT and Windows 95:	\WIN32\Install\Install.exe	New mail template file name:	mail45.ntf
Path for Windows 3.x:		Ignore 200 category limit:	☒ Yes
Path for OS/2:			
Path for Macintosh 68K:			
Path for Macintosh PPC:			

Additional Information:
Your administrator has set up this message to perform these steps for you automatically when you hit the buttons.

Do not upgrade Notes if the workstation uses build 145 or later.

Notify Administrator when users complete mail conversion: ◉ Yes ○ No

4. Within the **TO:** field, enter the recipients to receive the Notes client upgrade notification.

5. Fill the **Root path for Install kits** field with the path including server name of the root of the install kit. Using our example above, this would be **\\ACME01\APPS\Notes**. It is recommended that you use UNC names for the server and resource, if drive letters are used, some users may not have the same drive mappings. Also, the end of the path statement must end with a ****.

6. **Paths and program names for Notes client installs**. In each of these fields, enter the path for the client(s) that will be used within your organization. Using our exjample again for Windows 95 and NT users, this would be **\WIN32\Install\Install.exe**.

7. The **Old design template name for your mail files** field should contain the name of the template that was used for the user's current mail file. An asterisk (*) within this field defaults to any.

8. The **New mail template file name** field should include the name of the new mail template. If the default is going to be used within your organization for version 4.5 of Lotus Notes, this field will contain the entry **mail45.ntf**.

9. The **Ignore 200 category limit** checkbox should be checked if you wish to ignore the 200 category limit within the user's mail file.

10. The **Additional Information** field should contain any additional information you wish the user to see when the message is opened.

11. The **Do not upgrade Notes if the workstation uses build XXX or later** field determines whether or not the specified Notes user's client should be upgraded. If a Notes user's build number of his or her client is less than the specified number, the Notes client will receive the first button that will enable the Notes user to perform an upgrade. A Notes user's build number can be determined by performing the **@Version** function on a Notes user's desktop.

Sys. Admin. I

12. The **Notify Administrator when users complete mail conversion** field will notify the Notes administrator when a Notes user's mail file is upgraded.

Once all fields are configured, the Notes administrator can e-mail the message to the intended recipients. They will have to open the Notes mail message, and if the Notes user's build number is less than the specified number that the Notes administrator set, the user will see the two buttons.

The Notes user should click the first button, and the user's Notes client will close and the Notes installation program will run. The user then should follow the steps to install the Notes client on his or her machine, making sure to install Notes within the same directory that the older version resides. The installation program will fill the target fields with the current location of Lotus Notes on the user's machine based on settings in the user's **NOTES.INI** file. Once the upgrade is complete, the Notes user may restart the Notes client.

Once the upgraded Notes client is running, the Notes user should enter his or her Notes mail file and open the original Notes mail message. The Notes user should now click the second button, which will upgrade the user's Notes mail file based upon the template that the Notes administrator set within the Notes mail upgrade notification message. When this button is pressed, a background program will start and the user will be prompted for his or her Notes password. Once the password is entered, the user's Notes mail file will be upgraded and if the Notes administrator has specified an e-mail alert, a Notes mail message will inform the administrator that the upgrade has been performed.

Chapter 13 Sample Questions

Objective: Group Records.

Jeanine wishes to create a group record for a mailing list for the entire sales department. All sales department users will use the group. The list will not be used for ACL entries within Notes applications. What type of group should she create?

> A. A Multi-Purpose Group within the public Name and Address book
>
> B. A Mail Only Group within the public Name and Address book
>
> C. A Mail Only Group within her personal Name and Address book
>
> D. A Deny Access Group within the public Name and Address book

Answer: B

A Mail Only group within the public Name and Address book can be used for mailing lists to be used by all Notes administrators. A Multi-Purpose group would work as well, but will provide an additional burden to the Notes server as it would be indexed by the Notes server for resolving database ACL access. If a group is created within a personal address book, only the local user would have access to the group.

Objective: Location Records.

Lee wishes to configure his laptop so that he will have multiple configurations for Lotus Notes. This includes a configuration for remotely dialing into the office Notes server, a configuration while he is connected to the office LAN, and a configuration when he is disconnected. How could this be accomplished?

> A. Create a location document for each type of configuration by clicking **Create – Location** from his personal address book
>
> B. Create a location document for each type of configuration by entering the server administration panel and clicking the **Location** icon

C. Create a connection document within his personal address book for each type of configuration by clicking **Create – Connection**

D. Create a workstation document within his personal address book for each type of configuration by clicking **Create – Connection**

Answer : A
Location documents within the personal address book can be used to configure multiple configurations for Notes workstations.

Objective: Person Records.

Wayne wishes to create person records within Lotus Notes for some users so that their Notes mail can be forwarded to their Internet mail accounts. How can Wayne accomplish this?

A. Create new Notes user accounts and the person records will be automatically created

B. Within the public Name and Address book, manually create connection documents by clicking **Create – Connection** and fill in the proper value for forwarding Internet mail

C. Within the public Name and Address book, manually create person documents by clicking **Create – Person** and fill in the proper value for forwarding Internet mail

D. Within each user's personal address books manually create person documents by clicking **Create – Person** and fill in the proper value for forwarding Internet mail

Answer: C
For non-Notes users, such as Internet mail users, you would not want to create a new Notes account. Instead, you would want to manually create person records within the public Name and Address book and enter each user's Internet mail address within the forwarding address field. This way, Notes users may use the directory functions of Notes to address the mail messages.

Objective: Server Records.

Corey has just added another active network port on his Notes server from the Notes users interface on his Notes server. Where else does he have to add this port?

> A. Within the public Name and Address book, edit the **Ports** field within the network configuration section of the server record of the Notes server
>
> B. Within the public Name and Address, book edit the **Ports** field of the network record of the Notes server
>
> C. Within the administrator's personal Name and Address book, edit the **Ports** field within the network configuration section of the server record of the Notes server
>
> D. Edit the Notes server's **NETWORK.INI** file to add the Notes network port

Answer: A
On a Notes server, after a network port is active, the port should also be added to the public Name and Address book server record within the port field within the network configuration section. It should be noted that COM ports do not need to be added to this section.

Objective: Server Records.

By default, which of the following is true?

> A. All users can create new databases on a Notes server
>
> B. All users can create new replica databases on a Notes server
>
> C. All users cannot create new databases on a Notes server
>
> D. All users cannot create new replica databases on a Notes server

Answer: A and D
Based on the server record, if the **Create new databases** and **Create replica databases** fields are left blank, then users are able to create new databases on the Notes servers but are *not* allowed to create new replica databases.

Objective: Certifier Records.

How should a certifier record within the public Name and Address book be created for a new organizational unit certifier?

> A. Within the public Name and Address book, click **Create – Server – Certifier**
>
> B. A certifier record within the public Name and Address book is automatically created when an organizational unit certifier is created
>
> C. The Notes server automatically creates the record when another Notes server sharing a common ancestor within its naming hierarchy connects
>
> D. Certification records are created within the certification log, not the public Name and Address book

Answer: B

When new hierarchical certifiers are registered, a certifier record is created within the public Name and Address book. Also, when an administrator cross-certifies another hierarchical certifier, a certifier record is created, but cross-certification is covered only in the System Administration II exam.

Objective: Server Configuration Records.

Wayne wishes to configure all of his Notes servers within his domain so that the ADMINPINTERVAL environment variable is consistent. What is the most efficient means in accomplishing this?

> A. Edit the **NOTES.INI** variable on each Notes server
>
> B. Use the Notes remote server console and perform a **set config ADMINPINTERVAL** on each Notes server

C. Use the Notes remote server console and perform a **set config ADMINPINTERVAL ALL** so that the configuration is set on all Notes servers within the Notes domain

D. Create a Server Configuration record within the public Name and Address book for each Notes server to set the ADMINPINTERVAL variable

E. Create a single Server Configuration record within the public Name and Address book containing a wildcard entry for the server name to set the ADMINPINTERVAL variable

Answer: E

A Notes administrator may create a server configuration document with a wildcard entry for the server name to modify a **NOTES.INI** variable on all Notes servers within the Notes domain.

Objective: Server Connection Record.

Susie has two Notes servers within the same Notes domain and Notes named network. What type of connection records are needed to replicate Notes applications and route Notes mail between the servers?

A. No connection records are needed, as replication and mail routing are automatic between Notes servers on the same Notes named network

B. Mail and replication connection records are automatically created upon server creation

C. Susie needs to create a replication connection record and mail connection record for each Notes server

D. Susie needs to create only a single replication connection record

E. Susie needs to create only two replication connection records, one for each server

Answer: D

Notes servers on the same Notes named network do not need mail connection records. For replication to occur, Notes administrators must configure a single replication record between the two Notes servers. This is done by entering the public Name and Address book and clicking **Create – Server – Connection**.

Objective: Server Domain Record.

Steve wishes to stop Notes mail messages from external Notes domains from using his Notes server to route to other companies where he has Notes connections. What document should he edit to prevent external Notes domain mail messages from using his domain as an intermediary?

> A. He should edit the adjacent domain record within the **Allow mail only from domains** field
>
> B. He should edit the Notes server document that connects to other Notes servers
>
> C. He should edit the Notes connection document within the **Allow mail only from domains** field
>
> D. You cannot limit Notes mail from external Notes domains

Answer: A

Adjacent and Non-Adjacent domain records can be used to allow or disallow Notes mail from entering and/or exiting your Notes domain.

Objective: Mail-In Database Record.

Amy wishes to have Notes mail messages delivered to her Notes application as a part of a workflow operation that her marketing department will be using. How can she do this?

> A. She can design her Notes application to poll the Notes router for Notes mail messages
>
> B. She can create a mail-in database record by performing a **Create – Server – Mail-In Database** within the public Name and Address book

C. She can create a connection record by performing a
Create – Server – Connection

D. She can create a mail-in database record by performing a
Create – Server – Mail-In Database within her personal
Name and Address book

Answer: B
Mail-In Database records can be used within the public Name and Address book to route e-mail to a Notes application.

Objective: Program Record.

Jim wishes to run the Notes server task **compact** on his Notes server every evening. How can he accomplish this?

A. He can create a program record within the public Name and Address book to run the program at a specified time

B. He can create a program record within his personal Name and Address book to run the program at a specified time

C. A program record is not necessary, as he can load **compact** from the Notes server console to run at a specified time

D. Programs can be specified to run within the server record of the Notes server

Answer: A
Program records can be created within the public Name and Address book to run programs at a specified time on a Notes server.

Objective: Setup Profile Record.

Debbie wishes to set the InterNotes server for all of her new Notes users within her organization. How can she accomplish this most efficiently?

A. She will have to install each new Notes workstation and edit the location document on each Notes workstation to add the Inter-Notes server entry

B. She will have to install each new Notes workstation and edit the connection document on each Notes workstation to add the Inter-Notes server entry

C She can create a Setup Profile record within the public Name and Address book and set an InterNotes server for that profile to register new Notes users

D. She can create a Setup Profile record within her personal Name and Address book and set an InterNotes server for that profile to register new Notes users

Answer: C

The most efficient means to set an InterNotes server for new Notes users is to create a setup profile record within the public Name and Address book and use that profile to register new users.

Objective: Setup Profile Record.

Pete wishes to upgrade all of his Notes version 4.0 users with version 4.12 of Lotus Notes. How can he accomplish this most efficiently?

A. Visit each workstation and perform a Notes workstation upgrade

B. Load the **upgrade** utility on the Notes server console

C. Send a **Mail Notifcation** upgrade from the public Name and Address book

D. Send a **Mail Notifcation** upgrade from the user's Notes mail file

Answer: C

A Notes workstation upgrade message may be sent from the public Name and Address book to Notes mail users to upgrade their Notes workstation.

Notes Infrastructure Security

This final chapter for the System Administration I exam covers the security topics of Lotus Notes as they relate to this exam. As with previous topics, only those security aspects directly related to topics on the exam will be covered.

This chapter includes discussion on Notes server and database access, Notes passthru access, and securing the public Name and Address book.

Notes Server Access

There are several layers of security when a Notes workstation attempts to access a Notes server. These include physical security, certification and authentication, server access, and database access. Each of these issues is explained in the following sections.

Physical Security

Although not an important topic for the exam, *physical security* refers to the physical security of the Notes server machine, server room, and associated ID files.

Certification and Authentication

Certification is the mechanism by which user ID files are certified. Certification is an integral part of the authentication process.

Every Notes ID, whether it be a server or user ID, contains a certificate. If one Notes ID is to authenticate with another (user to server or server to server) then the two IDs must share a certificate in common. This is the first level of security. If the two IDs share a certificate in common, an authentication process occurs. If the authentication "handshake" between the two IDs is successful, then the security is passed up to the next layer.

Authentication is the process used to validate that a user ID can access a given Notes server. This process occurs as a challenge and response between a workstation and a server, or between two servers. When a client attempts to establish a connection with a server, validation first occurs. This validation process establishes trust of the client's public key. The second step is authentication. Authentication is the actual challenge and response interaction that uses the public/private keys of the client and server (or server to server). This is done by the Notes servers in a client/server challenge (the target Notes server performs this if two Notes servers are attempting a connection). The target Notes server sends a random number to the initiating ID file (server or client). The initiating ID file then encrypts the random number with the ID's private key and sends it back to the target ID file. The target ID file then encrypts the challenge message with the initiator's public key. If successful, this process is then reversed. If this reverse scenario is then successful, authentication between the two ID files is granted.

Notes

Please see Chapter 11 for complete details on how to create and utilize certifier ID files.

Server Access Lists

After successful authentication takes place, the server then checks its server record in the public Name and Address book, as well as any **NOTES.INI** variables that secure the server.

Tips

*There are some variables within **NOTES.INI** that have equivalent settings within the public Name and Address book. The Server document's access list within the public Name and Address book will override any **NOTES.INI** variables.*

Server access lists add an additional layer of security to Notes servers. By using access lists, access can be granted or denied to a server—or particular ports on the server—even if the user is certified to access the server. Server access lists are controlled through the Server Record in the public Name and Address book and/or in the server's **NOTES.INI** file. Port level access is achieved through a **NOTES.INI** variable on each server.

Table 14.1 lists the different settings available to secure a Notes server within the server document in the public Name and Address book. It is recommended that you use Notes groups, rather than individual server and/or user names within the fields, for easier administration.

Tips

*For the exam, it is important to understand the effects of leaving fields blank within the server document and the resulting effect on security access. Every field listed in Table 14.1 that exists in the public Name and Address book (N&A Book) should be studied. Those listed only in **NOTES.INI** are not deemed as important.*

Sys. Admin. I

Table 14.1
Notes Server
Access Settings

Access List	Description
Only allow server access to users listed in this Address Book (N&A Book)	This field is found in the public Name and Address book. If set to **yes**, only people within the same domain of the server will be allowed access to the server. If set to **yes** you must add other servers that need access to this server into the Access Server field.
Access Server (N&A Book **INI**)	Place any users and/or server that need access to this Notes server within this field. If you set the field above this field to **yes** you must enter other users not within your domain and any server within or outside your domain in this field; otherwise access will not be granted. If this field is left blank, all certified users and/or servers will be allowed access assuming the field above is set to **no**.
Not access server (N&A Book)	Denies access to users, servers, and groups to this Notes server.
Create new databases (N&A Book)	Enter a Notes group that will be allowed to create new database applications on this Notes server. If the field is left blank, **all users** will be allowed to create new databases.
Create replica databases (N&A Book)	Enter the Notes group that will be allowed to create new replica databases on this server. If the field is left blank, **no one** will be able to create new replica applications.
Access this server through passthru (N&A Book)	Enter the users, servers, or groups that are allowed access to this server via a passthru server. If this field is left blank, **no one** will be allowed access via passthru.
Use this server as a passthru server (N&A Book)	Enter the users, server, or groups that may use this server as a passthru server to reach another server. If this field is left blank, **no one** will be allowed to use this server as passthru server.
Allow Anonymous Notes Connections (N&A Book)	If you set this field to **yes** within a Notes server document, all Notes users will be allowed access to the Notes server, regardless of certificates held. In other words, authentication will not take place between the two ID files. Access will be granted with these types of connection using the user name "Anonymous," which can be placed within ACLs of databases and other server access fields.
Compare public keys against those stored in the public Name and Address book (N&A Book)	Select this field to **yes** to check users' public keys within their user ID files against those public keys stored within your domain's public Name and Address book. This is useful in the event a "dummy" or "fake" ID has been created to access the Notes server.
Allow_Access (**NOTES.INI**)	Same function as Allow Access field within the public Name and Address book, and only used if that field is left blank.
Allow_Access_portname (**NOTES.INI**)	Specifies the servers, users, and groups that may access this server at the specified port. There is no equivalent setting within a server record.

Table 14.1
Notes Server
Access Settings
(cont'd.)

Access List	Description
Allow_Passthru_Access (**NOTES.INI**)	Same function as the server record equivalent. Only used if the server record field is left blank.
Allow_Passthru_Callers (**NOTES.INI**)	Same function as the server record equivalent. Only used if the server record field is left blank.
Allow_Passthru_Clients (**NOTES.INI**)	Same function as the server record equivalent. Only used if the server record field is left blank.
Allow_Passthru_Targets (**NOTES.INI**)	Same function as the server record equivalent. Only used if the server record field is left blank.
Create_File_Access (**NOTES.INI**)	Same function as the server record equivalent. Only used if the server record field is left blank.
Create_Replica_Access (**NOTES.INI**)	Same function as the server record equivalent. Only used if the server record field is left blank.
Deny_Access (**NOTES.INI**)	Same function as the server record equivalent. Only used if the server record field is left blank.
Deny_Access_portname (**NOTES.INI**)	Specifies the servers, users, and groups that are denied access to this server at the specified port. There is no equivalent setting within a server record.
Server_Restricted (**NOTES.INI**)	Specifies whether or not the Notes server will accept requests to Open Database requests. There is no equivalent setting with the public Name and Address book.

Sys. Admin. I

Notes Directory Links

Directory links on a Notes server may also be used to limit access to directories on a Notes server. *Directory links* are text files that allow you to create a database directory that is unrelated to the server's Notes data directory. Directory links can be used to locate databases to a new drive without user confusion and, more importantly, to control access to a directory tree. By using directory links, you are adding an additional layer of security to database access.

Directory links end with a .DIR extension and exist within the Notes server's data directory. Their contents include the physical location (drive and directory) of the databases and a list of members that are able to access the link. Following is a sample Notes directory link file:

```
E:\HR
Human Resource Department
Notes Admin
Jim Carlson/ACME
```

Notes Database Access

In order for a user or server to gain access to a Lotus Notes application, the user or server must be listed in the access control list (ACL) of the database or be a member of a group in the ACL of the database. If a user is listed in the ACL of a database, they will be granted access to the database at the level specified. The levels of access control in Notes version 4 are No Access, Depositor, Reader, Author, Editor, Designer, and Manager (in descending order). For entries of Author access and higher, each level attains those privileges of the level below it (e.g. Author access has all privileges of Reader access plus those of Author access). Database ACLs are used to limit access to Notes applications as well as controlling how replication occurs between two servers and between servers and clients.

Tips

The concept of the different levels of Access Control for a Notes application is extremely important. Each level should be memorized and completely understood for the System Administration I exam.

Also, it is highly recommended that you use group names from the public Name and Address book to assign access rights to a Notes application. Using specific user names will become very tedious to manage once the number of Notes applications within a company grows. This group naming concept will be tested upon the System Administration I exam as well.

The different levels of access control that may be assigned to a Notes application are listed (assuming no Roles or Reader or Author Fields):

Sys. Admin. I

- **No Access:** The user is not granted access to the database.

- **Depositor:** The user is able to create documents, but not view any documents within the database—even documents the user creates.

- **Reader:** The user is able to read documents but not create any documents within the database. Users with this access level may also create personal agents within the Notes application that may run against any document to which they have proper access.

- **Author:** The user is able to read all documents as well as create new documents. However, the server or user is only able to edit those documents the user or server created itself. This setting should be used rather than Editor access to avoid replication and save conflicts.

- **Editor:** The user is able to read, create, and edit all documents.

- **Designer:** The user is able to read, create, and edit all documents. In addition, the user is able to edit and create Forms, Views, and create a Full-Text Index.

- **Manager:** The user is able to read, create, and edit all documents. In addition, if using the Notes client, the manager is able to edit and create Forms, Views, and Full-Text Indices. Manager access also allows the editing of the ACL of the database itself. Each Notes application requires at least one entry with MANAGER access.

To configure the access control list for a Notes database application, follow these steps:

1. Highlight the Notes database and click **File – Database – Access Control...** The screen shown in Figure 14-1 appears:

Sys. Admin. I

Figure 14-1

Notes Database Access
Control List Settings

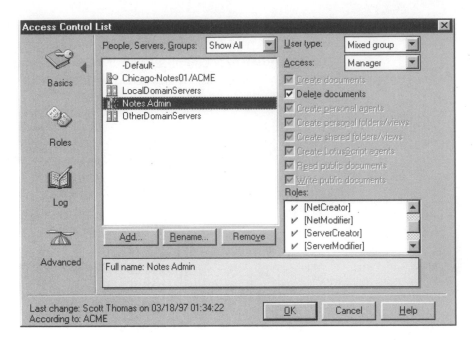

2. Highlight each entry to configure the access for each server, user, or group. The access field assigns the rights per entry.

3. For each entry in the ACL, it is recommended that you assign what type it is. Choices include: Person, Server, Mixed Group, Person Group, and Server Group.

4. Click the **Add**, **Rename**, or **Remove** buttons to add, rename, or remove an ACL entry for the database. Entries allowed are groups, servers, users, or hierarchical wildcards (e.g. ***/ACME** would allow all ID files with the /ACME certifier). The entry **Default** is applied to any user or server not specifically listed or a member of any group.

Tips

For the examination, the use of wildcards within database ACL entries should be understood.

5. Assign any additional settings that you desire such as the ability to create or delete documents within the dialog box. Also assign any roles if available.

6. Click **OK**.

Tips

If a user appears specifically within the ACL of a Notes database ACL and also is a member of a group that appears in the ACL of the database, the user's name will prevail. If a user belongs to two or more groups that all appear within the ACL of the database, the group with HIGHER ACL access will prevail.

There are also additional ACL settings that are available within a Notes application. To access these settings, click the **Advanced** icon within the access control list dialog box as shown in Figure 14-2.

Figure 14-2
Notes Database
Advanced Access
Control List Settings

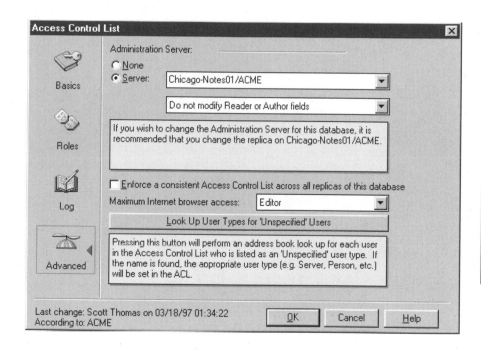

The following fields are available:

- **Administration Server:** As explained in Chapter 12, this is the field that specifies which Notes server will act as this database's administration server.

- **Enforce a consistent ACL across all replicas of this database:** When enabling this dialog box, ACL settings on all replica copies of this Notes application will remain the same; however, every server or user replicating the application must have Manager access or the database will not replicate with this box enabled. Also, with the box enabled, the ACL will be enforced on local machines. It is not intended to be a security feature, as a Notes add-on product may bypass this feature. This option must be selected to utilize Roles on a local machine.

- **Look up User Types for "Unspecified" Users** button: It is highly recommended that you use this button if there are any entries within the database's ACL with an unspecified entry. This button will look up these entries within the public Name and Address book and assign a type to the entry.

Tips

A type should be assigned for each entry within the database's ACL. If an entry is left unspecified—for example, a person is left unspecified—another person could create a group with the same name as that person and be allowed access to the database with that person's rights. By specifying that a person listed is of type person, a group with the same name as the person would not be allowed. See the section "Specifying ACL Types" later within this chapter for more explanation.

Notes Passthru Security

Tips

Although covered in previous chapters, the passthru Notes server record fields are covered here again, as they are very important to know for the System Administration I exam.

The Notes administrator must configure the proper fields on the passthru Notes server's and any destination Notes server's server document within the public Name and Address book to allow client passthru access. These fields include:

- **Access this server through Passthru:** This field allows users, groups, and servers to access this server as a passthru destination. If this field is left blank, then *no* users or servers can access this Notes server as a passthru destination.

- **Passthru route through:** This field should be populated with users, servers, or groups you wish to access the Notes server for passthru to another Notes server destination. If this field is left blank, then *no* user or server will be able to use this Notes server as a passthru server.

- **Passthru cause calling:** This field designates which servers, groups, or users may force the Notes server to "call" or contact another server and act as an intermediary (passthru) contact to another Notes server. If this field is left blank, then *no* destinations are allowed to be called.

- **Passthru destinations allowed:** This field lists all destination Notes servers that are allowed. If this field is left blank then *all* Notes servers are possible destinations via passthru.

Traps

By default, NO ACCESS is allowed to passthru Notes servers and to connect to destination servers via passthru Notes servers. The restrictions must be configured within the server documents of the respective Notes servers. However, the **Passthru destinations allowed** *default access is ALL.*

ACL Database Settings and Effect on Replication

Just like Notes users, Notes servers are limited access to Notes applications based upon the access control list security settings of Notes applications. If two Notes servers have replica database application(s) in common but do not have proper access, replication will not occur between the applications. Table 14.2 lists the different ACL settings for a Notes application and the effect upon replication between two Notes machines. The table shows a Notes database residing on Server B. Server A has been assigned the following ACL rights to the Notes application on Server B. The second column shows the replication results to the application on Server B.

Table 12.2
Database ACL Effects
upon Replication

Replica Notes Application Residing on Server B	
ACL Assigned to Server A	**Result to Notes Application on Server B**
No Access	No changes or updates sent or received from Server A.
Depositor	This ACL setting only applies to users and not servers.
Reader	Changes and Updates are sent to Server A, No New documents or Updates to current documents are received from Server A.
Author	Changes and Updates are sent to Server A, New documents are received from Server A, Updates to existing documents are not received from Server A.
Editor	Changes and Updates are sent to Server A, New documents and Updates to existing documents are received from Server A.
Designer	Changes and Updates are sent to Server A, New documents are received from Server A, Updates to existing documents are received from Server A. Design changes to the Notes application are received from Server A.
Manager	Changes and Updates are sent to Server A, New documents are received from Server A, Updates to existing documents are received from Server A. Design changes to the Notes application are received from Server A. All ACL settings to the Notes application are received from Server A.

Tips

Many companies assign the LocalDomainServers group with Manager access for all Notes applications within the Notes domain. This allows all documents to be replicated and will keep the ACL of the application consistent. For databases that will be replicated outside of your Notes domain, the highest level of access ever recommended is Editor for the external servers. Many times Reader access is sufficient if no updates are going to be received from the external Notes server.

Traps

If the setting **Enforce a consistent ACL across all replicas of this database** *is enabled on a Notes application, replication will not occur for the application unless both replicating Notes servers have Manager access to the database. This setting is found within a Notes application in the Advanced ACL settings of a Notes application.*

Tips

If an ACL change is made on two different replica copies of a Notes database application where the replicating Notes servers both have Manager access, the most recent change will prevail on both replica copies at the next scheduled replication.

Other Security Measures

Other security measures include specifying ACL types and local database encryption. Both methods are described below.

Specifying ACL Types

As mentioned earlier within this chapter, within release 4.0 and higher of Lotus Notes, administrators are able to assign a "type" for each ACL entry for a Notes application. These include:

- Person

- Server

- Person Group

- Server Group

- Mixed Group

- Unspecified

It is highly recommended that you assign a type for each entry within the database's ACL. If an entry is left unspecified—for example a person is left unspecified—another person could create a group with the same name as that person and be allowed access to the database with that person's rights. By specifying that a person listed is of type "person," a group with the same name as the person would not be allowed.

Local Database Encryption

Version 4.0 and higher of Lotus Notes now supports encryption of local databases with a user ID or server ID. Once encrypted, only the ID that encrypted the database is able to access the data. This is especially useful for remote users, where a local copy of Notes databases do not follow the Notes security model as they do not exist on Notes servers. To encrypt a Notes application, follow these procedures:

1. Highlight the Notes application and select **File – Database – Properties** from the Notes menu.

2. Click the **Encryption** button. The dialog box shown in Figure 14-3 appears:

Figure 14-3

Notes Database
Encryption Dialog Box

3. Select the level of encryption and change the user if necessary by pressing the **For** button.

4. Click **OK**.

Securing the Public Name and Address Book

By default, the ACL (access control list) setting for the public Name and Address book is set to Author. This lets individual users edit their own person records and update any personal information they wish to store within their record. Many organizations, however, choose *not* to let users modify their records. This is due to the fact a user's mail information and public keys are stored within the user's person record. If a user changes any of this important information, mail routing and encryption procedures will be disrupted. For these reasons, many companies choose to set the default access to Reader. The decision you make within your company should be based on the comfort level you have with your users' understanding of the person record in the public Name and Address book and whether or not you feel it is necessary for them to add information to their person records.

With the release 4 of Notes, there are a number of new and improved items within the Notes public Name and Address book—particularly in the areas related to security and administration.

New to the public Name and Address book are administration roles governing who can create and modify different parameters within the public Name and Address book. If you are upgrading your Notes server from release 3 to release 4, there is a macro (agent—macros are now *agents* in release 4 of Notes) that adds roles to the public Name and Address book. The agent is called **Add Admin Roles to Access Control List**. For upgrades from release 3 of Notes, it is imperative that this agent is run, as new documents on the new version 4 environment will not be able to be created. For new version 4 Notes servers that are not involved in an upgrade from version 3 of Notes, the roles are automatically included with the public Name and Address book.

As with all Notes applications in all versions of Lotus Notes, a Notes user must have at least Author access in order to create a Notes document with the **Create Documents** box checked. Within the public Name and Address book for version 4 Lotus Notes networks, additional roles now also determine what a user can view, create, and edit within the database. Figure 14-4 shows what the configuration looks like:

530

Chapter 14

Figure 14-4

Notes 4 Public Name
and Address Book
ACL and Role List

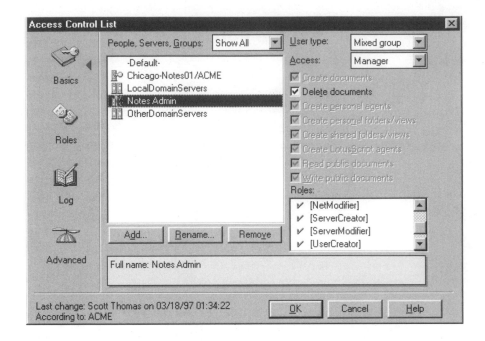

There are 2 sets of roles; modifier and creator. The creator role must be granted to any user or group to allow the creation of that type of document in the public Name and Address book. If a creator role is not granted, no user or group may create a document in the public Name and Address book even if that user or group has Manager privileges to the database. For example, if the Notes Admin group of ACME has Manager access to the public Name and Address book, and wishes to create a new person document, it will be denied access until the role **UserCreator** is granted.

The modifier set of roles will let a Notes user or group edit the specified type of document with only Author access privileges granted. This enables Notes administrators to grant certain users or groups the ability to modify certain types of Notes documents while restricting modification access to other documents. For example, the ACME Notes administration team can grant the **GroupModifier** role to a Notes user or group, enabling the user or group to edit group documents in the public Name and Address book without having to grant them Editor access. However, since the other modifier roles are not granted, these users or groups will not be able to edit any other type of document, such as person or server records.

The roles can be selected for a user or group by highlighting the user or group in the ACL and then clicking the role you wish that user or group to perform. If a Notes user is not a member of the role, they will not be able to create a document in the public Name and Address book as it will not appear in the list under the Create menu of the Notes GUI. What these new roles provide is the ability for the core Notes administration team to distribute the Notes administration tasks.

Tips

It should be noted that as in Notes version 3, anyone with Editor or higher privileges can still edit all documents in the public Name and Address book, regardless of whether or not they are a member of a modifier role. Users with Editor or higher ACL access to the public Name and Address book automatically have modifier role access. However, the creator roles must be granted to users in order to create documents in the public Name and Address book, even if the user or group has Manager access to the database.

For example, let us look at our example corporation, ACME. The ACME Notes administration team can grant a specific group of users, say a Notes development team, the ability to only modify group listings within the public Name and Address book by granting the group **GroupModifier** privileges with Author access to the public Name and Address Book. The Notes development team would have the ability to add and delete users from groups, but not be able to create new groups or perform any other task to the Name and Address book, as none of the other roles have been assigned.

The following lists the eight new roles in the version 4 Notes public Name and Address book.

Notes

For the exam, it is important to understand each of the roles for the public Name and Address book and their functions.

- **GroupCreator:** This role enables users to create groups within the public Name and Address book. Normally, this role

Sys. Admin. I

will only be granted to a select few users as to prevent an explosion of unauthorized groups from being created. Again, this role must be assigned in order to create groups regardless of ACL access to the database.

- **GroupModifier:** A user or group with this role assigned may modify groups even with only Author access granted. This includes all groups within the public Name and Address book, not just groups where owner access is granted.

- **NetCreator:** This role must be assigned, regardless of access, in order to create Server Configuration documents, Connection documents, Domain documents, Mail-In Database documents, Program documents, or Setup Profile documents. The central Notes administration team is the only group within a company that should have these privileges.

- **NetModifier:** This role is assigned to users who need to modify Server Configuration documents, Connection documents, Domain documents, Mail-In Database documents, Program documents, or Setup Profile documents. Again, this is normally the central Notes administration team, or in some instances, a remote Notes administration team.

- **ServerCreator:** Administrators who need to create new server documents within the public Name and Address book need to have the **ServerCreator** role assigned to them. This includes an instance when an administrator is registering a new Notes server from the administration console.

- **ServerModifier:** The **ServerModifier** role is assigned to administrators who need to modify all Notes server documents within the public Name and Address book. Again, users with Editor access or higher automatically assume this role. The role should only be granted to the core Notes Administration team, and possibly to those administrators in remote locations where multiple server administration is necessary.

- **UserCreator:** The **UserCreator** role is granted to those administrators who need to create person records in the public Name and Address book. This includes the instances when administrators create new user IDs when registering a new person from the administration console of the Notes GUI. Without this role, regardless of ACL access, a new Notes user cannot be created.

- **UserModifier:** The **UserModifier** role should be granted to those administrators with Author access in order to maintain and edit all person documents within the public Name and Address book.

Sys. Admin. I

Chapter 14 Sample Questions

Objective: Notes Server Access—Authentication.

Chad has configured his Notes server not to allow anonymous Notes server connections. Jenny is a Notes user created with the /ACME organization certifier. Chad's Notes server was created with the /ABCompany organization certifier. There is no cross-certification between the two certifiers. Can Jenny access the Notes server?

> A. Jenny will only be able to access the Notes server if Chad has listed Jenny within the Server Access field of the Notes server document within the public Name and Address book
>
> B. Jenny will only be able to access the Notes server if Chad has listed Jenny within the Server Access line within the **NOTES.INI** file of the Notes server
>
> C. Jenny will not be able to authenticate with the Notes server as they do not share certificate in common
>
> D. Yes, Jenny will be able to successfully authenticate with Chad's Notes server

Answer: C

A Notes user and server must share a certificate in common (or cross-certificate) in order to authenticate. This is the first level of security and if not satisfied, regardless of other security layers, access will be denied.

Objective: Notes Server Access—Server Access Lists.

Tom wishes to configure his Notes server so that only a select list of Notes users and servers can access his Notes server. How can he accomplish this most efficiently?

> A. He can authenticate those users and servers that need access
>
> B. He can list those users and servers individually within the **Access Server** field within the server record of the Notes server within the public Name and Address book

C. He can list those users and servers within a Notes group(s), and then place that group name(s) within the **Access Server** field within the server record of the Notes server in the public Name and Address book

D. He can list those users and servers individually within the **Access Server** line in the Notes server's **NOTES.INI** file

Answer: C

Although server and user names can be listed specifically, it is better to use a group or a series of group names to control access to a Notes server within the **Access Server** field of the Notes server record. The **NOTES.INI** file can be used to grant access as well; however, the Notes server record will take precedence over any settings within the **NOTES.INI** file.

Objective: Notes Server Access—Directory Links.

Wayne has just created a directory link on his Notes server. What features are available to him using a directory link?

A. He may limit access to Notes users and servers to the directory itself

B. He can place Notes applications within another directory other than within the Notes **DATA** directory

C. He can place Notes applications within another physical drive other than within the Notes **DATA** directory

D. Directory links cannot be used on Notes servers, only Notes workstations

Answer: A, B, and C

Directory links can be used to house Notes applications on a separate physical drive and/or directory. They can also be used to limit access for Notes users and server to the directory itself.

Sys. Admin. I

Objective: Notes Database Access.

Jeanine wants to configure her Notes application so that every user can edit each others' documents, but not be able to make design changes or modifications to the ACL of the database. What access should she set for users?

A. Reader

B. Author

C. Depositor

D. Editor

Answer: D

Editor access will enable users to edit all documents, but not allow design or ACL changes to the application.

Objective: Notes Database Access.

Pete's assistant wishes to check his Notes mail while he is out of the office. How can she do this?

A. Click **File – Database – Open** from her desktop and open his mail file

B. She needs to add her name to the ACL of his Notes mail application with Reader access, using her Notes ID from her Notes desktop

C. Pete needs to add her name to the ACL of his Notes mail application with Reader access, using his Notes ID from his Notes desktop

D. Mail file applications cannot be read by any user other than by the owner

Answer: C

By default, Notes applications have **Default** access set to none, with the owner set to Manager. Like any other Notes application, the manager of the application may modify the ACL of the database to grant others specific levels of access.

Objective: Notes Database Access.

Server A is receiving an error message that it is unable to deliver mail messages to server B because of insufficient ACL access to server B's mail router box (**MAIL.BOX**). What should the default ACL access be for the **MAIL.BOX** of a Notes server?

> A. Editor
>
> B. NO ACCESS
>
> C. Author
>
> D. Depositor

Answer: D
The mail router database (**MAIL.BOX**) has default access set to Depositor so that any server or user may send mail (deposit messages to the database), but not read any message in transit.

Objective: Notes Passthru Security.

What fields within a Notes server document need to be modified in order to allow Notes passthru to function?

> A. **Passthru route through** on the passthru Notes server document, **Passthru cause calling** on the passthru Notes server document, and **Passthru destinations allowed** on the target Notes server document
>
> B. **Access this server through Passthru** on the target Notes server document, **Passthru route through** on the passthru Notes server document, **Passthru cause calling** on the target Notes server document, and **Passthru destinations allowed** on the passthru Notes server document
>
> C. **Access this server through Passthru** on the target Notes server document, **Passthru route through** on the passthru Notes server document, **Passthru cause calling** on the passthru Notes server document, and **Passthru destinations allowed** on the target Notes server document

D. **Access this server through Passthru** on the target Notes server document, **Passthru route through** on the passthru Notes server document, and **Passthru cause calling** on the passthru Notes server document.

Answer: D

By default, on the passthru server(s) document(s), if the fields **Passthru route through** and **Passthru cause calling** are left blank, then *no* passthru access is allowed for any of the fields. Also, on the target Notes server, if the field **Access this server through Passthru** is left blank, then *no* access is allowed to this server.

However, the field **Passthru destinations allowed** on the passthru server(s) document(s) left blank will allow *all* destinations.

Objective: Notes Database ACL settings with Replication.

Notes server A is replicating with Notes server B. The Sales Notes application on server A lists server B with Editor access. The Sales Notes application on server B lists server A with Reader access. What documents in the Sales application will be replicated between the servers?

A. The Notes server A application will let server B pull all documents and receive all edits and new documents; the Notes server B application will only let server A pull all documents. No edits and new documents will be allowed.

B. The Notes server B application will let server A pull all documents and receive all edits and new documents; the Notes server A application will only let server B pull all documents. No edits and new documents will be allowed.

C. The Notes server A application will send and receive all new documents; the Notes server B application will send and receive all new documents.

D. Replication cannot occur with these settings

Answer: A

Reader access will only let a server read documents and no updates or new documents will be allowed. Editor access will allow server reads, as well as accept new updates and documents.

Objective: Notes Database ACL Types.

The Notes group LocalDomainServers should have what type of ACL setting?

A. Mixed Group

B. Server Group

C. Server

D. Unspecified

Answer: B
The Notes group LocalDomainServers should contain only those Notes servers within your Notes domain, and should be set to a **Server Group** type in all ACL settings of Notes applications.

Objective: Notes Local Database Encryption.

If a Notes user encrypts a local Notes database with his or her user ID file, how can the data be viewed?

A. The Notes database can be viewed using the encryptor's user ID file

B. The Notes database can be viewed using the Notes server ID file

C. The data may be viewed by a third party application without the user of an ID file

D. Once a database is locally encrypted, it may no longer be viewed

Answer: A
Once a Notes database is locally encrypted, it may only be viewed using the ID file that encrypted the database.

Sys. Admin. I

Objective: Securing the Public Name and Address Book.

What type of ACL setting and roles must be assigned to a user in order to create a new group within the public Name and Address book?

> A. Author and higher ACL access is needed to create a new group within the public Name and Address book
>
> B. Author and higher ACL access along with the **GroupCreator** role is needed to create a new group within the public Name and Address book
>
> C. Editor and higher ACL access is needed to create a new group within the public Name and Address book
>
> D. Any user or group with Manager ACL access may create a new group with the public Name and Address book

Answer: B

In order to create a group within the public Name and Address book, you must have at least Author access *with* the GroupCreator role assigned. Without this role, no one may create a new group document, regardless of ACL settings. However, to modify a group, the **GroupModify** role is only necessary for those with Author access. Editor access and higher may also modify a group without the role assigned.

System

Administration II

Chapter **15**

Advanced Notes Server Installation and Setup

In this chapter, we begin to discuss those issues related to the System Administration II exam. It should be noted that all topics covered for the System Administration I exam (Chapters 10–14) should be understood in even greater detail for System Administration II. The System Administration II covers many of those topics in greater detail, along with the additional topics covered in the final two chapters of this book.

Topics discussed within this chapter include database and log analysis, using and configuring statistics and events reporting, and discussion of Lotus' NotesView product. We will also examine advanced domain routing and configurations, including merging two separate Notes domains. Finally, we will look at the InterNotes and Web Publisher products.

Configure Database Analysis

A Notes administrator or manager may analyze a particular database by running a database analysis. This tool will gather information from the replication history, user activity dialog box, the statistics database (if it exists), and the Notes log, and stores the gathered information within a results database. To run a database analysis:

1. Click **File – Tools – Server Administration**.

2. Click the **Database Tools** icon (Figure 15-1).

Figure 15-1
Database Analysis
Settings

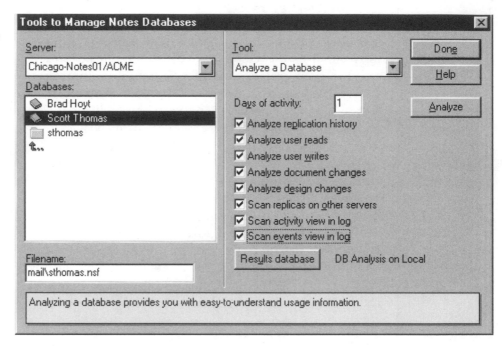

3. Within the **Tool** field, select **Analyze a Database**.

4. Within the **Server** field, select the Notes server to administer.

5. Within the **Databases** field, select the database to analyze.

6. Within the **Days of activity** field, select the number of days to evaluate.

7. Select any other settings you wish reports on from the radio boxes.

8. Click the **Results database** button to change the location of the results database.

9. Click **Analyze**.

The following items may be selected for analysis:

● Replication History

● User Reads

● User Writes

● Changes to documents

● Changes to design

Configure Log Analysis

The Lotus Notes logs of each server represent the complete audit trail in terms of the actions of each server. The Notes log is created automatically the first time a Notes server is run. Replication, mail routing, database size and usage, phone calls, and all events and errors are recorded within this database. Every morning and periodically throughout the day, the Notes administrator(s) should scan the

Notes logs on each Notes server for any errors or inconsistencies that may be a reason for concern.

The Notes log may be opened by simply performing a **File – Database – Open** on the specified Notes server, and then highlighting the selection and clicking **Open**.

You may also open the Notes log on a Notes server in this manner:

1. Click **File – Tools – Server Administration**.

2. Select the Notes server with the notes log you wish to view.

3. Click the **System Databases** icon.

4. Click **Open Log**.

Tips

The Notes Log on every Notes server is one of the most important tools for a Notes administrator. The Notes administrator should make it a point to monitor the Notes logs throughout the day to ensure proper overall health of each server.

The Notes log file can become quite large. To speed searches for specific events, you may perform a log analysis from the Notes server administration panel to search for a string of words within a Notes log file. To do so, follow these procedures:

1. Click **File – Tools – Server Administration**.

2. Select the Notes server to administer.

3. Click the **Servers** icon.

4. Choose **Log Analysis**. The screen shown in Figure 15-2 appears:

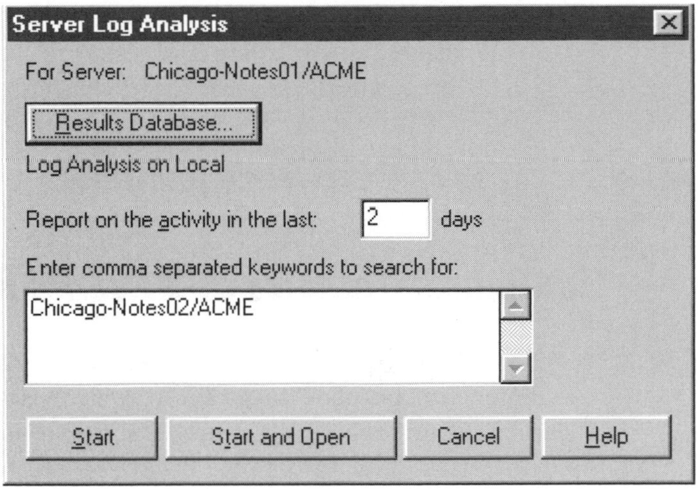

Figure 15-2
Log Analysis
Dialog Box

5. Click the **Results Database** button. The screen shown in Figure 15-3 appears:

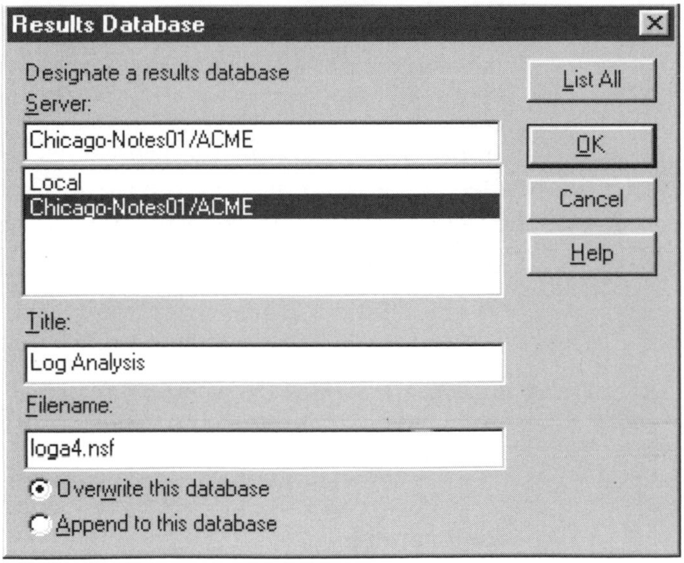

Figure 15-3
Results Database
Dialog Box

6. Specify the location to store the results of the search within this dialog box and click **OK**.

Sys. Admin. II

7. Enter the number of days and the search criteria and click the **Start** button to start the search, or the **Start and Open** button to start the search and then open the results database.

Configure Statistics and Events Reporting

The statistic reporting and event monitoring procedures within Notes can be used to monitor such items as communications, mail, replication, resources, Notes database security changes, and server statistics. The information can be reported to a central database repository for all Notes servers within the infrastructure or on each server individually. Alerts can also be e-mailed to a particular person.

These mechanisms within Notes makes it easy for a Notes administrator to get a quick snapshot of the "health" of all Notes servers within the environment. Also, replication and security problems can be quickly observed.

In order to configure the process, the server task **report** must be loaded on each server. The report server task collects the statistics of the Notes server and reports them to the statistics reporting database (**STATREP.NSF**).

This can be done from the console or remote console by typing the following line:

load report

The task should also be added to each Notes server's **ServerTasks** setting within the **NOTES.INI** file on the Notes server(s).

This report server task will automatically create the following when loaded:

- Statistics and Events database (**EVENTS4.NSF**) in the server's data directory. This database is used to configure the Statistics and Reporting.

- Statistics collection database (**STATREP.NSF**)

- Mail-In record within the public Name and Address book.

The following statistics are gathered by the **report** server task:

- Session information

- Disk statistics

- Memory statistics

- Server configuration information

- Server load statistics

- Replication statistics

- Database statistics

- Notes Mail statistics

- Mail gateway statistics

- Communications

- NetBIOS

Within the Statistics and Events database (**EVENTS4.NSF**) is where you specify the Notes server(s) to monitor for statistics and where to specify the location to log the data. This is shown in Figure 15-4:

Figure 15-4

Notes Server
Statistics Configuration

💻 Save Server To Monitor	🗒 Delete	☞ Exit

Server to Monitor

Chicago-Notes01/ACME

Basics:

Server name:	Chicago-Notes01/ACME		Server administrators:	Notes Admin
Server title:	Chicago Notes Mail Server		Report method:	Log to Database
Domain name:	ACME		Enter server name: Database to receive reports:	Chicago-Notes01/ACME statrep.nsf
Collection interval in (minutes):	120		Analysis interval:	○ Daily ○ Monthly ● Weekly ○ Never
Server description:				

Description:

Report statistics for server Chicago-Notes01/ACME, to database 'statrep.nsf' on server Chicago-Notes01/ACME.
Sample statistics every 120 minutes.
Analize statistics weekly.

The Statistics database then collects the statistics from the Notes server(s) within your domain. You may specify a statistics collection database (**STATREP.NSF**) for each server in the Notes domain, or a single master collection database for all Notes servers. This specification is done as shown in Figure 15-4.

Tips

For larger Notes installations, it may be beneficial not to use a master collection database, as it will grow quite large and the mail router on each Notes server may have to be used to deliver the statistics to the single collection database.

The **event** server task can be used along with the **report** server task to collect more information about a Notes server, as well as alert Notes administrators of specific events. The **event** server task is responsible for monitoring statistics and events that appear within the Notes server console. These include:

- Communication

- Mail

- Miscellaneous

- Replica

- Resource

- Security

- Server

- Statistics

- Database update console events

For each of the above events, the following severity levels are available:

- Fatal

- Failure

- Warning (high)

- Warning (low)

- Normal

To run the **event** server task, type the following at the Notes server prompt:

```
load event
```

For each type of event you wish to report, you must create an Event Monitor document within the Statistics and Events database (**EVENTS4.NSF**). These events then can be configured within this document to notify via e-mail, log to a database, relay to another server, through SNMP, or be logged to the Windows NT Event Viewer.

Table 15.1 lists each type of notification methods:

Table 15.1
Event Reporting
Methods

Notification Method	Description
Mail	Mail events to a person or a database on a different server. Used where incompatible protocols exist between Notes servers.
Log to Database	Reports events to a database local to the Notes server.
Relay to other Server	Reports events to a database on another Notes server within the same Notes domain sharing a protocol in common. Does not use the Notes mail router.
SNMP	Reports events to a SNMP host.
Windows NT Event Viewer	Reports events to the Windows NT event viewer.

Figure 15-5 shows a security event that may be configured when using the **event** server task:

Figure 15-5
Notes Server
Event Configuration

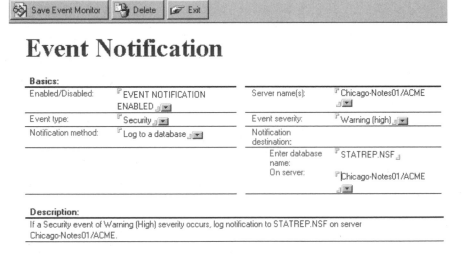

The **event** server task will perform the following once it is first loaded:

- Create the Statistics and Events database if it already does not exist.

- Copy the list of servers from the Server documents in the public Name and Address book to the Servers to Monitor view within the Statistics and Events database.

- Copy all version 3 Notes views and documents from the public Name and Address book to the Statistics and Events database.

- Create the Statistics Reporting database if it does not currently exist.

The Statistics and Events database (**EVENTS4.NSF**) database may also be used to create the following types of documents:

- Statistics monitors to report thresholds reached on specific Notes server statistics.

- Event monitors to specify the types of events to monitor.

- ACL monitors to monitor ACL changes on specific Notes applications.

- Replication monitors to monitor replication frequencies of specific Notes applications.

Tips

Statistics and Event reporting can be a confusing topic. To summarize, the Statistics Reporting database (STATREP.NSF) is the collection database, and the Statistics and Events database (EVENTS4.NSF) is used to configure event and statistics reporting.

Tips

Statistics and Event reporting is a very important topic for the System Administration II examination. You should understand the differences between statistics and events and what happens when the report and event server tasks are loaded, along with the tasks' functions.

Trouble Tickets

A Notes administrator may choose to assign people the responsibility of correcting problems that the Notes statistics and event reporting programs find. This is done by manually creating a trouble ticket within the Statistics Reporting database. There are two types of trouble tickets:

- **Alarm:** An alarm trouble ticket is composed when a statistic reaches a threshold.

- **Event:** An event trouble ticket is composed when a specific event occurs on a Notes server.

Once completed, a Notes trouble ticket is mailed to the appropriate person and is saved within the Statistics Reporting database.

NotesView

NotesView is an add-on program that runs on HP's Openview as well as IBM's Netview products. It is SNMP-compliant and can be used to monitor Notes servers within an organization's environment. It does give the administrator a little more control over the Notes environment, but it is more of a graphical monitoring tool that can be used in the event a threshold is surpassed.

The main advantage to the product when used with SNMP is that it provides administrators with real-time event monitoring data. NotesView also provides the following types of maps of your Notes network:

- Notes Network Topology

- Mail Routing

- Replication

Understanding and Configuring Multiple Domain Configurations

Within this section, we will be discussing multiple Notes domain configurations. A multiple domain configuration for a single company is a Notes environment where multiple Name and Address books exist within a Notes infrastructure. We will also be looking at multiple Notes domain situations for different companies in the example of routing mail and replicating applications between two or more companies' Notes domains.

Domain and Organization Discussion

Before discussing a multiple Notes domain configuration, we should clarify the differences between a Notes domain and a Notes organization. In simple terms, a Notes *domain* is a grouping of Notes servers, users, and groups within a single public Name and Address book. An *organization* is a certifier that is used to create users and servers. Listed below are the major points of each.

Notes Domain

- The major purpose is for server and user grouping as well as mail routing.

- All servers, users, and groups are managed centrally within a single domain (public Name and Address book).

- All mail routing and replication between Notes servers grouped within the same domain are configured within the public Name and Address book (domain).

- The domain name usually represents the company's name and is how the company is known to the outside world.

- An example of a domain name for the company ACME would have a public Name and Address book named ACME. All Notes mail messages would have @ACME appended to all user names when sent to Notes users external to the ACME Notes domain.

Sys. Admin. II

Notes Organization

- An organization is the top-level certifier that creates servers, users, and organizational unit certifiers.

- An organization is responsible for the first layer of security (authentication) between two Notes servers or a Notes server and a Notes client.

- All certifiers are recorded within the public Name and Address book.

- The top level organization certifier usually takes the name of the company and has the same name as the domain.

- Using the example for ACME, the organization would be "/ACME". User names would then be "Scott Thomas/ACME" and server names would be "Chicago-Notes01/ACME".

Tips

It is very important for the examination to understand the differences between a Notes domain and a Notes organization.

Now that we have discussed the major differences between a Notes domain and a Notes organization, we will continue with an in-depth discussion of how to understand and configure a multiple Notes domain configuration. Detailed discussion of organizations will be continued in the next chapter.

Multiple Notes Domains

Notes domains may either be adjacent or non-adjacent to one another. An *adjacent Notes domain* is one where a connection record exists between two Notes servers of two different domains. A *non-adjacent domain* is where intermediary Notes domain(s) exist between an initiating server and a target server. Within this section, we will look at both at adjacent and non-adjacent domains.

Adjacent Notes Domains

Notes mail routers may route Notes mail to other Notes servers within other Notes domains, assuming there is a connection record path for the Notes routers to successfully deliver the message. In order for a user to send a Notes mail message to a user within another Notes domain, each domain must be appended to the recipient's name from left to right. For example, Notes mail user Scott Thomas within the ACME domain wants to send a Notes mail message to Amy Peasley, who exists in the ABCompany Notes domain. If a Notes mail connection record existed between a Notes server within the ACME domain to a Notes server within the ABCompany domain, a Notes mail message could be delivered successfully. Notes user Scott Thomas within the ACME Notes domain would need to address his message as:

```
Amy Peasley @ ABCompany
```

Scott's Notes mail server would look within its public Name and Address book to determine which Notes server in the ACME domain had a mail connection record to a Notes server within the ABCompany Notes domain. Once determined, Scott's Notes mail server would deliver the message to the router mailbox of the Notes server within the ACME domain where the mail connection existed. This ACME Notes server would then deliver the message to the ABCompany Notes server.

From there, the ABCompany Notes server would look within its public Name and Address book to determine the location of Amy's Notes mail database. The Notes server's mail router would then deliver the Notes mail message to Amy's mail Notes server's router mailbox. The router on Amy's server would then deliver the message to her mail database.

Non-Adjacent Notes Domains

Notes mail may also be addressed across multiple Notes domain paths. In other words, intermediary Notes domain(s) may exist between the sender and receiver, assuming proper connection

Sys. Admin. II

records along the path. To take our example again, let us consider a third Notes domain called *Middledomain*. Let us assume that an ACME Notes server has a mail connection record to a Notes server in the Middledomain. Also let us assume that a Notes server in the Middledomain has a mail connection record to a Notes server in the ABCompany domain. For Scott to address a Notes mail message to Amy, the following format would be needed:

```
Amy Peasley @ ABCompany @ Middledomain
```

Within our example, no Notes server within the ACME domain knows how to route Notes mail to the ABCompany Notes domain. Because of the way Scott has addressed his e-mail message, Scott's Notes mail server would look only at the *last* domain appended to the recipient. Scott's Notes mail server will look within its public Name and Address book to determine which Notes server in the ACME domain had a mail connection record to a Notes server within the Middledomain Notes domain. Once determined, Scott's Notes mail server would deliver the message to the router mailbox of the Notes server within the ACME domain where the mail connection existed. This ACME Notes server would then deliver the message to the Middledomain Notes server.

At this point, the ACME Notes server has stripped the last portion of the appended domain from the Notes mail message. From here, the Middledomain Notes server looks within its public Name and Address book to determine which Notes server in its domain has a connection record to a Notes server in the ABCompany domain. This Middledomain Notes server delivers the message to the router mailbox that has a mail connection record to the ABCompany domain. This Notes server then delivers the message to the ABCompany's mail router mailbox.

From here, the ABCompany Notes server would look within its public Name and Address book to determine the location of Amy's Notes mail database. The Notes server's mail router would then deliver the Notes mail message to Amy's mail Notes server's router mailbox. The router on Amy's server would then deliver the message to his mail database.

Figure 15-6 depicts this multiple domain path:

Figure 15-6
Notes Mail Routing—
Multiple Notes
Domain Hops

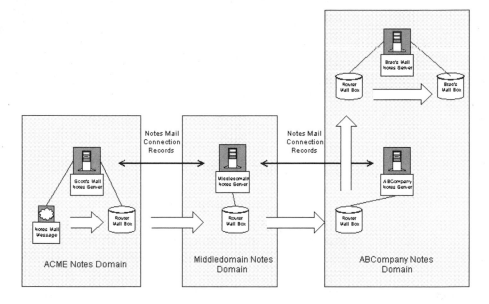

To avoid confusion for Notes mail users where there will be Notes mail routing to external domains and the target domain is not adjacent to the users' Notes domain, a Notes administrator may create a non-adjacent domain record in the public Name and Address book. This would make it so that Notes mail users only need to type the user name and append only the recipient's Notes domain to the message. To illustrate, instead of Scott addressing his memo as:

```
Amy Peasley @ ABCompany @ Middledomain
```

He would only have to address the memo as:

```
Amy Peasley @ ABCompany
```

The non-adjacent domain record in ACME's public Name and Address book would handle the translation. Figure 15-7 shows an example of such a record in ACME's public Name and Address book:

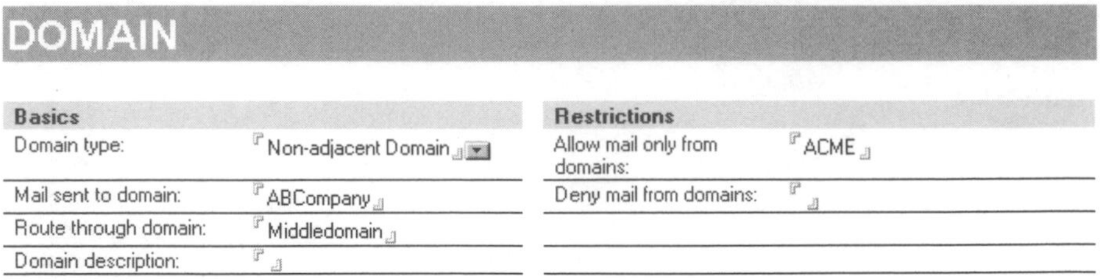

Figure 15-7

Non-Adjacent
Connection Record

DOMAIN

Basics		Restrictions	
Domain type:	Non-adjacent Domain ▾	Allow mail only from domains:	ACME
Mail sent to domain:	ABCompany	Deny mail from domains:	
Route through domain:	Middledomain		
Domain description:			

Controlling Mail Access

Within a non-adjacent and adjacent document, you may also limit which domains may use your domain for routing mail. This is done within the Restrictions Section, as shown in Figure 15-7. Many companies do not wish to have their domains used to route e-mail messages to another company. These restrictions are also useful in limiting other companies from using your gateways, such as fax, SMTP Internet and pager gateways.

Merging Multiple Domains

The merging of domains simply means combining of two or more public Name and Address books into a single public Name and Address book that will be used by all Notes servers and users.

The main reasons for merging domains include:

- One company acquires another

- A company has multiple Notes installations within different departments and wishes to consolidate all installations into a single domain.

To merge multiple Notes domains, a Notes administrator needs to consider all domain references within public Name and Address, book including:

- Server documents

- Connection documents

- Domain documents

- Person documents

- Location documents

- Mail-In database documents

- Group documents

A Notes administrator also needs to consider all domain references within Notes users' personal Name and Address books:

- Location documents

- Group documents

Finally, a Notes administrator needs to consider all domain references within Notes applications and the **NOTES.INI** files, including:

- **CERTLOG.NSF**

- **ADMIN4.NSF**

- **EVENTS4.NSF**

- **STATREP.NSF**

- Notes Custom Applications with hard coded entries containing the old domain name

- DOMAIN= line within the **NOTES.INI** file of Notes machines.

The following lists the steps necessary in order to merge domains. The "winner" domain refers to the domain that will exist once the merge is complete. The "loser" domain(s) refer to those old domain(s) that will no longer be used.

Sys. Admin. II

1. Determine the domain winner and loser(s).

2. Identify all documents within the public Name and Address book that will need to be modified.

3. Shut down all involved Notes servers and clients.

4. Back up the public Name and Address book in all domains.

5. Bring up all involved Notes servers and clients.

6. Modify all documents in public Name and Address book(s) of the loser domain(s) to reflect the winner domain name.

7. Delete any unneeded connection documents.

8. Delete any unneeded adjacent and non-adjacent domain documents.

9. Copy and paste modified documents from loser domain(s) public Name and Address book(s) to the winner domain's Name and Address book.

10. Change **DOMAIN=** line in **NOTES.INI** file for loser domain Notes servers to reflect the winner domain name.

11. Test the new public Name and Address book.

12. Make replica copies of new winner public Name and Address book to all old loser domain Notes servers.

13. Remove loser domain public Name and Address books from the loser domain Notes servers.

Cascaded Address Books

Multiple public Name and Address books may be cascaded upon a Notes server to provide users the ability to search and resolve user and group names for e-mail purposes. Cascaded address books may be replica copies of other Notes domain address books that are replicated to a company's own domain. Non-replicating, departmental Name and Address books may also be developed to house additional user and group names. Cascaded Name and Address books have the following properties:

- Notes servers search cascaded Name and Address books in the order they are cascaded following the public Name and Address book. This order is set within the **NAMES=** setting within the **NOTES.INI** file.

- The **NAMES=** setting may only have 256 characters, so the number of cascaded Name and Address books is limited.

- ACL settings cannot use user names or groups from cascaded Name and Address books.

In order to establish cascading Name and Address books, the Notes administrator must make a replica copy of each public Name and Address book from each domain on his or her home Notes server. The filename cannot be **names.nsf** if placed in the Notes data directory, as this is the filename used by the home Notes server. Once all replica copies are established on the Notes server, the administrator can add a line to the servers **NOTES.INI** file similar to the following:

```
NOTES=NAMES,WESTNAME,EASTNAME
```

This entry would cascade two additional public Name and Address books with database names of **WESTNAME.NSF** and **EASTNAME.NSF**. The search order would first be the NAMES address book, then the WESTNAME address book, and finally the EASTNAME address book.

InterNotes Web Navigator

You may configure a Notes server to act as an InterNotes server. This makes the Notes server responsible for connecting to Web servers and pulling HTML pages into a central repository Notes application, so that any Notes client may view the information. Because the Web pages are stored within a Notes application on the InterNotes server, a Notes client does not have to run TCP/IP and does not have to connect to the target Web server directly. Figure 15-8 shows this type of connectivity:

Figure 15-8

InterNotes Server
Connectivity

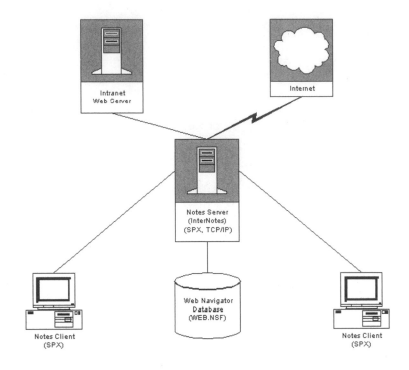

Requirements for the InterNotes server include:

- TCP/IP must be enabled as well as any other protocol for Notes client connectivity.

- The Notes server must run the Web Navigator server program.

- The Web Navigator must be configured within the Web Navigator database (**WEB.NSF** is the default filename).

- For Internet Web connectivity, the InterNotes server must have a direct connection to the target Web servers (an Internet connection).

Installation and Configuration

To start the Web server task a Notes server, type the following command from the Notes server console:

```
load web
```

If you wish this task to begin every time the Notes server is started, the task must be added to the **ServerTasks** line in the **NOTES.INI** file of the Notes server. Once the server task begins, the Web Navigator database (**WEB.NSF**) is created. Within this database, the administration document is also created. It is within this document that you should configure the settings for the InterNotes server. To open the document, follow these procedures:

1. Open the Web Navigator database (**WEB.NSF**) on the Notes server running the **web** server task.

2. Click the **Database Views** icon from within the home navigator page.

3. Click on the **All Documents** button.

4. Click **Actions – Administration**. The screen shown in Figure 15-9 appears:

Figure 15-9
InterNotes Server
Configuration Settings

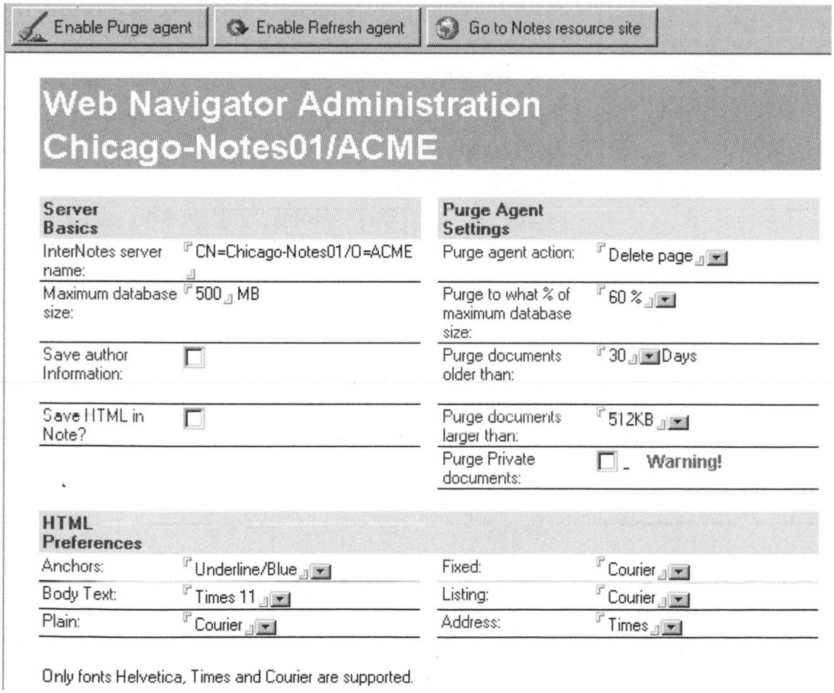

| Enable Purge agent | Enable Refresh agent | Go to Notes resource site |

Web Navigator Administration
Chicago-Notes01/ACME

Server Basics		Purge Agent Settings	
InterNotes server name:	CN=Chicago-Notes01/O=ACME	Purge agent action:	Delete page
Maximum database size:	500 MB	Purge to what % of maximum database size:	60 %
Save author Information:	☐	Purge documents older than:	30 Days
Save HTML in Note?	☐	Purge documents larger than:	512KB
		Purge Private documents:	☐ _ **Warning!**

HTML Preferences			
Anchors:	Underline/Blue	Fixed:	Courier
Body Text:	Times 11	Listing:	Courier
Plain:	Courier	Address:	Times

Only fonts Helvetica, Times and Courier are supported.

Tips

You must have Manager access with the WebMaster role assigned in order to view this configuration document. Also, the document can only be viewed from within the All documents view of the application.

The following fields can be configured:

- **InterNotes server name:** This field is configured by default once the **web** server task is loaded on the Notes server. To change the name, enter the new Notes server name with its fully distinguished name.

- **Maximum database size:** Enter the maximum size in megabytes the Web Navigator Notes application may reach.

- **Save author information:** If you wish to save the Notes user name of the individual who retrieved the Web page into the Web Navigator application, click the box.

- **Save HTML in Note:** If you wish to have the HTML code stored for the retrieved Web page within the Notes document, check the box.

- **Purge agent action:** When the purge agent is run upon this database, you may have the agent either delete the document or reduce the document. Deleting the document will remove all contents of the Notes document from the Web Navigator database. Reducing the document will remove all portions of the document and will leave only a URL pointing to the original Web page.

- **Purge to what % of maximum database size:** Enter the percentage amount you wish to have the purge agent reach.

- **Purge documents older than:** Specify the number of days old the documents within the Notes application should be that the purge agent should delete.

- **Purge documents larger than:** Specify the maximum size a document may be before the purge agent will delete the document.

- **Purge Private documents:** Specify whether or not the purge agent should be allowed to delete documents stored in Notes users' private folders.

- **HTML Preferences:** Specify the appearance of Web page documents within the Notes application.

5. Documents within the Web Navigator database may be refreshed automatically on an InterNotes server by running the Refresh agent. Click the **Refresh Agent** button to run this agent.

Tips

You must have proper security rights within the server document of the InterNotes server in the public Name and Address book to run restricted LotusScript agents.

6. Exit the document and save your changes.

To further configure the settings for the InterNotes server, follow these procedures:

1. Open the server document housing the **web** server task within the public Name and Address book.

2. Move to the Web Retriever Administration section of the document. Figure 15-10 shows this section:

Figure 15-10
InterNotes Server
Administration Settings

▼ **Web Retriever Administration**

Web Retriever Management		Internet Site Access Control	
Web Navigator database:	web.nsf	Allow access to these Internet sites:	*
Services:	HTTP, FTP, GOPHER	Deny access to these Internet sites:	*.playboy.com *.mtv.com
Concurrent retrievers:	25		
Retriever log level:	Terse		
Update cache:	Once per session		
SMTP Domain:	acme.com		

Sys. Admin. II

The following fields should be configured:

- **Web Navigator database:** This field represents the Notes database application that will host all remote Web site pages.

- **Services:** This field controls what services can be accessed using the InterNotes server. These include FTP, GOPHER, HTTP, HTTPS, and FINGER.

- **Concurrent retrievers:** This field represents the maximum number of processes or threads that are permitted to access remote Web sites.

- **Retriever log level:** This field represents the level of logging that will be recorded to the Notes log database on the Notes server. The levels include None, Terse, and Verbose.

- **Update cache:** This entry controls how often the document within the Web Notes application is updated.

- **SMTP Domain:** This field represents the domain used to route SMTP mail.

- **Allow access to these Internet sites:** This field controls what sites users are able to connect to. Wildcards (*) may be used if desired. For example, ***.com** allows users to connect to any site ending with **.com**.

- **Deny access to these Internet sites:** This field controls what sites users are not allowed to connect to. As with the allow access field, wildcards may be used. ***.acme.com** would prevent users from connecting to any server within **acme.com**. You may also enter the IP address of a target site directly. This field overrides any sites that may be available within the allow access field listed above.

3. Exit and save your changes.

You may unload the **web** retriever task by typing the following line from the server console:

```
tell web quit
```

On each Notes client, you also must specify the InterNotes server for the client to use. This setting can be found within the location document within each user's personal Name and Address book. Before the creation of a Notes user, the Notes administrator may specify an InterNotes server within a Profile Record within the public Name and Address book. When the new user is then created, the profile can be assigned to the user, thus populating this field on the user's Notes workstation.

Web Publisher

The InterNotes Web publisher task enables Notes administrators to convert Notes applications to HTML files. These converted files then can be moved or copied onto a Web server for Web browser access. This program is being phased out by Lotus in favor of the Domino server. The Web Publisher add-on program can still be used, but the HTTP program is now a better solution for serving Notes applications to Web browsers. The Web Publisher program must be installed on the target Notes server. Once installed, the following server task must be started from the Notes server console:

```
load webpub
```

This line can also be added to the **ServerTasks** entry within the **NOTES.INI** file of the server so that the task will begin automatically upon server startup.

Once the task is loaded, the Web Configuration database (**WEBCFG.NSF**) is created. It is from within this Notes application that you will configure the settings for the Web Publisher. This includes target directory locations for the converted Notes application(s) (HTML files), Notes applications in which to convert, and schedules as to when and how often to publish the Notes applications.

Tips

The Domino server task should not be confused with the web publisher server task. At the time this book's printing, understanding the Domino server task is not required for the exam.

Sys. Admin. II

Chapter 15 Sample Questions

Objective: Configuring Database Analysis.

What items can be viewed when performing a database analysis on a Notes application?

> A. User Reads
>
> B. User Writes
>
> C. Database Size
>
> D. Replication History

Answer: A, B, and D

The database analysis tools can report back to an administrator user read, writes, and changes. In addition, it will report back replication history and design changes.

Objective: Configuring Log Analysis.

How can a Notes administrator view all server activity for the past few days?

> A. The administrator can take "screen shots" of the server console and save them to disk
>
> B. The administrator can pipe all server console output to an ASCII file and set the location with the server record of the public Name and Address book
>
> C. The administrator can look within the log view of the public Name and Address book
>
> D. The Notes administrator can open the Notes Log database on the Notes server

Answer: D

By default, the Notes server creates and appends to a Notes log database upon server startup. The log will provide the administrator with a complete audit trail of the Notes server's activity.

Objective: Configuring Log Analysis.

Tom is having connectivity problems with one of his Notes servers, Chicago-Notes02/ACME, connecting to his hub Notes server, Chicago-Notes01/ACME. How can he most efficiently find instances within his Notes log for the problem Notes server?

> A. Open the Notes log on server Chicago-Notes01/ACME and open each view and search for server Chicago-Notes02/ACME
>
> B. Perform a Log Analysis on Notes server Chicago-Notes01/ACME and search for Chicago-Notes02/ACME
>
> C. From the Notes server console, watch for error messages pertaining to Chicago-Notes02/ACME
>
> D. Open the Notes error log application and open the view by servers, looking for the Chicago-Notes02/ACME entry

Answer: B
The Log Analysis tool enables Notes administrators to search for specific strings throughout the entire Notes log application, and returns the result(s) to the results Notes application as specified by the Notes administrator.

Objective: Configuring Statistics and Event Reporting.

Which statement is true?

> A. The Statistics Collection database (**STATREP.NSF**) is used to collect statistics for Notes servers, and the Statistics and Events database (**EVENTS4.NSF**) is used to configure statistic reporting
>
> B. The Statistics and Events database (**EVENTS4.NSF**) is used to collect statistics for Notes servers and the Statistics Collection database (**STATREP.NSF**) is used to configure statistic reporting
>
> C. The Statistics Collection database (**STATREP.NSF**) is used to collect statistics for Notes servers, and the public Name and Address book (**NAMES.NSF**) is used to configure statistic reporting

D. The Statistics and Events database (**EVENTS4.NSF**) is used
to collect statistics for Notes servers, and the public Name and
Address book (**NAMES.NSF**) is used to configure statistic
reporting

Answer: A
The Statistics Collection database (**STATREP.NSF**) is used to collect statistics for Notes
servers, and the Statistics and Events database (**EVENTS4.NSF**) is used to configure statistic reporting. The Statistics Collection database can be used on each Notes server, or a
master collector may be used. The Statistics and Events database is used to configure statistic reporting.

Objective: Configuring Statistics and Event Reporting.

Debbie wishes to configure her Notes server to report events to a collection database
residing on a different Notes server within the same Notes domain running the same protocol. What is the most efficient means of accomplishing this?

A. Using Notes Mail

B. Relaying to another server

C. Logging to a database

D. Through a SNMP agent

Answer: B
For Notes servers within the same Notes domain running the same protocol, events
should be relayed so that the Notes mail router is not burdened with the transfer.

Objective: Configuring Statistics and Event Reporting.

What happens when the **Report** server task first loads on a Notes server?

A. The Statistics and Events database (**EVENTS4.NSF**) is created

B. The Statistics Collection database (**STATREP.NSF**) is created

C. The **Event** server task automatically loads

D. ACL Monitors are automatically created

Answer: A and B
When the **Report** server task first loads, the Statistic and Events database (**EVENTS4.NSF**) and Statistic Collection database (**STATREP.NSF**) are created. Also, a Mail-In database record is created within the public Name and Address book that points to the **STATREP.NSF** database. The **Event** server task is not called by the **Report** server task. ACL monitors are manually configured within the Statistic and Events database (**EVENTS4.NSF**).

Objective: Configuring Statistics and Event Reporting.

Which of the following are configured with the Statistic and Events database (**EVENTS4.NSF**)?

A. Trouble Tickets

B. ACL Monitors

C. Event Monitors

D. Statistic Monitors

Answer: B, C, and D
ACL, Statistic, Replication, and Event monitors may be configured within the Statistic and Events database by a Notes administrator. Trouble Tickets are created within the Statistics Collection database (**STATREP.NSF**).

Objective: Configuring Statistics and Event Reporting.

Which two statements are true?

A. An alarm trouble ticket is composed when a statistic threshold is met

B. An event trouble ticket is composed when a statistic threshold is met

C. An event trouble ticket is composed when a specific event
   occurs

D. An alarm trouble ticket is composed when a specific event
   occurs

Answer: A and C
Alarm trouble tickets are for statistic thresholds and event trouble tickets are for specific events. They are created within the Statistic Collection database (**STATREP.NSF**).

Objective: NotesView.

Which of the following can NotesView can be used for?

A. Real-time Notes event monitoring

B. Notes replication maps

C. Notes mail routing maps

D. Registering new Notes users

Answer: A, B, and C.
NotesView is an SNMP compliant tool that may be used with HP's Openview and IBM's Netview products to provide real-time Notes server event monitoring. It may also be used to provide maps of Notes network, replication, and mail environments.

Objective: Multiple Domain E-Mail Routing.

Which is true about a non-adjacent domain?

A. A connection record exists between two non-adjacent domains

B. A non-adjacent domain cannot be on the same physical network

C. A connection record does not exist between two non-adjacent
   domains

Answer: C

Two non-adjacent Notes domains do not have connection records between them. At least one Notes domain exists between the two domains where Notes mail may pass through. Non-adjacent domains may exist on the same physical network.

Objective: Multiple Domain E-Mail Routing.

Corey, who resides in Notes domain A, wishes to send a Notes mail message to Genet, who resides in Notes domain C. An intermediary Notes domain B exists between the two domains. No non-adjacent domain record exists within Corey's domain. How should Corey address the Notes mail message to Genet?

> A. Genet @ C
>
> B. Genet @ B
>
> C. Genet @ C @ B
>
> D. Genet @ B @ C

Answer: C

Without a non-adjacent domain record, Corey must explicitly address the Notes mail message for every Notes domain it will cross.

Objective: Multiple Domain E-Mail Routing.

Using the above scenario again, the Notes administrator in Corey's domain has created a non-adjacent domain record so that all Notes mail destined for domain C routes through domain B. Now how can Corey address the Notes mail message?

> A. Genet
>
> B. Genet @ B
>
> C. Genet @ C
>
> D. Genet @ B @ C

Answer: C
With a non-adjacent domain record in place, users can address Notes mail messages to recipients in the target domain using only the target domain's name appended.

Objective: Controlling Mail Routing from External Domains.

Wayne has been noticing lately that Notes users from an external Notes domain have been using his fax gateway. How can he prevent this from happening?

> A. Within the Notes connection document, he may specify the external domain within the **deny mail from domain** field
>
> B. Within the Notes server document, he may specify the external domain within the **deny mail from domain** field
>
> C. Wayne may create an adjacent domain document and specify the external domain within the **deny mail from domain** field
>
> D. If a non-adjacent domain document exists, Wayne may specify the external domain within the **deny mail from domain** field

Answer: C or D
Wayne may either create an adjacent or non-adjacent domain record, depending on how the Notes connection will be used (domain to domain, or domain to intermediary domain e-mail routing). Then within the **deny mail from domain** field, Notes mail messages may be blocked from a specific domain.

Objective: Cascading Address Books.

Bill wishes to cascade a second address book, **WESTNAMES.NSF**, on his Notes server. What must he do to accomplish this?

> A. The **NOTES.INI** file on his Notes server must have the line: **NAMES=WESTNAMES.NSF**
>
> B. The **NOTES.INI** file on his Notes server must have the line: **ADDRESSBOOK=NAMES.NSF, WESTNAMES.NSF**

C. Within the server document of the Notes server, the field **address book(s)** must have NAMES, WESTNAMES

D. The **NOTES.INI** file on his Notes server must have the line: **NAMES=NAMES.NSF, WESTNAMES.NSF**

Answer: D
In order to cascade multiple address books, the variable **NAMES=NAMES.NSF**, <<< *new address book(s) names*>>> must exist within the Notes server's **NOTES.INI** file. The server must be restarted for the change to take effect.

Objective: Cascading Address Books.

Using the scenario where Bill's home Notes server has 3 address books cascaded with the **NOTES.INI** variable of **NAMES=NAMES.NSF, WEST.NSF, EAST.NSF**, what is the search order for resolving Notes mail users?

A. EAST then WEST then NAMES

B. NAMES then WEST then EAST

C. Only NAMES is resolved for Notes mail purposes

Answer: B
For Notes mail user name resolutions, cascaded address books are searched from left to right as configured within the Notes server's **NOTES.INI** file within the **NAMES=** line.

Objective: InterNotes.

Web pages for Notes InterNotes users are stored where?

A. Within Web Navigator database (**WEB.NSF**) on the Notes users' InterNotes server

B. Within the public Name and Address book on the Notes users' InterNotes server

C. Within Web Navigator database (**WEB.NSF**) on the Notes users'
Notes mail server

D. Within the Notes users' Notes mail files

Answer: A

The Web Navigator database (**WEB.NSF**) on the InterNotes server is the store for
HTML pages for InterNotes users.

Objective: Web Publisher.

Delynne wishes to publish her Notes application into HTML format so that a Web server
can host the application. How can she accomplish this?

A. Load the InterNotes server task (**load web**).

B. Load the Web Publisher server task (**load webpub**) and
configure the settings with Web publisher configuration
database (**WEBCFG.NSF**)

C. This cannot be done within Notes

Answer: B

The Lotus Notes Web Publisher can be used to convert Notes applications into Web
(HTML) format, and then be used on a Web server for Web browser access.

16

Advanced Notes Infrastructure Security

This chapter concludes the advanced security topics that will be covered on the System Administration II exam. As with Chapter 15, it is essential that all topics covered within Chapters 10–14 are completely understood, along with contents of this chapter. Ideas are built upon those original topics and are covered in greater detail for the System Administration II exam.

Topics in this chapter include Notes external connectivity, understanding and configuring cross-certification, understanding and configuring flat certification, and configuring Notes server access.

Notes External Connectivity

With many companies, there comes a time where the desire and/or need arises to connect your company's Notes environment with another company's Notes infrastructure in order to route Notes mail or replicate Notes database applications. Lotus Notes was designed to enable a Notes administrator to perform this function very easily. The main concern facing a Notes administrator is the manner in which an external Notes connection is established. There are several security concerns that must be addressed to keep your company's internal Notes infrastructure secure.

There are a number of ways from a physical standpoint to connect your organization's Notes server to another company's Notes server. These include:

- An analog connections using a Notes-supported analog modem. Connection speeds will be up to 33.6 Kbps.

- A digital ISDN connection using a Notes-supported ISDN modem. Connection speeds will be up to 128 Kbps, depending on the configuration of the modem and BRI ISDN line.

- A network connection through a private network that is connected to both your company and the target company (e.g. CompuServe).

- A network connection through a public network such as the Internet. This type of connection is usually a dedicated phone link such as a T1 or fractional T1.

All above instances require that proper configurations be set, in particular dealing with the security issues surrounding opening up your Notes environment to other companies.

For direct private line connections such as modem connections, Notes takes control over the COM port, analog modem, or ISDN modem upon Notes server startup. For this reason, Notes will not allow any other type of connection except for that of a Notes client or server. Once a Notes client or server connects to a Notes server, all of the world-class security features of Notes are deployed. This includes authentication, port-access lists, server-access lists, database ACL settings, and any encryption mechanisms enabled on either the Notes server or client. If a Notes client or server does not pass any of these security mechanisms, the call will be dropped.

For Notes servers that will be running on public networks such as the Internet, additional measures should be put into place. Like an analog connection, all of the security measures will be in place, including server access lists and database ACL settings. However, two items should be highly considered when connecting a Notes server to another Notes server or client through a public network such as the Internet.

The first issue is that the internal Notes server should be behind what is called a *network firewall application*. A firewall application is a program that runs on a machine that sits between the internal network and the public network. It examines each packet of data that enters or leaves the internal network and, based upon a set of predefined rules, determines whether or not that particular packet of data is allowed in or out of the network. Industry leaders in terms of firewall applications include Raptor and Checkpoint. For a TCP/IP connection to an external Notes server, the main issue concerning a firewall application is that the predefined rule set should be set to only allow packets from the external Notes server. Also, all Notes servers listen for TCP/IP packets on port 1352. The firewall application administrator should adjust the rule set on the firewall machine accordingly.

The second issue in dealing with a network connection over a public network records encrypting the data over the network. Once this option is enabled on a Notes server or client, all data passing over that particular port will be encrypted regardless of the receiver's settings. In other words, if only the initiator is set to encrypt data over a network or COM port, the setting will force the receiver to encrypt data as well. It should be noted that encrypting data over a port will cause a performance decrease but the benefit of encrypted data far outweighs the performance hit.

Understanding and Configuring Cross-Certification

Tips

We assume the candidate has a very good understanding of Notes hierarchical naming. More detailed questions for the System Administration II examination will be asked concerning hierarchical naming. Also, cross-certification cannot be comprehended without a thorough understanding of hierarchical naming, covered in Chapter 10.

Sys. Admin. II

There comes a time that two or more companies need to share Notes resources (databases) or route Notes mail to one another. For this action to happen, cross-certification is necessary between the two Notes organizations.

Cross-certification is the action of enabling two hierarchical ID files with the ability to authenticate through the certification of each other's public keys or an ancestor of the ID files. The results of cross-certification include:

- Cross-Certificates are stored within the public Name and Address book.

- No user or server ID is ever altered.

- Individual Notes users store cross-certificates within their personal Name and Address book.

Cross-Certification does not:

- Work with flat ID files.

- Alter either company's hierarchical organization structure.

- Alter any ID file.

- Necessarily give another company access to all Notes servers

Cross-certification applies to hierarchical ID files that do not share a certificate in common so that they may authenticate. If authentication is needed between a hierarchical and flat ID, cross-certification is not used. Most companies will only have one organization certifier ID, so cross-certification within a company is never needed.

Tips

Most companies will only need to cross-certify ID files in the event they wish to connect to an external Notes infrastructure to replicate Notes application or route Notes mail.

As the name implies, cross-certification is a two way process. One company must certify an external ID file in which the result is stored within certifying company's Name and Address book. The external company then must repeat this process with the other companys' ID file. Unless certification is done on both company's ID files, authentication between the two Notes servers will not take place. Unlike flat certificates, cross-certificates are stored within the public Name and Address book of each company. If the cross-certification document is ever deleted from either address book, authentication between the two Notes servers will not occur. This feature gives a Notes administrator control in the event he or she wishes to cease connectivity with an external company. Shown in Figure 16-1 is a sample cross-certification document between /ACME and /ABCompany:

Figure 16-1
Notes Cross-
Certificate Record

CROSS CERTIFICATE:/ACME -/ABCompany

Basics

Certificate type:	Notes Cross-Certificate
Issued By:	/ACME
Issued To:	/ABCompany
Combined Name:	O=ACME:O=ABCompany
Comment:	
Organizations:	O=ACME:O=ABCompany

Administration

Owners:	Scott Thomas/Marketing/Chicago/ACME
Administrators:	Notes Admin

Cross-certification may occur between the following ID files:

● **Notes server ID to Notes server ID.** This is the most secure method of cross-certification (see Figure 16-2). It allows authentication only between two server ID files. For example, if ACME certifies ABCompany's server ID (NY-Notes01/ABCompany) and ABCompany certifies ACME's server ID (Chicago-Notes01/ACME), authentication can only take place between the two servers IDs. If another Notes server within the ABCompany tries to connect to an ACME Notes server, authentication will fail.

Figure 16-2

Cross-Certification—
Notes Server to
Notes Server

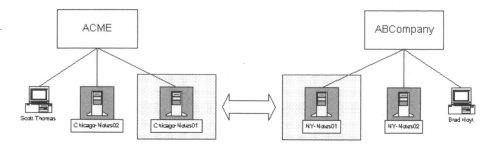

- **Notes server ID to Notes user ID.** This type of cross-certification (Figure 16-3) only allows authentication between a single Notes server and a single external Notes user. For example, a Notes administrator could certify an ABCompany's Notes user (**Joe User/ABCompany**), and Joe User/ABCompany could certify ACME's Notes server (**Chicago-Notes01/ACME**). In this manner Joe User from ABCompany would only be able to authenticate with **Chicago-Notes01/ACME**. The actual cross-certificate documents would exist in the public Name and Address book for the **Chicago-Notes01/ACME** Notes server and in the personal Name and Address book on the Joe User/ABCompany's machine.

Figure 16-3

Cross-Certification—
Notes Server to
Notes User

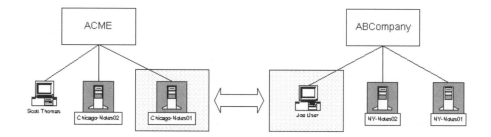

- **Notes organization ID to Notes organization ID.** This type of cross-certification (Figure 16-4) is the most wide-open certification model and is not recommended unless used internally within a company between two organization certifiers. With this type of cross-certification, all users and servers in both companies will be able to authenticate with one another, regardless of position in the hierarchy tree. For example, if the ACME Notes administrator certifies the **/ABCompany** certifier and the ABCompany Notes administrator certifies the **/ACME**

certifier, all Notes servers and users in both organizations will be able to authenticate with one another. If Notes server access lists and ACL lists on each Notes server permits, access to Notes applications can occur.

Figure 16-4
Cross-Certification—
Organization to
Organization

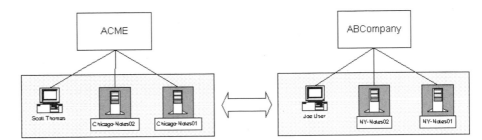

- **Notes organization ID to Notes organizational unit ID.** This type of cross-certification (Figure 16-5) is still a wide-open certification model and applies to one or both companies where certification occurs at an organizational unit level. In other words, a Notes administrator may have created a Notes ID hierarchy where there are 2 or more levels of a naming structure, for example, `Chicago-Notes01/Finance/ACME`. In this type of cross-certification, all users and servers within a given tree hierarchy will be able to authenticate on one end with all servers and users. On the other side, all servers and users will only be able to authenticate with servers and users at the organizational unit level.

To illustrate, the ACME Notes administrator certifies the `/ABCompany` certifier and the ABCompany Notes administrator certifies the `/Finance/ACME` certifier. With this scenario, all users and servers within ACME's `/Finance/ACME` tree will be able to authenticate with *all* users and servers within the ABCompany Notes infrastructure. All users and servers within the ABCompany organization, though, will only be able to authenticate with users and servers within the `/Finance/ACME` tree. A Notes server, say `Chicago-Notes02/HR/ACME`, would be inaccessible from users and servers in the ABCompany Notes infrastructure. See Figure 16-5.

Figure 16-5

Cross-Certification—
Organization to
Organizational Unit

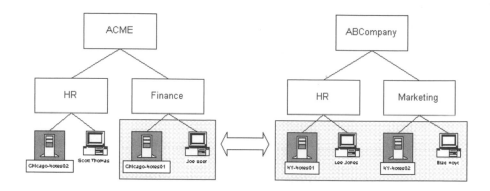

- **Notes organization ID to Notes server ID.** This type of cross-certification (Figure 16-6) will enable one company to authenticate with all users and servers within its organization. The other company, however, will only be able to authenticate with the single Notes server.

  To illustrate, the ACME Notes administrator certifies the `/ABCompany` certifier ID. The ABCompany Notes administrator certifies the `Chicago-Notes01/ACME` server ID file. In this example, all servers and users within ACME will be able to authenticate with all users and servers in the ABCompany Notes infrastructure. All users and servers though in the ABCompany will only be able to authenticate with the `Chicago-Notes01/ACME` Notes server. See Figure 16-6.

Figure 16-6

Cross-Certification—
Organization to Server

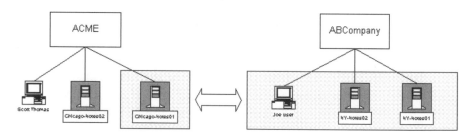

- **Notes organization ID to Notes user ID.** With this type of cross-certification, (Figure 16-7) a single external Notes user will be able to authenticate with all Notes servers within the organization. Because this is a cross-certification between a Notes user ID file, the other organization will not be able to authenticate with any other Notes server within the second company.

To illustrate, the ACME Notes administrator certifies the `Joe User/ABCompany` user ID file. Joe User/ABCompany then certifies the `/ACME` certifier. Joe User/ABCompany then would be able to authenticate with all Notes servers within the ACME organization. However, because the other end of the cross-certification is with a single Notes user ID file, no server or user within ACME will be able to authenticate with Notes servers within ABCompany. See Figure 16-7.

Figure 16-7
Cross-Certification—
Organization to User

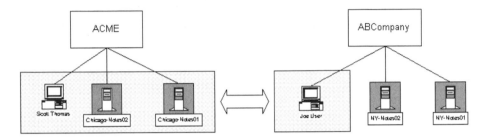

- **Notes organizational unit ID to Notes organizational unit ID.** Within this type of cross-certification (Figure 16-8), all Notes servers and users within both companies will be able to authenticate with Notes servers and users at the certified organizational unit level.

To illustrate, the ACME Notes administrator certifies the `/HR/ABCompany` certifier ID file. The ABCompany Notes administrator certifies the `Finance/ACME` certifier. In this scenario, all ACME Notes users and servers within the `/Finance/ACME` tree will be able to authenticate with all Notes users and servers within ABCompany's `/HR/ABCompany` hierarchy tree and vice versa. Any users or servers outside of either hierarchy will not be able to authenticate. See Figure 16-8.

Figure 16-8
Cross-Certification—
Organizational Unit to
Organizational Unit

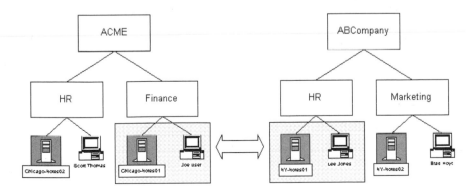

Sys. Admin. II

● **Notes organizational unit ID to Notes server ID.** This type of cross-certification (Figure 16-9) enables all users and servers within a given level of hierarchy to authenticate with a single external Notes server.

To illustrate, the ACME Notes administrator certifies the `NY-Notes01/HR/ABCompany` Notes server ID file. The ABCompany Notes administrator certifies the `/Finance/ACME` certifier ID file. In this scenario, the `NY-Notes01/HR/ABCompany` Notes server can authenticate with all ACME Notes servers and users within the `/Finance/ACME` tree hierarchy. See Figure 16-9.

Figure 16-9

Cross-Certification—
Organizational Unit
to Notes Server

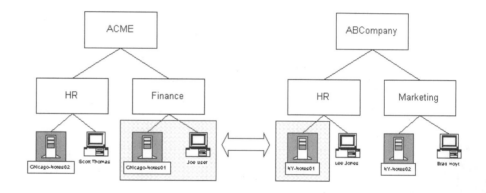

● **Notes organizational unit ID to Notes user ID.** This type of cross-certification (Figure 16-10) enables a single external Notes user to authenticate with Notes servers within a given level of hierarchy.

To illustrate, the ACME Notes administrator certifies the external Notes user `Lee Jones/HR/ABCompany`. The ABCompany Notes administrator certifies the `/Finance/ACME` certifier ID file. In this scenario, the Notes user `Lee Jones/HR/ABCompany` can authenticate with all ACME Notes servers and users within the `/Finance/ACME` tree hierarchy. See Figure 16-10.

Figure 16-10
Cross-Certification—
Organizational Unit
to Notes User

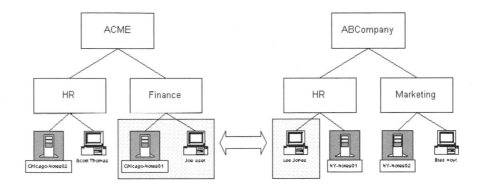

Notes

Users and administrators should never send copies of their certifier, user, or server ID files to other companies. Users and administrators may create what is called a safe copy of an ID file, which cannot be used by anyone to perform Notes functions other than those necessary for cross-certification.

In order to cross-certify hierarchical ID files, Lotus Notes offers **four** different methods.

1) Through Notes Mail

Send Safe Copy of ID File

If a Notes mail connection exists either directly or through an intermediary Notes network, cross-certification of Notes IDs through Notes mail may be used. Each Notes administrator at each company must perform the following steps:

1. Click **File – Tools – User ID**.

2. Click the **Certificates** icon and then click the **Request Cross Certificate** button.

3. Select the ID file you wish to have cross-certified.

4. Once the ID file is selected, a dialog box will appear in which you need to address the Notes mail message.

5. Click **Send** to send the safe copy to the other Notes administrator.

Cross-Certify the Safe Copy of the ID Received through Notes Mail

1. Open the mail document containing the cross-certificate request.

2. Click **Actions – Cross Certify – Attached ID File**.

3. Choose the certifier ID file you wish to use to certify the attached ID file and click **OK**.

4. Within the **Subject name** field, select which level of cross-certification you desire for the external company. For example, if the ABCompany sends the ACME Notes administrator a safe-copy of its server ID file, it will contain information for that Notes server as well as any higher level of hierarchy it belongs to. In other words for Notes server, `NY-Test/ABCompany`, the selections `NY-Test/ABCompany` and `/ABCompany` will appear. Care should be taken if `/ABCompany` is selected, as all users and servers within ABCompany will be able to authenticate. If only `NY-Test/ABCompany` is selected, then only that server will be able to authenticate (See Figure 16-11 for an example).

5. The **Certifier** button may be clicked to change the certifier that will be issuing the cross-certificate.

6. The **Server** button may be used to change the registration server.

7. Within the expiration field, the date for expiration may be changed.

8. Once all is selected, the Notes administrator may click the **Cross Certify** button to perform certification.

Once certification is complete, the other Notes administrator at the other company must perform these same steps. Mailing back the safe copy of the ID file is not necessary, as the cross-certification information is stored within the public Name and Address book and not in the ID files itself.

2) *On Demand*

Cross-certification on demand enables users and administrators to certify with an external hierarchical Notes server on the fly when cross-certification has already been performed on the target Notes server. Cross-certification on demand also occurs when a user opens a signed mail message and the user is not cross-certified with the hierarchy of the sender.

If you wish to cross-certify a Notes server from a different organization (assuming cross-certification has already been performed on the other end), follow these steps:

1. Start the Notes server GUI on the Notes server running the Notes server process. For Notes user workstations, simply start Lotus Notes.

2. Perform a **File – Database – Open** and type in the target Notes server within the server field.

3. Notes will display the name of the organization, its public key, and three buttons.

4. Click the **Yes** button to cross-certify the root certifier of the other company's hierarchy and put the cross-certificate in the public Name and Address book of the Notes server. For Notes users, the cross-certificate will be placed in their personal Name and Address books. This process is fine for Notes users; however, certifying the other company's root certifier on the Notes server may not be desired. The **Advanced Options** button gives the option to select only to certify the target Notes server and not the root certifier. Again, this process can only happen if the other company has performed certification on your company's ID file.

5. Click the **No** button to prevent a cross-certificate from being created.

6. Click the **Advanced Options** button to change cross-certification options.

   Within the **Subject name** field, select which level of cross-certification you desire for the external company. For example, if the ACME Notes administrator is accessing the ABCompany Notes server, it will contain information for that Notes server as well as any higher level of hierarchy it belongs to. In other words for Notes server, `NY-Test/ABCompany`, the selections `NY-Test/ABCompany` and `/ABCompany` will appear. Care should be taken if `/ABCompany` is selected, as all users and servers within ABCompany will be able to authenticate. If only `NY-Test/ABCompany` is selected, then only that server will be able to authenticate (See Figure 16-11 for an example).

7. Click **Cross Certify** to cross-certify the ID File.

3) Verbally, Over the Phone

Cross-certification can be performed verbally over the phone between two Notes administrators by reading validation codes to each other. Both administrators must perform these actions on their respective Notes networks:

1. Click **File – Tools – Server Administration**.

2. Click **Certifiers** and choose **Cross Certify Key**.

3. Choose the certifier ID file of your organization that you will use to create the cross-certificate.

4. A cross-certify key dialog box will appear. Within the **Subject name** field, select which level of cross-certification you desire for the external company. For example, if the ACME Notes administrator wishes to only cross-certify the `NY-Test/ABCompany` Notes server, he or she would type in that entry as given by the ABCompany's Notes administrator.

If the Notes administrator types in /ABCompany, then cross-certification will happen at that level of the hierarchy. Care should be taken if /ABCompany is selected, as all users and servers within ABCompany will be able to authenticate (See Figure 16-11 for an example).

5. Within the **Key** field, type in the public key of the ID file you are cross-certifying, including space. The Notes administrator of the other company will provide you with this number.

6. The **Certifier** button may be clicked to change the certifier that will be issuing the cross-certificate.

7. The **Server** button may be used to change the registration server.

8. Within the expiration field, the date for expiration may be changed.

9. Once all is selected, the Notes administrator may click the **Cross Certify** button to perform certification.

Again, these steps must be performed on both sides by Notes administrators for this procedure to work properly.

4) Physically Mailing an ID File through Snail Mail (the Post Office)

Since the release of Notes version 4, this is the least desirable method in terms of speed, considering the other 3 options to cross-certify. However, if you wish to use this method of cross-certification, each Notes administrator must create a safe copy of his or her ID file (certifier, server, or user ID file depending on the desired level of access—see above sections discussing cross-certification). A safe copy of an ID file cannot be used for accessing a Notes server; it only contains enough information to perform certification. Once the safe copy of the ID file is made, each Notes administrator must copy the file to a diskette and mail it to the intended recipient.

Once each Notes administrator receives the safe copy of the ID file, each administrator must certify that ID file. Again, this is a two-way process, so if only one Notes administrator certifies the other's safe copy, authentication will not take place.

Create Safe Copy of Notes ID File

In order to create a safe copy of an ID file, the following steps should be followed:

1. Click **File – Tools – Server Administration.**

2. Click **Administration – ID File...** and select the ID file you wish to make a safe copy of.

3. Click the **More Options** icon and then click **Create Safe Copy**.

4. Enter a filename and path to store the safe copy of the ID file. The default filename is **SAFE.ID**.

5. Copy the safe copy of the file to a diskette and mail it to the other company's Notes administrator.

Again, a safe copy cannot be used to perform Notes activities. The file only contains enough information to perform certification procedures.

Cross-Certify Safe Copy ID File

Once you receive a safe copy of an ID file from another company's Notes administrator, the following steps should be taken to cross-certify the ID file:

1. Click **File – Tools – Server Administration**.

2. Click the **Certifiers** icon and click **Cross Certify ID File**.

3. Choose the certifier ID file of your organization that you will use to certify the ID file.

4. Next, select the other company's safe copy ID file that was sent on diskette. The dialog box shown in Figure 16-11 appears:

Figure 16-11
Cross-Certification
Dialog Box

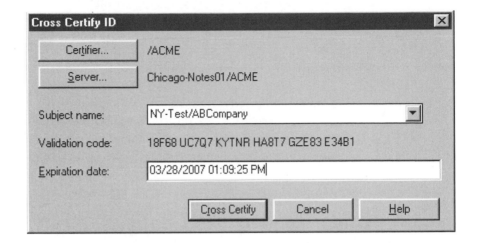

5. Within the **Subject name** field, select which level of cross-certification you desire for the external company. For example, if the ABCompany sends the ACME Notes administrator a safe-copy of its server ID file, it will contain information for that Notes server as well as any higher level of hierarchy it belongs to. In other words for Notes server, `NY-Test/ABCompany`, the selections `NY-Test/ABCompany` and `/ABCompany` will appear. Care should be taken if `/ABCompany` is selected, as all users and servers within ABCompany will be able to authenticate. If only `NY-Test/ABCompany` is selected, then only that server will be able to authenticate.

6. The **Certifier** button may be clicked to change the certifier that will be issuing the cross-certificate.

7. The **Server** button may be used to change the registration server.

8. Within the expiration field, the date for expiration may be changed.

9. Once all is selected, click the **Cross Certify** button to perform certification.

Once certification is complete, the other Notes administrator at the other company must perform these same steps. Mailing back the safe copy of the ID file is not necessary, as the cross-certification information is stored within the public Name and Address book and not in the ID file itself.

Tips

Cross-Certification is a very important topic for the System Administration II exam. Security aspects, administrative tasks, and end results of cross-certification should be thoroughly understood by the candidate.

Understanding and Configuring Flat Certification

For backwards compatibility for older version of Lotus Notes (v2), flat certification is still supported. A flat certifier may be created by a Notes administrator and then used to create a new flat Notes user or server. A flat certifier may also be applied to an existing flat or hierarchical ID file. An ID file may contain multiple flat certificates. A flat ID file can be compared to just the common name (CN) of a hierarchical ID file (no O or OU within the name of the server or user).

Any two flat ID files may authenticate as long as they have at least one flat certificate in common. Also, a hierarchical ID file and a flat ID file may authenticate as long as they have at least one flat certificate in common. However, two different hierarchical ID files may *not* authenticate if they share a flat certifier in common. Cross-certification must be used between two different hierarchical ID files in order to authenticate.

Configuring Notes Server Access

In order for another Notes server or user to access a Notes server after successful authentication takes place, the server then checks its server record in the public Name and Address book as well as any **NOTES.INI** variables that secure the server.

Tips

*There are some variables within the **NOTES.INI** that have equivalent settings within the public Name and Address book. The Server document's access list within the public Name and Address book will override any **NOTES.INI** variables.*

Server access lists add an additional layer of security to Notes servers. By using access lists, access can be granted or denied to a server, or particular ports on the server even if the user is certified to access the server. Server access lists are controlled through the Server Record in the public Name and Address book and/or in the **NOTES.INI** file of the server. Port level access is achieved through a **NOTES.INI** variable on each server.

Table 16.1 lists the different settings available for securing a Notes server. It is recommended that you use Notes groups rather than individual server and/or user names within the fields for easier administration. More details on fields within a Notes server document within the public Name and Address book can be found in Chapter 13—*The Name and Address Book Structure.*

Table 16.1
Notes Server
Access Settings

Security Setting	Description
Only allow server access to users listed in this Address Book (N&A Book)	This field is found in the public Name and Address book. If set to **yes**, only people within the same domain of the server will be allowed access to the server. If set to **yes** you must add other servers that need access to this server into the Access Server field.
Access Server (N&A Book)	Place any users and/or server that need access to this Notes server within this field. If you set the field above this field to **yes** you must enter other users not within your domain and any server within or outside your domain in this field, otherwise access will not be granted. If this field is left blank, all certified users and/or servers will be allowed access assuming the field above is set to **no**.
Not access server (N&A Book)	Denies access to users, servers, and groups to this Notes server.
Create new databases (N&A Book)	Enter a Notes group that will be allowed to create new database applications on this Notes server. If the field is left blank, **all** users will be allowed to create new databases.
Create replica databases (N&A Book)	Enter the Notes group that will be allowed to create new replica databases on this server. If the field is left blank, **no one** will be able to create new replica applications.

Table 16.1

Notes Server
 Access Settings
(cont'd.)

Security Setting	Description
Access this server through passthru (N&A Book)	Enter the users, servers, or groups that are allowed access to this server via a passthru server. If this field is left blank, **no one** will be allowed access via passthru.
Use this server as a passthru server (N&A Book)	Enter the users, server, or groups that may use this server as a passthru server to reach another server. If this field is left blank, **no one** will be allowed to use this server as passthru server.
Allow Anonymous Notes Connections (N&A Book)	If you set this field to **yes** within a Notes server document, all Notes users will be allowed access to the Notes server, regardless of certificates held. In other words, authentication will not take place between the two ID files. Access will be granted with these types of connection using the user name "Anonymous," which can be placed within ACLs of databases and other server access fields.
Compare public keys against those stored in the public Name and Address book (N&A Book)	Select this field to **yes** to check users' public keys within their user ID files against those public keys stored within your domain's public Name and Address book. This is useful in the event a "dummy" or "fake" ID has been created to access the Notes server.
Allow_Access (NOTES.INI)	Same function as Allow Access field within the public Name and Address book, and only used if that field is left blank.
Allow_Access_portname (NOTES.INI)	Specifies the servers, users, and groups that may access this server at the specified port. There is no an equivalent setting within a server record.
Allow_Passthru_Access (NOTES.INI)	Same function as the server record equivalent. Only used if the server record field is left blank.
Allow_Passthru_Callers (NOTES.INI)	Same function as the server record equivalent. Only used if the server record field is left blank.
Allow_Passthru_Clients (NOTES.INI)	Same function as the server record equivalent. Only used if the server record field is left blank.
Allow_Passthru_Targets (NOTES.INI)	Same function as the server record equivalent. Only used if the server record field is left blank.
Create_File_Access (NOTES.INI)	Same function as the server record equivalent. Only used if the server record field is left blank.
Create_Replica_Access (NOTES.INI)	Same function as the server record equivalent. Only used if the server record field is left blank.
Deny_Access (NOTES.INI)	Same function as the server record equivalent. Only used if the server record field is left blank.
Deny_Access_portname (NOTES.INI)	Specifies the servers, users, and groups that are denied access to this server at the specified port. There is no equivalent setting within a server record.
Server_Restricted (NOTES.INI)	Specifies whether or not the Notes server will accept Open Database requests. There is no equivalent setting with the public Name and Address book.

Chapter 16 Sample Questions

Objective: External Notes Connectivity.

Dylynne is able to ping a target Notes server across the Internet via TCP/IP, but is unable to access the target Notes server via the Notes client. What is a possible problem?

> A. The target Notes server is not running
>
> B. A firewall is set not to allow Notes traffic to pass, but is allowing "ping" traffic to pass
>
> C. The Internet uses the SPX protocol

Answer: A or B

The target Notes server may be up but may not be running the Notes server task. Also, a firewall network application may be configured on Dylynne's network or the target Notes server's network to not allow passage of Notes traffic via TCP/IP (port 1352). The Internet uses the TCP/IP protocol, not SPX.

Objective: Understanding and Configuring Cross-Certification.

Cross-Certification between two Notes server IDs will do the following:

> A. Grant access to all servers and users between the two organizations
>
> B. Alter the ID files involved
>
> C. Store the cross-certification documents within the public or personal address book(s)
>
> D. Work with flat ID files

Answer: C

Cross-certification documents are stored within either the personal or public Name and Address book(s) and never alter the ID file itself. Cross-certification only occurs between two unlike hierarchical ID files. Flat ID files require flat certifiers in common to authenticate.

Objective: Understanding and Configuring Cross-Certification.

The ACME corporation certified the ABCompany's Notes Server `Notes01/ABCompany`. The ABCompany certified the `/Finance/ACME` organizational unit certifier. What authentication levels are possible?

> A. All users and servers within the ABCompany may authenticate with all users and servers within the `/Finance/ACME` organizational hierarchy
>
> B. Only the Notes server `Notes01/ABCompany` may authenticate with users or servers within ACME company
>
> C. Only users and servers within the `/Finance/ACME` hierarchy may authenticate with users and servers within the ABCompany
>
> D. All users and servers within the `/HR/ACME` hierarchy may authenticate with users and servers within the ABCompany

Answer: B and C

ACME has only certified that the Notes server, `Notes01/ABCompany` authenticate with the ABCompany. However, ABCompany has certified all servers and users within the `/Finance/ACME` hierarchy may authenticate.

Objective: Understanding and Configuring Cross-Certification.

What methods are available in Notes for cross-certifying two ID files?

> A. Verbally over the phone exchanging keys
>
> B. Using safe copies of the two ID files
>
> C. On demand after the one side of the cross-certification has been completed
>
> D. By creating a certification record within the public Name and Address book and entering the target Notes server name

Answer: A, B, and C
Cross certification may be done by exchanging safe copies of the two ID files and then certifying them. Cross-certification may also be done on demand after certification has been established one of the two ways. Finally, cross-certification may be done verbally over the phone by exchanging each other's keys.

Objective: Understanding and Configuring Flat Certification.

Amy has just created a flat certifier ID and certified her Notes server, `Notes01/ACME`. She also just certified another company's Notes server, `Chicago-01/ABCompany`, with the same flat certifier ID file. When she tries to communicate with the external server, authentication will not take place. Why not?

> A. She forgot to create a certification document within the public Name and Address book
>
> B. She didn't certify `Chicago-01/ABCompany` using encryption
>
> C. A flat certifier cannot be used between two hierarchical ID files to authenticate
>
> D. Flat certifiers may no longer be used in version 4 and higher of Lotus Notes

Answer: C
A flat certifier cannot be used between two hierarchical ID files to authenticate. A flat certifier may only be used between two flat ID files, or a flat ID file and a hierarchical ID file.

Objective: Understanding and Configuring Flat Certification.

Kristine created a flat certifier called `Chicago-Access` and applied it to her flat Notes server ID file, `Chicago-Notes01`. Her Notes server already has another flat certifier, `HR-Access`. In New York, she also has another Notes server called `NY-Notes01` with two flat certifiers, `NY-Access` and `Finance-Access` applied to the server ID file. Both Notes servers are in the same Notes domain. Will the `Chicago-Notes01` and `NY-Notes01` be able to authenticate?

A. Yes, because the two servers are flat ID files

B. Yes, because the two servers are in the same Notes domain

C. No, because the two server ID files are not hierarchical

D. No, because the two server ID files do not share a flat certificate in common

Answer: D

Because the two ID files do not share a flat certificate in common, they will not be able to authenticate. If the `Chicago-Access` certifier were applied to the `NY-Notes01` server, then the two Notes servers would be able to authenticate.

Objective: Configuring Notes Server Access.

Brad has configured his Notes server within the server document so that the field **Only allow server access to users listed in this Address Book** is set to **YES**. The server document field **Access Server** is left blank. Other Notes servers in his Notes domain are no longer able to access his Notes server. Why not?

A. The field **Only allow server access to users listed in this Address Book** can only be used where there is one Notes server within a domain

B. If the field **Only allow server access to users listed in this Address Book** is set to **YES**, then the **Access Server** field must contain Notes servers that are able to access the Notes server

C. The field **Only allow server access to users listed in this Address Book** must also be set within the Notes server's **NOTES.INI** file

D. The field **Access Server** must also be set within the Notes server's **NOTES.INI** file

Answer: B

If the field, **Only allow server access to users listed in this Address Book** is set to **YES**, then the **Access Server** field must contain Notes servers that are able to access the Notes server.

Objective: Configuring Notes Server Access.

Pete is trying to create a new replica Notes application on his Notes server from his workstation. However, the Notes server is denying him from doing so. What is wrong?

     A. The field **Create Replica Databases** on the Notes server document has been left blank

     B. Pete has not logged into the Notes server as administrator

     C. The field **Create Replica Databases** on the Notes configuration document has been left blank

     D. Replica databases cannot be created from a Notes workstation

Answer: A

By default, if the field **Create Replica Databases** within a Notes server document is left blank, no users or servers will be able to create replica copies of Notes applications on that Notes server.

Objective: Configuring Notes Server Access.

Chad has noticed everyone within his company has been creating new Notes applications on his Notes server. How can he prevent this?

     A. Leave the field **Create New Databases** blank within the Notes server document.

     B. Add the line **Prevent Database Creation** to the **NOTES.INI** file on the Notes server.

     C. Within the field **Create New Databases** place only those people he wishes to have create new database applications on his Notes server.

     D. Within the field **Prevent Database Creation** in the Notes server document, add those people he does not wish to be able to create new applications on his server.

Sys. Admin. II

Answer: C

By default, if the server field **Create New Databases** is left blank, all users and servers will be able to create new Notes applications. Therefore, he must add those users and servers that will be able to create new Notes applications.

Index

About the Authors

Scott L. Thomas currently is a Senior Network Specialist at Sprint Paranet specializing in Lotus Notes and Windows NT architectures. He has his Master's degree in Computer Telecommunications from DePaul University and holds certifications as a Certified Lotus Professional (CLP), Certified Microsoft Systems Engineer (MCSE), and a Certified NetWare Administrator (CNA). He has been designing and configuring enterprise Lotus Notes networks since 1991 for numerous Fortune 1000 organizations.

Before Sprint Paranet, Scott was a Senior Network Consultant for Price Waterhouse LLC's Management Consulting Services where he specialized in Lotus Notes and Windows NT network design and analysis. While at Price Waterhouse, he also performed several presentations at Price Waterhouse conferences on Lotus Notes and other networking technology topics. He is also the co-author of *Lotus Notes and Domino Architecture, Administration, and Security* and a technical reviewer of *Windows NT Security* by Charles B. Rutstein. Both books are also published by McGraw-Hill. Scott can be reached at *slthomas@earthlink.net*.

Amy E. Peasley is currently a Senior Consultant for Whittman-Hart, Inc. She specializes in designing and integrating Lotus Notes applications that provide advanced business solutions for Whittman-Hart's Fortune 1000 client base. She is a Certified Lotus Professional (CLP) in Lotus Notes version 3.x and 4.x.

Prior to working for Whittman-Hart, Inc., Amy was employed by Price Waterhouse Tax Technology Group where she was responsible for Lotus Notes Application development, Lotus Notes System Administration, and Novell network infrastructure support. Amy is a technical reviewer of *Lotus Notes and Domino Architecture, Administration, and Security* by Scott L. Thomas and Brad Hoyt, published by McGraw-Hill. Amy can be reached at *apeasley@earthlink.net*.